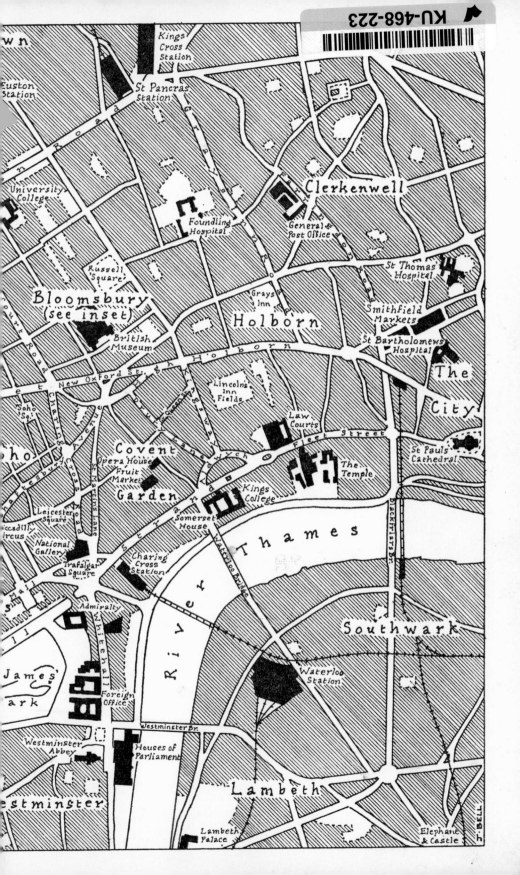

THE DIARY OF
VIRGINIA WOOLF

Volume III: 1925-1930

Edited by
ANNE OLIVIER BELL

Assisted by
ANDREW McNEILLIE

1980
THE HOGARTH PRESS
LONDON

Published by
The Hogarth Press Ltd
40 William IV Street
London WC2N 4DG

*

Clarke, Irwin & Co. Ltd
Toronto

British Library Cataloguing
in Publication Data

Woolf, Virginia
The Diary of Virginia Woolf
Vol. III: 1925-1930
1. Woolf, Virginia
I. Title   II. Bell, Anne Olivier
III. McNeillie, Andrew
823'.9'12   PR6045.072
ISBN 0-7012-0466-4

Printed in Great Britain by
T. & A. Constable Ltd
Hopetoun Street, Edinburgh

Contents

Editor's Preface

The division of this edition of Virginia Woolf's diaries into five volumes arises, it must be confessed, largely from practical considerations; nevertheless the span covered by this third volume—that is to say the years 1925 to 1930—has a unity which, though largely undesigned, is real and which corresponds to a distinct period in her life. It is the period in which she attained full maturity as an artist and at the same time achieved a secure and respected position in the world of letters. As a corollary, she became financially more stable and socially more adventurous. These are perhaps the most fruitful and satisfying years of her life.

This volume opens with Virginia revising and preparing both *The Common Reader* and *Mrs Dalloway* for their publication in the late spring of 1925. Her last book, *Jacob's Room*, which had appeared towards the end of 1922, had achieved a certain *succès d'estime*, but as a novelist she was still very unsure of herself; Middleton Murry's opinion that in that novel she had reached a dead end was a perpetual source of disquiet, and she awaited the reception of her new books—*Mrs Dalloway* in particular—with marked apprehensiveness. Her fluctuations of feeling as the opinions of individuals and the press reached her are almost obsessively recorded; but as she also wrote at this time: 'The truth is that writing is the profound pleasure & being read the superficial.' That this was true for her one cannot doubt.

But 'being read' brought its rewards, superficial or otherwise, in the way of greatly enhanced reputation (what she dubiously referred to as her 'fame', a condition she both relished and mistrusted); it brought acknowledgment by the literate public on both sides of the Atlantic that Virginia Woolf was an artist of authentic quality and originality, and a creative and illuminating critic. And this certainly reassured her and gave her greater confidence in following her own path; she could scarcely contain her impatience to start the writing of *To The Lighthouse* which had been simmering in her brain for many months. Fame also brought a greater demand for her books, for her opinions, and for her company; maintaining a balance between the pleasures and rewards of society and those of solitude became an ever more difficult operation.

In the spring of 1927, in the torpid period between finishing *To The Lighthouse* and its publication in May, Virginia began to amuse herself with an idea to which she attached a provisional title: *The Jessamy*

Brides. This protean concept developed finally, by way of *The Moths*, into *The Waves*, which she had almost completed as this volume closes; but it also branched out in a slighter form as *Orlando*, a work written at breakneck speed between October 1927 and March 1928. Although sterner critics, and among them Virginia herself, regarded this as little more than a *jeu d'esprit*, it delighted a large number of people and sold far better than any of her previous books. It is perhaps the most accessible of all of them and comes nearest to the simpler human passions.

Orlando may be regarded as an offering of love to Vita Sackville-West who, during these years, was to hold sway in both Virginia's heart and her imagination. They had first met at the end of 1922, but it was not until late in 1925 that their somewhat guarded interest in each other (Virginia had been told that Vita was a pronounced Sapphist who might have her eye on her) developed into an intensely absorbing passion. Virginia is at first reticent in her diary about her feelings for Vita, which may rather be inferred from the frequency of her letters to her; but gradually the paramount importance of the attachment becomes apparent. This is a passage in Virginia's life which has attracted a good deal of attention, but with the publication of her letters and her diary there is little more that I would wish to say concerning that delicate sentimental transaction of which *Orlando* is the permanent monument; and yet these sources reveal a seeming paradox: Virginia's one serious infidelity is remarkable in that it exhibits clearly the secure strength of her marriage. Nothing in the letters or the diary during her love affair with Vita is more manifest than her constant affection for Leonard, and his for her. Vita represented romance, the champagne and gold-dust aspect of the world by which Virginia always was fascinated; but with Leonard she could depend completely upon that spirit of trusting affection and mutual respect, of intimacy and ease, upon the solid comfort of day-to-day happiness which she described as the core of her life. It is a characteristic anomaly of the situation that if Leonard was discomposed by any of Virginia's lovers, it was not by Vita but by that formidable old egotist and eccentric Dame Ethel Smyth. He really liked Vita; but Ethel both exasperated and bored him.

The proximate cause of this later friendship, which was to absorb— and demand—so much of Virginia's time after their first meeting in February 1930, was *A Room of One's Own*. This little book, Virginia's most persuasive essay in feminist propaganda, had branched and flowered from the root-stock of two papers read to student societies at the two women's colleges at Cambridge in October 1928, and was published a year later. Ethel Smyth, a veteran in the struggle for women's suffrage, convinced that her failure as a musician could be ascribed to male prejudice, discerned in the author of *A Room of One's Own* a natural ally, resolved to claim her as such, and bore down upon her with all flags flying. Already predisposed, Ethel fell in love with Virginia at once; and Virginia, fascinated and impressed by the old campaigner's vigour and spirit, found her impossible to withstand. However, in this volume of the diary we see only the beginning of this relationship.

Virginia's relations with individual women, and her interest in the whole subject of women—in their particular qualities, their hidden and unrecorded lives, their disadvantages and struggles and triumphs in a male-dominated society—has become the focus for a great deal of attention, and she is rightly seen to have been both a profound analyst of women and an eloquent advocate of their rights. Yet the attention devoted to the 'feminist' aspect of her life and work threatens at times to distort and obscure the whole, and it seems almost necessary to insist that Virginia was not essentially a feminist zealot. A measure of the very wide-ranging and catholic nature of her thought and interest is given by her diary—the most direct and unpremeditated record of her immediate concerns—which is relatively little occupied with these matters.

Although Virginia continued to feel most at ease with her old Bloomsbury intimates, she extended her social circle and, always curious about people, embraced the opportunities her growing fame afforded her to observe or meet the eminent, particularly in her own profession of letters (though she did not disdain an invitation to dine in company with the Prime Minister). Her impressions of, for example, Thomas Hardy or W. B. Yeats, of Max Beerbohm, George Moore, or H. G. Wells, provide some of the most vivid and interesting pages in this volume. And her literary success brought more material advantages: amenities and comforts could be added to 52 Tavistock Square and to Monks House; Virginia could afford to buy nice clothes (always an agitating matter) and works of art, to give presents and parties, to buy a second-hand motor-car, to travel abroad. Leonard and Virginia were both frugal by nature and by habit, and what to them appeared free-handed spending would seem modest enough today; but their years of stringency and scraping were over; they had earned the liberty to order their lives free from the harsher restraints of financial anxiety.

This was indeed a period of new achievements, new affluence, new pleasures. There are inevitable vexations and dejections, illnesses and anxieties; nevertheless, allowing for Virginia's tendency to use her diary as a vent for ill humour, this volume is on the whole the record of a fortunate time: the record of a woman happy in her marriage, happy in her friendships, but above all happy in her work, in the fertility of her imagination, in the growing assurance of her own powers of expression, in the continued expansion of her genius.

EDITORIAL NOTE

In 1953 Leonard Woolf published *A Writer's Diary*, a selection of excerpts from his wife's manuscript diaries, before making the dispositions which brought the originals to America after his death. They are now preserved in the Henry W. and Albert A. Berg Collection of English and American Literature in the New York Public Library (Astor, Lenox, and Tilden Foundations). Through a concord between the copyright holders, Virginia Woolf's English and American publishers, and the Curator of the Berg Collection, the series of diaries she kept from 1915 until her death in 1941 are now being published in their entirety in five volumes. The text for the six years included in this third volume is transcribed from Diaries XIV to XIX inclusive, plus a few pages from the end of Diary XIII, and the first forty pages of Diary XX. (See Volume I, Appendix I, in which the whole series is listed.)

The transcription follows the manuscript as closely and completely as possible, though it has to be said that Virginia Woolf's rapid handwriting gets progressively more difficult to decipher; my uncertainties or total defeats are revealed by the use of square brackets (reserved throughout for editorial interpolations) and question marks. Where she has crossed out or altered words or passages I have followed her reconsidered version, although when they seem of sufficient interest, the cancelled words are given within angled brackets: ⟨ ⟩. Her spelling is so consistently good that her rare aberrations are preserved; so is her often phonetic spelling of proper names, when the correct form is supplied between square brackets or in a footnote. Virginia Woolf's almost invariable use of the ampersand has been retained to suggest the pace of her writing (although the symbol in its printed form unfortunately rather negates this intention), and to give point to the occasions where she chooses to spell out the conjunction.

I have made some concession to the convenience of reader and printer in respect of certain features of the manuscript:

I have standardised the dating of the entries, and they are set out: day, date, month, and italicised thus: *Tuesday 6 January*; the month is repeated in the running headline on each page, together with the year. Virginia Woolf's own dating is inconsistent, and sometimes wrong, and there seems no particular point in perpetuating it. Where, from internal and external evidence, I have found her to be mistaken, I have indicated the fact.

Inconsistencies of punctuation, in particular a heedless insufficiency of inverted commas, brackets, and of apostrophes in the possessive case, have been amended. It is not always easy to determine what intention is implied by a single or double mark made at speed, but I have tried to interpret these faithfully. I have allowed myself some latitude in distinguishing paragraphs where they may not always be clearly apparent on the written page.

Autographical idiosyncrasies—in particular the habit of forming abbreviations with superior letters as in M^{rs}, Sq^{re}, 19th, and the like—have been brought as it were down to earth, the stops and dashes omitted; and the variety of marks following the single letter to which names are frequently abbreviated have been standardised to a full point.

Such annotations as I have thought could be helpful or interesting to readers are given at the foot of the page to which they relate; they are numbered in sequence *within each month*. (All methods of presenting annotations seem to me to have disadvantages, and this is admittedly a compromise solution.) I am of course aware that it is virtually impossible to suit everyone in the provision of supplementary information, and that much of my rather *terre-à-terre* annotation will prove superfluous to one or another reader. Readers' wants differ, and I can only remind them of their own power to choose to read, or to ignore, footnotes.

As in the previous volumes I have attempted to identify every person referred to in the diary; those regular players who must already be familiar to most readers I have relegated to Appendix I on p 349; the others—and as Virginia moved more into the world they become more numerous—are introduced in footnotes on their first appearance; the index should discover them. The summary information provided does not in general extend beyond the period covered by this volume.

I have where possible identified Virginia's own published writings according to B. J. Kirkpatrick's indispensable *Bibliography of Virginia Woolf*, prefixing the numbers therein by *Kp*; I use the abbreviation *HP Checklist* and number to indicate the books issued by Leonard and Virginia Woolf in their capacity as publishers, particulars of which are given in J. Howard Woolmer's *Checklist of the Hogarth Press, 1917-1938*; and *M & M* represents the volume on Virginia Woolf, edited by Robin Majumdar and Allen McLaurin, in *The Critical Heritage* series. A complete list of abbreviations employed for books and names is to be found on p 347; other books are cited by their author, full title, and date of publication in England, except for Virginia Woolf's own works, when reference is made, unless otherwise stated, to the uniform edition published in London by the Hogarth Press and in New York by Harcourt Brace Jovanovich.

ACKNOWLEDGMENTS

Once again the greater part of the research for this volume (outside my home) has been pursued in the London Library and in the Library and Documents Centre of the University of Sussex; to the ever helpful staff, and to the incomparable facilities, of those institutions, I wish to pay tribute. My work is greatly eased by the publication in advance of this diary of *The Letters of Virginia Woolf* edited by Nigel Nicolson and Joanne Trautmann, now approaching its sixth and final volume; besides bestowing this great natural advantage, Nigel Nicolson has been unfailingly generous in providing me with information that only he could supply. Harry (Sir Henry) Lintott has solved several puzzles for me, and has nobly read through my notes and saved me from innumerable errors of fact and form, for which I am deeply grateful. Trekkie Parsons has again permitted me to make use of Leonard Woolf's laconic diaries, an inestimable assistance. And the following friends and correspondents have generously responded to my need for help of various kinds:

Anastasia Anrep; Igor Anrep; Barbara Bagenal; Rachel Cecil; David and Elisabeth Elwyn; Alan Clark; David Garnett; Richard Garnett; John Gere; Anthony Harris; Michael Henley; Grace Higgens; Michael Jamieson; John Jones; Dr John Kelly; Milo Keynes; Paul Levy; Averil Lysaght; Norman and Jeanne McKenzie; G. H. G. Norman; Ian Parsons; Frances Partridge; Angela Richards; S. P. Rosenbaum; Daphne Sanger; Desmond Shawe-Taylor; Brenda Silver; George Spater; Olivier Todd; John le Forest Thompson; and Veronica Wedgwood.

I also wish to acknowledge the courtesy and assistance I have received from librarians, officials, or staff of the following: Cambridge University Library; Cheltenham Art Gallery and Museum Service; Christie's, London; *Country Life*; Dorset County Museum; The English Association; Girton College Library; Goethe Institute, London; King's College Library, Cambridge; The National Maritime Museum, Greenwich; Newnham College Library; Oxford University Press; The Royal Academy of Arts; The Victoria and Albert Museum (Departments of Metalwork, of Prints and Drawings, and Textiles and Dress, and the Theatre Museum); *Vogue*.

The portion of the letter from W. B. Yeats which appears on p 331 does so with the kind permission of Michael and Anne Yeats and A. P. Watt Ltd.

I have referred to concessions made for the sake of reader and printer. I would like however to observe that Messrs T. &. A. Constable of Edinburgh need no concessions from me; they could print anything they were asked to—and indeed have most faithfully done so.

The maps forming the endpapers for the English edition have been specially drawn by my son Julian Bell.

The indispensability of my assistant Andrew McNeillie is, I trust, evidenced by his name on the title-page of this work. Essential preparation and research have been carried out by Virginia Bell and Victoria Walton. Sandra Williams has again borne the onerous responsibility of typing the final copy. To have such excellent and dependable helpers is an immeasurable asset for which I am constantly grateful.

My greatest debt is to those who have entrusted me with this task: the copyright holders Angelica Garnett and Quentin Bell, Lola Szladits the Curator of the Berg Collection, John Ferrone of Harcourt Brace Jovanovich, and Norah Smallwood of the Hogarth Press. Although naturally I sometimes curse both them and the day I was so bold and foolhardy as to undertake it, they have severally been so helpful, so encouraging, and above all so patient, that I count myself fortunate in my taskmasters, salute them for their virtues, and thank them for their confidence.

ANNE OLIVIER BELL

Sussex, November 1979

— 1925 —

1925

The Woolfs returned to London from Monks House on 2 January. VW continued to use her 1924 book (Diary XIII).

Tuesday 6 January

The disgraceful truth is that I shall run year into year, for I cant waste so many blank pages.

What a flourish I began 1924 with! And today, for the 165th time, Nelly has given notice— Won't be dictated to: must do as other girls do. This is the fruit of Bloomsbury.[1] On the whole, I'm inclined to take her at her word. The nuisance of arranging life to suit her fads, & the pressure of 'other girls' is too much, good cook though she is, & honest, crusty old maid too, dependable, in the main, affectionate, kindly, but incurably fussy, nervy, unsubstantial. Anyhow, the servant question no longer much worries me.

Last night we dined at 3 Albert Road Mary's new villa.[2] I like the new year to begin with warm friendly feelings—& it was a superb dinner. There were the children too, a nice girl & boy; a girl with lovely *womans* eyes, sympathetic, startled; & wild like a girl. (I want to begin to describe my own sex.) What do I mean about the expression? Extreme youth, & yet, one felt, this feeling has been existing forever; very feminine. Here I conceive my story—but I'm always conceiving stories now. Short ones —scenes—for instance The Old Man (a character of L.S.) The Professor on Milton—(an attempt at literary criticism)[3] & now The Interruption, women talking alone. However, back to life. Where are we?

I spent this morning writing a note on an E[lizabe]than play—for

1. The Woolfs had employed Nelly Boxall and Lottie Hope as living-in servants since 1916; they took Nelly with them when they moved to Tavistock Square, Bloomsbury, in 1924, and Lottie went to work for the Adrian Stephens in neighbouring Gordon Square.
2. For Mary Hutchinson and her husband St John Hutchinson see Appendix I. The Hutchinsons had recently moved to 3 Albert (now Prince Albert) Road, Regent's Park, from their previous home at River House, Hammersmith. The children were Barbara (b. 1911) and Jeremy (b. 1915).
3. VW was already envisaging her father Leslie Stephen as the subject of a 'scene' the previous autumn (see *II VW Diary*, 17 October 1924); it was to develop into *To the Lighthouse*. The professor is incorporated in *Mrs Dalloway*, pp 193-4.

3

which I have been reading plays all this year.[4] Then I found the minute hand of my watch had come off (this was talking to Lytton about [Samuel] Richardson last night—I found it off then): so I went into the printing room to see the time—found Angus & Leonard doing Simkin's bill. Stayed & laughed. L. went off to the office, when we had dog-walked round the Square. I came in & set a page of Nancy. Then out to Ingersoll to get my watch mended.[5] Then dog walked. Then here. It being a black grained winter day; lengths of the pavement ink black where not lighted. Never shall I describe all the days I have noticed. I cannot hit it off, quite, & yet perhaps if I read this again I shall see what I meant then.

Rodmell was all gale & flood; these words are exact. The river over-flowed. We had 7 days rain out of 10. Often I could not face a walk. L. pruned, which needed heroic courage. My heroism was purely literary. I revised Mrs D[alloway]: the dullest part of the whole business of writing; the most depressing & exacting. The worst part is at the beginning (as usual) where the aeroplane has it all to itself for some pages, & it wears thin. L. read it; thinks it my best—but then has he not *got* to think so? Still I agree. He thinks it has more continuity than J[acob]s R[oom]. but is difficult owing to the lack of connection, visible, between the two themes.

Anyhow it is sent off to Clarks, & proofs will come next week. This is for Harcourt Brace, who has accepted without seeing & raised me to 15 p.c.[6]

I did not see very much at Rodmell, having to keep my eyes on the typewriter.

Angus was with us for Christmas, a very quiet, very considerate, unselfish deliberate young man, with a charming sense of humour—colourless, Lytton says: passive. But I think well of him, all the same.

4. VW's 'Notes on an Elizabethan Play' was published in the *TLS* of 5 March 1925 (Kp C259).

5. For Lytton Strachey see Appendix I. Angus Henry Gordon Davidson (b. 1898), graduate of Magdalene College, Cambridge, came to work at the Hogarth Press in December 1924 as successor to G. H. W. Rylands and stayed until the end of 1927. Simpkin, Marshall, Hamilton, Kent & Co were book wholesalers and distributors. The *Nation* office was at 38 Great James Street, WC1. Nancy Cunard (1896-1965), the rebellious daughter of the immensely wealthy Sir Bache and Lady Cunard; her long poem *Parallax* was to be published by the Hogarth Press in April 1925 (*HP Checklist* 57). The Ingersoll Watch Company had two establishments in Kingsway.

6. R & R Clark Ltd, the Edinburgh firm of printers. Harcourt, Brace and Company, VW's publishers in America.

Wednesday 18 March

These last pages belong to the Common Reader, & were written in bed with influenza;[1] & now, at last, having sent off the last proofs today, I have got my new diary made, & shall close this, with a thousand apologies, & some ominous forebodings at the sight of all the blank pages.

VW here begins a new book, Diary XIV, on the title-page of which is written:

52 Tavistock Square WC

1925

Wednesday 18 March[2]

This disgrace has been already explained—I think: two books to see through the press, mainly between tea & dinner; influenza, & a distaste for the pen.[3]

At the moment (I have 7½ before dinner) I can only note that the past is beautiful because one never realises an emotion at the time. It expands later, & thus we don't have complete emotions about the present, only about the past. This struck me on Reading platform, watching Nessa & Quentin kiss, he coming up shyly, yet with some emotion. This I shall remember; & make more of, when separated from all the business of crossing the platform, finding our bus &c. That is why we dwell on the past, I think.

We went to see the children at school: the young men, I should say. Julian was shut up in a pound, pounding Mr Eliot's tennis court by way of punishment. (That suggests a story about a man whose ambition it was to buy a field; this kept him alive; when he bought it, he died.) Mr Goddard came up, & Julian shouted out, "I'm at it till 5" as though they were undergraduates.[4] Not much public school about this; but oh

1. This entry follows a one-page, extensively rewritten draft of the final paragraph (on Sir Thomas Browne) of 'The Elizabethan Lumber Room', published as part of the *Common Reader* on 23 April 1925.
2. VW has written *Saturday 18 March*; Saturday was either 14 or 21 March, but the date rather than the day here seems more likely to be right.
3. Nancy Cunard's *Parallax* and R. C. Trevelyan's *Poems and Fables* (*HP Checklist* 78) were both hand-printed at the Hogarth Press and published in April 1925. VW probably caught influenza from LW, who was ill from 11-13 March.
4. Quentin Bell had followed his elder brother Julian to Leighton Park School, near Reading, and was now in his second term there. T. C. Elliott (d. 1969) taught French at the school from 1915-30; Scott Goddard (1895-1965) was music master, 1921-26, and later became a well-known music critic. For *pounding* read *rolling*.

the horror of being Mr Goddard, & wandering out, this bitter day (it snowed) to welcome home the steeplechasers. When they ran in, they at once rolled on the ground, & were covered with rugs & coats. The last lap, their legs rose very weakly. J. & Q. were utterly cynical about this, & said no one enjoyed it, but it was thought the right thing to do. But this nib scratches.

The Woolfs travelled from Victoria, via Newhaven-Dieppe, to Paris on Thursday 26 March, then on by overnight train to Marseilles and to Cassis, where they stayed at the Hotel Cendrillon; they returned to London on 6/7 April.

Wednesday 8 April

Just back from Cassis. Often while I was there I thought how I would write here frequently & so get down some of the myriad impressions which I net every day. But directly we get back, what is it that happens? We strip & dive into the stream, & I am obsessed with a foolish idea that I have no time to stop & write, or that I ought to be doing something serious. Even now, I pelt along feverishly, thinking half the time, but I must stop & take Grizzle [*dog*] out; I must get my American books in order;[1] the truth is, I must try to set aside half an hour in some part of my day, & consecrate it to diary writing. Give it a name & a place, & then perhaps, such is the human mind, I shall come to think it a duty, & disregard other duties for it.

I am under the impression of the moment, which is the complex one of coming back home from the South of France to this wide dim peaceful privacy—London (so it seemed last night) which is shot with the accident I saw this morning & a woman crying Oh oh oh faintly, pinned against the railings with a motor car on top of her. All day I have heard that voice. I did not go to her help; but then every baker & flower seller did that. A great sense of the brutality & wildness of the world remains with me—there was this woman in brown walking along the pavement— suddenly a red film car turns a somersault, lands on top of her, & one hears this oh, oh, oh. I was on my way to see Nessa's new house, & met Duncan in the square, but as he had seen nothing, he could not in the

---

1. VW's article 'American Fiction' appeared in the *Saturday Review of Literature*, New York, on 1 August 1925 (Kp C265).

least feel what I felt, or Nessa either, though she made some effort to connect it with Angelica's accident last spring. But I assured her it was only a passing brown woman; & so we went over the house composedly enough.[2]

Since I wrote, which is these last months, Jacques Raverat has died; after longing to die; & he sent me a letter about Mrs Dalloway which gave me one of the happiest days of my life.[3] I wonder if this time I have achieved something? Well, nothing anyhow compared with Proust, in whom I am embedded now. The thing about Proust is his combination of the utmost sensibility with the utmost tenacity. He searches out these butterfly shades to the last grain. He is as tough as catgut & as evanescent as a butterfly's bloom. And he will I suppose both influence me & make me out of temper with every sentence of my own. Jacques died, as I say; & at once the siege of emotions began. I got the news with a party here— Clive, Bee How, Julia Strachey, Dadie.[4] Nevertheless, I do not any longer feel inclined to doff the cap to death. I like to go out of the room talking, with an unfinished casual sentence on my lips. That is the effect it had on me—no leavetakings, no submission—but someone stepping out into the darkness. For her though the nightmare was terrific. All I can do now

2. For Vanessa Bell and Duncan Grant see Appendix I. An account of their daughter Angelica's accident is given in *II VW Diary*, 5 April 1924. 'Nessa's new house' was part of no. 37 Gordon Square.

3. Jacques Pierre Raverat (1885-1925), a Frenchman who had studied mathematics at Cambridge and was one of the group of friends called by VW the 'neo-Pagans', another of whom, the wood-engraver Gwendolen Mary Darwin (1885-1957), he married in 1911. They lived at Vence in the Alpes-Maritimes, and he became a painter. He had suffered for some years from a form of disseminated sclerosis, a paralysing disease, and his letters were dictated to his wife. About a month before his death on 7 March 1925, VW had sent him advance proofs of *Mrs Dalloway*, and he responded: 'Almost it's enough to make me want to live a little longer, to continue to receive such letters and such books . . . I am flattered & you know how important an element that is in one's sensations, and proud & pleased . . .' The correspondence between VW and Jacques and Gwen Raverat is preserved in MHP, Sussex.

4. For Clive Bell see Appendix I. Beatrice Isabel Howe, later Mrs Mark Lubbock, author of *A Fairy Leapt Upon My Knee* (1927); she was painted by Duncan Grant in 1926 (see *Shone*, p 228) Julia Frances Strachey (1901-79), daughter of Oliver Strachey and his first wife Ruby Mayer, was to become a writer of unusual character and quality if of scant quantity. George Humphrey Wolferston ('Dadie') Rylands (b. 1902), Scholar of Eton and King's College, Cambridge, and an Apostle; he worked in the Hogarth Press for the last six months of 1924 and then left to work for his Cambridge Fellowship. His poem *Russet and Taffeta*, dedicated to VW, was published in December 1925 (*HP Checklist* 75).

is to keep natural with her, which is I believe a matter of considerable importance. More & more do I repeat my own version of Montaigne "Its life that matters".[5]

I am waiting to see what form of itself Cassis will finally cast up in my mind. There are the rocks. We used to go out after breakfast & sit on the rocks, with the sun on us. L. used to sit without a hat, writing on his knee. One morning he found a sea urchin—they are red, with spikes which quiver slightly. Then we would go a walk in the afternoon, right up over the hill, into the woods, where one day we heard the motor cars & discovered the road to La Ciota[t] just beneath. It was stony, steep & very hot. We heard a great chattering birdlike noise once, & I bethought me of the frogs. The ragged red tulips were out in the fields; all the fields were little angular shelves cut out of the hill, & ruled & ribbed with vines; & all red, & rosy & purple here & there with the spray of some fruit tree in bud. Here & there was an angular white, or yellow or blue washed house, with all its shutters tightly closed; & flat paths round it, & once rows of stocks; an incomparable cleanness & definiteness everywhere. At La Ciota[t] great orange ships rose up out of the blue water of the little bay. All these bays are very circular, & fringed with the pale coloured plaster houses, very tall, shuttered, patched & peeled, now with a pot & tufts of green on them, now with clothes, drying; now an old old woman looking. On the hill, which is stony as a desert, the nets were drying; & then in the streets children & girls gossiped & meandered all in pale bright shawls & cotton frocks, while the men picked up the earth of the main square to make a paved court of it. The Hotel Cendrillon is a white house, with red tiled floors, capable of housing perhaps 8 people. There were Miss Toogood, the Howards, Miss Betsy Roberts, Mr Gurney, Mr Francis &, finally, Mr Hugh Anderson & Mr Garrow Tomlin.[6] All deserve pages of description. And then the whole hotel atmosphere provided me with many ideas: oh so cold, indifferent, superficially polite, & exhibiting such odd relationships: as if human nature were now reduced to a kind of code, which it has devised to meet these emergencies, where people who do not know each other meet, & claim their rights as members of the same tribe. As a matter of fact, we got into touch all round; but our depths were not invaded. But L. & I were too too happy,

5. See 'Montaigne' in *The Common Reader*, p 95: 'But enough of death; it is life that matters.' VW wrote this day to Gwen Raverat; see *III VW Letters*, no. 1547; also no. 1550 of 1 May 1925.
6. Hew Anderson, see below, 19 July 1925; the Hon George Garrow Tomlin (1898-1931), elder brother of Stephen Tomlin, the sculptor (see below, 27 March 1926); other hotel guests unidentified.

as they say; if it were now to die &c.[7] Nobody shall say of me that I have not known perfect happiness, but few could put their finger on the moment, or say what made it. Even I myself, stirring occasionally in the pool of content, could only say But this is all I want; could not think of anything better; & had only my half superstitious feeling as the Gods who must when they have created happiness, grudge it. Not if you get it in unexpected ways though.

Sunday 19 April

It is now after dinner, our first summer time night, & the mood for writing has left me, only just brushed me & left me. I have not achieved my sacred half hour yet. But think—in time to come I would rather read something here than reflect that I did polish off Mr Ring Lardner success-fully.[8] I'm out to make £300 this summer by writing, & build a bath & hot water range at Rodmell. But, hush, hush—my books tremble on the verge of coming out, & my future is uncertain. As for forecasts—its *just* on the cards Mrs Dalloway is a success (Harcourt thinks it "wonderful"), & sells 2,000—I dont expect it: I expect a slow silent increase of fame, such has come about, rather miraculously, since Js R. was published; my value mounting steadily as a journalist, though scarcely a copy sold. And I am not very nervous—rather; & I want as usual to dig deep down into my new stories, without having a looking glass flashed in my eyes— Todd, to wit; Colefax to wit et cetera.[9]

7. '...... If it were now to die,
    'Twere now to be most happy; for, I fear,
    My soul hath her content so absolute,
    That not another comfort like to this
    Succeeds in unknown fate.'   *Othello*, II, i

8. Ringgold Wilmer (Ring) Lardner (1885-1933), American short-story writer whose work is discussed by VW in her article 'American Fiction' (Kp C265); see above, 8 April 1925, n 1.

9. VW wrote several 'stories' concerned with 'the party consciousness, the frock consciousness' (see below, 27 April 1925) at this period, seven of which are collected in *Mrs Dalloway's Party* (1973) edited by Stella McNichol (whose editorial procedures were severely criticised by J. F. Hulcoop in the *VW Miscellany*, no. 3, Spring 1975, and defended in *ibid*, no. 9, Winter 1977). Manuscript and typescript versions of these stories are both now in the Berg. Dorothy Todd, who edited British *Vogue* from 1922-26, sought to make it an authoritative and sophisticated guide to high fashion in clothes and culture, and commissioned contributions from *avant-garde* writers (including VW) and artists in both France and England. Lady Colefax (*née* Sibyl Halsey, d. 1950) was celebrated for her indefatigable pursuit of 'interesting' people, whom she and her husband Sir Arthur entertained at their home, Argyll House, Chelsea.

Lytton came in the other night. He seemed to me autumnal; with that charming rectitude of spirit which no one else attains so perfectly I think. His justice of mind is considerable. But Christ is dismissed, to his disappointment, for he grows more & more fussy about subjects: Christ, he says did not exist: was a figment; & so much is known that really he couldn't pull it all together in one book. Then perhaps Philip Ritchie is waning.[10] We talked of old buggers & their lack of attraction for young men. My anti-bugger revolution has run round the world, as I hoped it would. I am a little touched by what appears their contrition, & anxiety to condone their faults. Yet if I cant say what's in my mind, & have a fling with Clive's Colonel now & then, what's the use of me?[11] The pale star of the Bugger has been in the ascendant too long. Julian agrees emphatically. We had Good Friday at Rodmell—June weather, & again this downy billowy wave beneath us: ah, but how quickly I sink; what violet shadows there are between the high lights, & one, perhaps, as unreasonable as another. But this properly belongs to a story.[12]

Yesterday we went to Max's show with dear shabby old Angus, who seems to me an elder brother, 20 years younger than I am.[13] We came back to tea (over all this the bloom of the past descends as I write—it becomes sad, beautiful, memorable) & ate a great many buns, & then discussed Murphy.[14] Alas!—she has a temper. She is an ill-conditioned mongrel woman, of no charm, a Bohemian scallywag, something like Irish stew to look at, & not destined for a long life here, I suppose. But Angus, though plaintive is gentlemanly; does not insist, & sees the drawbacks;

10. The Hon. Philip Charles Thomson Ritchie (1899-1927), eldest son of Lord Ritchie of Dundee, had been called to the Bar in 1924, and since the previous summer had engaged Lytton Strachey's affections.
11. The meaning is here equivocal. In most contexts 'Clive's Colonel' would mean his elder brother Lt. Col. William Cory Bell (1875-1961), Unionist MP for Devizes from 1918-23, whose views on buggery were likely to be more emphatic than VW's own. However, Clive Bell had recently published an article entitled 'The Colonel's Theory' (N & A, 7 March 1925), discussing Tolstoy on Art by Aylmer Maude, and referring to Tolstoy as 'a retired colonel—or lieutenant was it?'; but it is not easy to see in what way this was relevant to the matter in hand.
12. The Woolfs had motored down to Sussex with Clive Bell and Duncan Grant, and were at Rodmell from Maundy Thursday to Easter Monday, 9-13 April.
13. The Woolfs went to the opening day on 18 April of an exhibition of new caricatures by Max Beerbohm at the Leicester Galleries; it included the series 'The Old and the Young Self' and an unusual number of cartoons of political interest.
14. Bernadette Murphy came to work as secretary in the Hogarth Press on 4 February 1925.

Leonard will have to pull out the tooth on Thursday. I suspect some hidden grievance: I suspect she harbours scores.

Marjory & her Tom looked in at the basement this evening, very happy, L. says, & indeed I think she must enjoy her situation to the last ounce—money, food, security, & a supply of young men, & her faithful Tom, & a little dress allowance, & breakfast late, & consideration. She is a nice trusty creature into the bargain, & if I wished to see anyone, I daresay it would be her.[15]

At this moment, all we wish is to escape seeing anyone. Tomorrow I shall buy a new dress. I observe here that I am becoming jerky & jumpy, & my con[s]cience is asserting that I ought to read Mr Ring Lardner & earn my 50 guineas.

Monday 20 April

Happiness is to have a little string onto which things will attach themselves. For example, going to my dressmaker in Judd Street, or rather thinking of a dress I could get her to make, & imagining it made— that is the string, which as if it dipped loosely into a wave of treasure brings up pearls sticking to it. Poor Murphy is in the glumps, owing to Leonard's fiery harshness—each of which epithets he would most certainly deny. She has no string dipping into the green wave: things don't connect for her; & add up into those entrancing bundles which are happiness. And my days are likely to be strung with them. I like this London life in early summer—the street sauntering & square haunting, & then if my books (I never speak of L.'s pamphlet) were to be a success; if we could begin building at Monks, & put up wireless for Nelly, & get the Skeats to live at Shanks' cottage—if—if—if[16]—What will happen is *some* intensities of pleasure, some profound plunges of gloom. Bad reviews, being ignored; & then some delicious clap of compliment. But really what I should like would be to have £3 to buy a pair of rubber soled boots, & go for country walks on Sundays.

15. Marjorie Thomson (*c*. 1900-1931), at that time ostensibly married to C. E. M. Joad, had worked in the Hogarth Press from January 1923 until February 1925; she was about to marry Thomas Humphrey Marshall (b. 1893), Fellow of Trinity College, Cambridge, economist and social scientist, who taught at the London School of Economics. He was an elder brother of Frances Marshall (see below, 30 April, n 6).

16. LW's pamphlet *Fear and Politics. A Debate at the Zoo*, no. 7 in the first series of Hogarth Essays, was published in July 1925 (*HP Checklist* 79). The 'surly poet' and journalist Edward Shanks (see *II VW Diary*) had lived at Charnes Cottage, next door to Monks House. 'Skeats' unidentified.

One thing in considering my state of mind now, seems to me beyond dispute, that I have at last, bored down into my oil well, & can't scribble fast enough to bring it all to the surface. I have now at least 6 stories welling up in me, & feel, at last, that I can coin all my thoughts into words. Not but what an infinite number of problems remain; but I have never felt this rush & urgency before. I believe I can write much more quickly: if writing it is—this dash at the paper of a phrase, & then the typing & retyping—trying it over, the actual writing being now like the sweep of a brush; I fill it up afterwards. Now suppose I might become one of the interesting—I will not say great—but interesting novelists? Oddly, for all my vanity, I have not until now had much faith in my novels, or thought them my own expression.

Monday 27 April

The Common Reader was out on Thursday:[17] this is Monday, & so far I have not heard a word about it, private or public: it is as if one tossed a stone into a pond, & the waters closed without a ripple. And I am perfectly content, & care less than I have ever cared, & make this note just to remind me next time of the sublime progress of my books. I have been sitting to Vogue, the Becks that is, in their mews, which Mr Woolner built as his studio, & perhaps it was there he thought of my mother, whom he wished to marry, I think.[18] But my present reflection is that people have any number of states of

second selves is
what I mean

consciousness: & I should like to investigate the party consciousness, the frock consciousness &c. The fashion world at the Becks—Mrs Garland was there superintending a display—is certainly one;[19] where people secrete an envelope which connects them & protects

17. *The Common Reader* was published by the Hogarth Press on 23 April in an edition of 1250 copies (*HP Checklist* 81).
18. Maurice Adams Beck (1886-1960) and his partner Helen Macgregor were *Vogue*'s chief photographers at this period. Their studios at 4 Marylebone Mews had been built in 1861 at the rear of his new house at 29 Welbeck Street by the pre-Raphaelite sculptor Thomas Woolner (1825-1892), who about that time had sought leave to make a bust of Julia Jackson, for whom he cherished 'a more than artistic admiration', and to whom he made an offer of marriage; both overtures were declined. (See Leslie Stephen, *The Mausoleum Book*, edited by Alan Bell, 1977, p 28.) Beck and MacGregor had photographed VW the previous year, and one was reproduced by *Vogue* in its feature 'We Nominate for the Hall of Fame' in late May, 1924 (see also *In Vogue*, edited by Georgina Howell, 1975, p 61). A portrait from the present sitting was to appear in *Vogue*'s early May issue, 1926. (See also *QB II*, pl. 6a; Cecil Beaton, *British Photographers*, 1944, p 61.)
19. Madge Garland was Fashion Editor of *Vogue* under Dorothy Todd's editorship.

them from others, like myself, who am outside the envelope, foreign bodies. These states are very difficult (obviously I grope for words) but I'm always coming back to it. The party consciousness, for example: Sybil's consciousness. You must not break it. It is something real. You must keep it up; conspire together. Still I cannot get at what I mean. Then I meant to dash off Graves before I forget him.[20]

Figure a bolt eyed blue shirted shockheaded hatless man in a blue overcoat standing goggling at the door at 4.30, on Friday. "Mrs Woolf?" I dreading & suspecting some Nation genius, some young man determined to unbosom himself, rushed him to the basement, where he said "I'm Graves". "I'm Graves". Everybody stared. He appeared to have been rushing through the air at 60 miles an hour & to have alighted temporarily. So he came up, &, wily as I am, I knew that to advance holding the kettle in a dishclout was precisely the right method, attitude, pose. The poor boy is all emphasis protestation & pose. He has a crude likeness to Shelley, save that his nose is a switchback & his lines blurred. But the consciousness of genius is bad for people. He stayed till 7.15 (we were going to Caesar & Cleopatra—a strange rhetorical romantic early Shaw play[21]) & had at last to say so, for he was so thick in the delight of explaining his way of life to us that no bee stuck faster to honey. He cooks, his wife cleans; 4 children are brought up in the elementary school; the villagers give them vegetables; they were married in Church; his wife calls herself Nancy Nicolson; won't go to Garsington, said to him I must have a house for nothing; on a river; in a village with a square church tower; near but not on a railway—all of which, as she knows her mind, he procured. Calling herself Nicolson has sorted her friends into sheep & goats. All this to us sounded like the usual self consciousness of young men, especially as he threw in, gratuitously, the information that he descends from dean rector, Bishop, Von Ranker &c &c &c: only in order to say that he despises them. Still, still, he is a nice ingenuous rattle headed young man; but why should our age put this burden of

20. Robert Ranke Graves (b. 1895), poet and novelist; in 1918 he had married eighteen-year-old Nancy, daughter of the painter William Nicholson. The information concerning Graves's heredity and way of life here summarised by VW is amplified in his autobiography *Goodbye To All That* (1929). The Hogarth Press had already published two, and were to publish a further four, books by him (see *HP Checklist*, nos. 33, 46, 59, 63, 92 and 93).

21. Bernard Shaw's play, with Cedric Hardwicke and Gwen Ffrangcon-Davies in the name parts, was given by the Birmingham Repertory Theatre Company at the Kingsway Theatre; the Woolfs went on the evening of 23 April—a Thursday, which implies that VW was mistaken in supposing Graves's visit to have been on a Friday.

proof on us? Surely once one could live simply without protestations. I tried, perhaps, to curry favour, as my weakness is. L. was adamant. Then we were offered a ticket for the Cup tie, to see wh. Graves has come to London after 6 years; cant travel in a train without being sick; is rather proud of his sensibility. No I don't think he'll write great poetry: but what will you? The sensitive are needed too; the halfbaked, stammering stuttering, who perhaps improve their own quarter of Oxfordshire.

And on Sunday we had our first walk, to Epping.[22]

Wednesday 29 April

Hastily (Moore waiting[23]) I must record the fact of Tom's long gaslit emotional rather tremulous & excited visit last night, which informed us of his release (But I have not yet sent in my demission) from the Bank; some heavensent appointment, providing "4/5th's of my present salary" & a guarantee, being "humanly speaking" certain, to take effect next October—whether Lady Rothermere (who has become 'very nice') or the 4ly review, he sayeth not. Then he has a house near Sloane Sqre in view, rent £58 only, & so hopes to start fresh, & has been thinking over his state these past weeks, being alone, with time on his hands.[24] He has seen his whole life afresh, seen his relations to the world, & to Vivien in particular, become humbler suppler more humane—good, sensitive honourable man as he is, accusing himself of being the American husband, & wishing to tell me privately (L. gone to fetch the letters) what store V. sets by me, has done nothing but write since last June, because I told her to! He then defended not writing which is her device he said, & went into her p[s]ychology. Then he said to L. (having told us that he must space his remarks very carefully to fit in all he had to say) Do you know

22. Of this outing LW noted in his diary: 'Went Loughton train, & walked Epping Forest, High Beech & Chingford, & back by bus.'

23. VW was presumably reading for her article on George Moore's *Hail and Farewell* which was to be published in *Vogue*, early June, 1925 (Kp C263.1).

24. For T. S. Eliot and his wife Vivienne, see Appendix I. Heaven was sending Eliot, through several benevolent intermediaries, an appointment to the editorial board of the publishers Faber & Gwyer (later Faber & Faber), which he was to occupy from November 1925 until his death. The literary quarterly *The Criterion*, created for and edited by Eliot since 1922, had been subsidised by Lady Rothermere (d. 1937), wife of the newspaper proprietor Alfred Harmsworth, 1st Viscount Rothermere; Faber & Gwyer now undertook to share, and later to shoulder, the financial responsibility and it continued as *The New Criterion*, subsequently *The Monthly Criterion*, and once again as *The Criterion*, until its dissolution in 1939. The Eliots were to move to 57 Chester Terrace (now Row), a short distance from Sloane Square.

anything about psycho-analysis? L. said yes, in his responsible way; &
Tom then told us the queer story—how Martin the dr. set V. off thinking
of her childhood terror of loneliness, & now she cant let him, Tom, out
of her sight. There he has sat mewed in her room these 3 months, poor
pale creature, or if he has to go out, comes in to find her in a half fainting
state.[25]

"Tomorrow will be wretched" he said, for he was now away from
8 to 11. We advised another doctor. But whether its doctors or sense or
holiday or travel or some drastic method unknown thats to cure that
little nervous self conscious bundle—heaven knows. She has the abstract,
he the historic mind he said. The upshot was a queer sense of his emotion
in coming to tell us all this—something not merely touching to my vanity
but to my sense of human worth, I think; his liking for us, affection,
trust in Leonard, & being so much at his ease in some subconscious way
he said, not in conversation, with me, all making me lay my arm on his
shoulder; not a very passionate caress, but the best I can do.

And now I'm a little fidgety about the *Common Reader*; not a single
word of it from a soul, & perhaps a Review in the Lit Sup tomorrow.
But this is quite recognisably superficial; beneath my fidgets being
considerable stability.

Friday 1 May

This is a note for future reference as they say. The Common Reader
came out 8 days ago, & so far not a single review has appeared, & no body
has written to me or spoken to me about it or in any way acknowledged
the fact of its existence; save Maynard, Lydia, & Duncan. Clive is
conspicuously dumb; Mortimer has flu & cant review it; Nancy saw him
reading it, but reported no opinion: all signs which point to a dull chill
depressing reception; & complete failure.[1] I have just come through the
hoping fearing stage, & now see my disappointment floating like an old

25. Sketches by Vivienne Eliot, using the pseudonyms Feiron Morris or Fanny
Marlow, appeared in each quarterly issue of *The Criterion* between October 1924
and July 1925. Dr Marten was a physician and lay-psychologist of Freiburg much
favoured by Lady Ottoline Morrell; Eliot had written to VW on 22 May 1924
(MHP Sussex, copy) warmly recommending him as a remarkable doctor who had
done Vivienne a great deal of good the previous year—'in fact, made the turning
point in that serious illness'; by 10 July 1925 he was writing to LW that he should
consider suing Dr Marten did it not entail the necessity of going to Germany to
do so.
1. For Maynard Keynes, Lydia Lopokova, Raymond Mortimer and Duncan Grant
see Appendix I.

bottle in my wake & am off on fresh adventures. Only if the same thing happens to Dalloway one need not be surprised. But I must write to Gwen.[2]

Monday 4 May

This is the temperature chart of a book. We went to Cambridge, & Goldie said he thought me the finest living critic: the paralysed man, Hayward, said, in his jerky angular way: "Who wrote that extraordinarily good article on the Elizabethans 2 or 3 months ago in the Lit. Sup.?" I pointed to my breast.[3] Now there's one sneering review in Country Life, almost inarticulate with feebleness, trying to say what a Common reader is, & another, says Angus, in the Star, laughing at Nessa's cover.[4] So from this I prognosticate a good deal of criticism on the ground that I'm obscure & odd; & some enthusiasm; a slow sale, & an increased reputation. Oh yes—my reputation increases. But I am headachy, & cannot go to a concert with Angus, & Leonard is giving Randall his farewell dinner,[5] & it [is] a relief to sit quiet (the joy of giving up an engagement is supreme) & I wish I could describe Pernel, Cambridge, Braithwaite & Hayward, with a postscript for Thompson. A lovely place full, like all places, now, of this wave of the past. Walking past the Darwins I noticed the willows; I thought with that growing maternal affection which now comes to me, of myself there; of Rupert; then I went to Newnham, & kindled Mrs Palmer with talk of Pernel marrying an Archbishop.[6]

2. She did: see *III VW Letters*, no. 1550.
3. The Woolfs went to Cambridge on Saturday afternoon so that LW might attend an Apostles' meeting that evening; they returned to London on Sunday evening. Goldsworthy ('Goldie') Lowes Dickinson (1862-1932), Fellow of King's College and an Apostle, had resigned his lectureship in Political Science in 1920. John Davy Hayward (1905-65), who was to become a notable bibliophile and editor, was in his final year at King's; he suffered from muscular dystrophy.
4. *Country Life*, 2 May 1925, contained an unsigned review, 'What Does the "Common Reader" Read?' The critic in the *Star*, 1 May 1925, was Horace Thorogood; of the jacket design he wrote that 'only a conscious artist could have done it so badly'.
5. On 3 May 1925 John Randall completed fifty years of service as proof-reader on the *Athenaeum* (now amalgamated with the *Nation*); he finally retired the following January, when LW, on behalf of his colleagues, presented him with a barometer.
6. As LW was dining with his brother Apostles, VW walked to Newnham College to dine with the Principal, (Joan) Pernel Strachey (1876-1951), the fourth of Lytton's five sisters, passing Newnham Grange, the Darwin's house by the river, on her way. (Cf *A Room of One's Own*, chapter I.) Helen Elizabeth Palmer (1887-1954), Tutor at Newnham, was a widowed sister of VW's old admirer Walter Lamb (see *VW Diary* Volumes I and II). VW presumably saw Thompson and

No, I can't fire it off [?]; Mrs Asquith sticks in my gizzard;[7] I shall read Moore till dinner, & ⟨a paper⟩ then again till Leonard comes in. No, I dont want to hear Bach, & by giving Angus the tickets, secured him a charming young man for company.

Pernel was easier than I've ever known her. We sat over her fire, gossiping—how Kate died, taking the dog for a walk till a week of the end; entirely reserved; like a skeleton, like a dead person walking with sarcoma; no doctor. No mention of herself & the 58 brown diaries burnt, I suppose.[8]

Saturday 9 May

Just back from the Greek play at Chiswick with Lydia & Berta Ruck; a fine spring day, all the trees out driving across the Park; that transient journey being founded on a walk with Nessa Clive & Thoby, & Thoby & I agreed in calling Hyde Park 'urbane'.[9]

As for the Common Reader, the Lit. Sup. had close on 2 columns sober & sensible praise—neither one thing nor the other—my fate in the Times. And Goldie writes that he thinks "this is the best criticism in English—humorous, witty & profound."[10]—My fate is to be treated to all extremes & all mediocrities. But I never get an enthusiastic review in the Lit. Sup. And it will be the same for Dalloway, which now approaches.

Braithwaite, both Apostles, next day, as LW breakfasted with the one and lunched with the other. George Derwent Thompson (b. 1903) was a Fellow of King's who in 1937 became Professor of Greek at Birmingham; Richard Bevan Braithwaite (b. 1900), also a Fellow of King's, was to become a University lecturer and then Knightbridge Professor of Moral Philosophy at Cambridge, 1953-67.

7. VW's review, entitled 'Gipsy or Governess?', of Margot Asquith's *Places and Persons* appeared in the *N & A* on 16 May 1925 (KpC262·4).

8. VW's cousin Katherine Stephen (1856-1924) had been Principal of Newnham from 1911-20. See *II VW Diary*, 19 February 1924: '... there in a row on a shelf were her diaries from Jan 1 1877. ... And on her last day she will say to the charwoman who attends her, Bring me the diaries which you will find in the cabinet; & now, put them on the fire.'

9. The Cambridge Amateur Dramatic Company performed Euripides' *Helen* and *Cyclops* at the Chiswick Empire on 9 May in versions by J. T. Sheppard, who gave an introductory talk on 'Euripides and Comedy'. VW had unconsciously killed off the popular novelist Berta Ruck (Mrs Oliver ('Sally') Onions, 1878-1978) in *Jacob's Room* (see *II QB*, pp 91-2, where in her letter to the author Mrs Onions misremembers the performance as being of *The Frogs*). Thoby was VW's elder brother, who had died in 1906.

10. 'Mrs Woolf as Critic' appeared in the *TLS* of 7 May 1925 (see *M & M*, p 148); G. L. Dickinson's letter of the same date (accurately quoted) is in MHP, Sussex.

I'm jangled & jaded, having sat next the sea horse Sally Onions, who oozes lust at the sight of young men dancing. Last night we made a meagre meal with the Sangers,[11] whose mediocrity of comfort & taste saddens me: oh for a little beauty in life, as Berta Ruck might say—a lewd woman that, deposited in a lewd South Kensington House, like an equestrienne, in pale Jacon with a carnation, & her front teeth with a red ridge on them where her lips had touched them.[12] Little Lydia I liked: how does her mind work? Like a lark soaring; a sort of glorified instinct inspires her: I suppose a very nice nature, & direction at Maynard's hands.

Last night we had Morgan & Brace;[13] Morgan pleading with Leonard to come & see him—operated on for a broken bone in the wrist, I should have added, but it is now

Thursday 14 May

The first day of summer, leaves visibly drawing out of the bud, & the Square almost green. Oh what a country day—& some of my friends are now reading Mrs D. in the country.[14]

I meant to register more of my books temperatures. C.R. does not sell; but is praised. I was really pleased to open the Manchester Guardian this morning & read Mr Fausset on The Art of V.W. Brilliance combined with integrity; profound as well as eccentric.[15] Now if only the Times would speak out thus, but the Times mumbles & murmurs like a man sucking pebbles—did I say that I had nearly 2 mumbling columns on me there? But the odd thing is this: honestly I am scarcely a shade nervous about Mrs D. Why is this? Really I am a little bored, for the first time, at thinking how much I shall have to talk about it this summer. The truth is that writing is the profound pleasure & being read the superficial. I'm now all on the strain with desire to stop journalism & get on to *To the Lighthouse*. This is going to be fairly short: to have father's character done complete in it; & mothers; & St Ives; & childhood; & all the usual things I try to put in—life, death &c. But the centre is father's character,

11. C. P. (Charlie) Sanger (1871-1930), Chancery Barrister and an Apostle, and his wife Anna Dorothea (Dora), *née* Pease (1865-1955), lived in Oakley Street, Chelsea. VW had known them since before her marriage, and was very fond of him, but less so of his wife.
12. Jacon = jaconet, a plain light-weight cotton fabric, like muslin.
13. For E. Morgan Forster, see Appendix I. Donald Clifford Brace (1881-1955) was a co-founder of VW's American publishers, Harcourt, Brace; he came to tea.
14. *Mrs Dalloway* was published by the Hogarth Press on 14 May 1925.
15. The *Manchester Guardian*'s review of *The Common Reader* was by the author and literary critic Hugh I'Anson Fausset (1895-1965). It is reprinted in *M & M*, p 151.

sitting in a boat, reciting We perished, each alone, while he crushes a dying mackerel—However, I must refrain.[16] I must write a few little stories first, & let the Lighthouse simmer, adding to it between tea & dinner till it is complete for writing out.

Yesterday was a terrific chatter day—Desmond on top of Dr Leyes, Lord Olivier on top of Desmond, James & Dadie to finish off with, while L. had I forget how many press interviews & committees into the bargain. The League of Nations is booming (Innes, I mean.)[17] But I meant to describe my dear old Desmond, whom it rejoiced me to see again, & he held out both his hands, & I set him in his chair & we talked till 7 o'clock. He is rather worn & aged; a little, I think, feeling that here's 45 on him & nothing achieved, except indeed the children, whom he dotes on— Micky to write, Dermod & Rachel trilling & warbling on flute & piano:[18] all his human relations very fertile & flourishing, but oh, he said, talking of Houseman, don't let him give up the Corn Exchange & take to literature![19] I saw him thinking of his 50 articles for 5 years, his welter of old articles lying dusty in boxes, & now Geoffrey Scott promoted to do Donne, which Desmond should have done in the year 1912. I

16. From the last verse of William Cowper's poem, 'The Castaway':
    'No voice divine the storm allay'd,
      No light propitious shone,
    When, snatch'd from all effectual aid,
      We perish'd, each alone:
    But I beneath a rougher sea,
      And whelm'd in deeper gulfs than he.'

17. For Desmond MacCarthy and James Strachey, see Appendix I. Dr Norman Maclean Leys (d. 1944), had spent sixteen years in the Public Health Service in East and Central Africa; his controversial book *Kenya* had been published by the Hogarth Press six months earlier (*HP Checklist* 48). Sydney Olivier (1859-1943), 1st Baron Olivier of Ramsden, Fabian socialist and colonial administrator, had been ennobled in order that he might serve as Secretary of State for India in the shortlived Labour administration of 1924; four books by him were to be published by the Hogarth Press (*HP Checklist* 138, 139, 204 and 327). Kathleen E. Innes's book *The Story of the League of Nations told for Young People* had been published in April 1925 (*HP Checklist* 65).

18. The MacCarthy children were Michael (1907-1973), Rachel (b. 1909), and Dermod (b. 1911); Michael became a farmer and Dermod a doctor; Rachel was to marry a writer (Lord David Cecil) and to publish a novel.

19. This may be interpreted as Desmond's way of expressing his hope that his son Michael—whose ambition was to become a farmer—should stick to so useful and rewarding a profession (i.e. growing or selling corn) rather than suffer the financial and ethical doubts and insecurities of the literary life. (A. E. Housman had spent ten years in the Patent Office before becoming an academic and publishing his poetry.)

remember him telling me the story at Brunswick Square. So I said I would
take the thing in hand & see it through which touched him, for children
are not enough, after all; one wants something to be made out of oneself
alone—& 5 boxes of dusty articles are rather raggy & rotten for 45 years.
And he praised the C.R. with enthusiasm; & will write on it,[20] & so we
chattered along; Vernon Lee, with her cheap rings in exquisite taste; &
her idiomatic Italian; & her spiteful way of seeing things, so that she
dare not write her memoirs; Lily Langtry coming down the playhouse
steps & her daughter looming behind her, loveliness that "struck me in
the breast"; also Logan & Ottoline—how Alys is ill of the cancer again—
"a most unhappy miserable life poor woman—" L. having the new Mrs
B.R. on one side, would be chafed to death by Ott. next door; but like a
fool, Logan made none of this clear, & only complained that the village
peace of Chelsea would be destroyed by O. wh. naturally she resented.[21]
In all this, Desmond acts as solvent & go between, everyone sponging
on his good nature & sense. What else did we discuss? The E[lizabe]thans?
The Phoenix; poor Ray Litvin's miserable big mouth, & little body;[22]

20. Geoffrey Scott (1883-1929), whose second book *The Portrait of Zélide* appeared
    this year, never 'did' Donne. Desmond's aspirations in this respect are referred
    to in *I VW Letters*, no. 617 of 21 May [1912]: '. . . we go over the story of Donne's
    life. As the greater part of the history of England is somehow coming in, the
    book will be apoplectic.' His essay on Donne was republished in his book *Criticism*
    (1932), 'a selection from a selection made for me from the accumulation of many
    years of literary journalism'. VW went through his articles at this time (see below,
    15 May and 1 June 1925, and *III VW Letters*, no. 1553, probably of 20, not 17,
    May) to encourage him to make a book from them, but her efforts were ineffective.
    'Affable Hawk' (Desmond MacCarthy) reviewed *The Common Reader*—'a most
    uncommon book'—in the *New Statesman* of 30 May 1925.
21. Vernon Lee was the pseudonym of Violet Paget (1856-1935), a prolific writer,
    notably on Italian cultural history; she lived in Florence but made frequent visits
    to London. Emilie (Lillie), *née* Le Breton, widow of Edward Langtry and now
    Lady de Bathe (1853-1929), actress and famous beauty, was known as 'The Jersey
    Lily'; her daughter Jeanne-Marie was the child of Prince Louis of Battenberg.
    Logan Pearsall Smith (1865-1946), American-born man of letters, lived in
    St Leonard's Terrace, Chelsea, with his sister Alys (1867-1951), divorced wife of
    the Hon.Bertrand Russell, who with his second wife Dora now lived near by in
    Sydney Street. Lady Ottoline Morrell (see Appendix I), who was at this time
    thinking of moving from Garsington to Chelsea, was credited by Logan with
    the break-up of his sister's marriage to Russell, with whom she had had a long
    affair.
22. The Woolfs had been to see the Phoenix Society's production at the Adelphi
    Theatre (Sunday 10 May) of *The Orphan* by Thomas Otway. Rachel (Ray)
    Litvin (d. 1977) played Monimia, the orphan; VW who knew her slightly had
    called her 'a Bohemian'; and indeed the action of the play is set in Bohemia.

when L. came, & then the dinner party, I just having time for a race round the Square; both Dadie & James very easy & affable, indeed for Dadie I feel considerable affection—so sensitive & tender is he, & one of these days will get a pull on himself, & be less of a quicksilver. Indeed, staying on he talked very seriously & excitedly of his dissertation & poets use of words, how they fix on to a word & fill it out with meaning & make it symbolic. But what these scholars want is to get at books through writing books, not through reading them.[23]

But I must remember to write about my *clothes* next time I have an impulse to write. My love of clothes interests me profoundly: only it is not love; & what it is I must discover.

Friday 15 May

Two unfavourable reviews of Mrs D (Western Mail & Scotsman[24]): unintelligible, not art &c: & a letter from a young man in Earls Court "This time you have done it—you have caught life & put it in a book . . ." Please forgive this outburst, but further quotation is unnecessary; & I dont think I should bother to write this, if I weren't jangled what by? The sudden heat, I think, & the racket of life. It is bad for me to see my own photograph. And I have been lunching with Desmond, & reading that dear old Owl's journalism. The thing is, he cant thrust through an article. Now, Lytton or I, though we mayn't think better or write better, have a drive in us, which makes an article whole. And yet there are things worth keeping, & he becomes moved, & irrational when he thinks of it, & I want him to be pleased— So we lunched in the grill of the Connaught Rooms where other men were talking business, had a bottle of wine & delved into the filth packets as he calls them.[25] Home to find Vogue sending photographs—more photographs: T.P. wants one, the Morning Post another.[26] & the C.R. sells 2 or 3 copies a day.

23. Rylands' Fellowship dissertation was to be published by the Hogarth Press in May 1928 as the first part of his book *Words and Poetry* (*HP Checklist* 175).
24. *Mrs Dalloway* was reviewed in the *Western Mail* of 14 May 1925. The reviewer said the book did not interest him 'very much' but supposed that 'readers of preternaturally nimble intellect may discover a consecutive story', while in *The Scotsman* of the same date the critic warned that 'None but the mentally fit should aspire to read this novel' and concluded: 'It may be said such is life, but is it art?'
25. The Connaught Rooms were in Great Queen Street, as were the offices of the *New Statesman*, of which Desmond MacCarthy was literary editor.
26. *Vogue* sent prints of the Beck-MacGregor photographs (see above, 27 April). No picture of VW appeared in either *T.P.'s Weekly* or the *Morning Post*.

MAY 1925

We are going to the play out into this tawny coloured London—but journalism is the devil. I cannot write after reading it. No time—& I must change, & write about clothes some day soon.

Sunday 17 May[27]

A wire from Raymond in Paris—just read Mrs D. it is quite beautiful— & a very good, outspoken wholly praising review of C. R. in the Observer —"no living critic" &c.[28] But this is not all vanity; I'm recording for curiosity: the fate of a book. The only judgment on Mrs D. I await with trepidation (but thats too strong) is Morgan's. He will say something enlightening.

Just back (all my days here begin with this) from Sutton.[29] Oh it is full summer weather—so hot one can't walk on the sunny side, & all London—even Lavender Hill Lambeth which peels visibly in the sun— transmogrified. We had a bad walk, all along the cinder track, with soft footpaths inviting wh. we could not take, owing to L.'s lecture, delivered in a semi-religious sanctuary, with hymns & prayers & a chapter from the Bible. The whole of Sutton was hymning something: soft intense strains of human [*word omitted by VW*] went warbling about, as I sat; & I was touched & moved by it: the world so beautiful, God's gift to us, said the Chairman, who looked poor man as if he had never had an ounce of pleasure in his life. Things become very familiar to me, so that I sometimes think humanity is a vast wave, undulating: the same, I mean: the same emotions here that there were at Richmond. Please have some tea—we shall be hurt if you don't accept our hospitality. Accordingly we do; & the same queer brew of human fellowship, is brewed; & people look the same; & joke in the same way, & come to these odd superficial agreements, wh. if you think of them persisting & wide spread—in jungles, storms, birth & death—are not superficial; but rather profound, I think. We came home on top of a bus all the way for a shilling, with the usual glimpses down lanes, into farmyards, at running streams, persisting in between villas, & behind sunbaked yellow or black motor roads. A little girl on the bus asked her mother how many inches are there in a mile. Her mother repeated this to me. I said you must go to school &

27. VW has misdated this entry *Sunday May 16th*.
28. The anonymous reviewer in *The Observer* of 17 May 1925 wrote: 'Few books . . . can show a deeper enjoyment, a wider range, or a finer critical intelligence than the volume of Mrs Woolf's.'
29. LW's diary note for 17 May reads: 'Train to Epsom. Walked Banstead. Bus Sutton. Address Adult School. Bus home.'

22

they'll tell you. But she is at school said her mother. She's seven; & *he* (the baby on her knee) goes to school. He's three. So I gave them two biscuits left over, & the little girl (see my egotism) with her bright excitable eyes, & eagerness to grasp the whole universe reminded me of myself, asking questions of my mother. We saw Lambeth, & I imagined the frolics of clergymen in the boscage, which is very thick; crossed Westminster Bridge; admired the Houses of Parliament & their fretted lacy look; passed the Cenotaph, which L. compromised by sitting with his hat off all the way up Whitehall,[30] & so home, passing a nigger gentleman, perfectly fitted out in swallow tail & bowler & gold headed cane; & what were his thoughts? Of the degradation stamped on him, every time he raised his hand & saw it black as a monkeys outside, tinged with flesh colour within?

Yesterday we had tea with Margaret in her new house. There are three poplars, & behind them St Paul's. But I don't want to live in the suburbs again. There we sat, & I teased her, & she me, & she minded a little, & got red & then white, as if her centre were not very firm. She is severe to Lilian, who has the small rooms & is not allowed to plant flowers, she said bitterly, for it worries Margaret, & so nothing is done to the garden, which too worries Margaret. For these worries, she takes Ethel M. Dell & Dickens. Why, she said, should D.s characters be like people, when he can create people?—an interesting criticism, I think. We hit it off very well, chiefly owing to my wildness & harum scarumness, I think; & I am very fond of her, & sorry for her, since how awful it would be to 'retire' at 60: to sit down & look at poplar trees? Moreover, she once said she had 'compromised'; her father making entire work impossible; & she now regrets things, I imagine; has seen so little of the world, & carried nothing to the extreme. Lilian irritates too, compared with what she might have had. But, after all, thats enough.[31]

The time is now ripe for dinner. And I must answer some of my admirers. Never have I felt so much admired—so tomorrow, snubs will snub me back again into trim.

30. Lambeth Palace in its extensive park has been the seat of the Archbishops of Canterbury since about 1200. It used to be the custom for men to raise their hats on passing the Cenotaph in Whitehall as a mark of respect for the fallen.

31. Margaret Caroline Llewelyn Davies (1861-1944), General Secretary of the Women's Co-operative Guild from 1889-1921. She had recently moved the short distance to Well Walk, Hampstead, from the house she had shared with her father until his death, aged ninety, in 1916. She was an old and staunch friend of the Woolfs. Her colleague and constant companion Lilian Harris (c. 1866-1949) had been Assistant Secretary to the Guild and had retired at the same time as Margaret. Ethel M. Dell (1881-1939) was an enormously popular romantic novelist.

Wednesday 20 May[32]

Well, Morgan admires. This is a weight off my mind. Better than Jacob he says; was sparing of words; kissed my hand, & on going said he was awfully pleased, very happy (or words to that effect) about it. He thinks—but I wont go into detailed criticism: I shall hear more; & this is only about the style being simpler, more like other peoples this time.

I dined with the Sitwells last night.[33] Edith is an old maid. I had never conceived this. I thought she was severe, implacable & tremendous; rigid in her own conception. Not a bit of it. She is, I guess, a little fussy, very kind, beautifully mannered, & a little reminding me of Emphie Case![34] She is elderly too, almost my age, & timid, & admiring & easy & poor, & I liked her more than admired or was frightened of her. Nevertheless, I do admire her work, & thats what I say of hardly anyone: she has an ear, & not a carpet broom; a satiric vein; & some beauty in her. How one exaggerates public figures! How one makes up a person immune from one's own pleasures & failings! But Edith is humble: has lived in a park alone till 27, & so described nothing but sights & sounds; then came to London, & is trying to get a little emotion into her poetry—all of which I suspected, & think promising. Then how eager she was to write for the Press, which had always been her great ambition, she said. Nothing could be more conciliatory & less of an eagle than she; odd looking too, with her humorous old maids smile, her half shut eyes, her lank hair, her delicate hands, wearing a large ring, & fine feet, & her brocade dress, blue & silver. Nothing of the protester or pamph[l]eteer or pioneer seemed in her—rather the well born Victorian spinster. So I must read her afresh. There were Francis [Birrell], Raymond [Mortimer], [Arthur] Waley & a little American toad called Towne, who soaked himself in liquor & became almost loving to us all.[35] The three Sitwells have

32. This entry is mistakenly dated *May 18th.*

33. VW had been (without LW, who dined with his mother) to a dinner party at 2 Carlyle Square, Chelsea, given by Osbert Sitwell (1892-1969) with his brother Sacheverell (b. 1897) and sister Edith (1887-1964), the poet. Since their production of *Façade* (see *II VW Diary*, 13 June 1923), the Sitwells had enjoyed wide notoriety in the popular press as eccentrics and poseurs, and had been the inspiration of a revue sketch by Noel Coward. The Woolfs were to publish Edith Sitwell's essay *Poetry and Criticism* later this year (*HP Checklist* 76).

34. Euphemia Case kept house with her youngest sister Janet (1862-1938), VW's old Classics teacher and friend.

35. For Francis Birrell, see Appendix I. Arthur David Waley (1889-1966) had already published several books of translations from the Chinese and Japanese. He

considerable breeding about them; I like their long noses, & grotesque faces. As for the house, Osbert is at heart an English squire, a collector, but of Bristol glass, old fashion plates, Victorian cases of humming birds, & not of foxes brushes & deers horns. His rooms are all stuck about with these objects. And I liked him too. But why are they thought daring & clever? Why are they the laughing stocks of the music halls & the penny a liners?

Not much talk; all easy goodnatured generalities after dinner, Francis bawling, Waley sombre & demure, & I very indulgent with my compliments: & now tomorrows Supt [*TLS*] & then (here L. came in & told me about R. Macdonald at the Labour party meeting).

Monday 1 June

Bank holiday, & we are in London. To record my books fates slightly bores me; but now both are floated, & Mrs D. doing surprisingly well. 1070 already sold. I recorded Morgan's opinion: then Vita was a little doubtful;[1] then Desmond, whom I see frequently about his book, dashed all my praise by saying that Logan thought the C.R. well enough, but nothing more. Desmond has an abnormal power for depressing one. He takes the edge off life in some extraordinary way; I love him; but his balance & goodness & humour, all heavenly in themselves, somehow diminish lustre. I think I feel this not only about my work, but about life. However, now comes Mrs Hardy to say that Thomas reads, & hears the C.R. read, with "great pleasure". Indeed, save for Logan, & he's a salt veined American, I have had high praise. Also Tauchnitz asks about them.[2]

---

was still at this time on the staff of the British Museum. The American was Charles Hanson Towne (1877-1949), novelist and editor, who in 1925 visited England in the capacity of a literary agent, specifically to meet 'new writers who were coming along'. In his book *So Far So Good* (New York, 1945), Towne related that he was invited to dine by Somerset Maugham, who 'asked me whom I should most care to meet, of all the writers. I begged for Arnold Bennett and H. G. Wells; and they both came. And, as a generous extra attraction, that wonderful writer, Virginia Woolf.' There is no record that VW ever met Somerset Maugham, and Towne has evidently confused different occasions.

1. For Vita Sackville-West, see Appendix I.
2. A copy of Florence Hardy's letter, dated 31 May 1925, is in MHP Sussex; it enclosed a poem by Thomas Hardy, 'Coming up Oxford Street: Evening' which was published in the *N & A* on 13 June 1925. Bernhard Tauchnitz of Leipzig published paper-cover editions in English of a very large number of British and American authors, from whom they acquired the European rights. Both *Mrs Dalloway* and *Orlando* were to be published by Tauchnitz in 1929 (Kp E1, E2).

We are now considering a change to a widow called by courtesy Smith, Jones' sister; which will despatch poor Murphy, but one can't be very sentimental over her, & to settle in with a placid powerful professional woman is precisely what we want to pull us together. Angus is a little languid—not that we in any way, I hasten to say, complain of him; but Murphy is temperamental, untidy, sloppy, & turns crusty about accounts.[3]

A week ago we had a great invasion—Ottoline surprising us with Julian Philip & a Gathorne Hardy.[4] Ottoline was very affectionate, & perhaps affection being so much time & habit, I too have some real affection for her. But how can I analyse my feelings? I like everyone, I said at 46 the other night; & Duncan said I liked everyone, & thought everyone quite new each time. That was at dinner to meet Miss Warner, the new Chatto & Windus poetess, & indeed she has some merit—enough to make me spend 2/6 on her, I think.[5] It is a sunny fitful day, & standing in Hyde Park to listen to the socialists, that furtive Jew, Loeb, who dogs my life at intervals of 10 years, touched us on the shoulder, & took 2 photographs of us, measuring his distance with a black tape, provided by his wife. He usually tells people to hold one end next their hearts: but this is a joke. He had been hanging about Covent Garden to photograph singers & had lunched at 2.30. I asked if he were a professional, which hurt his pride: he owned to taking a great interest in it, & said he had a large collection.[6]

Tom came in yesterday, rather rockier than last time, not quite so flushed with emotion, & inclined to particularise the state of Vivien's bowels too closely for my taste. We both almost laughed; she has a queer rib, a large liver, & so on. What is more to the point is that Tom is to be

3. Alice Louisa Jones, called by courtesy 'Mrs' (see *II VW Diary*, 29 August 1923), was secretary to the editor of the *N & A*; her sister did not succeed Murphy in the Hogarth Press.
4. For Lady Ottoline and Philip Morrell and their daughter Julian, see Appendix I. The Hon. Robert Gathorne-Hardy (1902-1973), third son of the 3rd Earl of Cranbrook, had got to know them while he was at Christ Church, Oxford, and became a very close friend of Lady Ottoline, whose memoirs he was to edit and publish in two volumes in 1963 and 1974.
5. Sylvia Townsend Warner (1893-1978), whose first book of poems, *The Espalier*, had just been published. 46 Gordon Square was Maynard Keynes's house.
6. Sydney J. Loeb (1876-1964), stockbroker and ardent Wagnerian. VW referred to him and his 'collection of operatic photographs' in a letter to Lytton Strachey written in 1910 (*I VW Letters*, no. 492); in 1912 he married Matilde (1881-1978), a daughter of the great Wagnerian conductor Dr Hans Richter. His vast collection remains in the family.

the editor of a new ⟨mag⟩ quarterly, which some old firm is issuing in the autumn, & all his works must go to them—a blow for us.[7]

He said nothing of my books. With great dignity, I did not ask for his opinion. People often dont read books for weeks & weeks. And anyhow, for my part I hate giving an opinion.

[Friday 5 June][8]

To work off the intense depression left by Desmond. What does this come from? But I have just made this beautiful image—how he is like a wave that never breaks, but lollops one this way & that way & the sail hangs on ones mast & the sun beats down—& its all the result of dining & sitting talking till 3 in the morning with El[izabe]th Bibesco, with whom I had tea yesterday.[9] She is a fat housekeeper of a woman, excellent manager, bustling, economical, entirely without nerves, imagination, or sensibility, but what a good housekeeper, how she keeps the books down, & what a good woman of business, how well she would suit an innkeeper, & how she would see to his interests—entertain his customers with her; sprightly rather broad jokes, standing with her thumbs in her armpits on the other side of the bar, with all her false   arms akimbo diamonds flashing, & her little pig eyes, & her broad fat hips & cheeks. This is the spiritual truth about Bibesco: the fact being that she lies in bed, in green crepe de chine, with real diamonds on her fingers, & a silk quilt, & thinks she talks brilliantly to the most intellectual set in London—so she does, to Desmond, & Mortimer, & poor Philip Ritchie, & I was half in a rage, having sacrificed my Mozart 5tet to her, from which I should have got gallons of pure pleasure instead of the break-fast cup of rather impure delight. For it had its fun. There was old Asquith in [*page ends*].

And then I was ruffled by Nelly, but got over it, by spending £50 of charm. And now I remember—how fatal this is to remember after a quarrel what one did not say—how I might have said, If you have Lottie every day, why should I not have my friends? But one can't—& she is *jealous*, that is the truth. And next time I will say it—& it was Miss Mayor

7. See above, 29 April 1925 n 24, and below, 14 September 1925 n 5.
8. This entry is undated, but the date may be deduced from the fact that the Mozart recital here referred to was given at the Æolian Hall on Thursday 4 June.
9. Elizabeth Charlotte Lucy Bibesco (1897-1945), the only daughter of the former Liberal leader H. H. Asquith, recently created Earl of Oxford and Asquith, and his second wife Margot, had married the Roumanian diplomat Prince Antoine Bibesco in 1919. She wrote stories, plays and poems and had already published four books.

coming that upset us; 'always people when we have dinner parties". And we had Vita, Edith Sitwell, Morgan, Dadie, Kitty Leaf[10]—old Vita presenting me with a whole tree of blue Lupins, & being very uncouth & clumsy, while Edith was like a Roman Empress, so definite clear cut, magisterial & yet with something of the humour of a fishwife—a little too commanding about her own poetry & ready to dictate—tremulously pleased by Morgan's compliments (& he never praised Vita, who sat hurt, modest, silent, like a snubbed schoolboy).[11]

Monday 8 June

This is the hottest June on record. Do not take this seriously—only it is very hot. & we were at Karin's yesterday. There was Irene & her Phil [Noel-Baker]. I am too sleepy having got up at $\frac{1}{4}$ to 6 this morning to describe her. She has spread a little, has a double chin, an emphatic nose, & the feet of gulls on sand round her eyes, which are of the old staring sea green blue. And she has her old ways—her straightforwardness, downrightness, ideals; love of adventure, but none of this is so becoming as of old. For in fact she's grown stereotyped, metallic, harsh; her voice brazen, & her cheeks crude. She suspected me, & suspected Bloomsbury, & adored Leonard, whom she thought so salutary for Phil, but we both suspect [a] scheme for making Phil the foreign sec. in the next Labour Government. I liked her best when she talked about the Greek peasants, & that side may retain some charm. But she talks, talks, talks; thrusts her way with a hard kind of energy into whatever may be going forward— would like, I imagine, to wire pull, & be hostess, & know the right people, but instead protests a horror of success, & wants to keep Phil unspoilt. She also wants to be the mistress of men, I imagine, & a little resents that age should have unseated her from that familiar post, as it very obviously has. She veered, as usual, towards Desmond, professed her horror of "hurting Molly—a very gallant creature", & almost drove L. distracted by asking him what he thought of the character of every politician.[12]

10. Katherine ('Kitty') Leaf was the only daughter of Walter and Charlotte Leaf (see below, 9 April 1926). Fiona MacDonald Mayor (1872-1932), was the author of *The Rector's Daughter*, which the Woolfs had published in 1924 (*HP Checklist* 49).

11. The words in parenthesis were added on the date of the subsequent entry.

12. The Woolfs spent Saturday and Sunday in Essex with Adrian and Karin Stephen (see Appendix I) in their cottage, once an inn, on the tidal waters equidistant from Thorpe-le-Soken and Walton-on-the-Naze (where they kept their yacht). Their fellow-guests were Philip and Irene Noel-Baker. Irene (1889-1956) was the only child and heiress of Frank Noel of Achmetaga where VW and her brothers had

No, she has not worn well; the plating has come off & she's rather steely & common underneath. Needless to say, I had some waves of ancient emotion, chiefly at the sound of her voice & sight of her hands—hands expressing motherhood, perhaps; but mostly felt very flat, unable to pump up anything, & thus uncomfortable. To this, the sordid East End country, the woman who whispers with a gashed throat, the terrific pound home along the hot road, added. And the taxi never came, & we had a second night of it, hearing good, pure hearted Phil, with his principles & his ability, & his athleticism, read aloud to Irene till late.

Sunday 14 June

A disgraceful confession—this is Sunday morning, & just after ten, & here I am sitting down to write diary & not fiction or reviews, without any excuse, except the state of my mind. After finishing those two books, though, one can't concentrate directly on a new one; & then the letters, the talk, the reviews, all serve to enlarge the pupil of my mind more & more. I cant settle in, contract, & shut myself off. I've written 6 little stories, scrambled them down untidily, & have thought out, perhaps too clearly, To the Lighthouse. And both books so far are successful. More of Dalloway has been sold this month than of Jacob in a year. I think it possible we may sell 2,000. The Common one is making money this week. And I get treated at great length & solemnity by old gentlemen.

A powerful, heavy, light blue eyed woman of 50, Mrs Cartwright wants to succeed Murphy; & Murphy wants to stay.[13] How people want work! How tremendous a pull a very little money has in the world! But what the solution is to be, & how we are to find it, I know not. Here I salute Leonard with unstinted, indeed childlike, adoration. Somehow he will gently & firmly decide the whole thing, while Angus & I wobble & prevaricate. But then I have a child's trust in Leonard. Waking this morning, rather depressed that Mrs D. did not sell yesterday, that we

---

stayed on their visit to Greece in 1906. There had been some attachment between Irene and Desmond MacCarthy (see I VW Diary, 27 January 1918; and for Molly MacCarthy see Appendix I), but in 1915 she had married Philip Noel-Baker (b. 1889), who had been a scholar and noted athlete at King's College, Cambridge; he had subsequently worked for the League of Nations, and since 1924 had been Professor of International Relations at London University. He was seeking election to Parliament in the Labour interest, and was elected in 1929, when he became Parliamentary Private Secretary to the Secretary of State for Foreign Affairs.

13. Mrs Cartwright did succeed Bernadette Murphy in July, and remained at the Hogarth Press until 31 March 1930.

had Peter [Lucas], Eileen Power & Noll & Ray [Strachey] last night[14] & found it hard work, & not a single compliment vouchsafed me, that I had bought a glass necklace for £1, that I had a sore throat & a streaming nose, rather under the weather, I say, I snuggled in to the core of my life, which is this complete comfort with L., & there found everything so satisfactory & calm that I revived myself, & got a fresh start; feeling entirely immune. The immense success of our life, is I think, that our treasure is hid away; or rather in such common things that nothing can touch it. That is, if one enjoys a bus ride to Richmond, sitting on the green smoking, taking the letters out of the box, airing the marmots, combing Grizzle, making an ice, opening a letter, sitting down after dinner, side by side, & saying "Are you in your stall, brother?"—well, what can trouble this happiness? And every day is necessarily full of it. If we depended upon making speeches, or money, or getting asked to parties—which reminds me of Ottoline's ghastly party the other night. What possessed me to talk all the time to Helen Anrep? Partly that the plethora of young men slightly annoys me. Really, I am not a good lioness. With all my vanity, I'm come now to be a little cynical, or why don't I so much relish the admiration of the Turners, Kitchins, & Gathorne Hardys? A woman is much more warmly sympathetic. She carries her atmosphere with her. And Ott.'s powers of hostesry are all worn threadbare. People sat about at great distances, & one had a sense of the clock ticking & Ott. saying This is a failure, a failure, & not knowing how to pick the pieces up.[15]

Now I must answer Gerald Brenan, & read the Genji; for tomorrow

14. Frank Laurence (Peter) Lucas (1894-1967), an Apostle, and since 1920 a Fellow of King's College, Cambridge, was in 1926 to be appointed University Lecturer in English Literature. He was a prolific writer. Eileen Power (1889-1940), mediaeval historian, had studied and taught at Girton and was now Reader in Economic History in the University of London. They dined with the Woolfs, and were joined afterwards by Lytton's brother Oliver Strachey (1874-1960) and his second wife Rachel ('Ray', 1887-1940), Karin Stephen's elder sister, who had edited the *Woman's Leader* and was Chairman of the Women's Service Bureau.

15. Ottoline's 'ghastly party' was given in Ethel Sands' house, 15 The Vale, Chelsea, which she had rented for the season in order to launch her daughter Julian in society. The entrance hall was decorated by the Russian mosaicist Boris von Anrep (1883-1969), whose second wife Helen, *née* Maitland (1885-1965), a beautiful and perspicacious half-American woman trained as an opera singer in Europe, had gravitated into Augustus John's Bohemian circle, had married Anrep in 1917, and was soon to leave him for Roger Fry. W. J. Turner (1889-1946), author, critic, and journalist. C. H. B. Kitchin (1895-1967), whose first book *Streamers Waving* had been published by the Woolfs in April (*HP Checklist* 68). VW reverts to her unsocial behaviour on this occasion in *III VW Letters*, nos. 1560 and 1561.

I make a second £20 from Vogue.[16] Did I say that I am rejected by Sybil? From being Sybil, she has become Lady Colefax. No invitations for a month.

Tuesday 16 June

This is the fag end of my morning's work on Genji, which runs a little too easily from my pen & must be compressed & compacted. Dalloway, I fear, has hit her head against some impassable barrier of the public, just as Jacob did, & scarcely sells these last 3 days. Yet my friends are enthusiastic—really so, I think; & ready to acclaim me successful, arrived, triumphant with this book: Clive, Mary, Molly, Roger, my latest allies. We have sold 1240, I think; so the wave spread further than Jacob, & has a ripple left perhaps.

Tonight is Leonard's festival night, the feast of the Brethren Apostles, & presumably some overflow of them here. "Why do human beings invent these ways of torturing themselves?" Them's his words; for he has to preside & speak.[17] Old Lytton, I am reminded, has fairly passed from our lives. No word about my books; no visits since Easter. I imagine that when he takes a new love, & he has Angus, he gets surly, like a stag; he feels a little ridiculous, uneasy, & does not relish the company of old cynical friends like ourselves. And in fact, when I hear the story from Angus, of his agony & entreaty & despair, I only feel slightly nauseated. He makes the young men pity him & laugh at him, & there is a touch of senility in this exposure of himself, while, practically speaking, his amours land him in society of the most tepid, milk & watery kind; nothing that taxes his mind or stimulates; poor feeble Philip for instance, who is precisely like an Eton boy in an Eton jacket: give him an ice & a sovereign.

"Them's his words"—this reminds me I must get back to D. Copper-

16. Gerald Brenan (b. 1894) who had been the Woolfs' host in Spain in April 1923 (see *II VW Diary*, p 240), was temporarily living in lodgings in Wiltshire pursuing his tormented love affair with Carrington and his literary researches. His letter to VW, about her novels, is in MHP Sussex; for her reply, see *III VW Letters*, no. 1560. VW's review of Arthur Waley's translation of the first volume of *The Tale of Genji* by Lady Murasaki appeared in *Vogue*, late July 1925 (Kp C264).

17. In his address to the Society, of which he was current President, LW referred to an occasion in Cambridge when 'all of us, except Goldie, agreed that we had suffered the most extraordinary agonies connected with the Society', and with this in mind had taken as his subject 'the connection between reality and happiness and misery'. See LWP, Sussex.

field.[18] There are moments when all the masterpieces do no more than strum upon broken strings. It is very rare—the right mood for reading—in its way as intense a delight as any; but for the most part pain.

Thursday 18 June

No, Lytton does not like Mrs Dalloway, &, what is odd, I like him all the better for saying so, & don't much mind. What he says is that there is a discordancy between the ornament (extremely beautiful) & what happens (rather ordinary—or unimportant). This is caused he thinks by some discrepancy in Clarissa herself; he thinks she is disagreeable & limited, but that I alternately laugh at her, & cover her, very remarkably, with myself. So that I think as a whole, the book does not ring solid; yet, he says, it is a whole; & he says sometimes the writing is of extreme beauty. What can one call it but genius? he said! Coming when, one never can tell. Fuller of genius, he said than anything I had done. Perhaps, he said, you have not yet mastered your method. You should take something wilder & more fantastic, a frame work that admits of anything, like Tristram Shandy. But then I should lose touch with emotions, I said. Yes, he agreed, there must be reality for you to start from. Heaven knows how you're to do it. But he thought me at the beginning, not at the end. And he said the C.R. was divine, a classic; Mrs D. being, I fear, a flawed stone. This is very personal, he said & old fashioned perhaps; yet I think there is some truth in it. For I remember the night at Rodmell when I decided to give it up, because I found Clarissa in some way tinselly. Then I invented her memories. But I think some distaste for her persisted. Yet, again, that was true to my feeling for Kitty,[19] & one must dislike people in art without its mattering, unless indeed it is true that certain characters detract from the importance of what happens to them. None of this hurts me, or depresses me. Its odd that when Clive & others (several of them) say it is a masterpiece, I am not much exalted; when Lytton picks holes, I get back into my working fighting mood, which is natural to me. I don't see myself a success. I like the sense of effort better. The sales collapsed completely for 3 days; now a little dribble begins again. I shall be more than pleased if we sell 1500. Its now 1250.

July 20th. Have sold about 1550

18. VW's article 'David Copperfield', a review of *The Uncommercial Traveller; Reprinted Pieces and Christmas Stories* by Charles Dickens, appeared in the *N & A* of 22 August 1925 (Kp C266).
19. Katherine (Kitty) Maxse, *née* Lushington (1867-1922), a figure of considerable social consequence in VW's Kensington youth, had served as a model for Clarissa Dalloway.

Saturday 27 June

A bitter cold day, succeeding a chilly windy night, in which were lit all the Chinese lanterns of Roger's garden party. And I do not love my kind. I detest them. I pass them by. I let them break on me like dirty rain drops. No longer can I summon up that energy which when it sees one of these dry little sponges floating past, or rather stuck on the rock, sweeps round them, steeps them, infuses them, nerves them, & so finally fills them & creates them. Once I had a gift for doing this, & a passion, & it made parties arduous & exciting. So when I wake early now I luxuriate most in a whole day alone; a day of easy natural poses, a little printing, slipping tranquilly off into the deep water of my own thoughts navigating the underworld; & then replenishing my cistern at night with Swift. I am going to write about Stella & Swift for Richmond, as a sign of grace, after sweeping guineas off the Vogue counter. The first fruit of the C.R. (a book too highly praised now) is a request to write for the Atlantic Monthly.[20] So I am getting pushed into criticism. It is a great stand by—this power to make large sums by formulating views on Stendhal & Swift.

Jack dined here last night; & we said how many years is it since we three were alone in a room together? he & Nessa & I, waiting for dinner, & a little nervous.[21] I'm more nervous of these encounters than she is. She has a sweet cordiality (odd term to use) which impressed me, recalling mother, as she led him on; & laughed; so sincere, so quiet, & then, when we went on to Roger's rather dismal gathering, gay & spirited, kissing Chrissie & flirting with Mrs Anrep, so careless & casual & white-haired—but enough of this.[22] The truth is I am too random headed to describe Jack, yet he is worth describing. He made us laugh of course. He said such Wallerish things. "There are two kinds of biography, my dear Ginia"—in his old opinionative sententious way with enormous emphasis. He is red-copper coloured, with a pouch under his chin which rests on his collar; trusty brown eyes, a little hazy now, & one ear deaf, he said,

20. VW's article 'Swift's Journal to Stella' appeared in the *TLS* (of which Bruce Richmond was editor) on 24 September 1925 (Kp C268). Her first contribution to the *Atlantic Monthly* did not appear until November 1927.

21. John (Jack) Waller Hills (1867-1938), Unionist MP from 1906-22, and re-elected in December 1925. He was the widower of VW's half-sister Stella Duckworth; after her early death, he and Vanessa had injudiciously fallen in love. He it was who had encouraged the bug-hunting Stephen children to become serious lepidopterists (see *I QB*, p 33); he was also a keen fisherman.

22. Roger Fry (see Appendix I)'s party was at his home, 7 Dalmeny Avenue, Holloway. Christabel, the Hon. Mrs Henry McLaren (1890-1974), became Lady Aberconway on the death of her father-in-law in 1934.

& proceeded to tell us how he is cured by a Swiss every year, & gives the Nuns who keep the clinic a box of chocolates, which they love, being underfed. He looks in at the window & sees them handing the box round, & picking in turn. Then he told us, driving back from Roger's—I insist upon paying this taxi my dear Leonard—how he sugared for moths last summer & caught perhaps 150—& the man he was with (on a fishing club) left his electric light on & the moths came & sat on the curtain. He exaggerates, illuminates, appreciates everyone very generously. L. thinks he "might become a bit of a bore". Then we discussed his writing an autobiography: upon which he became very intent, & almost emotional. "But could one tell the truth? About one's affairs with women? About one's parents? My mother now—she was a very able woman—we all owe her an awful lot—but hard." She said an odd thing to Nessa once— that she hated girls, especially motherless girls. "There you go very deep— It was the terror of her life—that she was losing her charm. She would never have a girl in the house. It was a tragedy. She was a very selfish woman."[23] (But while I try to write, I am making up "To the Lighthouse"—the sea is to be heard all through it. I have an idea that I will invent a new name for my books to supplant "novel". A new —— by Virginia Woolf. But what? Elegy?)

Sunday 19 July

By bringing this book down here to the Studio, I have rather stinted it I think, as my mornings have all been spent writing—Swift or letters. So a whole tribe of people & parties has gone down the sink to oblivion[1] —Ott's parties & complaints; Gwen Raverat set sturdy dusty grim black, yesterday; Tom hedging a little over the Bank; Sybil Colefax drinking tea & protesting her desire to give up parties; her party when Olga Lynn dropped her music in a rage & had to be pacified by Balfour;[2] & Ott lost

23. Such autobiographical truths as J. W. Hills found proper to reveal are to be found in his books A Summer on the Test (1924) and My Sporting Life (1936). The motherless girls Vanessa and Virginia Stephen had encountered his mother when, following Stella's death in 1897, they had stayed at the Hills' family home, Corby Castle, near Carlisle. For VW's reactions then, see I QB, p 61, and her 1897 Diary (Berg).

1. The veil of oblivion is lifted in II QB, p 113.

2. This scene, at a Colefax party probably given on 1 July at Argyll House, is described by Olga Lynn (1882-1957), a diminutive Lieder singer much favoured by Society, in her memoirs Oggie (1955); her rage was occasioned by the entry of Margot Asquith (Lady Oxford), who created such a disturbance that the singer had to stop. A somewhat different version of what appears to have been the same occasion is given in IV LW, pp 104-5.

her shawl; & the garden was lit like a stage, & Clive & Mary could be seen to the least eyelash; & so home to bed; & Mrs Asquith, Lady Oxford, called me the most beautiful woman in the room, which compliment was repeated to me the next night (so thick have parties been) by Jack Hutch. at Dadie's, where there were many faces again, & drink, & again home to bed; & then little Eddie Sackville-West & Julian Morrell to dine (& I am to have his piano) & Philip in to fetch her; & then a party at Ott's with Ching playing the piano; & the news of Hew Anderson's death there broken to Angus;[3] & Murphy going; & Mrs Cartwright coming; & my books—oh yes, the Calendar has abused Mrs D. which hurt me a little; & then the tide of praise has flowed over me again, & they both sell well, & my fears were ungrounded; & Maynard has brought us a pamphlet, wh. is called The Economic Consequences of Mr Churchill, & we are having 10,000 printed for Monday week to sell at a shilling.[4]

On Friday I went on a river party & we dined at Formosa, & Eddie [Sackville-West] played in the round drawing room, & there was George Young in a punt.[5] Not a moments reflection has gone to any of these statements; but I take them together, never knowing what withered straw doesn't vivify the whole bunch of flowers. They have shone bright & gay this summer in the incessant heat. For the first time for weeks I sit by a fire, but then I am in the thinnest silk dress; & for once, it is watery & windy though I see blue sky through my skylight. A happy summer, very busy; rather overpowered by the need of seeing so many people. I never ask a soul here; but they accumulate. Tonight Ottoline; Tuesday Jack Hutch; Wednesday Edith Sitwell, Friday dine with Raymond. These are my fixed invitations; & all sorts of unforseen ones will occur. I run out after tea as if pursued. I mean to regulate this better

3. The Hon. Edward Charles Sackville-West (1901-1965), the son and heir of 4th Baron Sackville and Vita's cousin, was a writer and extremely musical. James Ching was a young aspiring classical pianist who was to give three public concerts in the Wigmore Hall in the autumn. Hew Skelton Anderson (1900-1925), who had graduated from New College, Oxford, in 1923, died of meningitis on 15 July 1925; he had been at the Hotel Cendrillon at Cassis, when VW was there in April (see III VW Letters, no. 1546).

4. J. F. Holms wrote in the Calendar of Modern Letters, July 1925, that 'despite its pure and brilliant impressionism' Mrs Dalloway is 'sentimental in conception and texture, and is accordingly aesthetically worthless'. (See M & M, pp 169-71.) John Maynard Keynes's pamphlet The Economic Consequences of Mr Churchill was published this month in an edition of 7000 copies (HP Checklist 66).

5. Formosa Fishery, on the Thames near Cookham, was the home of the Youngs, old family friends of the Stephens. The present (4th) Baronet was the diplomat George Peregrine Young (1872-1952).

in future. But I dont think of the future, or the past, I feast on the moment. This is the secret of happiness; but only reached now in middle age.

Monday 20 July

Here the door opened, & Morgan came in to ask us out to lunch with him at the Etoile, which we did, though we had a nice veal & ham pie at home (this is in the classic style of journalists).[6] It comes of Swift perhaps, the last words of which I have just written, & so fill up time here.

I should consider my work list now. I think a little story, perhaps a review, this fortnight; having a superstitious wish to begin To the Lighthouse the first day at Monks House. I now think I shall finish it in the two months there. The word 'sentimental' sticks in my gizzard (I'll write it out of me in a story—Ann Watkins of New York is coming on Wednesday to enquire about my stories).[7] But this theme may be sentimental; father & mother & child in the garden: the death; the sail to the lighthouse. I think, though, that when I begin it I shall enrich it in all sorts of ways; thicken it; give it branches & roots which I do not perceive now. It might contain all characters boiled down; & childhood; & then this impersonal thing, which I'm dared to do by my friends, the flight of time, & the consequent break of unity in my design. That passage (I conceive the book in 3 parts: 1. at the drawing room window; 2. seven years passed; 3. the voyage:) interests me very much. A new problem like that breaks fresh ground in ones mind; prevents the regular ruts.

Last night Clive dined with us; & Nelly is rather waspish about it this morning; & tried to run away before Ottoline came; but it proved to be Adrian; & then we talked of cancer, & Clive got set, & Ottoline came, in tea kettle taffeta, all looped & scolloped & fringed with silver lace, & talked about Rupert & Jacques, & re-told, with emendations, the story of Ka & Henry Lamb & herself.[8] She has been working over these old stories so often, that they hold no likeness to the truth—they are stale, managed, pulled this way & that, as we used to knead & pull the

6. The Etoile Restaurant, then as now at 30 Charlotte Street.
7. The galling word 'sentimental' is the keynote of the criticism of VW in *The Calendar* (see above, 19 July 1925, n 4). Ann Watkins was a New York literary agent.
8. The painter Henry Lamb (1883-1960), one-time protégé of Ottoline and a noted philanderer, had in 1911/12 attracted Ka Cox's love; this had excited an obsessive passion for her in her hitherto merely affectionate friend Rupert Brooke, and precipitated his nervous breakdown. (See Christopher Hassall, *Rupert Brooke*, 1964, pp 296-8.) Ka—Katherine Laird Cox (1887-1938), a friend of VW's since 1911, had married Will Arnold-Forster in 1918.

crumb of bread, till it was a damp slab. Then the old motor was heard hooting & there was Philip & Julian [Morrell], at which, at Julian that is, Clive cheered up, & was very brisk & obliging as he knows how. We argued the case of the aristocracy v. the middle class. I rather liked it. But one seldom says anything very profound. I like the sense of other people liking it, as I suppose the Morrells do, for they settle on us like a cloud of crows, once a week now. My vanity as a hostess is flattered. Sometimes a buttery crumb of praise is thrown to me—"Lady Desborough admires your books enormously—wants to meet you"—& then Clive, looking at my photographs in Vogue says of the one last year—"That is charming—but must be taken very long ago, I suppose"⁹—so you see how I switch back from pleasure to pain, & time was when I should have ended the evening fast stuck in black despair, gone to bed like a diver with pursed lips shooting into oblivion. But enough, enough—I coin this little catchword to control my tendency to flower into phrase after phrase. Some are good though.

What shall I read at Rodmell? I have so many books at the back of my mind. I want to read voraciously & gather material for the Lives of the Obscure—which is to tell the whole history of England in one obscure life after another. Proust I should like to finish. Stendhal, & then to skirmish about hither & thither. These 8 weeks at Rodmell always seem capable of holding an infinite amount. Shall we buy the house at Southease? I suppose not.

Thursday 30 July

I am intolerably sleepy & annulled, & so write here. I do want indeed to consider my next book, but I am inclined to wait for a clearer head. The thing is I vacillate between a single & intense character of father; & a far wider slower book—Bob T. telling me that my speed is terrific, & destructive.¹⁰ My summer's wanderings with the pen have I think shown me one or two new dodges for catching my flies. I have sat here, like an improviser with his hands rambling over the piano. The result is perfectly inconclusive, & almost illiterate. I want to learn greater quiet, & force. But if I set myself that task, don't I run the risk of falling into the flatness of N[ight]. & D[ay].? Have I got the power needed if quiet

9. Lady Desborough (1867-1952) held a pre-eminent position in the world of wit and fashion. For *Vogue*'s photographs of VW, see above, 27 April 1925, n 18.
10. Robert (Bob) Calverly Trevelyan (1872-1951), poet and classical scholar, an Apostle, and an old friend.

is not to become insipid. These questions I will leave, for the moment, unanswered.

I should here try to sum up the summer, since August ends a season, spiritual as well as temporal. Well; business has been brisk. I don't think I get many idle hours now, the idlest being, oddly enough, in the morning. I have not forced my brain at its fences; but shall, at Rodmell. When the dull sleep of afternoon is on me, I'm always in the shop, printing, dissing addressing; then it is tea, & Heaven knows we have had enough visitors. Sometimes I sit still & wonder how many people will tumble on me without my lifting a finger: already, this week, uninvited, on the verge of the holidays too, have come Mary, Gwen, Julian & Quentin, Geoffrey Keynes, & Roger. Meanwhile we are dealing with Maynard. All Monday Murphy & I worked like slaves till 6 when I was stiff as a coal heaver. We get telegrams & telephones; I daresay we shall sell our 10,000. On Tuesday at 12.30 Maynard retires to St Pancras Registry office with Lydia, & Duncan to witness (against his will.) So that episode is over.[11] But, dear me, I'm too dull to write, & must go & fetch Mr Dobrée's novel & read it, I think.[12] Yet I have a thousand things to say. I think I might do something in To the Lighthouse, to split up emotions more completely. I think I'm working in that direction.

The Woolfs went to Monks House on the afternoon of Wednesday, 5 August. On Sunday 16 August they lunched with the newly-married Keyneses at Iford where they had rented a house; and on Wednesday 19 August they bicycled to Charleston for tea and dinner, it being Quentin's fifteenth birthday. The Keyneses were there too. During dinner VW fainted and was taken home by car, and remained in a delicate state of health for some time to come.

Saturday 5 September

And why couldn't I see or feel that all this time I was getting a little used up & riding on a flat tire? So I was, as it happened; & fell down in a faint at Charleston, in the middle of Q.'s birthday party: & then have lain about here, in that odd amphibious life of headache, for a fortnight. This has rammed a big hole in my 8 weeks which were to be stuffed so

11. Maynard Keynes and Lydia Lopokova were married at St Pancras Central Registry Office on 4 August 1925. Geoffrey Langdon Keynes (b. 1887), surgeon and bibliographer, was Maynard's younger brother.
12. Presumably a manuscript submitted by the writer and academic Bonamy Dobrée (1891-1974), whom the Woolfs were publishing in their Hogarth Essays series; but they published no novel by him until 1932.

full. Never mind. Arrange whatever pieces come your way. Never be unseated by the shying of that undependable brute, life, hag ridden as she is by my own queer, difficult nervous system. Even at 43 I dont know its workings, for I was saying to myself, all the summer, "I'm quite adamant now. I can go through a tussle of emotions peaceably that two years ago even, would have raked me raw."

I have made a very quick & flourishing attack on To the Lighthouse, all the same—22 pages straight off in less than a fortnight. I am still crawling & easily enfeebled, but if I could once get up steam again, I believe I could spin it off with infinite relish. Think what a labour the first pages of Dalloway were! Each word distilled by a relentless clutch on my brain.

I took up the pen meaning to write on "Disillusionment". I have never had any illusion so completely burnt out of me as my illusion about the Richmonds.[1] This they effected between 4 & 6 yesterday. But Elena has no beauty, no charm, no very marked niceness even! Any country parsons wife is her match. Her nose is red, her cheeks blowsed: her eyes without character. Even her voice & movements which used to be adorable, her distinction, her kindly charm—all have vanished; she is a thick, dowdy, obliterated woman, who has no feelings, no sympathies, prominences & angles are all completely razed bare. Seriously, one has doubts for her complete mental equipment. The conversation was practically imbecile: for instance: (E). I think I could get very fond of a house. But we are so lucky. There are some delightful people near. People who like the same sort of things we do. (B). We are very lucky. There are two fellows within 4 miles who were at Winchester with me. One went to Ceylon as a tea planter. They both farm now. Are you lucky in your clergyman? So much depends in the country on one's clergyman. (E). I really forget anything more from the lips of E. I believe it was all the same: how she would like a house with a piano: & they mean to retire & buy a house with a piano. She sees flowers, dogs, houses, people with the same quiet, stolid, almost coarse, at any rate dull indifference. Her hands are thick. She has a double chin. She wears a long American looking blueish coat, with a nondescript dowdy scarf, a white blouse, fastened with a diamond lizard—oh the colourlessness, drabness, & coldness of her personality—she whom I used to think arch & womanly & comforting! She is white haired too. Bruce is completely

1. Bruce Lyttelton Richmond (1871-1964), editor since 1902 of the *TLS* and VW's most regular employer, and his wife Elena, *née* Rathbone (1878-1964), who were married in 1913. She had formed part of the young Stephens' social circle in Kensington, and had been admired by VW's elder brother Thoby.

circular: round head, eyes, nose, paunch, mind. You can't stop him rolling from thing to thing. He never stops, he glides smoothly. It would shock him to mention writing, money, or people. All has to be dissolved in slang & kindliness.

Now the curious thing was that these qualities infected us both to such an extent that we were acutely miserable. I have sometimes felt the same when walking in the suburbs. Castello Avenue made me angry like this once.[2] As for L. he was indignant. That human nature should sink so low, he said; & then that people should lead such aimless evil lives—the most despicable he could imagine. They took the colour, the sting, the individuality out of everything. And to think that I have ever wasted a thought upon what that goodtempered worldly little grocer thought of my writing! But E. is the great disillusionment. Partly on Thoby's account, partly through my own susceptibility to certain shades of female charm, I had still some glow at the thought of her. Now that glow is replaced by a solid tallow candle. And I feel, this morning, having pitched into bed exhausted, physically worn out, mentally bankrupt, scraped; whitewashed, cleaned. An illusion gone.

Monday 14 September[3]

A disgraceful fact—I am writing this at 10 in the morning in bed in the little room looking into the garden, the sun beaming steady, the vine leaves transparent green, & the leaves of the apple tree so brilliant that, as I had my breakfast, I invented a little story about a man who wrote a poem, I think, comparing them with diamonds, & the spiders webs (which glance & disappear astonishingly) with something or other else: which led me to think of Marvell on a country life, so to Herrick, & the reflection that much of it was dependent upon the town & gaiety—a reaction. However, I have forgotten the facts. I am writing this partly to test my poor bunch of nerves at the back of my neck—will they hold or give again, as they have done so often?—for I'm amphibious still, in bed & out of it; partly to glut my itch ('glut' and 'itch'!) for writing. It is the great solace, & scourge. Leonard is in London this solitary perfect day; this day of the peculiar September mintage; talking to Murphy in the basement, while the vans rumble by, & peoples skirts & trousers appear at the top of the area. This leads us to think of selling Monks, & spending our summers, quit of Press, quit of Nelly, quit of Nation, quit

2. See *II VW Diary*, 31 January 1920. LW's brother Edgar and his wife lived at 7 Castello Avenue, Putney.
3. VW has written 'Monday Sept 13th perhaps'.

of polar blasts, in the South of France. The news that Mr Wilkinson is longing to buy Monks shakes our resolution to sell it.[4] A walk, in pearly mottled weather, on the marshes, plunges me in love again. Leonard then finds his potato crop good, & his autumn crocuses rising. We have been in the throes of the usual servant crisis—varied this time it is true: Nelly says Lottie wants to come back; we offer to have her; she denies it—to Karin; to Nelly she prevaricates. I was flung into a passion with Karin, & so precipitated another headache. But we are on the laps of the Gods: we don't intend to raise a finger either way. Only it is a curious reflection that a little strain with servants more effectually screws the nerves at the back of the head than any other I am aware of. Now why? It is because it is subterranean, partly.

Tom has treated us scurvily, much in the manner that he has treated the Hutchinsons. On Monday I get a letter that fawns & flatters, implores me to write for his new 4ly; & proposes to discuss press matters as soon as we get back; on Thursday we read in the Lit. Supt. that his new firm is publishing Waste Land & his other poems—a fact which he dared not confess, but sought to palliate by flattering me. also (Sept 23rd) that Read is being asked to write for Tom's Press He treated Jack in the same way over Vivien's story in the *Criterion*.[5] The Underworld—the dodges & desires of the Underworld, its shifts & cabals are at the bottom of it. He intends to get on by the methods of that world; & my world is really not the underworld. However, there is a kind of fun in unravelling the twists & obliquities of this remarkable man. How far will they make his poetry squint? Anyhow, at my age, without illusions of that sort any more—I mean in the greatness of Tom, or the greatness of any of us, or our power to influence each other intellectually—I remain detached, & composed. Plenty of other illusions remain to me—emotional, personal; the pleasures of inventing Wednesday walks this winter is now uppermost. I'm going to Greenwich, to Caen Woods, to Gunnersbury, all in the dripping autumn weather, with tea at an

4. Clennell Anstruther Wilkinson (1883-1936), journalist and writer of popular biographies, and brother-in-law of J. C. Squire, editor of the *London Mercury*. Squire and his cronies made a considerable and, as VW felt, wholly regrettable contribution to the social life of Rodmell village.

5. VW's reply to Eliot's entreaty is *III VW Letters*, no. 1577, misdated *3rd* for *8th* September; in it she adverts to the need for a reprint of the Hogarth Press edition of *The Waste Land* (1923). On 10 September the *TLS* carried an announcement by Faber & Gwyer of their forthcoming publication of T. S. Eliot's *Collected Poems* 'containing *The Waste Land*, now out of print, together with many other pieces no longer available and some not previously collected'. The parallel with Jack Hutchinson and Mrs Eliot has defied explanation. Read, see below, p 45 n 13.

A.B.C. & home to a hot bath.[6] Really I am going to let myself slacken in social ways: instead of feeling that I shirk a hedge, in refusing Lord Berners or Lady Colefax, I am going to allow myself to do so approvingly;[7] saying that I strengthen a paragraph in The Lighthouse thereby, or add another hour to the shabby crony talk which I love best. Not but what I shall dip here & there; but without anxiety or preparation of clothes or any of that struggle. This gives me a delicious sense of ease. And I have earned it, too, for I spread my £35 dress allowance to its furthest, & braved many a party spartanly 'on principle' as the marmots would say. The 'principle' which I find intermittently guiding my life is—to take one's fences. Heaven knows how I've dreaded them! Now, with my Studio habitable, & another servant perhaps, I shall aim at haphazard, bohemian meetings, music (we have the algraphone, & thats a heavenly prospect—music after dinner while I stitch at my wool-work—I go to Lewes this afternoon to meet Nessa & buy wools[8]) people of our own standard dropping in; ease, slippers, smoke, buns, chocolate. For I'm naturally sociable; it cannot be denied.

Tuesday 22 September

How my handwriting goes down hill! Another sacrifice to the Hogarth Press. Yet what I owe the Hogarth Press is barely paid by the whole of my handwriting. Haven't I just written to Herbert Fisher refusing to do a book for the Home University Series on Post Victorian?[9]—knowing

6. For VW's visit to Greenwich, see below, 27 March 1926. Ken (formerly Caen) Wood in Highgate was opened to the public by King George V on 18 July 1925; these meadows and woods surrounding the Adam mansion had, after protracted negotiations, been bought from Lord Mansfield and vested in the London County Council. (The house and collections were be to bequeathed by the 1st Earl of Iveagh in 1927.) The purchase by the Boroughs of Acton and Ealing of Gunnersbury Park, some 200 acres and two mansions, the property of a branch of the Rothschild family since 1876, was imminent; but it was not opened to the public until May 1926. A.B.C.: one of the chain of tea-rooms operated by the Aerated Bread Company.
7. Gerald Hugh Tyrwhitt-Wilson, 14th Baron Berners (1883-1950), was a witty and accomplished composer, author, and painter, whom VW had met in 1924.
8. *The Algraphone*, 'Gramophone Superior', was manufactured by Alfred Graham & Co of South London; it was at about this time that LW began to review gramophone records for the *N & A*, and this may have been part of his apparatus for so doing. VW was embroidering a cross-stitch chaircover from a design by Vanessa Bell; see *III VW Letters*, no. 1576 *et seq*.
9. Herbert Albert Laurens Fisher (1865-1940), the historian and one of the editors of the 'Home University Library', was VW's first cousin. He had been President

that I can write a book, a better book, a book off my own bat, for the Press if I wish! To think of being battened down in the hold of those University dons fairly makes my blood run cold. Yet I'm the only woman in England free to write what I like. The others must be thinking of series' & editors. Yesterday I heard from Harcourt Brace that Mrs D. & C.R. are selling 148 & 73 weekly—Isn't that a surprising rate for the 4th month? Doesn't it portend a bathroom & a w.c. either here, or Southease? I am writing in the watery blue sunset, repentance of an ill tempered morose day, which vanished, the clouds, I have no doubt, showing gold over the downs, & leaving a soft gold fringe on the top there.

Today is
Thursday 24 September

—sad to think a week only left whole of this partially wrecked summer; however, I don't complain, seeing as how I have dipped my head in health again & feel stabilised once more about the spinal cord, which is always the centre of my being. Maynard & Lydia came here yesterday— M. in Tolstoi's blouse & Russian cap of black astrachan—A fair sight, both of them, to meet on the high road![10] An immense good will & vigour pervades him. She hums in his wake, the great mans wife. But though one could carp, one can also find them very good company, & my heart, in this the autumn of my age, slightly warms to him, whom I've known all these years, so truculently pugnaciously, & unintimately. We had very brisk talk of Russia: such a hotch-potch, such a mad jumble, M. says, of good & bad, & the most extreme things that he can make no composition of it—can't yet see how it goes. Briefly, spies everywhere, no liberty of speech, greed for money eradicated, people living in common, yet some, L[ydia]'s mother for instance with servants, peasants contented because they own land, no sign of revolution, aristocrats acting showmen to their possessions, ballet respected, best show of

---

of the Board of Education in Lloyd George's coalition government from 1916 to 1922, and was still a Liberal MP; he was appointed Warden of New College, Oxford, in 1925 and gave up his seat in 1926.

10. Early in September the Keyneses had gone to Russia, officially for Maynard to attend the bicentenary celebrations of the Academy of Sciences in Leningrad as the representative of the University of Cambridge, and unofficially, to visit Lydia's family. His reactions to the Soviet régime were recorded in three articles in the *N & A*, subsequently published as a Hogarth Press pamphlet *A Short View of Russia* in December 1925 (*HP Checklist* 67).

Cezanne & Matisse in existence. Endless processions of communists in top hats, prices exorbitant, yet champagne produced, & the finest cooking in Europe, banquets beginning at 8.30 & going on till 2.30; people getting slightly drunk, say about 11, & wandering round the table. Kalinin getting up, & perambulating followed by a little crowd who clapped him steadily as he walked; then the immense luxury of the old Imperial trains; feeding off the Tsars plate; interview with Zinoviev who (I think) was a suave cosmopolital Jew, but had two fanatical watch dogs with square faces, guarding him, & mumbling out their mysteries, fanatically. One prediction of theirs, to the effect that in 10 years time the standard of living will be higher in Russia than it was before the war, but in all other countries lower, M. thought might very well come true. Anyhow they are crammed & packed with sights & talks: Maynard has a medal set in diamonds, & L. a gold sovereign wh. she was allowed to take from the bags at the mint.[11]

But the Keynes', I need hardly say, renewed my headache, & when Lytton came, I was drooping over the fire, & could not do much battle with that old serpent. What was said I think was to the effect that he had had a fire at Hamspray, which blistered the wall, but did not touch his books—& what fire could have the heart to do that? Then he had read Bunny "Really its very extraordinary—so arty,—so composed— the competence terrific, but . . . well, its like a perfectly restored Inn—Ye Olde . . . everything tidied up & restored." No Bunny in it, as there were signs of being in The Man in the Zoo; no humour; a perfect restoration.[12]

But to tell the truth, I am exacerbated this morning. It is 10.25, on a fine grey still day; Lily is doing my bedroom; the starlings are in the apple tree; Leonard is in London, & Nelly I suppose is settling the greatest question of her whole life—what marriage is to a woman—with Lottie. Lily is a wide eyed sheep dog girl who comes from Iford to

11. Mikhail Ivanovich Kalinin (1875-1946) was made a member of the Politburo and the Communist Party's Central Committee in 1925. Grigori Evseevich Zinoviev (1883-1936), a Ukrainian of Jewish parentage—the alleged author of the 'Zinoviev Letter'—was at the time of Keynes's visit chairman of the Executive Committee of the Communist International; dismissed by Stalin in 1926, he was shot in August 1936, a victim of the Great Purge.

12. Lytton this year stayed first at Charleston and then with the Keyneses at Iford, from whence he visited the Woolfs. David (Bunny) Garnett's recently published third book was The Sailor's Return; his second, A Man in the Zoo, had been published in 1924. Born in 1892, Garnett was an old, if younger, friend of both Lytton and VW; in the summer of 1924 he had given up his partnership in the bookshop he had started in 1919 with Francis Birrell to devote himself to writing and country life.

'do'; but can't scramble an egg or bake a potato, & is thus ill armed for life, so far as I can see.

Beginning at 9.45 I wrote two pages of a story, as a test again; & passed it well, I think, anyhow my cistern is full of ideas. But to the point: why am I exacerbated? By Roger. I told him I had been ill all the summer. His reply is—silence as to that; but plentiful descriptions of his own front teeth. Egotism, egotism—it is the essential ingredient in a clever man's life I believe. It protects; it enhances; it preserves his own vital juices entire by keeping them banked in. Also I cannot help thinking that he suspects me of valetudinarianism & this enrages me: & L. is away & I cant have my thorn picked out by him, so must write it out. There! it is better now; & I think I hear the papers come; & will get them, my woolwork, & a glass of milk.

[*Wednesday 30 September*]

This was I suppose successfully accomplished; & it is now Wednesday morning, damp & close & over all the sense already of transmigration, of shedding one habit for another. My autumn coat is grown. I begin to sympathise with Nelly's longing for the ease & speed of civilisation. But I vow here not to be misled into thinking this is life—this perpetual frenzy & stretch; or I shall again be deposited in a heap, as I was in August.

Today we are on Tom's track, riddling & reviling him. He won't let Read off that book, has been after him 3 or 4 months.[13] Dignity is our line; & really, as far as the poaching of authors goes, he won't harm us. Then there is the fascination of a breach; I mean, after feeling all this time conscious of something queer about him, it is more satisfactory to have it on the surface. Not that I want a breach: what I want is a revelation. But L. thinks the queer shifty creature will slip away now.

I actually forgot to record the finish of the Lottie drama—she's in love with the cowman at Thorpe [-le-Soken]! This emerged after an hours violent argument with Nelly. This explains & excuses all: & we are, for private reasons, thoroughly content. What is worse, is poor unfortunate Karin—in operating, they cut a nerve in her face, which is

13. Herbert Read (1893-1968), poet and critic, at this time an Assistant-Keeper in the Victoria & Albert Museum. The Woolfs had published his first book *Mutations of the Phoenix* in 1923, and were publishing his *In Retreat* in October 1925; his first book for Faber & Gwyer was to be *Reason & Romanticism. Essays in Literary Criticism* (1926).

half paralysed. She can't speak, I gather, without being all screwed up.[14] She refuses to see the children for fear of frightening them. This final malignancy on the part of fate seems to me her knock out blow; save that somehow she will, I suppose, find a way round, as people mostly do. This softens the heart towards her. It makes one think of her courage. But how quickly the *intense* feeling of sympathy passes, & she resumes her place in ones mind as a person one is conscious of being permanently, dully, sorry for. But then propinquity will revive it: Tavistock Sqre, being next door, will make one more conscious of the horror of screwing up one's own face.

The Woolfs returned to Tavistock Square on Friday 2 October; by Monday VW felt so unwell that her doctor, Elinor Rendel, was sent for, and for the rest of this month and most of November she was more or less ill, in and out of bed, with occasional walks or drives with LW and seeing a very limited number of visitors. She managed to write On Being Ill, *for T. S. Eliot's* New Criterion, *and a few reviews for the* Nation & Athenaeum.

Friday 27 November

Oh what a blank! I tumbled into bed on coming back—or rather Ellie tumbled me; & keeps me still prostrate half the day.[1] Next week I shall go to the ballet, my first night out. One visitor a day. Till 2 days ago, bed at 5. So visitors have become as usual, pictures hung on the wall. On the whole, I have not been unhappy; but not very happy; too much discomfort; sickness, (cured by eating instantly); a good deal of rat-gnawing at the back of my head; one or two terrors; then the tiredness of the body—it lay like a workman's coat. Sometimes I felt old, & spent. Madge died. Rustling among my emotions, I found nothing better than dead leaves. Her letters had eaten away the reality—the brilliancy, the warmth. Oh detestable time, that thus eats out the heart & lets the body go on. They buried a faggot of twigs at Highgate, as far as I am concerned.

14. The operation was intended to alleviate Karin Stephen's deafness. Her servant Lottie's *amour* (see *III VW Letters*, no. 1590) was likewise ill-fated.
1. Frances Elinor Rendel (1885-1942), daughter of Lytton's eldest sister Elinor, studied history and economics at Newnham College, Cambridge, and worked until 1912 for the National Union of Women's Suffrage Societies; she then qualified as a doctor, and after war service in Roumania and the Balkans, set up as a General Practitioner in London. She became VW's doctor when the latter moved to Tavistock Square in 1924.

I drove to the gate, & saw Nessa & Leonard, like a pair of stuffed figures, go in.[2]

My walks are extended to Oxford Street; only once so far; & then what about talks. Vita has been twice. She is doomed to go to Persia; & I minded the thought so much (thinking to lose sight of her for 5 years) that I conclude I am genuinely fond of her.[3] There is the glamour of unfamiliarity to reckon with; of aristocracy (Raymond says, But she's half a peasant—) of flattery. All the same, after sifting & filing, much, I am sure, remains. Shall I stay with her? Shall we go to Charleston for Christmas? The best of these illnesses is that they loosen the earth about the roots. They make changes. People express their affection. Nessa wants to have us— Indeed, I have seen more of her & Duncan than for many a day. Gwen [Raverat] comes in: threatens to dissolve, her hearty direct stodgy manner in floods of tears, as if the rivets that hold her must give way—such tragedies have beaten her, together for the moment; but suddenly she will break down & tell me something that she has not told anyone. She finds me understanding. And I suppose she is in love—or Marchand in love—& I don't altogether want to hear it.[4]

Reading & writing go on. Not my novel though. And I can only think of all my faults as a novelist & wonder why I do it—a wonder which Lytton increases, & Morgan decreases. Morgan is writing an article on me.[5] This may be very helpful. It may shove me off again. Then I want to write 'a book' by which I mean a book of criticism for the H.P. But on what? Letters? Psychology? Lytton is off: The Loves of

2. Margaret (Madge) Vaughan, née Symonds (1869-1925), wife of VW's cousin W. W. Vaughan, headmaster since 1921 of Rugby School. She was buried at Highgate Cemetery on 7 November after a service in Rugby School Chapel the previous day. Madge Vaughan had once been very much alive in VW's emotions; indeed she had been the first woman 'to capture her heart', see *I QB*, pp 60-1.

3. Vita Sackville-West had in 1913 married Harold George Nicolson (1886-1968), third son of the 1st Baron Carnock and, like his father, a career diplomatist. From 1920 he was at the Foreign Office in London, but had now been posted as Counsellor to the British Legation in Teheran. Vita, who had a horror of the constraints and formalities of the diplomatic life, remained at Long Barn, their Kentish home, but joined him in Persia for two months in the Spring of 1926, and again in 1927.

4. Jean-Hippolyte Marchand (1883-1914), French painter, whose work was shown at the Second Post-Impressionist Exhibition in 1912, and subsequently at the Carfax Gallery, in London, where he was much admired. He was a friend of the Raverats in Vence, Alpes-Maritimes.

5. 'The Novels of Virginia Woolf' by E. M. Forster was published in *The New Criterion* of April 1926 (and subsequently reprinted as 'The Early Novels of Virginia Woolf' in *Abinger Harvest*, 1936). For VW's 'book' see below, 7 December 1925, n 5.

the Famous. Q. Elizabeth &c. I thought him at his most intimate last night; all plumy, incandescent, soft, luminous. Something slightly repels (too strong) Leonard. His character is not so good as Morgan's, he said, walking round the square in the snow today. "There is something about all Stracheys—" Then, when we talk, L. & I, we rather crab Lytton's writing I observe. But all this vanishes, with me, when he comes, as yesterday, to talk, & talk, & talk. That Nessa is still most beautiful— that comes over me. That Ka is thinner—& very self conscious: but nothing, in my sentimental heart, can stand against these old loyalties. I cannot keep my wits altogether about me in talk. I begin to glitter & englobe people with a champagne mist. And then it fades. I was talking of this to Raymond—whose blunt nose & flashy clothes are, I think, one's chief grudge against him—the other day. That there is no substance in ones friendships, that they fade like—For instance, did he regret Harold [Nicolson] in Persia?* Nothing like a coin is struck & left for ever in one's possession. People die; Madge dies, & one cannot beat up a solitary tear. But then, if 6 people died, it is true that my life would cease: by wh. I mean, it would run so thin that though it might go on, would it have any relish? Imagine Leonard, Nessa Duncan Lytton, Clive Morgan all dead.

* A shrewd guess— he does regret Harold in Persia

Monday 7 December

I want to lie down like a tired child & weep away this life of care— & my diary shall receive me on its downy pillow.[1] Most children do not know what they cry for; nor do I altogether. It is 12 o'clock on Monday morning, a very cold day, but sunny, healthy, cheerful. Bells ring downstairs; doors are slammed. I should be in full feather, for after all these drowsy dependent weeks I am now almost quit of it again; & can read & write, & walk a little, & mildly entertain. Well, it is partly that devil Vita. No letter. No visit. No invitation to Long Barn. She was up last week, & never came. So many good reasons for this neglect occur to me that I'm ashamed to call this a cause for weeping. Only if I do not see her now, I shall not—ever: for the moment for intimacy will be gone, next summer. And I resent this, partly because I like her; partly

Poor woman! she did try to come— prevented, fog &c.

1. 'I could lie down like a tired child,
    And weep away the life of care
    Which I have borne and yet must bear,
    Till death like sleep might steal on me.'
    Shelley, *Stanzas Written in Dejection near Naples.*

because I hate the power of life to divide. Also, I am vain. Clive will know *why* Vita did not come to see me. That old rat chased to his hole, there is Tom's postcard about *On Being Ill*—an article which I, & Leonard too, thought one of my best: to him characteristic &c: I mean he is not enthusiastic; so, reading the proof just now, I saw wordiness, feebleness, & all the vices in it.[2] This increases my distaste for my own writing, & dejection at the thought of beginning another novel. What theme have I? Shan't I be held up for personal reasons? It will be too like father, or mother: &, oddly, I know so little of my own powers. Here is another rat run to earth. So now for news.

We shall spend Xmas at Charleston, which I'm afraid Leonard will not like much. We walked at Hampstead on Saturday. It was very cold— skating everywhere, save there, L. having brought his skates. It had a foggy winter beauty. We went in to Ken Wood (but dogs must be led) & there came to the duelling ground, where great trees stand about, & presumably sheltered the 18th Century swordsmen (how I begin to love the past—I think something to do with my book) & it was here that we discussed Lytton, gravely, like married people. But my God—how satisfactory after, I think 12 years, to have any human being to whom one can speak so directly as I to L.! Well, it was a question of L[ytton]'s change of feeling. He has the faults of a small nature said L. He is ungenerous. He asks, but never gives. But I have always known that— often I have seen the dull eyelid fall over him, if one asked a little too much: some sheath of selfishness that protects him from caring too much, or committing himself uncomfortably. He is cautious. He is a vale-tudinarian. But—there are, as usual, the other things; & as I say, I have known about Lytton's leathern eyelid since I was 20. Nothing has ever shocked me more, I think. But L. said when they were at Cambridge Lytton was not like that to him. First there was the I[nternationa]l Review: & Lytton refused to write; then Ralph; then never a word of praise for other people.[3] Morgan, said Leonard, as we trod back over the

2. In response to T. S. Eliot's letter imploring her to write for his new quarterly (see above, 14 September 1925), VW had sent him her article 'On Being Ill' on 14 November. His unenthusiastic postcard has not been located, but the article appeared in *The New Criterion* in January 1926 (Kp C270).

3. LW had been editor of the monthly *International Review* from its inception in 1919 until its amalgamation with the *Contemporary Review* at the end of the year. Ralph Partridge (1894-1960) had distinguished himself academically and in the 1914-18 war, from which he returned to Oxford disillusioned with militarism. He became an intimate of Lytton Strachey's household with his devoted companion (Dora) Carrington (whom Partridge prevailed upon to marry him in 1921), and from October 1920 to March 1923 had worked with the Woolfs in the Hogarth Press; but

slippery hillocks seeing so little as we talked (& yet all this part of Hampstead recalls Katherine to me—that faint ghost, with the steady eyes, the mocking lips, &, at the end, the wreath set on her hair:[4]) Morgan has improved. Morgan is I think naturally more congenial to L. than Lytton is. He likes "Sillies"; he likes the dependent simplicity of Morgan & myself. He likes settling our minds, & our immense relief at this. Well, well.[5]

I am reading The Passage to India; but will not expatiate here, as I must elsewhere. This book for the H.P.: I think I will find some theory about fiction.[6] I shall read six novels, & start some hares. The one I have in view, is about *perspective*. But I do not know. My brain may not last me out. I cannot think closely enough. But I can—if the C.R. is a test— beat up ideas, & express them now without too much confusion. (By the way, Robert Bridges likes Mrs Dalloway: says no one will read it; but it is beautifully written, & some more, which L. who was told by Morgan, cannot remember.[7])

I don't think it is a matter of 'development' but something to do with prose & poetry, in novels. For instance Defoe at one end: E. Brontë at the other. Reality something they put at different distances. One would have to go into conventions; real life; & so on. It might last me—

---

his character and behaviour together with Lytton's covert promotion of his interests had been a source of increasing irritation to them. See *II VW Diary*, *passim*.

4. On learning of Katherine Mansfield's death, VW had written (*II VW Diary*, 16 January 1923); 'Then, as usual with me, visual impressions kept coming and coming before me—always of Katherine putting on a white wreath, & leaving us, called away; made dignified, chosen.'

5. For LW's definition of the 'silly' see *II VW Diary*, 11 September 1923, n 5.

6. Forster's last novel had been published eighteen months earlier; VW did not publish any comment upon it until the end of 1927 (Kp C292, 'The Novels of E. M. Forster'). LW and Dadie Rylands had planned a series, to be called 'Hogarth Lectures on Literature' (see *HP Checklist*, Appendix I, p 139), to which VW was intended to contribute a book on fiction. She refers to this several times in her diary between now and September 1928, and in letters during 1927, and it was announced as 'in preparation' in the introductory booklet *A Lecture on Lectures* by Sir Arthur Quiller-Couch (published ostensibly in 1927 but actually in February 1928; *HP Checklist* 144). VW's book never appeared in the series, but was eventually published as three articles under the title 'Phases of Fiction' in the New York *Bookman* in 1929 (Kp C312, reprinted in *Granite and Rainbow*). See also MHP, Sussex, B6 & 7.

7. Robert Seymour Bridges (1844-1930) was a long-standing friend of Roger Fry; he was appointed Poet Laureate in 1913. VW was to meet him on her visit to Garsington in 1926 (see below, 1 July 1926).

this theory—but I should have to support it with other things. And death—as I always feel—hurrying near. 43: how many more books?

Katie came here;[8] a sort of framework of discarded beauty hung on a battered shape now. With the firmness of the flesh, & the blue of the eye, the formidable manner has gone. I can see her as she was at 22 H[yde] P[ark] G[ate] 25 years ago: in a little coat & skirt; very splendid; eyes half shut; lovely mocking voice; upright; tremendous; shy. Now she babbles along.

"But no duke ever asked me, my dear Virginia. They called me the Ice Queen.

And why did I marry Cromer? I loathed Egypt; I loathed invalids. I've had two very happy times in my life—childhood—not when I grew up—but later, with my boys club, my cottage, & my chow—& now. Now I have all I want. My garden—my dog."

I don't think her son enters in very largely. She is one of these cold eccentric great Englishwomen, enormously enjoying her rank, & the eminence it lends her in St John's Wood, & now free to poke into all the dusty holes & corners, dressed like a charwoman, with hands like one, & finger nails clotted with dirt. She never stops talking. She lacks much body to her. She has almost effused in mist. But I enjoyed it. Though I think she has few affections, & no very passionate interests. Now, having cried my cry, & the sun coming out, to write a list of Christmas presents. Ethel Sands comes to tea.[9] But no Vita.

Monday 21 December

But no Vita! But Vita for 3 days at Long Barn, from which L. & I returned yesterday.[10] These Sapphists *love* women; friendship is never untinged with amorosity. In short, my fears & refrainings, my 'impertinence' my usual self-consciousness in intercourse with people who mayn't want me & so on—were all, as L. said, sheer fudge; &, partly

8. Katie was the Countess of Cromer, *née* Lady Katherine Thynne (1865-1933), second wife and since 1917 widow of Evelyn Baring, 1st Earl of Cromer, the British administrator and Consul-General in Egypt.

9. Ethel Sands (1873-1962), American-born painter who divided her year between the Château d'Auppegard, near Dieppe, which she shared with her lifelong friend Nan Hudson, and her house at 15 The Vale, Chelsea. Wealthy and gregarious, she was an active and benign hostess and patron of the arts.

10. VW went to stay with V. Sackville-West at Long Barn on 17 December; it was, according to Nigel Nicolson (*III VW Letters*, p 223), 'the beginning of their love affair'. LW joined them on the afternoon of 19 December, and Vita motored them to London next day.

thanks to him (he made me write) I wound up this wounded & stricken year in great style. I like her & being with her, & the splendour—she shines in the grocers shop in Sevenoaks with a candle lit radiance, stalking on legs like beech trees, pink glowing, grape clustered, pearl hung. That is the secret of her glamour, I suppose. Anyhow she found me incredibly dowdy, no woman cared less for personal appearance—no one put on things in the way I did. Yet so beautiful, &c. What is the effect of all this on me? Very mixed. There is her maturity & full breastedness: her being so much in full sail on the high tides, where I am coasting down backwaters; her capacity I mean to take the floor in any company, to represent her country, to visit Chatsworth, to control silver, servants, chow dogs; her motherhood (but she is a little cold & offhand with her boys[11]) her being in short (what I have never been) a real woman. Then there is some voluptuousness about her; the grapes are ripe; & not reflective. No. In brain & insight she is not as highly organised as I am. But then she is aware of this, & so lavishes on me the maternal protection which, for some reason, is what I have always most wished from everyone. What L. gives me, & Nessa gives me, & Vita, in her more clumsy external way, tries to give me. For of course, mingled with all this glamour, grape clusters & pearl necklaces, there is something loose fitting. How much, for example, shall I really miss her when she is motoring across the desert? I will make a note on that next year. Anyhow, I am very glad that she is coming to tea today, & I shall ask her, whether she minds my dressing so badly? I think she does. I read her poem; which is more compact, better seen & felt than anything yet of hers.[12]

Mary's stories, I fear, are bad.[13] Dear me—then Roger is in love with H[elen Anrep]. Morgan's article has cheered me very much.[14] L. is doing up rubber seals & fur rabbits at the moment. The workmen are hammering, their engines throbbing outside on the hotel. We go down to Charleston tomorrow, not without some trepidation on my part, partly because I shall be hung about with trailing clouds of glory from Long

11. Vita's sons were (Lionel) Benedict (1914-1978) and Nigel (b. 1917) Nicolson.
12. V. Sackville-West's journey from Cairo to Persia in March 1926 is described in her *Passenger to Teheran*, published by the Hogarth Press in 1926 (*HP Checklist* 107); the final four days travel, over high mountain passes and desert plains, was by Trans-Desert Mail car. Her poem was probably 'On the Lake' which appeared in the *N & A* on 26 December 1925.
13. Nonetheless the Hogarth Press published Mary Hutchinson's *Fugitive Pieces* in June 1927 (*HP Checklist* 122); only one of them is referred to by the author as a 'story', the others being categorized as 'Shuttlecocks' and 'Weathercocks'.
14. Forster sent his as yet unpublished article (see above, 27 November 1925) to VW to read.

Barn wh. always disorientates me & makes me more than usually nervous: then I am—altogether so queer in some ways. One emotion succeeds another.[15]

On 22 December the Woolfs went to Charleston for Christmas, as builders were making alterations to Monks House. Clive and Vanessa Bell and the three children were there; also, until 24th, Roger Fry. Vanessa reported to Duncan Grant (who was with his mother at Twickenham) that they had spent a fascinating evening reading VW's diary recalling early days at 46 Gordon Square, with the four Stephens' very full and 'rather high society' life there. (Berg, 1905 Diary). VW and Quentin Bell had again collaborated in a squib, called The Messiah, *purporting to depict scenes from Clive's life. On Boxing Day Vita Sackville-West came to lunch. LW returned to London on 27th, and VW followed him on 28th December.*

15. The entry for 21 December is written on two pages; but on an intervening and a succeeding page VW has twice written out the following passage:

> Such a being must have stood out conspicuously among his fellows; the facts of his life would have been the ground of the faith in his genius; & when his early death endeared & sanctified his memory, loving grief would generously grant him the laurels which he had never worn.   (written for Bridges)

Roger Fry was collaborating with Robert Bridges, one of the founders of the Society for Pure English, in producing two tracts on English Handwriting, and to this end was collecting specimens of handwriting from his friends; VW's sample was not however, included in the total of 65 facsimiles reproduced (Tracts nos. XXIII and XXVIII). See *II RF Letters*, no. 575 of 18 December 1925 to Robert Bridges.

1926

1926

VW wrote no diary between 21 December 1925 and 19 January 1926; her letters preserved from this interval are, with one exception, all to Vita Sackville-West, a significant indication of her preoccupation. After her return from Charleston to Tavistock Square on 28 December, she was again unwell, and on 8 January Dr Elinor Rendel diagnosed German Measles; but by 13th she was allowed out. Both the Woolfs and Vita were given dinner by Clive Bell at his favourite restaurant, the Ivy in West Street, WC2, on 18 January before his party, to which VW did not go.

The next entry was the last made in DIARY XIV; but there follow two pages of a preliminary version of the lecture she was to give at a private girls' school at Hayes Court in Kent on 30 January 1926 (later published as 'How Should one Read a Book?', Kp C277).

Tuesday 19 January

Vita having this moment (20 minutes ago—it is now 7) left me, what are my feelings? Of a dim November fog; the lights dulled & damped. I walked towards the sound of a barrel organ in Marchmont Street. But this will disperse; then I shall want her, clearly & distinctly. Then not— & so on. This is the normal human feeling, I think. One wants to finish sentences. One wants that atmosphere—to me so rosy & calm. She is not clever; but abundant & fruitful; truthful too. She taps so many sources of life: repose & variety, was her own expression, sitting on the floor this evening in the gaslight. We dined last night at the Ivy with Clive; & then they had a supper party, from which I refrained. Oh & mixed up with this is the invigoration of again beginning my novel, in the Studio, for the first time this morning. All these fountains play on my being & intermingle. I feel a lack of stimulus, of marked days, now Vita is gone; & some pathos, common to all these partings; & she has 4 days journey through the snow.

VW here begins DIARY XV, the title page of which is inscribed:

52 Tavistock Square
1926

Monday 8 February

Just back from Rodmell—to use again the stock opening. And I should explain why I've let a month slip perhaps. First, I think, the

57

German measles or influenza; next Vita; then, disinclination for any exertion, so that I never made a book till last week. But undoubtedly this diary is established, & I sometimes look at it & wonder what on earth will be the fate of it. It is to serve the purpose of my memoirs. At 60 I am to sit down & write my life. As rough material for that master-piece—& knowing the caprice of my own brain as record reader for I never know what will take my fancy, I here record that I come in to find the following letters waiting me. 1. Ottoline, on that wonderful essay On Being Ill. She is doing a cure. 2. A long letter of hysterical flattery from Miss Keiller [Kieffer] who is translating Jacob's Room. 3. a card, showing me her character in an unfavourable light from Miss Ethel Pye, who once met me in an omnibus & wishes to take a mask of my head; 4. a letter from Harcourt Brace enclosing cheque from the Forum for O[n]. B[eing]. Ill. 5. a letter asking me to become one of the Committee of the English Association; 6. a cutting on Hogarth Essays from the Dial; 7. a note from Clive asking me to dine to meet his brother.[1] I think this makes me out rather specially important. It is 3 days post. I am rather tired, a little tired, from having thought too much about To the Light-house. Never never have I written so easily, imagined so profusely. Murry says my works won't be read in 10 years time—Well, tonight I get a new edition of the V[oyage]. O[ut]. from Harcourt Brace—this was published 11 years ago.[2]

1. 1. VW's essay 'On Being Ill' had appeared in the January issue of Eliot's *New Criterion* (Kp C270). 2. Marie Kieffer and Claude Dravaine published their translation of two extracts from *Jacob's Room* in *La Revue nouvelle*, Paris, March 1927 (Kp D28) and *Revue politique et littéraire: Revue bleue*, Paris, 6 August 1927 (Kp D29). 3. Ethel Pye (c. 1882-1960) was an artist and sculptor peripherally connected with the 'neo-pagan' circle. 4. 'On Being Ill' was reprinted as 'Illness: An Unexplored Mine' in the New York *Forum* in April 1926 (Kp C270). 5. Mrs Leonard Woolf was co-opted on to the general committee of the English Association (founded in 1906 to promote the knowledge and appreciation of English language and literature) on 28 January 1926; though there is no record of her having ever attended a meeting, her name appeared each year until 1934. 6. *The Dial*, New York, commended the series in general and gave a fairly detailed comment upon each of the first six of the 'Hogarth Essays' (see *HP Checklist*), in its February number. 7. Clive's brother was Lt. Col. Cory Bell (see above, 19 April 1925, n 11).

2. John Middleton Murry (1889-1957), literary critic, author, widower of Katherine Mansfield (though now remarried), controlled and edited the *Adelphi*; in his article entitled 'The Classical Revival' in the issue of 9 February 1926, he wrote: 'Mrs Woolf's *Jacob's Room* and Mr Eliot's *The Waste Land* belong essentially to the same order. Both are failures; . . . Fifty, ten years hence no one will take the trouble (no small one) to read either of these works, unless there should be some revolutionary happening to their authors—some liberation into a real spontaneity—which will cause these records of their former struggle . . . to be studied.'

Tuesday 23 February

Here is the usual door bell/ & I think Gwen came in, & I was rather sodden & wretched, feeling that I had nothing to give her, & she everything to ask. As I foretold, she is enmeshed in a net of fire: that is the truth; loves net; the fiery net of—who was it?—that was scorched to death: & hers is more painful than his, & more enduring.[3] Yet how seldom one envisages what one knows! Her net lies on me; but it does not burn me. And I do little futile kindnesses to her, which are little good to anybody; & I don't do them, & I feel compunction. Of all this I have little appetite to write, being exacerbated 1. because Nelly won't make marmalade; 2. because a certain function impends; 3. because I can't go, in deference to L.'s wish, to Mortimer's farewell party, 4. because Dadie asked me to tea, & I did not go; 5. because—the last because I cannot now remember—a vague dissatisfaction: spring & funerals; yellow lights & white blossoms; beautiful black yellow pointed squares—& so on. Vita is a dumb letter writer, & I miss her. I miss the glow & the flattery & the festival. I miss her, I suppose, not very intimately. Nevertheless, I do miss her, & wish it were May 10th; & then I don't wish it; for I have such a razor edge to my palette that seeing people often disgusts me of seeing them.[4]

I am blown like an old flag by my novel. This one is To the Lighthouse. I think it is worth saying for my own interest that at last at last, after that battle Jacob's Room, that agony—all agony but the end, Mrs Dalloway, I am now writing as fast & freely as I have written in the whole of my life; more so—20 times more so—than any novel yet. I think this is the proof that I was on the right path; & that what fruit hangs in my soul is to be reached there.[5] Amusingly, I now invent theories that fertility & fluency are the things: I used to plead for a kind of close, terse, effort. Anyhow this goes on all the morning; & I have the devils own work not to be flogging my brain all the afternoon. I live entirely in it, & come to the surface rather obscurely & am often unable to think what to say when we walk round the Square, which is bad I know. Perhaps it may be a good sign for the book though. Of course

3. Semele was consumed by the fire of her lover Jupiter's full majesty; but it was Mars and Venus who were caught in a net by Vulcan.
4. Raymond Mortimer was shortly to set out for Teheran to join the Nicolsons; Vita was due to return to England on 10 May.
5.   'Hang there like fruit, my soul,
                        Till the tree die!'
                                Cymbeline, V v 262.

See also *I QB*, p 69.

it is largely known to me: but all my books have been that. It is, I feel, that I can float everything off now; & "everything" is rather a crowd & weight & confusion in the mind.

Then I have seen Lytton: seen Eddy; Mary; I forget: I have been discreet in my society, & enjoyed it. Perhaps I am again brisking, after my lethargy. The publishing season is about to begin. Nessa says Why don't you give it up? I say, because I enjoy it. Then I wonder, but do I? What about Rome & Sicily? And Manning Sanders is not worth the grind.[6] Am I a fanatical enthusiast for work, like my father? I think I have a strain of that, but I don't relish it. Tonight Francis Birrell & Rose Macaulay dine with us.[7] To celebrate the occasion, I have bought a toast rack & a bedspread, which covers that atrocious chest of drawers wh. has worried me these 2 years. I am now so pleased with the colour that I go out & look at it.

Wednesday 24 February

To continue, the second day running which is a rarity, they came last night, Francis & Rose Macaulay—I daresay I shall be calling her Rose one of these days. Francis didn't much relish meeting her: my gnats of worries gave me little peace: Gwen ringing up; I not cordial; she shying off: I repentant; ringing up again. Then Rose—too chattery chittery at first go off; lean as a rake, wispy, & frittered. Some flimsy smartness & taint of the flimsy glittery literary about her: but this was partly nerves, I think; & she felt us alien & observant doubtless. Anyhow in the middle of dinner the lights went out: only a few candles in saucers to be had, & I left her & Francis alone in the dark to talk. After all, she has no humbug about her; is exactly on a par as far as conventions go, I imagine; only frosted & rather cheaply gilt superficially with all that being asked to speak at dinners, to give opinions to newspapers, & so on; lunching at the League of Nations; dining with Iolo Williams, meeting Jack Squire who has grown whiskers & looks like a verger.[8]

Let me see, there's some failure of sympathy between Chiswick & Bloomsbury, I think, she said. So we defined Bloomsbury. Her part is to

6. The second booklet of Ruth Manning-Sanders' verse to be printed by the Woolfs, *Martha Wish-You-Ill*, was published by the Hogarth Press in July 1926 (*HP Checklist* 102).
7. (Emilie) Rose Macaulay (1881-1958), the drily entertaining novelist and popular literary lady, whom VW met occasionally.
8. Iolo Aneurin Williams (1890-1962), author, journalist, and collector, was from 1920-39 the bibliographical correspondent of the *London Mercury*, founded and edited by the egregious man of letters, John Collings Squire (1884-1958).

stick up for common sense she said. I elaborated her being Cambridge. She is writing an article for an American paper on London after the War.[9] It is [this] sort of thing that one distrusts in her. Why should she take the field so unnecessarily? But I fancy our 'leading lady novelists' all do as they are asked about this, & I am not quite one of them. I saw my own position, a good deal lowered & diminished; & this is part of the value of seeing new people—still more of going to people's houses. One is, if anything, minimised: here in the eternal Bloomsbury, one is apt, without realising it, to expand. Then Gwen came. I like Francis. I like his laughter; & his random energy. He is a Victorian. Indeed we talked a lot, when L. was in the basement with the electrician, of father, who, said Francis, dominates the 20th Century. "He made it possible for me to have a decent life" he said. "He pulled down the whole edifice, & never knew what he was doing. He never realised that if God went, morality must follow. A remarkable man; for though he would not believe in God, he was stricter than those who did."

"He loved lamentation" said L. coming up. R.M. said her parents called him always "poor Leslie Stephen" because he had lost his faith. Also they said he was very gentle & charming. Gwen said her father & uncles had a great respect for him. They had a very romantic feeling for my mother.[10]

Because she was so beautiful, I said, proud that R.M. should know this; & felt rather queer, to think how much of this there is in To the Lighthouse, & how all these people will read it & recognise poor Leslie Stephen & beautiful Mrs Stephen in it. Then we talked of knowing people. R.M. said she always knew why she liked people. Gwen being perhaps tired, was a little mystical; or perhaps she has acquired views which are yet hardly articulate. Anyhow Leonard thought her 'almost imbecile'. They got talking about whether one knew more about pictures or books. R.M. showed up rather well in argument, & maintained that a book is a subjective thing; she attacks authority in literature. But people know about painting as it is a more technical art. Then she said (this makes me think she will wish to be called Rose) how she had dreamt she was staying with us in a cottage in Surrey, a 15th century house, full of old beams & candle lit. In some lights she has the beautiful eyes

9. Rose Macaulay had studied at Somerville College, Oxford; but her father, George Macaulay, was a Cambridge man, and for the last ten years of his life, when she still lived at home, was lecturer in English there. Her article, 'New London Since 1914', appeared in the New York Times in May 1926.

10. Gwen Raverat's father and four uncles were the sons of the great Charles Darwin; see her Period Piece, A Cambridge Childhood, 1952.

of all us distinguished women writers; the refinement; the clearness of cut; the patience; & humbleness. It is her voice & manner that make one edgy.

Saturday 27 February

I think I shall initiate a new convention for this book—beginning each day on a new page—my habit in writing serious literature. Certainly, I have room to waste a little paper in this year's book. As for the soul: why did I say I would leave it out? I forget. And the truth is, one can't write directly about the soul. Looked at, it vanishes: but look at the ceiling, at Grizzle, at the cheaper beasts in the Zoo which are exposed to walkers in Regents Park, & the soul slips in. It slipped in this afternoon. I will write that I said, staring at the bison: answering L. absentmindedly; but what was I going to write?[11]

Mrs Webb's book has made me think a little what I could say of my own life. I read some of 1923 this morning, being headachy again, & taking a delicious draught of silence.[12] But then there were causes in her life: prayer; principle. None in mine. Great excitability & search after something. Great content—almost always enjoying what I'm at, but with constant change of mood. I don't think I'm ever bored. Sometimes a little stale; but I have a power of recovery—which I have tested; & am now testing for the 50th time. I have to husband my head still very carefully: but then, as I said to Leonard today, I enjoy epicurean ways of society; sipping & then shutting my eyes to taste. I enjoy almost everything. Yet I have some restless searcher in me. Why is there not a discovery in life? Something one can lay hands on & say "This is it?" My depression is a harassed feeling—I'm looking; but that's not it— thats not it. What is it? And shall I die before I find it? Then (as I was walking through Russell Sqre last night) I see the mountains in the sky: the great clouds; & the moon which is risen over Persia; I have a great & astonishing sense of something there, which is 'it'— It is not exactly beauty that I mean. It is that the thing is in itself enough: satisfactory; achieved. A sense of my own strangeness, walking on the earth is there too: of the infinite oddity of the human position; trotting along Russell Sqre with the moon up there, & those mountain clouds. Who am I,

11. i.e.: those beasts which the public could see from the park through the railings without having to pay for admission to the Zoo.
12. Beatrice Webb's *My Apprenticeship*, consisting of extracts from her diary from 1868 up to the time of her marriage in 1892, with connecting and explanatory passages, had just been published. VW had been rereading her *own* diary for 1923.

what am I, & so on: these questions are always floating about in me; & then I bump against some exact fact—a letter, a person, & come to them again with a great sense of freshness. And so it goes on. But, on this showing which is true, I think, I do fairly frequently come upon this 'it'; & then feel quite at rest.

Is that what I meant to say? Not in the least. I was thinking about my own character; not about the universe. Oh & about society again; dining with Lord Berners at Clive's made me think that. How, at a certain moment, I see through what I'm saying; detest myself; & wish for the other side of the moon; reading alone, that is. How many phases one goes through between the soup & the sweet! I want, partly as a writer, to found my impressions on something firmer. I said to Lord B. All you must do in writing is to float off the contents of your mind. Clive & Raymond laughed & said Thats exactly what you do anyhow. And I don't want that to be all. Nor is it. Theres a good deal of shaping & composing in my books. However—the main idea of them is that, then; & I dont like it.

Lord B. was stockish, resolute, quick witted: analysed his own instability. His father was a sea captain; wished him not on any account to be a long haired artist; his mother used to say "My little boy plays so nicely—you should hear him play" but she minded his not hunting & riding. So, he said, he was inhibited as a musician. His talent clung (I think he said) like a creeper to the edge of a cliff. One day he wrote two marches for fun. Stravinsky saw them, thought them good, & they were published. So he was accepted as a serious musician, with only 4 lessons from Tovey in counterpoint. He had an astonishing facility. He could write things that sounded all right. Suddenly, last year, all his pleasure in it went. He met a painter, asked him how you paint; bought 'hogsheads' —(meant hog's bristles) & canvas & copied an Italian picture, brilliantly, consummately, says Clive. Has the same facility there: but it will come to nothing he said, like the other.[13]

What did we talk about? Tom & the Sitwells; Eddie Marsh & Lady Colefax,[14] & I felt one cd. go on saying these things for ever, & they

13. VW dined with Clive on 25 February. Lord Berners' autobiographical *First Childhood* (1934), amplifies this summary of his parents' characters. Donald Francis Tovey (1875-1940), pianist, composer and scholar, was one of the greatest personalities in the musical world of his day; he had been Reid Professor of Music at Edinburgh University since 1914.

14. Edward ('Eddie') Marsh (1872-1952), again private secretary to Winston Churchill (now Chancellor of the Exchequer), was like Lady Colefax inveterately sociable; his interests and patronage embraced writers, painters and actors.

mean nothing. Sure enough, he asked me to dine: & now I say I have a headache & can't.

Wednesday 3 March

And I did have a bit of a headache—yes; all this time is rather weathering headaches. Nailing a flag to a mast in a gale, I have just compared writing a novel in London to that, in a letter to Vita. The glow is off my visit to Herbert & Freda at Cookham: a very memorable day.[1] From their windows you look down on the top of old Mr Watkins' bald head skulling on the Thames. You look at two twisted stakes in the river which I took for cranes; & across Marlow to some hills. They motored us up into the hills, & it was oddly strangely still & bright & empty & full of unblown flowers. We saw a Queen Anne house called—I forget; so high & remote, with turf to its door; & broad alleys; capacious windows, a woman. Well; no one gets more pleasure from these sights than I do; only the wave of pleasure leaves some regret—all this beauty going—going—going: & I in Tavistock Sqre not seeing it. And spiritually it was very interesting. I thought I had found the real human being— something so simple & fitted to its surroundings as to be almost irreflective, in Freda. She is nearer humanity than I am: eats her way into the heart of it, as I cannot. Her thighs are thick with honey. But the impression is dying, as they do, under others—how I lost my little mother of pearl brooch, bought a 16/ hat which I do not like, & must go to tea at Ethel [Sands]'s tomorrow in what then? My own lack of beauty depresses me today. But how far does the old convention about 'beauty' bear looking into? I think of the people I have known. Are they beautiful? This problem I leave unsolved.

Raymond gave a fancy dress party on Sunday night. I was torpid with a sleeping draught; & was dozing off, as the carriages arrived at no. 6. Still I envied them; & thought, when Raymond telephoned about the copy of Old Kensington which I gave him & said how lovely Nancy [Cunard] had looked, that I had missed the greatest sight of the season.[2] Happily, Lucas comes to tea, & he says he hears it was a terrible sticky dull party, with not room to turn round in, which greatly pleases me. Lucas, Peter, I should call him, came, from friendship; which friendship,

1. See *III VW Letters*, no. 1622 for VW's letter to Vita; it also describes the Woolfs' visit to LW's stockbroker brother Herbert Sidney Woolf (1879-1949) and his wife Alfreda, *née* Major, at Cookham Dean on Sunday 28 February.
2. Raymond Mortimer lived at 6 Gordon (now Endsleigh) Place, which connected Gordon and Tavistock Squares. His present was the book published in 1873 by Miss Thackeray—subsequently Lady Ritchie, VW's 'Aunt Anny'.

as I suppose, was gently stimulated by my praise of his novel.[3] He is a
bony rosy little austere priest; so whole, & sane, & simple throughout
one can't help respecting him, though when it comes to books we disagree.
He says Tom &c: have thrown intellect to the winds; given up the ghost;
he says Houseman & de la Mare are the real poets.[4] I say poetry is defunct;
& Tom &c anyhow try to animate it. The Sitwells, he says, advertise.
They're aristocrats, I say, thinking criticism upstart impertinence on the
part of flunkeys. No merit in their works anyhow, he says. But what
about this drawing room singer, de la Mare, I ask. The most charming
of men. Granted. Granted, on Peter's side, that he has no coherency
whatever—is always darting after strange monsters—goldfish in bowls,
I say. Well, but we cant all be great philosophical poets, he says.
Anyhow Tom ain't a drawing room singer, I say. Tom has been down
lecturing, & not creating a good impression at Cambridge, I fancy.[5]
He tells the young men, in private, how they cook fish in Paris: his
damned selfconsciousness again, I suppose. But Peter is, to my mind,
too entire in his judgments; founded on book learning & prettiness into
the bargain. He has no ascendency of brain: he is not, & now never will
be, a personage: which is the one thing needful in criticism, or writing of
any sort, I think; for we're all as wrong as wrong can be. But character
is the thing.

Tuesday 9 March

Then I was at two parties: Ethel's tea; Mary's dinner.

Ethel's was a ghastly frizzly frying pan affair. I chattering in front
of the footlights.

Well, said Ott. how are you? You look wonderfully well; as if you
had never had an illness in your life.

3. F. L. Lucas's first novel, *The River Flows*, was published by the Hogarth Press in
October 1926 (*HP Checklist* 99); written in the form of a diary, it betrayed,
according to the *TLS* (14 October 1926): 'inexperience which was not so obvious
from his criticism' but shed 'a not uninteresting light on the Cambridge scene'.
4. A. E. Housman (1859-1936), Professor of Latin at Cambridge 1911-36, was
eminent in the fields of classical scholarship and of original poetry, although of the
latter he published nothing between *A Shropshire Lad* in 1896 and *Last Poems* in
1922. Walter de la Mare (1873-1956), poet, storyteller, and man of letters.
5. T. S. Eliot gave eight lectures (the Clark Lectures) on 'The Metaphysical Poetry
of the Seventeenth Century' at Trinity College between 26 January and 9 March
1926. (The unpublished texts are in the Hayward Bequest in King's College
Library, P6.) As described by Lucas, who did not admire him, the impression made
by Eliot upon Cambridge was inevitably poor.

(Now what does she say that for? To get pity for herself, sure enough.) I can't say I'm any better.

But she is all dressed like a girl of 18; tomato coloured Georgette & fur.

Ethel says, tittering

What a nice hat.

I'm all windblown in my old felt, come through the snow, with Dadie.

Well, I say to myself, I'll see this through anyhow, take my seat as on a throne, & proceed, first to little smug Leigh Ashton: Read wrote that Times Leader this morning (quoting me & Joyce as examples of good prose versus death of Queen Victoria).[6]

I should so much like to know if you think its well written—such a charming man.

Then diversion: Ethel; Ottoline: Percy Lubbock.[7]

Are the Russians more passionate than we are?

No; I say; I have all the passions. Asked to define a dramatic scene; how Leonard says "I think the worse of you for ever" when I accept Ott's invitation. Suddenly I remember it was Ott's invitation. If Mr Lubbock had a daughter he would have scenes—this is sheer egotistical cruelty on Ott's part; so home, holding Dadie by the arm; talking about his fellowship, to be announced on Saturday, (But Peter thinks he won't get it[8]) & abusing Chelsea, & Ottoline; & saying how unpopular I made myself.

As for Mary's party, there, save for the usual shyness about powder & paint, shoes & stockings, I was happy, owing to the supremacy of literature. This keeps us sweet & sane, George Moore & me I mean.[9]

He has a pink foolish face; blue eyes like hard marbles; a crest of snowhite hair; little unmuscular hands; sloping shoulders; a high stomach;

6. (Arthur) Leigh Bolland Ashton (b. 1897) had joined the staff of the Victoria & Albert Museum (of which he was later to become Director) in 1922. The leading article in the *TLS* of 4 March 1926, entitled 'English Prose', discussed *The Oxford Book of English Prose* (1925), chosen and edited by Sir Arthur Quiller-Couch. The examples VW refers to here were taken from her own *Mrs Dalloway*, from Joyce's *Ulysses*, and from *Queen Victoria* by Lytton Strachey, who was the only one of the three to be represented in Quiller-Couch's anthology.

7. Percy Lubbock (1875-1965), man of letters.

8. Peter Lucas was right; G. H. W. Rylands was not elected a Fellow of King's College, Cambridge, until March 1927.

9. George Augustus Moore (1852-1933), the admired Anglo-Irish novelist and writer, author of *Esther Waters* (1894), was a friend of the Hutchinsons; VW now apparently met him for the first time. His views on Thomas Hardy and Anne Brontë had been expressed at length in his *Conversations in Ebury Street* (1924).

neat, purplish well brushed clothes; & perfect manners, as I consider them. That is to say he speaks without fear or dominance; accepting me on my merits; every one on their merits. Still in spite of age uncowed, unbeaten, lively, shrewd. As for Hardy & Henry James though, what shall one say?

"I am a fairly modest man; but I admit I think Esther Waters a better book than Tess."

But what is there to be said for that man? He cannot write. He cannot tell a story. The whole art of fiction consists in telling a story. Now he makes a woman confess. How does he do it? In the third person—a scene that should be moving, impressive. Think how Tolstoi would have done it!

But, said Jack [Hutchinson] War & Peace is the greatest novel in the world. I remember the scene where Natasha puts on a moustache, & Rostov sees her for the first time as she is & falls in love with her.

No, my good friend, there is nothing very wonderful in that. That is an ordinary piece of observation. But my good friend (to me—half hesitating to call me this) what have you to say for Hardy? You cannot find anything to say. English fiction is the worst part of English literature. Compare it with the French—with the Russians. Henry James wrote some pretty little stories before he invented his jargon. But they were about rich people. You cannot write stories about rich people; because, I think he said, they have no instincts. But Henry James was enamoured of marble balustrades. There was no passion in any of his people. And Anne Brontë was the greatest of the Brontës & Conrad could not write, & so on. But this is out of date.

Saturday 20 March

But what is to become of all these diaries, I asked myself yesterday. If I died, what would Leo make of them? He would be disinclined to burn them; he could not publish them. Well, he should make up a book from them, I think; & then burn the body. I daresay there is a little book in them: if the scraps & scratches were straightened out a little. God knows.

This is dictated by a slight melancholia, which comes upon me sometimes now, & makes me think I am old: I am ugly. I am repeating things. Yet, as far as I know, as a writer I am only now writing out my mind.

Dining with Clive last night to meet Lord Ivor Spencer Churchill— an elegant attenuated gnat like youth; very smooth, very supple, with the semi-transparent face of a flower, & the legs of a gazelle, & the white waistcoat & diamond buttons of a dandy, & all an Americans desire to understand psycho-analysis—I thought of my own age.[10] I made a horrid gaffe early on: said I liked a picture, which I did not like, & found I was wrong. Now if I had followed my instinct, as one should do, I should have been right. For some extraordinary reason, this poisoned my evening, slightly. The Lord analysed everything very ingeniously: he is a clever boy. I was greatly impressed by masculine cleverness, & their ability to toss balls swiftly & surely to & fro: no butter fingers; all clean catches. Adrian Bishop came in; a ruddy bull frog;[11] & then I went, & Clive, with a discrimination which was affectionate, but not just, apologised, thinking I had not talked enough for my pleasure; whereas I had said the wrong thing, & been depressed over that. Otherwise the evening amused me, & I wanted, like a child, to stay & argue. True, the argument was passing my limits—how if Einstein is true, we shall be able to foretell our own lives. Fortune tellers can now read one's mind exactly according to Lord Ivor, who, by the bye, had read neither Henry James nor V.W., is about 23, & came to the Press this morning, obediently, to buy my complete works. No intellectual would have done that. They are excessively anxious to save their souls—these aristocrats; witness Lord Berners the other night, sending out for Peacock—on my recommendation.

Otherwise, we had Bea Howe to dinner; & went to Philip [Woolf]'s one hot still day of the usual loveliness, & saw the place, & the horses, & the pepper box towers of Waddesdon, & I liked the immense directness & uncloudedness of Babs;[12] but says Eddy [Sackville-West] who came to tea on Sunday, this is "I assure you" all my imagination. She would be very dull if you knew her. He knows dozens of her. Who is not dull? Only B[loomsbur]'y according to Eddy.

Then there was Sybil Colefax: she comes to heel promptly: no, I won't go there; she may have a little cheap tea here, which she does, gratefully.

10. Lord Ivor (Charles Spencer-) Churchill (1898-1956), younger son of the 9th Duke of Marlborough and his first wife, Consuelo Vanderbilt; uninterested in public affairs, he was devoting himself to connoisseurship and to forming his remarkable collection, in particular of French Impressionist and Post-Impressionist painting.
11. Herbert Frank ('Adrian') Bishop (1898-1942) was a Dubliner educated at Eton and at King's College, Cambridge (1919-23), where he was prominent as a scholar, a wit, and an actor. After leaving Cambridge, he lived mostly abroad—in Vienna, Persia, Germany and Italy, teaching and writing—until 1935.
12. Philip Sidney Woolf (1889-1962), LW's youngest brother, was estate manager to a distant cousin, James de Rothschild, owner of Waddesdon Manor, Buckinghamshire—a conspicuous mansion built in 1880 in the style of a French château (now National Trust property). Philip had married Marjorie ('Babs') Lowndes in 1922.

She has done America with the usual dashing, joyless efficiency; could not analyse, merely report. Charlie Chaplin such a mixture of subtlety & common[n]ess: but why? No instances available, so I infer that she picked this up second hand, perhaps from Esme Howard; perhaps from Coolidge, or from Douglas Fairbanks or from the Italian boy who drove the car. Like a good housewife, which she is, she is making Peter begin life hard, cooking his breakfast, down on Wall Street by 9. There is a strain of hard, serious, professionalism in her, quite unmitigated by all the splendours of Argyll House.[13]

Wednesday 24 March

"I'm going to hand in my resignation this morning" said L. making the coffee.

To what? I asked.

"The Nation".

And it is done; & we have six months only before us. I feel 10 years younger; the shafts off our shoulders again & the world before us. I can't pretend to make much of a to-do about this either way. It was a temporary makeshift job, amusing at first, then galling, & last night, after an argument of the usual kind about literary articles & space & so on with Maynard & Hubert L. came to the decision to resign now. There was no quarrel. Oddly enough, having tea with Nessa, she had set me thinking the same thing. Phil [Noel-]Baker had said to her he thought L. the best living writer, & what a pity it was he spent so much time on the Nation & the Press. So there was I beginning, don't you think we might give them up! —when L. came in with his contribution to the question. He was dining with Clive, so the discussion waited till this morning; was decided by 10; in the hands of the Chief by 11—& now thank God no more chiefs for either of us so long as we live I hope.[14]

The situation appears to be that L. shall make £300; I £200—& really I don't suppose we shall find it hard; & then the mercy of having no ties, no proofs, no articles to procure, & all that, is worth a little more exertion elsewhere, should it come to that. I'm amused at my own

13. Esme Howard (1863-1939), created 1st Baron Howard of Penrith in 1930, was from 1924-30 British Ambassador to the USA. Peter was one of Sibyl Colefax's two sons.

14. LW was dissuaded by Keynes ('the Chief') and Henderson from carrying out this intention to resign as literary editor of the *N & A*—a position he had held since the end of April 1923—and in fact continued to hold until the end of 1930. See correspondence in LWP, Sussex, section I. Hubert Douglas Henderson (1890-1952), economist, was editor of the paper from 1923-1930.

sense of liberation. To upset everything every 3 or 4 years is my notion
of a happy life. Always to be tacking to get into the eye of the wind.
Now a prudent life is, as L. pointed out in the Square the opposite of
this. One ought to stick in the same place. But with £400 assured & no
children, why imitate a limpet in order to enjoy a limpets safety? The
next question will be, I see, the Press. Shall we give that up too, & so be
quit of everything? Its not such an easy question, or so pressing. I sometimes wish it. For, speaking selfishly, it has served my turn: given me a
chance of writing off my own bat, & now I doubt if Heinemann or Cape
would much intimidate me. But then there's the fun—which is considerable. The time will come, at this rate, when we have nothing in the
world to resign: then, to get the effect of change, one will have to accept.
We say we will travel & see the world. Anyhow I make my usual
prediction—we shall be richer this time next year without the Nation
than with it.

I rather like feeling that I *have* to earn money. I intensely dislike being
in office, in any post of authority. I dislike being in people's pay. This of
course is part of the reason why I like writing for the Press. But I suppose
freedom becomes a fetish like any other. These disjointed reflections I
scribble on a divine, if gusty, day; being about, after reading Anna
Karenina, to dine at a pot-house with Rose Macaulay—not a cheerful
entertainment; but an experience perhaps.

Lydia came into the room when L. was talking to Maynard this
morning to show him her Zebra shoes, which cost £5.8.6. & they were
really lizard, L. says. Also it is curious how a change like this destroys
formality[?]—dissipates the elements.

Saturday 27 March

To continue—I don't know why I should really tell the story of the
Nation—it doesn't figure largely in our lives. But Leonard met Phil
Baker, who says he will get £300 as lecturer at the School of Economics
easily if he wants it. He came in that night & said this & then we went
off on a blowing night to dine at Rose M.'s 'pothouse', as I so mistakenly
called it. There were 10 second rate writers in second rate dress clothes,
Lynds, Goulds, O'Donovan:[15] no, I won't in any spasm of hypocritical

15. Robert Wilson Lynd (1879-1949), journalist and essayist, regular contributor to
    the *New Statesman* and the Liberal *Daily News*; his wife, also a writer, was Sylvia,
    née Dryhurst (1888-1952). Gerald Gould (1885-1936), author and literary
    journalist; his wife Barbara Ayrton Gould (d. 1950), had worked on the *Daily
    Herald*, and was a Labour Party parliamentary candidate—finally elected in 1945.
    Jeremiah (Gerald) O'Donovan (1872-1942) had once been a Catholic priest in

humanity include Wolves. L. by the way was in his red brown tweed. Then the pitter patter began; the old yard was scratched over by these baldnecked chickens. The truth was that we had no interests private; literature was our common ground; & though I will talk literature with Desmond or Lytton by the hour, when it comes to pecking up grains with these active stringy fowls my gorge rises. What d'you think of the Hawthornden prize? Why isn't Masefield as good as Chaucer, or Gerhardi as good as Tchekov: how can I embark with Gerald Gould on such topics? He reads novels incessantly; got a holiday 3 years ago, & prided himself on reading nothing but Tchekhov; knows all about a novel in the first chapter. Sylvias & Geralds & Roberts & Roses chimed & tinkled round the table. A stout woman called Gould got steadily more & more mustard & tomato coloured. I said Holy Ghost? when Mr O'Donovan said the whole of the coast. Lodged on a low sofa in Rose's underground cheerful, sane, breezy room I talked to a young cultivated man, who turned out to be Hinks, Roger, British Museum, mild aesthete, variety of Leigh Ashton; but thank God, not a second rate journalist.[16] All the time I kept saying to myself Thank God to be out of that; out of the Nation; no longer brother in arms with Rose & Robert & Sylvia. It is a thinblooded set; so 'nice', 'kind', respectable, cleverish & in the swim.

Then our set at Nessa's last night, was hardly at its best. L. & Adrian silent & satirical; old Sickert rather toothless & set;[17] I driven to chatter, not well; but Nessa & Duncan don't consolidate & order these parties; so home in a spasm of outraged vanity, & not that altogether, for I had worked honestly if feebly, & L. had not; & then he was off early this morning to Rodmell where Philcox is in the thick of building & drains:[18]

Galway, had resigned, travelled, married, published novels and met Rose Macaulay while they were both working in the Ministry of Information towards the end of the war. Their ensuing clandestine love-affair lasted until his death.

16. Roger Packman Hinks (1903-1963), educated at Westminster School and Trinity College, Cambridge, had spent a year at the British School in Rome, and had just been appointed to an assistant-Keepership in the Department of Greek and Roman Antiquities in the British Museum.

17. Walter Richard Sickert (1860-1942), the painter, had suffered a long period of depression and misanthropy following the death of his second wife in 1920. He was living alone in a bed-sitting-room and studio at 15 Fitzroy Street. However in 1924 he had been elected ARA, much to his gratification, and later this year was to marry again.

18. Philcox Bros, builders, of 155 High Street, Lewes; they were carrying out alterations to Monks House.

so I had no time to uncrease my rose leaf; had to try & work, to finish the rather long drawn out dinner scene [in *To the Lighthouse*], & was just striking oil when in comes Angus to tell me Eddy was on the phone: would I go to Rimsky Korsakov with him on Tuesday.[19] I agreed—more, asked him to dinner. Then was all a whirl & flutter of doubts; detested the engagement; could not settle; suddenly shook my coat, like a retriever; faced facts; sent Eddy a wire, & a letter "Cant come—detest engagements", & pondered where shall I spend the day? decided on Greenwich, arrived there at 1; lunched; everything fell out pat; smoked a cigarette on the pier promenade, saw the ships swinging up, one two, three, out of the haze; adored it all; yes even the lavatory keepers little dog; saw the grey Wren buildings fronting the river; & then another great ship, grey & orange; with a woman walking on deck; & then to the hospital; first to the Museum where I saw Sir John Franklin's pen & spoons (a spoon asks a good deal of imagination to consecrate it)—I played with my mind watching what it would do,—& behold if I didn't almost burst into tears over the coat Nelson wore at Trafalgar with the medals which he hid with his hand when they carried him down, dying, lest the sailors might see it was him. There was too, his little fuzzy pigtail, of golden greyish hair tied in black; & his long white stockings, one much stained, & his white breeches with the gold buckles, & his stock—all of which I suppose they must have undone & taken off as he lay dying. Kiss me Hardy &c—Anchor, anchor,—I read it all when I came in, & could swear I was there on the Victory— So the charm worked in that case.[20] Then it was raining a little, but I went into the Park, which is all prominence & radiating paths; then back on top of a bus, & so to tea. Molly [McCarthy] came, a warm faithful bear, of whom I am really fond, judging from the steady accumulation of my desire to see her these last 3 or 4 weeks, culminating in my asking her to come, as I so rarely ask anyone to come. Saxon came, with his great grandfather's diary, which it pleases him I should like, & call like him;[21] & then reading & bed. I think my rose leaf is now uncrumpled. Certainly I shall remember

19. A concert performance of Rimsky Korsakov's opera *The Legend of the Invisible City of Kitezh* was to be given at the Royal Opera House, Covent Garden, on 30 March.

20. The relics of Sir John Franklin's ill-fated 1845 expedition to discover the North-West passage were displayed in the Naval Museum, at that time housed in King Charles' Block of the Royal Naval College (formerly hospital); the Nelson relics were exhibited in the Painted Hall. Since 1934 they have been assembled in the National Maritime Museum in the Queen's House, Greenwich.

21. Saxon had an idea that a book might be made of his great-grandfather Sharon Turner's diary, and be published by the Hogarth Press; but it never was.

the ships coming up (here Tomlin rings,[22] but I won't see him—solitude is my bride, & she is adulterated by Clive & Mary tonight) & Nelson's coat long after I have forgotten how silly & uncomfortable I was at Nessa's on Friday.

Friday 9 April

Life has been very good to the Leafs.[1] I should say it has been perfect. Why then all this pother about life? It can produce old Walter, bubbling & chubby; & old Lotta, stately & content; & little Kitty, as good & nice as can be; & handsome Charles, as loving & affectionate. Plunge deep into Walter's life & it is all sound & satisfactory. His son kisses him & says "Bless you father". He sinks back chuckling on his cushions. He chooses a maccaroon. He tells a story. Lotta purrs[?], in her black velvet dress. Only I am exiled from this profound natural happiness. That is what I always feel; or often feel now—natural happiness is what I lack, in profusion. I have intense happiness—not that. It is therefore what I most envy; geniality & family love & being on the rails of human life. Indeed, exaggeration apart, this is a very satisfactory form of existence. And it exists for thousands of people all the time. Why have we none of us got it, in that measure? Old & young agreeing to live together: & being normal; & clever enough of course; yet not stinted or self-conscious in emotion. Much of this may be the generalised & harmonious view which one gets of unknown people as a whole. I might not think it if I saw more of them. Writers do not live like that perhaps. But it is useless frittering away the impression which is so strong. Also I keep thinking "They pity me. They wonder what I find in life." Then I sink a little silent, & rouse myself to talk to Kitty. Also I know that nothing Leonard or I have done—not our books or the Press or anything means anything to Lotta & Walter & Charles & very little to Kitty. Charles has his

22. Stephen Tomlin (1901-1937), youngest son of a High Court judge, had abandoned study of the law to become a sculptor. He had become close friends with many of the younger adherents of 'Bloomsbury'. VW met him in 1924 when she recorded: 'Theres a little thrush like creature called Tomlin who wants to sculpt me.' (*II VW Diary*, 21 December 1924.)

1. The Woolfs had been to tea with the Leafs at Sussex Place, Regent's Park. Walter Leaf (1852-1927), Homeric scholar, Chairman since 1919 of the London & Westminster Bank, and President of the International Chamber of Commerce; he had married in 1894 Charlotte Mary (1867-1937), second daughter of John Addington Symonds and sister of Madge Vaughan (the wife of VW's cousin W. W. Vaughan) who had died the previous November. Their children were Charles (b. 1896), and Katherine (Kitty) (b. 1900), who was at Newnham College, Cambridge, from 1920-23.

motor at the door. They are perfectly happy, motoring off to Berk-
hamstead, which will take an hour, so they are among the lanes even now.
A spring night & so on.

Sunday 11 April

Cannot read Mrs Webb because at any moment S. Tomlin may ring
the bell. Also I wanted to go on about the Leafs. I have almost forgotten
the impression they made on me. I have wrapped myself round in my
own personality again. How does it come about—these sudden intense
changes of view? Perhaps my life, writing imagining, is unusually
conscious: very vivid to me: & then, going to tea with the Leafs destroys
it more completely than other people's lives because my life is saying to
itself "This is life—the only life". But when I enter a complete world of
its own; where Walter cracks a joke, I realise that this is existing whether
I exist or not; & so get bowled over. Violent as they are, these impressions
go quickly; leaving a sediment of ideas which I shall discuss with L.
perhaps when we go to Iwerne Minster. About natural happiness: how it
is destroyed by our way of life.

Mrs Webb's Life makes me compare it with mine. The difference is
that she is trying to relate all her experiences to history. She is very
rational & coherent. She has always thought about her life & the meaning
of the world: indeed, she begins this at the age of 4. She has studied
herself as a phenomenon. Thus her autobiography is part of the history
of the 19th Century. She is the product of science, & the lack of faith in
God; she was secreted by the Time Spirit. Anyhow she believes this to
be so; & makes herself fit in very persuasively & to my mind very
interestingly. She taps a great stream of thought. Unlike that self-
conscious poseur Walter Raleigh she is much more interested in facts &
truth than in what will shock people & what a professor ought not to
say.[2] Tomlin does not seem to be coming, & L. is at Staines, so I will
try a little reading.[3]

2. See in particular Chapter III of Beatrice Webb's *My Apprenticeship*: 'The Choice
of a Craft: the Religion of Humanity.' VW was also reading *The Letters of Sir
Walter Raleigh, 1879-1922*, edited by Lady Raleigh (2 vols., 1926); her withering
review appeared under the title 'A Professor of Life' in the early May number of
Vogue; it was reprinted in *A Captain's Deathbed* (Kp C273). Walter Raleigh
(1861-1922), knighted in 1911, had been successively Professor of English Literature
at Liverpool, Glasgow, and Oxford Universities.
3. LW, in one of his regular filial observances, launched with his mother at his brother
Harold's home near Staines, and drove with her to his brother Herbert's at
Cookham.

On Tuesday 13 April the Woolfs went by train to Blandford in Dorset, and motored out to the Talbot Inn at Iwerne Minster, where they stayed five nights; for the return journey on the 18th they went by bus to Bournemouth and took the train from there back to Waterloo.

Sunday 18 April

⟨This is written⟩

This is not written very seriously.—obviously not—to try a pen, I think. And it is now [*Friday*] *April 30th*, the last of a wet windy month, excepting the sudden opening of all the doors at Easter, & the summer displayed blazing, as it always is, I suppose; only cloud hidden. I have not said anything about Iwerne Minster. Now it would amuse me to see what I remember it by. Cranbourne Chase: the stunted aboriginal forest trees, scattered, not grouped in cultivations; anemones, bluebells, violets, all pale, sprinkled about, without colour, livid, for the sun hardly shone. Then Blackmore Vale; a vast air dome & the fields dropped to the bottom; the sun striking, there, there; a drench of rain falling, like a veil streaming from the sky, there & there; & the downs rising, very strongly scarped (if that is the word) so that they were ridged & ledged; then an inscription in a church "sought peace & ensured it", & the question, who wrote these sonorous stylistic epitaphs?—& all the cleanliness of Iwerne village, its happiness & well being, making me ask, as we tended to sneer. Still this is the right method, surely; & then tea & cream— these I remember: the hot baths; my new leather coat; Shaftesbury, so much lower & less commanding than my imagination, & the drive to Bournemouth, & the dog & the lady behind the rock, & the view of Swanage, & coming home.

And then it was horror: Nelly; faced her going; was firm yet desolate; on Tuesday she stopped me on the landing said "Please ma'am may I apologise?" & this time we had been so resolute & implicitly believed her that I had written 6 letters. No cooks however came; & I had enough look into the 'servant question' to be glad to be safe again with Nelly. Now I vow come what may, never never to believe her again. "I am too fond of you ever to be happy with anyone else" she said. Talking of compliments, this is perhaps the greatest I could have. But my mind is wandering. It is a question of clothes. This is what humiliates me— talking of compliments—to walk in Regent St, Bond Str &c: & be notably less well dressed than other people.

Yesterday I finished the first part of To the Lighthouse, & today began the second. I cannot make it out—here is the most difficult abstract piece of writing—I have to give an empty house, no people's characters, the passage of time, all eyeless & featureless with nothing to cling to: well, I rush at it, & at once scatter out two pages. Is it nonsense, is it brilliance? Why am I so flown with words, & apparently free to do exactly what I like? When I read a bit it seems spirited too; needs compressing, but not much else. Compare this dashing fluency with the excruciating hard wrung battles I had with Mrs Dalloway (save the end). This is not made up: it is the literal fact. Yes, & I am rather famous. For the rest, we dally about the Nation. Maynard, dressed in a light overcoat, is back; hums & haws about standing for the Provost of King's.[4] We tell him Lydia would like it. He says it means middle age & respectability. I feel some sympathy for him. This is because he is going grey, I tell Clive. Clive's back; Nessa departing,[5] & I worrying about my clothes, & how Roger last night upset me by saying that Nessa finds fault with my temper behind my back. Then (at Ralph's new left handed establishment[6]) Inez, rather like Vivien [Eliot] to look at, searches into my eyes with her greenish pink-rimmed ones, & says, I must tell you two things: then she tells me that she admires me. That swallowed (doubtfully) she says, Did you ever have an affair with Oliver?[7] The connection is this: she disliked me, from jealousy. I protest I never kissed him, & he never looked at me. She refuses to believe. So she has been refusing to believe for years— A queer little interview, stage managed by Oliver* & she: at last brought off. I called in Leonard, & I think convinced her.

* Oliver denied all knowledge of this; & said she invented it in order to have an excuse for an intimate conversation. "So many women are like that" said Rose Macaulay sitting spruce lean, like a mummified cat, in her chair (this is written Aug. 12th)

4. The Provostship of King's College was vacant because of the death on 7 April of Sir Walter Durnford; in the event the Rev. A. E. Brooke, Ely Professor of Divinity, was elected to succeed him.

5. Clive was back from Paris; Vanessa was about to go, with Duncan Grant and Angus Davidson, to Venice.

6. This was at 41 Gordon Square, where Ralph Partridge now lived during the week with Frances Marshall, returning each weekend to Ham Spray, his country home with his wife Carrington and Lytton Strachey. Frances Catherine Marshall (b. 1900), educated at Bedales and Newnham, worked in Birrell and Garnett's bookshop (David Garnett was her brother-in-law); she and Ralph Partridge were married after Carrington's death in 1932.

7. Inez Jenkins, née Ferguson (b. 1895), had had an affair with Oliver Strachey at the end of the war; she married in 1923. From 1919-29 she was General Secretary of the National Federation of Women's Institutes.

Wednesday 5 May

An exact diary of the Strike would be interesting.[1] For instance, it is now a ¼ to 2: there is a brown fog; nobody is building; it is drizzling. The first thing in the morning we stand at the window & watch the traffic in Southampton Row. This is incessant. Everyone is bicycling; motor cars are huddled up with extra people. There are no buses. No placards. no newspapers. The men are at work in the road; water, gas & electricity are allowed; but at 11 the light was turned off. I sat in the press in the brown fog, while L. wrote an article for the Herald. A very revolutionary looking young man on a cycle arrived with the British Gazette. L. is to answer an article in this.[2] All was military stern a little secret. Then Clive dropped in, the door being left open. He is offering himself to the Government. Maynard excited, wants the H[ogarth]. P[ress]. to bring out a skeleton number of the Nation.[3] It is all tedious & depressing, rather like waiting in a train outside a station. Rumours are passed round—that the gas wd. be cut off at 1—false of course. One does not know what to do. And nature has laid it on thick today—fog, rain, cold. A voice, rather commonplace & official, yet the only common voice left, wishes us good morning at 10. This is the voice of Britain, to wh. we can make no reply. The voice is very trivial, & only tells us that the Prince of Wales is coming back (*from Biarritz*), that the London streets present an unprecedented spectacle.

Thursday 6 May

(one of the curious effects of the Strike is that it is difficult to remember the day of the week). Everything is the same, but unreasonably, or

1. The General Strike was proclaimed by the Trades Union Congress on the evening of 2 May 1926 in support of the mineworkers who had struck on 1 May. Their dispute dated back to the summer of 1925. The coal strike that had seemed imminent then had been effectively postponed by a nine month government subsidy. This ran out on 30 April 1926. But any real hope of averting the coal strike had foundered with the rejection by both miners and coalowners of the Samuel Commission's recommendations published in March this year.
2. The *British Gazette* was the government-founded newspaper run for the duration of the strike under the management of Winston Churchill; no article by LW appeared at this period in the *Daily Herald*, which was published, in the same format and with identical contents, on eight occasions between 5 and 17 May.
3. The *N & A* was not published again until 15 May; but a special strike issue, consisting of a 'symposium of views' by Keynes, Gilbert Murray, Ramsay Muir, W. T. Layton and E. D. Simon, had been prepared for publication, but did not appear, the previous week. See *N & A* 15 May; also *III VW Letters*, no. 1635.

because of the weather, or habit, we are more cheerful, take less notice, & occasionally think of other things. The taxis are out today. There are various skeleton papers being sold. One believes nothing. Clive dines in Mayfair, & everyone is pro-men; I go to Harrison [*dentist*], & he shouts me down with "Its red rag versus Union Jack, Mrs Woolf" & how Thomas has 100,000.[4] Frankie dines out, & finds everyone pro-Government. Bob [Trevelyan] drops in & says Churchill is for peace, but Baldwin wont budge.[5] Clive says Churchill is for tear gas bombs, fight to the death, & is at the bottom of it all. So we go on, turning in our cage. I notice how frequently we break of[f] with "Well I don't know." According to L. this open state of mind is due to the lack of papers. It feels like a deadlock, on both sides; as if we could keep fixed like this for weeks. What one prays for is God: the King or God; some impartial person to say kiss & be friends—as apparently we all desire.

Just back from a walk to the Strand. Of course one notices lorries full of elderly men & girls standing like passengers in the old 3rd class carriages. Children swarm. They pick up bits of old wood paving. Everything seems to be going fast, away, in business[?]. The shops are open but empty. Over it all is some odd pale unnatural atmosphere—great activity but no normal life. I think we shall become more independent & stoical as the days go on. And I am involved in dress buying with Todd [*editor of* Vogue]; I tremble & shiver all over at the appalling magnitude of the task I have undertaken—to go to a dressmaker recommended by Todd, even, she suggested, but here my blood ran cold, with Todd. Perhaps this excites me more feverishly than the Strike. It is a little like the early hours of the morning (this state of things) when one has been up all night. Business improved today. We sold a few books. Bob cycled from Leith Hill, getting up at 5 a.m. to avoid the crowd. He punctured an hour later, met his tailor who mended him, set forth again, was almost crushed in the crowd near London, & has since been tramping London, from Chelsea to Bloomsbury to gather gossip, & talk, incoherently about Desmond's essays & his own poetry. He has secreted two more of these works which 'ought to be published'. He is ravenous greedy, & apelike, but has a kind of russet surly charm; like a dog one teases. He complained how Logan teased him. Clive calls in to discuss bulletins—indeed, more than anything it is like a house

4. James Henry Thomas (1874-1949), General Secretary of the National Union of Railwaymen 1918-24, 1925-31, had been Colonial Secretary in the Labour Government of 1924. He had directed and negotiated the settlement of a rail strike in 1919.
5. Stanley Baldwin (1867-1947) was Prime Minister in the current Conservative administration; Winston Churchill (1874-1965) his Chancellor of the Exchequer.

where someone is dangerously ill; & friends drop in to enquire, & one has to wait for doctor's news—Quennel, the poet, came; a lean boy, nervous, plaintive, rather pretty; on the look out for work, & come to tap the Wolves—who are said, I suppose to be an authority on that subject. We suggested Desmond's job.[6] After an hour of this, he left, —— here Clive came in & interrupted. He has been shopping in the West End with Mary. Nothing to report there. He & L. listened in at 7 & heard nothing. The look of the streets—how people "trek to work" that is the stock phrase: that it will be cold & windy tomorrow (it is shivering cold today) that there was a warm debate in the Commons—

Among the crowd of trampers in Kingsway were old Pritchard, toothless, old wispy, benevolent; who tapped L. on the shoulder & said he was "training to shoot him"; & old Miss Pritchard, equally frail, dusty, rosy, shabby. "How long will it last Mrs Woolf?" "Four weeks" "Ah dear!" Off they tramp, over the bridge to Kennington I think; next in Kingsway comes the old battered clerk, who has 5 miles to walk. Miss Talbot has an hours walk; Mrs Brown 2 hours walk.[7] But they all arrive, & clatter about as usual—Pritchard doing poor peoples work for nothing, as I imagine his way is, & calling himself a Tory.

Then we are fighting the Square on the question of leading dogs. Dogs must be led; but tennis can be played they say. L. is advancing to the fight, & has enlisted the Pekinese in the Square. We get no news from abroad; neither can send it. No parcels. Pence have been added to milk, vegetables &c. And Karin has bought 4 joints.

It is now a chilly lightish evening; very quiet; the only sound a distant barrel organ playing. The bricks stand piled on the building & there remain. And Viola was about to make our fortune. She dined here, Monday night, the night of the strike.[8]

6. Peter Quennell (b. 1905), who had had a precocious success as a schoolboy poet and became a protégé of Eddie Marsh and the Sitwells, had been rusticated from Balliol (to which he did not return) the previous October. LW had met him with the Sitwells; he did find reviewing work from Desmond MacCarthy on the *New Statesman*.

7. William Burchell Pritchard (d. 1940), admitted 1876, was the senior partner in the firm of solicitors, Dollman & Pritchard, which occupied the ground and first floors of 52 Tavistock Square; 'old Miss Pritchard' was his sister who acted as chief clerk. Rose Talbot (later Mrs Shrager) and Mrs Brown were clerks in the office.

8. Viola Tree (1884-1939), eldest daughter of the great actor-manager Sir Herbert Beerbohm Tree, was a performer in her own right. The expected success of her memoirs, *Castles in the Air. The Story of my Singing Days*, published by the Hogarth Press in April 1926 (*HP Checklist* 111), had miscarried owing to the general strike.

MAY 1926

Friday 7 May

No change. "London calling the British Isles. Good morning everyone". That is how it begins at 10. The only news that the archbishops
are conferring, & ask our prayers that they may be guided right. Whether
this means action, we know not. We know nothing. Mrs Cartwright
walked from Hampstead. She & L. got heated arguing, she being anti-
labour; because she does not see why they should be supported, &
observes men in the street loafing instead of working. Very little work
done by either of us today. A cold, wet day, with sunny moments. All
arrangements unchanged. Girl came to make chair covers, having walked
from Shoreditch, but enjoyed it. Times sent for 25 Violas.[9] Question
whether to bring out a skeleton Roneo Nation. Leonard went to the
office, I to the Brit[ish] Mus[eum]; where all was chill serenity, dignity
& severity. Written up are the names of great men; & we all cower like
mice nibbling crumbs in our most official discreet impersonal mood
beneath. I like this dusty bookish atmosphere. Most of the readers
seemed to have rubbed their noses off & written their eyes out. Yet
they have a life they like—believe in the necessity of making books, I
suppose: verify, collate, make up other books, for ever. It must be
15 years since I read here. I came home & found L. & Hubert [Henderson]
arriving from the office—Hubert did what is now called "taking a cup
of tea", which means an hour & a halfs talk about the Strike. Here is his
prediction: if it is not settled, or in process, on Monday, it will last 5 weeks.
Today no wages are paid. Leonard said he minded this more than the war &
Hubert told us how he had travelled in Germany, & what brutes they were
in 1912.[10] He thinks gas & electricity will go next; had been at a journalists meeting where all were against labour (against the general strike that
is) & assumed Government victory. L. says if the state wins & smashes
T[rades]. U[nion]s he will devote his life to labour: if the archbishop
succeeds, he will be baptised. Now to dine at the Commercio to meet Clive.

Sunday 9 May

There is no news of the strike. The broadcaster has just said that we
are praying today. And L. & I quarrelled last night. I dislike the tub

9. i.e. The Times Book Club, of 42 Wigmore Street, W1, a leading circulating library.
10. Troops had been used to maintain order during a brief but bitter coal strike in the
Ruhr in March 1912. Over 1500 charges were preferred against individual strikers
and a high proportion of these led to prison sentences. Reaction hardened and
throughout the remainder of the year the German authorities set their face against
the so-called 'red and gold international' of socialists and Jews and pursued
policies hostile to organised labour and in particular to the right to picket.

thumper in him; he the irrational Xtian in me. I will write it all out later—my feelings about the Strike; but I am now writing to test my theory that there is consolation in expression. Unthinkingly, I refused just now to lunch with the Phil Bakers, who fetched L. in their car. Suddenly, 10 minutes ago, I began to regret this profoundly. How I should love the talk, & seeing the house, & battling my wits against theirs. Now the sensible thing to do is to provide some pleasure to balance this, which I cd. not have had, if I had gone. I can only think of writing this, & going round the Square. Obscurely, I have my clothes complex to deal with. When I am asked out my first thought is, but I have no clothes to go in. Todd has never sent me the address of the shop; & I may have annoyed her by refusing to lunch with her. But the Virginia who refuses is a very instinctive & therefore powerful person. The reflective & sociable only comes to the surface later. Then the conflict.

Baldwin broadcast last night: he rolls his rs; tries to put more than mortal strength into his words. "Have faith in me. You elected me 18 months ago. What have I done to forfeit your confidence? Can you not trust me to see justice done between man & man?" Impressive as it is to hear the very voice of the Prime Minister, descendant of Pitt & Chatham, still I can't heat up my reverence to the right pitch. I picture the stalwart oppressed man, bearing the world on his shoulders. And suddenly his self assertiveness becomes a little ridiculous. He becomes megalomaniac. No I dont trust him: I don't trust any human being, however loud they bellow & roll their rs.

Monday 10 May

Quarrel with L. settled in studio. Oh, but how incessant the arguments & interruptions are! As I write, L. is telephoning to Hubert. We are getting up a petition.[11] There was a distinct thaw (we thought) last night. The Arch B. & Grey both conciliatory.[12] So we went to bed happy. Today ostensibly the same dead lock; beneath the surface all sorts of

11. The petition called upon the government to 'restart negotiations immediately on the lines suggested by the Archbishop of Canterbury . . .' LW had undertaken to organise the collection of signatures of writers and artists, in which task he was helped by a company of active young people, with bicycles. See *IV LW*, 217-18.

12. The Most Rev. Randall Thomas Davidson (1848-1930), Archbishop of Canterbury 1903-28; his sermon on Sunday 9 May at St Martin in the Fields, preached on a text from *Ephesians* iv 1: 'Walk worthy of the vocation wherewith ye are called', was broadcast. Viscount Grey of Fallodon (1862-1933), now an Elder Statesman of the Liberal Party, also broadcast on Sunday evening, appealing to the public to help the Government so that wage negotiations might be conducted freely and not under duress.

currents, of which we get the most contradictory reports. Dear old Frankie has a story (over the fire in the bookshop) of an interview between Asquith & Reading which turned Reading hostile to the men. Later, through Clive, through Desmond, Asquith is proved to be at the Wharfe, 60 miles from Lord Reading.[13] Lady Wimbore gave a party—brought Thomas & Baldwin together.[14] Meeting mysteriously called off today. Otherwise strike wd. have been settled. I to H of Commons this morning with L.'s article to serve as stuffing for Hugh Dalton in the Commons this afternoon.[15] All this humbug of police & marble statues vaguely displeasing. But the Gvt. provided me with buses both ways, & no stones thrown. Silver & crimson guard at Whitehall; the cenotaph, & men bare heading themselves. Home to find Tom Marshall caballing with L.; after lunch to [Birrell & Garnett's] bookshop, where the gossip (too secret for the telephone) was imparted; to London Library where Gooch—a tall, pale mule, affable & long winded, was seen, & Molly dustily diligently reading the Dublin Review for 1840,[16] walk home; Clive, to refute gossip; James to get St Loe to sign;[17] then Maynard ringing up to command us to print the Nation as the N. Statesman is printed; to wh. I agreed, & L. disagreed; then dinner; a motor car collision—more telephones ringing at the moment 9.5.

13. Asquith (Lord Oxford), still leader of the Liberal Party, had a house, The Wharf, on the Thames at Sutton Courtney near Oxford. Rufus Isaacs (1860-1935), 1st Viscount (and newly created 1st Marquis) Reading, had only just returned from India, where he was Viceroy 1921-26.

14. Lady Wimborne, *née* the Hon. Alice Grosvenor (1880-1948), was the wife of the wealthy Ivor Churchill Guest, 1st Viscount Wimborne; for an extended account of her part in the behind-the-scenes negotiations, see Chapter 3 'The General Strike' of Osbert Sitwell's *Laughter in the Next Room*, 1949.

15. Hugh Dalton (1887-1962), educated at Eton and King's College, Cambridge, Reader in Economics at London University and Labour MP for Camberwell. Dalton may or may not have received his 'stuffing' in time but either way his only utterance before the House of Commons on 10 May was: 'A statement by the head of the Established Church.' This exclamation he directed at Winston Churchill who was attempting to explain why the views of the Archbishop of Canterbury and other leading churchmen on how to settle the Strike had not been reported in the government-run *British Gazette*.

16. George Peabody Gooch (1873-1968), the eminent historian, was from 1911-60 editor of the *Contemporary Review*, to which LW had been a regular contributor in 1920-22. Molly MacCarthy was researching for her collection of biographical sketches, *Fighting Fitzgerald and other Papers*, published in 1930, in the *Dublin Magazine*.

17. (John) St. Loe Strachey (1860-1927), a first cousin of James and Lytton from the senior branch of the Strachey family, had been the influential proprietor and editor of the Unionist weekly *The Spectator* from 1898 until December 1925.

Tuesday 11 May

I may as well continue to write—this book is used to scandalous mistreatment—while I wait—here interruptions began which lasted till the present moment/ when I write   from 12.30 to 3 with Gerald Brenan in the study composing with infinite difficulty a letter to Mr Galsworthy.[18] Arguing about the Ar[chbisho]p of Canterbury with Jack Squire at 12 seems now normal, but not—how often do I repeat—nearly as exciting as writing To the Lighthouse or about de Q[uincey].[19] I believe it is false psychology to think that in after years these details willl be interesting. The war is now barren sand after all. But one never knows: & waiting about, writing serves to liberate the mind from the fret & itch of these innumerable details. Squire doesn't want to "knuckle under". To kneel is the duty of the Church. The Church has no connection with the nation. Events are that the Roneo workers refuse to set up L.'s article in the Nation, in which he says that the Strike is not illegal or unconstitutional. Presumably this is a little clutch of the Government throttle. Mr Baldwin has been visiting the Zoo.[20] In the middle of lunch admirable Miss Bulley arrives, having visited Conway unsuccessfully.[21] St Loe has joined. So Rose Macaulay & Lytton. Tonight the names are to be handed in; & then perhaps silence will descend upon us. Ralph & Gerald are our emissaries. But

18. According to *IV LW*, p. 218, John Galsworthy, the renowned author of *The Forsyte Saga*, was the only person approached who refused to sign the petition; however the editor of the *Observer*, J. L. Garvin, was certainly another (see LWP, Sussex).

19. VW's article on de Quincey, 'Impassioned Prose', was to appear in the *TLS* on 16 September 1926 (Kp C275).

20. It had been stated in the House of Commons on 6 May by Sir John Simon, Liberal MP and one-time Attorney-General, that the resolution of the General Council of the TUC to call a general strike was unlawful. The special Strike Issue of the *N & A* which had been prepared for publication this week was in any event scrapped since the strike ended; it appeared in a very truncated form dated 15 May.

    Although Regent's Park had been taken over by the authorities and closed, the Zoological Gardens were open, and were visited by the Prime Minister on Sunday afternoon.

21. Margaret H. Bulley, from a Northern Quaker family, rented the house at 19 Taviton Street, Bloomsbury, which had housed Birrell and Garnett's bookshop and several other congenial tenants. Much influenced by Roger Fry, she wrote several books on art, including *Art and Counterfeit* (1925). She was shortly to marry her cousin G. W. Armitage. Sir Martin Conway (1856-1937), raised to the Peerage by Ramsay MacDonald in 1931 as Lord Conway of Allington, mountaineer, art historian and collector, was Conservative MP for the Combined Universities, the seat which LW had unsuccessfully contested in 1922 (See *IV LW*, 46).

then everyone rings up—the most unlikely people—[Donald] Brace for instance, Kahan;[22] the woman comes with the new sofa cover. Yesterday Ralph & Frances Marshall were in a railway accident. She had her teeth jangled. One man was killed; another had his leg broken—the result of driving a train without signals, by the efforts of ardent optimistic undergraduates.[23] Billing has been in to say he will print anything, all his men being back & needing work. So, as poor MacDermott has been dead since January, perhaps the Nation will be done by them.[24] Come to think of it, almost all our type is standing, so our printing was in any case hardly feasible. Must I now ring up James? Day's Library boy was set upon by roughs, had his cycle overturned, but kept his books & was unhurt after calling here for 6 Tree. Tree dribbles along. There is an occasional order. Mrs C[artwright]. arrives on Faith's bicycle which is red with rust.[25]

Wednesday 12 May

Strike settled. (ring at bell)

The Strike was settled about 1.15—or it was then broadcast. I was in Tottenham Court Rd. at 1 & heard Bartholomew & Fletcher's megaphone declaim that the T.U.C. leaders were at Downing Street;[26] came home to find that neither L. or Nelly had heard this: 5 minutes later, the wireless. They told us to stand by & await important news. Then a piano played a tune. Then the solemn broadcaster assuming incredible pomp & gloom

22. Richard Ferdinand Kahn (b. 1905), Scholar, and in 1930 to be elected Fellow, of King's College, Cambridge, was at this period still an undergraduate; a member of the Political Economy Club which met weekly in Maynard Keynes's rooms in King's, he turned to the formal study of economics after graduating in Mathematics and Natural Sciences in 1927.
23. On the afternoon of 10 May a goods train had crashed into the rear of a stationary Cambridge-London passenger train at Bishop's Stortford, derailing two coaches; one man was killed, and another suffered a broken leg.
24. Billing & Sons Ltd were the printers of Philip Noel-Baker's *Disarmament* (*HP Checklist* 106), published in April 1926. F. J. McDermott, of the Prompt Press, Richmond, had advised and helped the Woolfs when they first embarked on their Hogarth Press venture, and had printed *Monday or Tuesday* for them in 1921—so badly that they had not employed him again.
25. Day's was the fashionable Mayfair circulating library to which VW had subscribed in 1915. Mrs Cartwright's vehicle was borrowed from Faith Henderson, *née* Bagenal (b. 1889), wife of the editor of the *N & A*, who like her lived in Hampstead.
26. Bartholomew & Fletcher was a firm of upholsterers, cabinet makers and decorators at 217-18 Tottenham Court Road. The General Council of the TUC decided on 12 May to terminate the general strike and resume negotiations with the Government; but directed affiliated unions to issue instructions to their own members.

& speaking one word to the minute read out: Message from 10 Downing Street. The T.U.C. leaders have agreed that Strike shall be withdrawn. Instantly L. dashed off to telephone to the office, Nelly to tell Pritchard's clerk, & I to Mrs C. (But N[elly]. was beforehand) then we finished lunch; then I rang up Clive—who proposes that we should have a drink tonight. I saw this morning 5 or 6 armoured cars slowly going along Oxford Street; on each two soldiers sat in tin helmets, & one stood with his hand at the gun which was pointed straight ahead ready to fire. But I also noticed on one a policeman smoking a cigarette. Such sights I dare say I shall never see again; & dont in the least wish to. Already (it is now 10 past 2) men have appeared at the hotel with drainpipes. Also Grizzle has won her case against the Square.

Thursday 13 May

I suppose all pages devoted to the Strike will be skipped, when I read over this book. Oh that dull old chapter, I shall say. Excitements about what are called real things are always unutterably transitory. Yet it is gloomy—& L. is gloomy, & so am I unintelligibly—today because the Strike continues—no railwaymen back: vindictiveness has now seized our masters. Government shillyshallies. Apparently, the T.U.C. agreed to terms wh. the miners now reject. Anyhow it will take a week to get the machinery of England to run again. Trains are dotted about all over England. Labour, it seems clear, will be effectively diddled again, & perhaps rid of its power to make strikes in future. Printers still out at the Nation. In short, the strain removed, we all fall out & bicker & backbite.[27] Such is human nature—& really I dont like human nature unless all candied over with art. We dined with a strike party last night & went back to Clive's. A good deal was said about art there. Good dull Janet Vaughan, reminding me of Emma, joined us.[28] I went to my

27. There had been no general resumption of work following the TUC General Council's decision to terminate the strike. The Cabinet declined to resume negotiations over miner's pay until all strikers had returned to work; the miners refused to be represented at discussions with the government; the TUC issued a memorandum saying that it no longer stood behind the miners; the miners repudiated the memorandum. The railway unions decided to continue to strike until satisfactory assurances as to re-instatement had been given by their employers; the railway companies considered that their employees had broken agreements and fresh ones must therefore be entered into. And so on.

28. Janet Maria Vaughan (b. 1899), daughter of VW's cousin W. W. Vaughan and his wife Madge (*née* Symonds); she was finishing her medical studies, and had been active in collecting signatures for the petition. Emma (1874-1960) was Janet's aunt, the youngest of VW's Vaughan cousins.

dressmaker, Miss Brooke, & found it the most quiet & friendly & even enjoyable of proceedings. I have a great lust for lovely stuffs, & shapes; wh. I have not gratified since Sally Young died.[29] A bold move this, but now I'm free of the fret of clothes, which is worth paying for, & need not parade Oxford Street.

Thursday 20 May

Waiting for L. to come back from chess with Roger: 11.25. I think nothing need be said of the Strike. As tends to happen, one's mind slips after the crisis, & what the settlement is, or will be, I know not.

We must now fan the books up again. Viola & Phil Baker were both struck on the wing. Viola comes, very tactfully, as a friend, she says, to consult after dinner. She is a flamboyant creature—much of an actress— much abused by the Waleys & Marjories; but rather taking to me. She has the great egotism, the magnification of self, which any bodily display, I think, produces. She values women by their hips & ankles, like horses. Easily reverts to the topic of her own charms: how she shd. have married the D. of Rutland. "Lord —— (his uncle) told me I was the woman John really loved. The duchess said to me 'Do make love to John & get him away from ——. At any rate you're tall & beautiful—' And I sometimes think if I'd married him—but he never asked me—Daddy wouldn't have died. I'd have prevented that operation: Then how he'd have loved a duke for a son in law! All his life was dressing up—that sort of thing you know."[30] So she runs on, in the best of clothes, easy & familiar, but reserved too; with the wiles & warinesses of a woman of the world, half sordid half splendid, not quite at her ease with us, yet glad of a room where she can tell her stories, of listeners to whom she is new & strange. She will run on by the hour—yet is very watchful not to bore; a good business woman, & floating over considerable acuteness on her charm. All this however, is not making her book move, as they say.

Eddy came in to tea. I like him—his flattery? his nobility? I dont know—I find him easy & eager. And Vita comes to lunch tomorrow, which will be a great amusement & pleasure. I am amused at my relations

29. Mrs Young made the rather grander dresses for VW and her sisters when they were Kensington young ladies.
30. John Henry Montagu Manners (1886-1940), who succeeded his father as 9th Duke of Rutland in 1925, married Kathleen Tennant in 1916; Viola Tree had married Alan Parsons, a civil servant, in 1912. Her daddy, Sir Herbert Beerbohm Tree, died unexpectedly after an operation on a ruptured tendon in his leg, on 2 July 1917, aged sixty-three.

with her: left so ardent in January—& now what? Also I like her presence & her beauty. Am I in love with her? But what is love? Her being 'in love' (it must be comma'd thus) with me, excites & flatters; & interests. What is this 'love'? Oh & then she gratifies my eternal curiosity: who's she seen, whats she done—for I have no enormous opinion of her poetry. How could I—I who have such delight in mitigating the works even of my greatest friends. I should have been reading her poem tonight:[31] instead finished Sharon Turner—a prosy, simple, old man; the very spit & image of Saxon. a boundless bore, I daresay, with the most intense zeal for "improving myself", & the holiest affections, & 13 children, & no character or impetus—a love of long walks, of music; modest, yet conceited in an ant like way. I mean he has the industry & persistency in recounting compliments of an ant, but so little character that one hardly calls him vain!

Tuesday 25 May

The heat has come, bringing with it the inexplicably disagreeable memories of parties, & George Duckworth; a fear haunts me even now, as I drive past Park Lane on top of a bus, & think of Lady Arthur Russell & so on.[32] I become out of love with everything; but fall into love as the bus reaches Holborn. A curious transition that, from tyranny to freedom. Mixed with it is the usual "I thought that when you died last May, Charles, there had died along with you"—death being hidden among the leaves: & Nessa's birthday among the little hard pink rosettes of the may, which we used to stop & smell on the pavement at the top of Hyde Pk. Gate & I asked why, if it was may, it did not come out on the 1st; it comes out now, & Nessa's birthday, which must be her 47th, is in a few days. She is in Italy: Duncan is said to have "committed a nuisance" for which he has been fined 10 lira.

31. V. Sackville-West, who had returned from Persia on 16 May, had finished but had not yet published her long poem *The Land* on which she had been working since 1923.
32. George Herbert Duckworth (1868-1934), the elder of VW's half-brothers, had entertained social ambitions for her and Vanessa. Lady Arthur Russell (d. 1910), a sister-in-law of their mother's cousin Adeline, Duchess of Bedford, was a hostess of considerable consequence in his eyes—and he was briefly engaged to her daughter Flora (see *I QB*, pp 81-2); she lived at 2 Audley Square, just behind Park Lane. VW described her as 'a rude, tyrannical old woman, with a blood-stained complexion and the manners of a turkey cock.' (*Moments of Being* (1976), p. 149)

L. has been having Nelly's poisonous cold, brought by Lottie—Do I hear him? Grizzle says Yes: stands tail wagging—She is right. Vita has it; or I should be dining—

Now we have been sitting in the Square. L. is better. I am happier. Tomorrow we go to Rodmell—to find the bath & the W.C. & the drawing room with the wall pulled down. This cherry has been dangled & withdrawn so often that I scarcely believe we shall now munch it. And I must notice that the Strike still makes it necessary for me to find out trains at Victoria.

I have finished—sketchily I admit—the 2nd part of To the Lighthouse —& may, then, have it all written over by the end of July. A record— 7 months, if it so turns out.

So Vita came: & I register the shock of meeting after absence; how shy one is; how disillusioned by the actual body; how sensitive to new shades of tone—something 'womanly' I detected, more mature; & she was shabbier, come straight off in her travelling clothes; & not so beautiful, as sometimes perhaps; & so we sat talking on the sofa by the window, she rather silent, I chattering, partly to divert her attention from me; & to prevent her thinking "Well, is this all?" as she was bound to think, having declared herself so openly in writing. So that we each registered some disillusionment; & perhaps also acquired some grains of additional solidity— This may well be more lasting than the first rhapsody. But I compared her state, justly, to a flock of birds flying hither thither, escaped, confused: returning, after a long journey, to the middle of things again. She was quieter, shyer, awkwarder than usual even. She has no ready talk—confronted by Nelly or Mrs Cartwright she stands like a schoolgirl. I think it quite likely she will get Harold out of his job. But then, as I always feel, with her 'grand life', Dotties & so on, whom I don't know at all, there may be many parts of her perfectly unillumined.[33] But I cannot write. For the most part I can write. Suddenly the word instinct leaves me. This is the permanent state of most people no doubt. Maynard met George & Lady M[argaret]. at the Darwins. He is a humbug & she a fiend, he writes. She now walks with a stick.[34] What a dreary world it is—these bubbles meeting once in 20 years or so.

33. Dottie was Dorothy (d. 1956), wife of Lord Gerald Wellesley, from whom she was soon to separate (he succeeded his nephew as 7th Duke of Wellington in 1943). She was a very wealthy woman in her own right, a poet, and an intimate friend of Vita, who dedicated The Land to her. VW had met her once in July 1922 when she visited Knole with Vita.

34. George Duckworth had married Lady Margaret Herbert (1870-1958) in 1904; she was a daughter of the 4th Earl of Carnarvon.

Wednesday 9 June

Then I got the flue, last Saturday; sat shivering at Lords, in the hot sunshine; so have seen no one, except basement dwellers, & put off Don Giovanni, Dadie & Hope tonight, & Osbert [Sitwell]'s dinner tomorrow.[1] All my bubbling up faculty at once leaves me. I grind out a little of that eternal How to read, lecture, as the Yale Review has bought it,[2] & cannot conceive what The Lighthouse is all about. I hope to whip my brains up either at Vita's or Rodmell this weekend.

Yes, Rodmell is a perfect triumph, I consider—but L. advises me not to say so. In particular, our large combined drawing eating room, with its 5 windows, its beams down the middle, & flowers & leaves nodding in all round us. The bath boils quickly; the water closets gush & surge (not quite sufficiently though). The weather again failed us, & we had a queer journey home, via Newhaven, Peacehaven & Brighton. Trains slow & scarce. The Strike, I should say, continues. We then went to a party at Edith Sitwell's (I in my new dress) 'to meet Miss Stein', a lady much like Joan Fry, but more massive; in blue-sprinkled brocade, rather formidable.[3] There was Morgan, Siegfried [Sassoon], Todd—to whom I proposed, wildly, fantastically, a book—which she accepts![4]—(& Viola so much criticised in the austere heights of Ham Spray) & Edith distraught; & cherries in handfulls, & barley water—as L. described it very brilliantly to Sybil the next day. She came: no one else; we sat & laughed—& wheres the harm in this stupidish, kindly, rather amusing woman, I asked? Then she expressed a wish to dine with us. L. is lunching with Wells today.

1. LW and VW had been to watch England v. The Rest at Lord's on 5 June. *Don Giovanni*, conducted by Bruno Walter, was given at Covent Garden on 7 June. Hope Mirrlees (1887-1978), whose poem *Paris* the Woolfs had printed in 1920, had since published two novels and was about to publish a third.
2. This was a revised version of the lecture she had given on 30 January at Hayes Court; it was published in the *Yale Review* in October 1926 (Kp C277).
3. The party, on 1 June at Edith Sitwell's Bayswater flat, was given for the American experimental writer Gertrude Stein (1874-1946), who had lived in Paris since 1903; she had been invited to lecture to literary societies at Cambridge and Oxford. Her address, entitled *Composition as Explanation*, was published as a Hogarth Essay in November 1926 (*HP Checklist* 110). Joan Mary Fry (1862-1955), the second of Roger's six unmarried sisters, had kept house for him at Guildford until 1919; she was an active Quaker.
4. Nothing came of this proposal, which was that Todd should write her own life (see *III VW Letters*, no. 1644). Siegfried Sassoon (1886-1967), poet.

Wednesday 9 June

Leonard back from Wells who chattered till ¼ to 4: likes to walk through the streets; has a house in France kept for him by a very intelligent Brazilian lady.[5] Called me "too intelligent—a bad thing": can't criticise; brings in social theories, because he says in an age when society is dissolving, the social state is part of the character. They lunched at Boulesteins. Leonard asked for him at the Automobile Club; "A very famous name" said the man.[6] And the warmth & clamour of Wells' fame seems to reach me, this chilly rainy evening; & I see how, if I stayed there, as he asks us, he would overwhelm me. (We are very hungry, by the way; Nelly is preparing a nice roast chicken & ices for dinner, which I shall enjoy. Then we shall play the Gramophone). I'm cheering up after my attack I'm glad to say, though a little undecided whether to stay with Vita or go to Monks House.

L. is going to make a book of his essays. I think of asking Lady Horner to write her memoirs.[7] Today we discussed the date of Nelly's holiday— & so we go on.

Following VW's influenza or 'nerve exhaustion headache' (III VW Letters, no. 1646), the Woolfs went to Rodmell on Saturday 11 June; LW returned to London on Sunday afternoon leaving Vita Sackville-West, who had come to lunch, to stay with VW until Tuesday. The next two weeks were very sociable, and included a dinner party at the Hutchinsons to meet Aldous Huxley who had just been round the world, and a visit to Garsington, when she met Robert Bridges, on 26-27 June.

Wednesday 30 June

This is the last day of June & finds me in black despair because Clive laughed at my new hat, Vita pitied me, & I sank to the depths of gloom.

5. For the past eighteen months H. G. Wells (1866-1946) had rented a provençal *mas* near Grasse, where he was about to build one of his own. The lady with whom he shared it he described as Levantine, not Brazilian; she was Odette Keun (1888-1978), a writer and journalist of Italo-Dutch parentage born in Constantinople.
6. Boulestin was (and is) a French restaurant in Southampton Street off the Strand; the Royal Automobile Club was (and is) in Pall Mall.
7. LW's *Essays on Literature, History, Politics, etc*, the majority of which were based upon material first published in the *N & A* and the *New Statesman*, were published by the Hogarth Press in May 1927 (*HP Checklist* 153). Frances Horner, *née* Graham (1860-1940), who had been a friend to many of the pre-Raphaelites, did write her memoirs, *Time Remembered*, but they were published by Heinemann in 1933.

This happened at Clive's last night after going to the Sitwells with Vita. Oh dear I was wearing the hat without thinking whether it was good or bad; & it was all very flashing & easy; & there I saw a man with braided hair, another with long red tongues in his button hole; & sat by Vita & laughed & clubbed. When we got out it was only 10.30—a soft starry night: I had refused to go to Colefax: it was still too early for her to go. So she said "Shall we go to Clive's & pick him up?" & I was then again so lighthearted, driving through the park, & seeing people scud before us. Also we saw all the Mayfair houses, & finally came to Gordon Sqre & there was Nessa tripping along in the dark, in her quiet black hat. So we had some lively talk. She said Duncan was having a sandwich at the public house: then he came, carrying an egg. Come on all of us to Clive's, I said; & they agreed. Well, it was after they had come & we were all sitting round talking that Clive suddenly said, or bawled rather, what an astonishing hat you're wearing! Then he asked where I got it. I pretended a mystery, tried to change the talk, was not allowed, & they pulled me down between them, like a hare; I never felt more humiliated. Clive said did Mary choose it? No. Todd said Vita. And the dress? Todd of course: after that I was forced to go on as if nothing terrible had happened; but it was very forced & queer & humiliating. So I talked & laughed too much. Duncan prim & acid as ever told me it was utterly impossible to do anything with a hat like that. And I joked about the Squires' party. & Leonard got silent, & I came away deeply chagrined, as unhappy as I have been these ten years; & revolved it in sleep & dreams all night; & today has been ruined.

Thursday 1 July

These reflections about the hat read rather amusingly I think. What a weathercock of sensibility I am! How I enjoy—or at least how (for I was acutely unhappy & humiliated) these gyrations interest me, conscious as I am of a strong lynch pin controlling them—Leonard in short. Coming out from lunching with Maynard today I ran (in the hat, in the dress) into Clive & Mary, & had to stand their fire: dress praised to the skies, hat passed. So thats over. Indeed the cloud began to lift at 7 last night.

But all this has obscured Garsington; Bridges; & Wells. These great men are so much like the rest of us. Wells remarkable only for a combination of stockishness with acuity: he has a sharp nose, & the cheeks & jowl of a butcher. He likes, I judge, rambling & romancing about the lives of other people; he romanced about the Webbs: said their books were splendid eggs, well & truly laid, but addled. Described Beatrice, as by a gipsy & a Jew: a flashing creature, become Quaker as we all do as we get on. That has nothing to do with ⟨God⟩ Christianity. Are you a Quaker, I asked. Of course I am. One believes that there is a reason for things (I think he said). But he did not rise steadily off the ground for long. Lunch is a hot stodgy hour too. I could see from the plaintive watery look on Mrs Wells' face (she has widely spaced teeth & in repose looks very worried, at the same time vacant) that he is arrogant lustful & bullying in private life.[1] The virtues he likes are courage & vitality. I said how ghastly! (That is the story of Dorothy Richardson's struggles.) No: nothing is ghastly where there is courage he said. He rambled over her life, amusingly. How she married Odel, a man who makes symbolical drawings—bubbles coming out of a human mouth & turning into womens legs & so on: which is so like life, Wells said: the heterogeneity— one thing leading to another, & the design so remarkable. But they dont sell. And now Duckworth won't publish any more of her books.[2]

As for Bridges: he sprang from a rhododendron bush, a very lean tall old man, with a curly grey hat, & a reddish ravaged face, smoky fierce eyes, with a hazy look in them; very active; rather hoarse, talking incessantly. We sat in his open room & looked past blue spikes of flowers to hills, which were invisible, but when they show, all this goes out he said—his one poetical saying, or saying that struck me as such. We talked about handwriting, & criticism; how Garrod had written on Keats; & they know a Petrarchan sonnet, but not why one alters it. Because they dont write sonnets, I suggested, & urged him to write criticism.[3] He is direct & spry, very quick in all his movements, racing

1. LW had seen a good deal of H. G. Wells during and after the war in connection with League of Nations matters and Wells's *Outline of History* (see *III LW*, pp 192-3); but it is not clear that VW had met him or his wife before this lunch party at the Keynes's on 1 July. Amy Catherine ('Jane') Wells, *née* Robbins (1872-1927) had for many years acquiesced in Wells's notorious infidelities, but always maintained her social position as his wife.

2. The novelist Dorothy Miller Richardson (1873-1957) had been at school in Putney with Mrs Wells, and through her met H. G., with whom she had an affair which ended with a miscarriage in 1907; in 1917 she had married Alan Odle, a tubercular artist fifteen years her junior (he died in 1948). Duckworth, who in the ten years up to 1925 had published eight successive volumes of her novel series *Pilgrimage*, were losing money on it, though they did in fact publish two further volumes.

3. Robert Bridges lived at Chilswell House on Boar's Hill near Oxford. On the subject of handwriting, see 21 December 1925, n 15, above. H. W. Garrod (1878-1960), at this time Professor of Poetry at Oxford, published his book on Keats in July 1926 (and his edition of the *Poetical Works* in 1939). Bridges himself had written on Keats in 1894, a critical essay published as the introduction to G. Thorn Drury's edition of the *Poems*, 1896.

me down the garden to look at pinks, then into his library, where he showed me the French critics, then said Michelet was his favourite historian; then I asked to see the Hopkins manuscripts; & sat looking at them with that gigantic grasshopper Aldous folded up in a chair close by. Ottoline undulated & vagulated.[4]

He asked me to come again: would read me his poems—not his early ones which want a beautiful voice, & aren't interesting he said: but his later ones, his hexameters. He skipped off & held the gate open. I said how much I liked his poems—true of the short ones: but was mainly pleased & gratified to find him so obliging & easy & interested. Ottoline flattered me on this point. But she had her points too; her dwindling charm reveals them, as we sat by the lake, discussing Mary Clive life, truth, literature. Then dressed, & Aldous & Eddie & Philip Nichols, & Miss Spender Clay, who can have £500 a year if she wants it Julian said.[5]

Sunday 4 July

Then Wells came again; & stayed till 4, when he had to meet an American.[6] He is getting to the drowsy stage: the 60s. Seems well wishing but not so spry as he used to be. He talked about his new book, the thoughts one has at 60. He brings in everything—a man called Lubin, for instance, who invented int^n agriculture (I think) a man who died in poverty & was shuffled out of the way to his grave in Rome the day that Wilson made his entry—"that shallow, pretentious empty headed

4. The public recognition of Gerard Manley Hopkins (1844-89) as a poet was due to Robert Bridges, his contemporary and close friend at Oxford, who had first published his poems (in an edition of only 750 copies of which the Woolfs possessed one, sold at Sotheby's, 27 April 1970, lot 67) in 1918. Bridges collected Hopkins' poems and letters and assembled his posthumous papers (now mostly in the Bodleian). Aldous Huxley (1894-1963) was a fellow guest at Garsington.

5. Philip Bouverie Bowyer Nichols (1894-1962) had been at Balliol, served throughout the war, and was now in the Foreign Service; in 1932 he was to marry Phyllis Mary Spender-Clay (b. 1905), a granddaughter of the fabulously wealthy William Waldorf, 1st Viscount Astor.

On the page opposite this last paragraph is a list, headed *Tavistock Cafe*!: '1 Nessa 2 Roger 3 Julia 4 Dadie 5 Eddie 6 V. 7 Clive 8 Raymond 9 Lytton.' This relates to one of VW's recurrent social projects, later this year to take shape as the 'Bloomsbury Bar'. (See *III VW Letters*, no. 1677.)

6. H. G. Wells and Desmond MacCarthy lunched with the Woolfs on Friday 2 July.

professor"— Lubin was the real thinker for peace.[7] What other ideas had he? Desmond asked. Well, to do away with Sunday. There should be [a] holiday once in 10 days. That was his own stint. 10 days work, then 4 or 5 days off. The present system is wasteful. The shadow of the week end begins on Friday, is not over till Monday afternoon. He said sometimes he wrote all day for days; sometimes not at all. He struck me again as an odd mixture of bubble & solidity—likes to blow a phrase now & then. We got him on to Hardy—a very simple, subtle old peasant man much impressed by clever people who write[;] very humble, delighted when Wells took Rebecca West to call on him, walked half way into Dorchester with them—"an impudent young journalist" Wells called her. Hardy had heard of her. Came to stay with Barrie to see an air raid— wrote his early books in chapters as the printers wanted them.[8] Then he got up to go: we asked him to stay & tell us about Henry James. So he sat down. Oh I should be delighted to stay & talk the whole afternoon, he said. Henry James was a formalist. He always thought of clothes. He was never intimate with anyone—not with his brother even: had never been in love. Once his brother wanted to see Chesterton, & climbed a ladder & looked over a wall. This angered Henry; who called in Wells & asked him for an opinion—as if I had one![9] Wells has learnt nothing from Proust—his book like the British Museum. One knows there are delightful interesting things in it, but one does not go there. One day it may be wet—I shall say God, what am I to do this afternoon? & I shall read Proust as I might go to the British Museum. Would not read Richardson—a man who knows all about feminine psychology (with some contempt) nobody ought to know that. I said on the contrary he

7. Book 5, § 6 of Wells's latest book, *The World of William Clissold* (to be published in the autumn of 1926), is a discourse upon 'that prophetic American Jew, David Lubin', a self-made man who by 1905 had set up the International Institute of Agriculture in Rome. He was buried in that city in January 1919, 'and his funeral passed disregarded through streets that were beflagged and decorated to welcome the visit of President Wilson'.

8. Rebecca West was the professional name of the writer Cicily Isabel Fairfield (b. 1892) who, as a young and ardent radical, wrote regularly for the militant feminist weekly *The Freewoman*; in 1912 her hostile review of one of H. G. Wells's novels led to their meeting and an extended love affair only terminated by her in 1923. In July 1917, Mr and Mrs Hardy had stayed with the novelist and playwright Sir J. M. Barrie, Bt, OM (1860-1937) and had watched the searchlights scanning the sky from his Adelphi flat overlooking the Thames.

9. Wells's story of Henry James's disapprobation of his brother William's unseemly behaviour is retold by Leon Edel in *Henry James. The Master. 1901-1916* (1972), pp 373-4. The elephantine figure of the writer G. K. Chesterton (1874-1936) perambulating the streets of Rye would indeed have been a sight to see.

knew very little: was conventional. Honour, chastity & so on. Wells said we had changed our ideas completely. That idea of chastity had vanished. Women were even more suggestible than men. Now they dont think about it—a chaste little couple (he talks of little couples) mixing with a promiscuous little couple. He said we are happier perhaps— children are certainly more at ease with their parents. But he thought they were beginning to miss restraints. They were wondering what things were for. They were very restless; discussing Henry James & Eliot, & how formal they are & overdone with manner—(he described H.J. pushing under a letter he was writing to talk to Wells "at the Reform"). I said it was American. They were alien to our civilisation. He said he had been that himself. His father was a gardener, his mother a ladies maid. He found it very strange to meet people who went to parties & wore dress clothes. Henry James could not describe love— there comes the ahh—laying on of hands. This Wells could do himself. I am a journalist. I pride myself upon being a journalist he said. Well I have a sort of feeling that all writing should be journalism—(done with an object)— One knows nothing of what posterity will want—may be a guide book. I tell Arnold [Bennett] they will read him for his topography.

In all this he showed himself, as Desmond said afterwards, perfectly content to be himself, aware of his powers,—aware that he need not take any trouble, since his powers were big enough.

Thursday 22 July

The summer hourglass is running out rapidly & rather sandily. Many nights I wake in a shudder thinking of some atrocity of mine. I bring home minute pinpricks which magnify in the middle of the night into gaping wounds. However, I drive my pen through de Quincey of a morning, having put The Lighthouse aside till Rodmell. There all virtue, all good, is in retreat. Here nothing but odds & ends—going to the dentist, buying combs; having Maynard & Bob to tea, & then Ralph & Frances to dinner, followed by Eddie & Kitchen [C. H. B. Kitchin]. But we are both jaded, & get no clear impression any more from the human face—must dine with Osbert Sitwell tonight though, & go to Hardy tomorrow. This is human life: this is the infinitely precious stuff issued in a narrow roll to us now, & then withdrawn for ever; & we spend it thus. Days without definite sensation are the worst of all. Days when one compels oneself to undergo this or that for some reason—but what reason?

There is nothing important at the moment to record: or if so, & one's state of mind is overwhelmingly important, I leave that, too for Rodmell. There I shall come to grips with the last part of that python, my book; it is a tug & a struggle, & I wonder now & then, why I let myself in for it. Rose Macaulay said "What else would one do with one's thoughts?" I have not seen her again nor Gwen, nor written to Violet [Dickinson]; nor learnt French, nor finished Clarissa.

Desmond came in; talked about Shakespeare. Now to settle my mind to Suspiria.[10]

Sunday 25 July

At first I thought it was Hardy, & it was the parlourmaid, a small thin girl, wearing a proper cap. She came in with silver cake stands & so on. Mrs Hardy talked to us about her dog.[11] How long ought we to stay? Can Mr Hardy walk much &c I asked, making conversation, as I knew one would have to. She has the large sad lack lustre eyes of a childless woman; great docility & readiness, as if she had learnt her part; not great alacrity, but resignation, in welcoming more visitors; wears a sprigged voile dress, black shoes, & a necklace. We cant go far now, she said, though we do walk every day, because our dog isn't able to walk far. He bites, she told us. She became more natural & animated about the dog, who is evidently the real centre of her thoughts—then the maid came in. Then again the door opened, more sprucely, & in trotted a little puffy cheeked cheerful old man, with an atmosphere cheerful & businesslike in addressing us, rather like an old doctors or solicitors, saying "Well now—" or words like that as he shook hands. He was dressed in rough grey with a striped tie. His nose has a joint in it, & the end curves down. A round whitish face, the eyes now faded & rather watery, but the whole aspect cheerful & vigorous. He sat on a three cornered chair (I am too jaded with all this coming & going to do more than gather facts) at a round table, where there were the cake stands & so on; a chocolate roll; what is called a good tea; but he only drank one cup, sitting on his

10. Violet Dickinson (1865-1948) was one of VW's oldest friends, a friendship now maintained more through loyalty than interest. VW wrote to her on 26 July (see *III VW Letters*, no. 1658). VW owned the 8-volume, 1792, edition of Samuel Richardson's *Clarissa Harlowe*. "Suspiria de Profundis" was one of de Quincey's 'dream-visions', first published in *Blackwood's Magazine* in 1845.

11. The Woolfs went to Dorchester and back by train on the afternoon of Friday 23 July, in order to have tea with Mr and Mrs Hardy at Max Gate. Florence Emily, *née* Dugdale (1878-1937), had married Thomas Hardy as his second wife in 1914; he was then over twice her age. The two volumes of her *Life* of her husband, written in effect by Hardy himself, were published in 1928 and 1930, after his death.

three cornered chair. He was extremely affable & aware of his duties. He did not let the talk stop or disdain making talk. He talked of father—said he had seen me, or it might have been my sister but he thought it was me, in my cradle. He had been to Hyde Park Place—oh Gate was it. A very quiet street. That was why my father liked it. Odd to think that in all these years he had never been down there again. He went there often. Your father took my novel—Far From the Madding Crowd. We stood shoulder to shoulder against the British public about certain matters dealt with in that novel—You may have heard. Then he said how some other novel had fallen through that was to appear—the parcel had been lost coming from France—not a very likely thing to happen, as your father said—a big parcel of manuscript; & he asked me to send my story. I think he broke all the Cornhill laws—not to see the whole book; so I sent it in chapter by chapter, & was never late.[12] Wonderful what youth is! I had it in my head doubtless, but I never thought twice about it—It came out every month. They were nervous, because of Miss Thackeray I think. She said she became paralysed & could not write a word directly she heard the press begin. I daresay it was bad for a novel to appear like that. One begins to think what is good for the magazine, not what is good for the novel.

You think what makes a strong curtain, put in Mrs Hardy jocularly. She was leaning upon the tea table, not eating gazing out.

Then we talked about manuscripts. Mrs Smith had found the MS of F. from the M.C. in a drawer during the war, & sold it for the Red Cross.[13] Now he has his MSS back, & the printer rubs out all the marks. But he wishes they would leave them, as they prove it genuine.

He puts his head down like some old pouter pigeon. He has a very long head; & quizzical bright eyes, for in talk they grow bright. He said when he was in the Strand 6 years ago he scarcely knew where he was, & he used to know it all intimately. He told us that he used to buy 2nd hand books—nothing valuable—in Wyck Street. Then he wondered why Great James Street should be so narrow & Bedford Row so broad.

12. Hardy contributed his own account of his relations with Leslie Stephen—who as editor of *The Cornhill Magazine* had commissioned and published his fourth novel in serial form in 1874—to F. W. Maitland's *The Life and Letters of Leslie Stephen*, 1906, pp 270-78.

13. Hardy's manuscript had been found by the widow of Reginald John Smith, son-in-law of the founder of *The Cornhill Magazine* and its editor from 1898, after his death in 1917; she persuaded Hardy to rewrite a missing page, had it bound in blue morocco, and sent it to the Red Cross Sale at Christie's on 22 April 1918. It is now the property of Mr Edwin Thorne in America.

He had often wondered about that. At this rate, London would soon be unrecognisable. But I shall never go there again. Mrs Hardy tried to persuade him that it was an easy drive—only 6 hours or so. I asked if she liked it, & she said Granville Barker had told her that when she was in the nursing home she had 'the time of her life'.[14] She knew everyone in Dorchester, but she thought there were more interesting people in London. Had I often been to Siegfried's flat? I said no. Then she asked about him & Morgan, said he was elusive, as if they enjoyed visits from him. I said I heard from Wells that Mr Hardy had been up to London to see an air raid. "What things they say!" he said. It was my wife. There was an air raid one night when we stayed with Barrie. We just heard a little pop in the distance— The searchlights were beautiful. I thought if a bomb now were to fall on this flat how many writers would be lost. And he smiled in his queer way, which is fresh & yet sarcastic a little: anyhow shrewd. Indeed, there was no trace to my thinking of the simple peasant. He seemed perfectly aware of everything; in no doubt or hesitation; having made up his mind; & being delivered of all his work; so that he was in no doubt about that either. He was not interested much in his novels, or in anybodies novels; took it all easily & naturally. "I never took long with them" he said. The longest was the *Din*nasts. (so pronounced). "But that was really 3 books" said Mrs Hardy. Yes: & that took me 6 years; but not working all the time. Can you write poetry regularly? I asked (being beset with the desire to hear him say something about his books); but the dog kept cropping up. How he bit; how the inspector came out; how he was ill; & they could do nothing for him. Would you mind if I let him in? asked Mrs Hardy, & in came We[s]sex, a very tousled, rough brown & white mongrel, got to guard the house, so naturally he bites people, said Mrs H.; Well, I dont know about that, said Hardy, perfectly natural, & not setting much stock by his poems either it seemed. Did you write poems at the same time as your novels? I asked. No. he said. I wrote a great many poems. I used to send them about, but they were always returned, he chuckled. And in those days I believed in editors. Many were lost—all the fair copies were lost. But I found the notes, & I wrote them from those. I was always finding them. I found one the other day; but I don't think I shall find any more.

Siegfried took rooms near here, & said he was going to work very hard, but he left soon.

14. Harley Granville Barker (1877-1946), actor, producer, dramatist and critic, was a friend of the Hardys. Mrs Hardy had spent ten days in a London nursing home in the autumn of 1924, when VW had visited her (see *II VW Diary*, 17 October 1924).

E. M. Forster takes a long time to produce anything—7 years, he chuckled. All this made a great impression of the ease with which he did things. "I daresay F. from the M. C. would have been a great deal better if I had written it differently", he said. But as if it could not be helped, & did not matter.

He used to go to the Lushingtons in Kensington Sqre & saw my mother there. She used to come in & out when I was talking to your father.[15]

I wanted him to say one word about his writing before we left & cd only ask wh. of his books he wd. have chosen, if like me, he had had to choose one to read in the train. I had taken the M[ayor] of C[asterbridge]. That's being dramatised, put in Mrs H. & then brought L[ove's]. L[ittle]. Ironies.[16]

And did it hold your interest? he asked.

I stammered that I could not stop reading it, which was true, but sounded wrong. Anyhow, he was not going to be drawn, & went off about giving a young lady a wedding present. None of my books are fitted to be wedding presents, he said. You must give Mrs Woolf one of your books, said Mrs Hardy, inevitably. Yes I will. But I'm afraid only in the little thin paper edition, he said. I protested that it would be enough if he wrote his name (then was vaguely uncomfortable).

Then there was de la Mare. His last book of stories seemed to them such a pity.[17] Hardy had liked some of his poems very much. People said he must be a sinister man to write such stories. But he is [a] very nice man—a very nice man indeed.

He said to a friend who begged him not to give up poetry, "I'm afraid poetry is giving up me." The truth is he is a very kind man, & sees anyone who wants to see him. He has 16 people for the day sometimes.

Do you think one can't write poetry if one sees people? I asked. "One might be able to—I dont see why not. Its a question of physical strength" said Hardy. But clearly he preferred solitude himself. Always however he said something sensible & sincere; & thus made the obvious business

15. Judge Vernon Lushington (1832-1912) and his wife had been close friends of Leslie and Julia Stephen in Kensington; and their daughters Katherine (Kitty Maxse), Margaret (Massingberd), and Susan played a not inconsiderable part in the social life of their children.

16. John Drinkwater's stage adaptation of *The Mayor of Casterbridge* opened for a limited run at the Barnes Theatre on 8 September 1926; a special matinée, attended by Mr and Mrs Hardy, was given in his honour at the Pavilion Theatre, Weymouth, on 20 September.

17. *The Connoisseur and other Stories*, published Spring 1926. LW had used it as the basis for his weekly article, 'The World of Books' in the *N & A* of 3 July 1926.

of compliment giving rather unpleasant. He seemed to be free of it all; very active minded; liking to describe people; not to talk in an abstract way: for example Col. Lawrence, bicycling with a broken arm "held like that" from Lincoln to Hardy listened at the door; to hear if there was anyone there.[18]

I hope he won't commit suicide, said Mrs Hardy pensively, still leaning over the tea cups, gazing despondently. He often says things like it, though he has never said quite that perhaps. But he has blue lines round his eyes. He calls himself Shaw in the army. No one is to know where he is. But it got into the papers.

He promised me ⟨to give up fly—⟩ not to go into the air, said Hardy. My husband doesn't like anything to do with the air, said Mrs Hardy.

Now we began to look at the grandfather clock in the corner. We said we must go—tried to confess we were only down for the day. I forgot to say that he offered L. whisky & water, wh. struck me that he was competent as a host, & in every way.

So we got up & signed Mrs H's visitors books; & Hardy took my L. Little Ironies off, & trotted back with it signed, & Woolf spelt Wolff, wh. I daresay had given him some anxiety.[19] Then We[s]sex came in again. I asked if Hardy could stroke him. So he bent down & stroked him, like the master of the house. We[s]sex went on wheezing away.

There was not a trace anywhere of deference to editors, or respect for rank, an extreme simplicity: What impressed me was his freedom, ease, & vitality. He seemed very "Great Victorian" doing the whole thing with a sweep of his hand (they are ordinary smallish, curled up hands) & setting no great stock by literature; but immensely interested in facts; incidents; & somehow, one could imagine, naturally swept off into imagining & creating without a thought of its being difficult or remarkable; becoming obsessed; & living in imagination. Mrs Hardy thrust his old grey hat into his hand & he trotted us out on to the road. Where is that? I asked him, pointing to a clump of trees on the down opposite, for his house is outside the town, with open country (rolling, massive downs, crowned with little tree coronets before & behind) & he said, with interest, "That is Weymouth. We see the lights at night—not the

18. Thomas Edward Lawrence (1888-1935), 'Colonel Lawrence of Arabia', had become a close friend of the Hardys during the two and a half years he spent as Private Shaw, serving with the Royal Tank Corps at Bovington Camp, Dorset. In 1925 he had been allowed to rejoin the R.A.F. as an aircraftsman, and was posted to Cranwell, Lincolnshire; in March 1926 he had fractured his right arm but nonetheless came on his motorbicycle to visit the Hardys soon afterwards.

19. This copy was sold at Sotheby's on 27 April 1970, lot 65.

lights themselves, but the reflection of them." And so we left, & he trotted in again.

Also I asked him if I might see the picture of Tess which Morgan had described, an old picture: whereupon he led me to an awful engraving of Tess coming into a room from a picture by Herkomer.[20] "That was rather my idea of her" he said. But I said I had been told he had an old picture. "Thats fiction" he said. "I used to see people now & then with a look of her."

Also Mrs Hardy said to me, do you know Aldous Huxley? I said I did. They had been reading his book, which she thought 'very clever'. But Hardy could not remember it. Said his wife had to read to him— his eyes were now so bad. ⟨"Was that the book where the⟩ "Theyve changed everything now he said. We used to think there was a beginning & a middle & an end. We believed in the Aristotelian theory. Now one of those stories came to an end with a woman going out of the room."[21] He chuckled. But he no longer reads novels.

The whole thing—literature, novels &c—all seemed to him an amusement, far away, too, scarcely to be taken seriously. Yet he had sympathy & pity for those still engaged in it. But what his secret interests & activities are—to what occupation he trotted off when we left him—I do not know.

Small boys write to him from New Zealand, & have to be answered. They bring out a "Hardy number" of a Japanese paper, which he produced. Talked too about Blunden.[22] I think Mrs H. keeps him posted in the doings of the younger poets.

On the eve of her eleven-week summer retreat from London, VW spent the night of Monday 26 July at Long Barn with Vita Sackville-West, who motored her over to Rodmell the next afternoon. They arrived before LW,

20. Sir Hubert von Herkomer, R.A. (1849-1914) had illustrated the serialisation of *Tess of the D'Urbervilles* which appeared in the *Graphic* in 1891; he gave two of the original drawings to Hardy at Christmas 1891 (they are now in the Dorset County Museum). 'Tess's return from the Dance' shows Tess coming into a room, but it is a drawing in pen and wash, not an engraving.

21. Aldous Huxley's book was his collection *Two or Three Graces* published in May 1926; the story in question was 'Half-Holiday' which ends with a man, not a woman, going out of a room.

22. Edmund Charles Blunden (1896-1974), poet and critic; he had been awarded the Hawthornden Prize for his poetry in 1922, and had been on the staff of the *N & A* before going to Japan in 1924 as Professor of English at Tokyo University, a post he held until 1927.

who also came by car, with Clive and Julian Bell who were going to Charleston. Vita presented the Woolfs with a spaniel bitch puppy called Fanny, which they renamed Pinker (or Pinka).

The headed notes which follow were written at different times, only occasionally datable, between the end of July and the beginning of September. VW appears to have eschewed company to work at To the Lighthouse, *although Raymond Mortimer stayed one week-end. On 20 August the Woolfs dined with Maynard and Lydia Keynes at Tilton, the farmhouse half a mile from Charleston which, with its farm lands, Keynes had leased for 99 years from the local landowner, Viscount Gage. After dinner they all attended the now customary firework party at Charleston in celebration of Quentin's birthday.*

Rodmell. 1926

As I am not going to milk my brains for a week, I shall here write the first pages of the greatest book in the world. This is what the book would be that was made entirely solely & with integrity of one's thoughts. Suppose one could catch them before they became "works of art."? Catch them hot & sudden as they rise in the mind—walking up Asheham hill for instance. Of course one cannot; for the process of language is slow & deluding. One must stop to find a word; then, there is the form of the sentence, soliciting one to fill it.

Art & Thought

What I thought was this: if art is based on thought, what is the transmuting process? I was telling myself the story of our visit to the Hardys. & I began to compose it: that is to say to dwell on Mrs Hardy leaning on the table, looking out, apathetically, vaguely; & so would soon bring everything into harmony with that as the dominant theme. But the actual event was different.

Next,

Writing by living people

I scarcely ever read it. but, owing to his giving me the books, am now reading C by M. Baring.[23] I am surprised to find it as good as it is. But how good is it? Easy to say it is not a great book. But what qualities does it lack? That it adds nothing to one's vision of life, perhaps. Yet it is hard to find a serious flaw. My wonder is that entirely second rate work

23. *C* [Clarence], a novel by Maurice Baring (1874-1945), diplomat and man of letters; the two-volume American edition of 1924, with a long inscription by the author to VW, was sold at Sotheby's on 27 April 1970, lot 5.

like this, poured out in profusion by at least 20 people yearly, I suppose, has so much merit. Never reading it, I get into the way of thinking it non-existent. So it is, speaking with the utmost strictness. That is, it will not exist in 2026; but it has some existence now; which puzzles me a little. Now Clarence bores me; yet I feel this is important. And why?

[*Saturday 31 July*]

My own Brain

Here is a whole nervous breakdown in miniature. We came on Tuesday. Sank into a chair, could scarcely rise; everything insipid; tasteless, colourless. Enormous desire for rest. Wednesday—only wish to be alone in the open air. Air delicious—avoided speech; could not read. Thought of my own power of writing with veneration, as of something incredible, belonging to someone else; never again to be enjoyed by me. Mind a blank. Slept in my chair. Thursday. No pleasure in life whatsoever; but felt perhaps more attuned to existence. Character & idiosyncracy as Virginia Woolf completely sunk out. Humble & modest. Difficulty in thinking what to say. Read automatically, like a cow chewing cud. Slept in chair. Friday. Sense of physical tiredness; but slight activity of the brain. Beginning to take notice. Making one or two plans. No power of phrase making. Difficulty in writing to Lady Colefax. Saturday (today) much clearer & lighter. Thought I could write, but resisted, or found it impossible. A desire to read poetry set in on Friday. This brings back a sense of my own individuality. Read some Dante & Bridges, without troubling to understand, but got pleasure from them. Now I begin to wish to write notes, but not yet novel. But today senses quickening. No 'making up' power yet; no desire to cast scenes in my book. Curiosity about literature returning: want to read Dante, Havelock Ellis, & Berlioz autobiography; also to make a looking glass with shell frame. These processes have sometimes been spread over several weeks.

Proportions Changed

That in the evening, or on colourless days, the proportions of the landscape change suddenly. I saw people playing stoolball in the meadow: they appeared sunk far down on a flat board; & the downs raised high up, & mountainous round them. Detail was smoothed out. This was an extremely beautiful effect; the colours of the womens dresses also showing very bright & pure in the almost untinted surroundings. I knew, also, that the porportions were abnormal—as if I were looking between my legs.

Second Rate Art

i.e. C. by Maurice Baring. Within its limits, it is not second rate, or there is nothing markedly so, at first go off. The limits are the proof of its non-existence.. He can only do one thing: himself to wit; charming, clean, modest sensitive Englishman: outside that radius, & it does not carry far nor illumine much, all is—as it should be; light, sure, proportioned, affecting even; told in so well bred a manner that nothing is exaggerated, all related, proportioned. I could read this for ever, I said. L. said one would soon be sick to death of it.

Wandervögeln

of the sparrow tribe. Two resolute, sunburnt, dusty girls, in jerseys & short skirts, with packs on their backs, city clerks, or secretaries, tramping along the road in the hot sunshine at Ripe.[24] My instinct at once throws up a screen, which condemns them: I think them in every way angular, awkward & self assertive. But all this is a great mistake. These screens shut me out. Have no screens, for screens are made out of our own integument; & get at the thing itself, which has nothing whatever in common with a screen. The screen making habit, though, is so universal, that probably it preserves our sanity. If we had not this device for shutting people off from our sympathies, we might, perhaps, dissolve utterly. Separateness would be impossible. But the screens are in the excess; not the sympathy.

Returning Health

This is shown by the power to make images: the suggestive power of every sight & word is enormously increased. Shakespeare must have had this to an extent which makes my normal state the state of a person blind, deaf, dumb, stone-stockish & fish-blooded. And I have it compared with poor Mrs Bartholomew almost to the extent that Shre has it compared with me.[25]

[Monday 2 August]

Bank Holiday

Very fat woman, girl & man spend Bank Holiday—a day of complete sun & satisfaction—looking up family graves in the churchyard. 23

24. LW, who did not as a rule record his activities whilst at Rodmell, noted under 31 July: 'Bicycled Ripe'.
25. Mrs Rose Bartholomew of Style Cottages, Rodmell, cooked for the Woolfs at Monks House when Nelly was not there; 'she has been mad, squints, & is singularly pure of soul.' (*III VW Letters*, no. 1462.)

youngish men & women spend it tramping along with ugly black boxes on shoulders & arms, taking photographs. Man says to woman "Some of these quiet villages don't seem to know its bank holiday at all" in a tone of superiority & slight contempt.

The Married Relation

Arnold Bennett says that the horror of marriage lies in its 'dailiness'. All acuteness of relationship is rubbed away by this. The truth is more like this. Life—say 4 days out of 7—becomes automatic; but on the 5th day a bead of sensation (between husband & wife) forms, wh. is all the fuller & more sensitive because of the automatic customary unconscious days on either side. That is to say the year is marked by moments of great intensity. Hardy's 'moments of vision'.[1] How can a relationship endure for any length of time except under these conditions?

Friday 3 September

Women in tea garden at Bramber—a sweltering hot day: rose trellises; white washed tables; lower middle classes; motor omnibuses constantly passing; bits of grey stone scattered on a paper strewn green sward all thats left of the Castle.[1]

Woman leaning over the table, taking command of the treat, attended by two elder women, whom she pays for, to girl waitress (a marmalade coloured fat girl, with a body like the softest lard, destined soon to marry, but as yet only 16 or so)

Woman   "What can we have for tea?"

Girl   (very bored, arms akimbo) Cake, bread & butter, tea: Jam?

Woman   Have the wasps been troublesome? They get into the jam—
         as if she suspected the jam would not be worth having.

Girl   agrees.

Woman: Ah, wasps have been very prominent this year.

Girl   Thats right.

So she doesn't have jam.

This amused me, I suppose.

---

1. Hardy's *Moments of Vision, and Miscellaneous Verses* had been published in 1917.
1. Bramber, once a centre of Norman administration on the river Adur in West Sussex, with an imposing castle and chapel, had declined into romantic overgrown ruins overlooking a village along a busy main road.

For the rest, Charleston, Tilton, To the Lighthouse, Vita, expeditions: the summer dominated by a feeling of washing in boundless warm fresh air—such an August not come my way for years: bicycling; no settled work done, but advantage taken of air for going to the river, or over the downs. The novel is now easily within sight of the end, but this, mysteriously, comes no nearer. I am doing Lily on the lawn: but whether its her last lap, I don't know. Nor am I sure of the quality; the only certainty seems to be that after tapping my antennae in the air vaguely for an hour every morning I generally write with heat & ease till 12.30: & thus do my two pages.

[*Sunday 5 September*]

So it will be done, written over that is, in 3 weeks, I forecast, from today. What emerges? At this moment I'm casting about for an end. The problem is how to bring Lily & Mr R[amsay]. together & make a combination of interest at the end. I am feathering about with various ideas. The last chapter which I begin tomorrow is In the Boat: I had meant to end with R. climbing on to the rock. If so, what becomes [of] Lily & her picture? Should there be a final page about her & Carmichael looking at the picture & summing up R.'s character? In that case I lose the intensity of the moment. If this intervenes, between R. & the light-house, there's too much chop & change, I think. Could I do it in a parenthesis? so that one had the sense of reading the two things at the same time?

I shall solve it somehow, I suppose. Then I must go in to the question of quality. I think it may run too fast & free, & so be rather thin. On the other hand, I think it is subtler & more human than J[acob's] R[oom] & Mrs D[alloway]. And I am encouraged by my own abundance as I write. It is proved, I think, that what I have to say is to be said in this manner. As usual, side stories are sprouting in great variety as I wind this up: a book of characters; the whole string being pulled out from some simple sentence, like Clara Pater's, "Don't you find that Barker's pins have no points to them?"[2] I think I can spin out all their entrails this way; but it is hopelessly undramatic. It is all in oratio obliqua. Not quite all; for I have a few direct sentences. The lyric portions of To the L.

2. Clara Ann Pater (1841-1910), younger of Walter Pater's two sisters, became the first Classics Tutor and eventually Vice-President of Somerville College, Oxford. After their brother's death in 1894, the sisters moved to Canning Place, Kensington, and Clara gave VW lessons in Greek. Her question provided the starting point for ' "Slater's Pins have no Points" ' (Kp C295), first published in the *Forum*, New York, in January 1928.

are collected in the 10 year lapse, & dont interfere with the text so much as usual. I feel as if it fetched its circle pretty completely this time: & I dont feel sure what the stock criticism will be. Sentimental? Victorian?

Then I must begin to plan out my book on literature for the Press.[3] Six chapters. Why not groups of ideas, under some single heading—for example. Symbolism. God. Nature. Plot. Dialogue. Take a novel & see what the component parts are. Separate this, & bring under them instances of all the books which display them biggest. Probably this would pan out historically. One could spin a theory which wd bring the chapters together. I don't feel that I can read seriously[?] & exactly for it. Rather I want to sort out all the ideas that have accumulated in me.

Then I want to write a bunch of 'Outlines' to make money (for under a new arrangement, we're to share any money over £200 that I make): this I must leave rather to chance, according to what books come my way. I am frightfully contented these last few days, by the way. I dont quite understand it. Perhaps reason has something to do with it. Charleston & Tilton knocked me off my perch for a moment: Nessa & her children: Maynard & his carpets. My own gifts & shares seemed so moderate in comparison; my own fault too—a little more self control on my part, & we might have had a boy of 12, a girl of 10: This always rakes me wretched in the early hours. So I said, I am spoiling what I have. And thereupon settled [?] to exploit my own possessions to the full; I can make money & buy carpets; I can increase the pleasure of life enormously by living it carefully. No doubt, this is a rationalisation of a state which is not really of that nature. Probably I am very lucky. Mrs Allinson says she would like to look like me.[4] Mary says I'm the only woman she loves. Nelly cooks admirably. Then, I am extremely happy walking on the downs. I dont want to be talking to Eddy at Charleston. I like to have space to spread my mind out in. Whatever I think, I can rap out, suddenly to L. We are somehow very detached, free, harmonious. I don't in the least want to hurry up & finish the time here. I want to go to Seaford & walk back over the downs; to go & see the house at East Chiltington; to breathe in more light & air; to see more grey hollows & gold cornfields & the first ploughed land shining white, with the gulls flickering. No: I dont want anyone to come here & interrupt. I am immensely busy. Hence I come to my moral, which is simply to enjoy what one does enjoy, without teasing oneself oh but Nessa has

3. See above, 7 December 1925, n 6.
4. Elsie Allison was the wife of the Australian J. Murray Allison, of Hill Farm House, Rodmell, advertising director of Allied Newspapers Ltd, a prominent and gregarious local landowner.

children, Maynard carpets. I might go & stay with Ethel [Sands, *in Normandy*]. For my own wishes are always definite enough to give me a lead, one way or another; & the chief joy in life is to follow these lights; I am now almost entirely surrounded by sheep. God knows, I wish we could buy the terrace, & have a garden all round the lodge—but this is not a serious diminution of joy.[5]

Clive & Mary came over yesterday in brilliant sun. We sat on the millstones. (one sheep has a tail like a bell-rope—the others are all bit short.) Wells. Hardy. Maynard. Richardson. [*word illegible*]. Christabel—going to Greece for a month with Lesley Jowitt. Maupassant's metaphors —The Questionnaire. Lytton's harem—Their dulness—Carrington a cook who doesn't go out on Sundays. Whether Eddy is clever or not. Tonks & Steer & Moore—Tonks in love with Mary, Clive insists; she is modest. So we talked.[6] Then I drove with them to the Laye, walked up the down behind Asheham & let all that wind & sun blow through the crazy sails of my old windmill, which gives me so much pleasure still.[7] I forget what I thought about: did not think, I suppose; was all in a thrill of emotion at my being liked by Mary & being a success, &c. Home to music, my new 15/- table, talk with L.: a sense of great happiness & ease. Went & looked at the stars, but could not get quite the right sense of amazement (I can get this really well at times) because L. said

"Now come in. Its too cold to be out"

5. The Woolfs had erected a wooden 'lodge' (often used by VW as a writing room) by the churchyard wall at the far end of their property; from it there was a view over the wide Ouse valley across a strip of land, adjoining theirs, which fell steeply away into a field. LW had for some time been trying to buy this 'terrace' and, if necessary, the rest of the field; and in 1928 he succeeded. (See below, 8 August 1928.)

6. Christabel McLaren (later Lady Aberconway) and Lesley Jowitt, wife of a future Lord Chancellor, were both ornaments of the smart artistic society in which Clive Bell and Mary Hutchinson were equally at home; the latter was also a great favourite with the elderly bachelor artists Henry Tonks and Philip Wilson Steer and their close friend the writer George Moore.

In successive issues in August and September 1926 the *N & A* had carried a supplement entitled 'Questionnaire on Religious Belief' which arose from an article by LW, 'Rationalism and Religion' published on 12 June; the results, finally reported in the *N & A* of 16 October 1926, gave as answer to the first question, "Do you believe in a personal God?" 743 affirmative and 1024 negative replies. (A wholly contrary result was obtained by the *Daily News* in a similar enquiry.) For Carrington (1893-1932), see above, 7 December 1925, n 3.

7. 'The Lay' was a farm cottage and buildings on the road half way between Asheham and Beddingham.

Monday 13 September

The blessed thing is coming to an [end] I say to myself with a groan. Its like some prolonged rather painful & yet exciting process of nature, which one desires inexpressibly to have over. Oh the relief of waking & thinking its done—the relief, & the disappointment, I suppose. I am talking of To the Lighthouse. I am exacerbated by the fact that I spent 4 days last week hammering out de Quincey, which has been lying about since June; so refused £30 to write on Willa Cather; & now shall be quit in a week I hope of this unprofitable fiction, & could have wedged in Willa before going back. So I should have had £70 of my years 200 ready made by October: (my greed is immense: I want to have £50 of my own in the Bank to buy Persian carpets, pots, chairs &c.) Curse Richmond, Curse The Times, Curse my own procrastinations & nerves. I shall do Cobden Sanderson & Mrs Hemans & make something by them however.[8] As for the book [*To the Lighthouse*]—Morgan said he felt 'This is a failure' as he finished The passage to India. I feel—what? A little stale this last week or two from steady writing. But also a little triumphant. If my feeling is correct, this is the greatest stretch I've put my method to, & I think it holds. By this I mean that I have been dredging up more feelings & character, I imagine. But Lord knows, until I look at my haul. This is only my own feeling in process. Odd how I'm haunted by that damned criticism of Janet Case's "its all dressing . . . technique. (Mrs Dalloway). The C.R. has substance". But then in ones strained state any fly has liberty to settle, & its always the gadflies. Muir praising me intelligently has comparatively little power to encourage —when I'm working that is—when the ideas halt.[9] And this last lap, in the boat, is hard, because the material is not so rich as it is with Lily on the lawn: I am forced to be more direct & more intense. I am making

8. VW's review of *The Journals of Thomas James Cobden-Sanderson, 1897-1922*, appeared in the *N & A* on 9 October 1926 under the title 'The Cosmos' (Kp C276). She wrote nothing on her contemporary Willa Cather (1876-1947), the American regionalist writer, nor on Felicia Hemans (1793-1835), chiefly remembered for 'The Boy Stood on the Burning Deck'; though there is an incomplete ms draft of an article on the latter in MHP, Sussex (B10a).

9. Edwin Muir (1887-1959), poet and critic, born and brought up in Orkney, came to London after his marriage in 1919 and worked on the Guild Socialist weekly *The New Age*. LW printed his poems at the Hogarth Press in 1925 and 1926, and employed him as a reviewer on the *N & A*, which first published his series of appraisals of contemporary writers which the Hogarth Press were about to issue in book form under the title *Transition* (HP Checklist 105). The long essay on VW had appeared in the *N & A* on 17 April 1926, and is also reprinted in *M & M*, p 178.

some use of symbolism, I observe; & I go in dread of 'sentimentality'. Is the whole theme open to that charge? But I doubt that any theme is in itself good or bad. It gives a chance to ones peculiar qualities—thats all. Then I'm concerned whether to stay with Ethel Sands or not: whether to buy a dress or not. Then I'm astonishingly happy in the country—a state of mind which, if I did not dislike hyphens, I should hyphen, to show that it is a state by itself.

We took Angus over the downs towards Falmer yesterday. After all these years, we have discovered some of the loveliest, loneliest, most surprising downland in these parts: lovelier I think than our rival the Seaford-Tilton down over which we walked in broiling sun last Thursday. How it beat on our heads, made poor puppy pant. Lydia & Maynard came to tea.

Wednesday 15 September

Sometimes I shall use the Note form: for instance this

A State of Mind

Woke up perhaps at 3. Oh its beginning its coming—the horror—physically like a painful wave swelling about the heart—tossing me up. I'm unhappy unhappy! Down—God, I wish I were dead. Pause. But why am I feeling this? Let me watch the wave rise. I watch. Vanessa. Children. Failure. Yes; I detect that. Failure failure. (The wave rises). Oh they laughed at my taste in green paint! Wave crashes. I wish I were dead! I've only a few years to live I hope. I cant face this horror any more—(this is the wave spreading out over me).

This goes on; several times, with varieties of horror. Then, at the crisis, instead of the pain remaining intense, it becomes rather vague. I doze. I wake with a start. The wave again! The irrational pain: the sense of failure; generally some specific incident, as for example my taste in green paint, or buying a new dress, or asking Dadie for the week end, tacked on.

At last I say, watching as dispassionately as I can, Now take a pull of yourself. No more of this. I reason. I take a census of happy people & unhappy. I brace myself to shove to throw to batter down. I begin to march blindly forward. I feel obstacles go down. I say it doesn't matter. Nothing matters. I become rigid & straight, & sleep again, & half wake & feel the wave beginning & watch the light whitening & wonder how, this time, breakfast & daylight will overcome it; & then hear L. in the passage & simulate, for myself as well as for him, great cheerfulness; &

generally am cheerful, by the time breakfast is over. Does everyone go through this state? Why have I so little control? It is not creditable, nor lovable. It is the cause of much waste & pain in my life.

Tuesday 28 September

Every day I have meant to record a state of mind. But it has always disappeared (characteristically) yet recurred often enough to make it one of some importance. It is raining hard this evening; we have entered the calm period of Nelly's departure. So I will try, before my fingers chill & my mind wanders to the fire, to write here what I can remember.

Intense depression: I have to confess that this has overcome me several times since September 6th (I think that, or thereabouts was the date.) It is so strange to me that I cannot get it right—the depression, I mean, which does not come from something definite, but from nothing. "Where there is nothing" the phrase came ⟨back⟩ to me, as I sat at the table in the drawing room. Of course I was interested; & discovered that, for the first time for many years, I had been idle without being ill. We had been walking, expeditioning, in the hot fine weather. I was writing the last pages of To the Lighthouse (finished, provisionally, Sept 16th). Somehow, my reading had lapsed. I was hunting no hares. One night I got hold of Geoffrey Scott's book on Architecture, & a little spark of motive power awoke in me.[10] This is a warning then; never to cease the use of the brain. So I used my brain. Then, owing to mismanagement, no one came to stay, & I got very few letters; & the high pure hot days went on & on; & this blankness persisted, & I began to suspect my book of the same thing; & there was Nessa humming & booming & flourishing over the hill; & one night we had a long long argument. Vita started it, by coming over with Plank,[11] & L. (I say) spoilt the visit by glooming because I said he had been angry. He shut up, & was caustic. He denied this, but admitted that my habits of describing him, & others, had this effect often. I saw myself, my brilliancy, genius, charm, beauty (&c. &c.— the attendants who float me through so many years) diminish & disappear. One is in truth rather an elderly dowdy fussy ugly incompetent woman vain, chattering & futile. I saw this vividly, impressively. Then he said our relations had not been so good lately. On analysing my state of mind

10. *The Architecture of Humanism. A Study in the History of Taste,* 1914.

11. George Plank (1883-1965), a Philadelphian Quaker who came to England in May 1914, stayed on and took British nationality in 1926. A modest but accomplished illustrator and wood-engraver, he regularly provided the covers for *Vogue*; and the wrapper of V. Sackville-West's poem *The Land*, published this month, was designed and cut on wood by him.

SEPTEMBER 1926

I admitted that I had been irritated, first by the prevalency of the dogs (Grizzle on heat too.[12]) Secondly by his assumption that we can afford to saddle ourselves with a whole time gardener, build or buy him a cottage, & take in the terrace to be garden. Then, I said, we shall be tying ourselves to come here; shall never travel; & it will be assumed that Monks House is the hub of the world. This it certainly is not, I said, to me; nor do I wish to spend such a measure of our money on gardens, when we cannot buy rugs, beds or good arm chairs. L. was, I think, hurt at this, & I was annoyed at saying it, yet did it, not angrily, but in the interests of freedom. Too many women give way on this point, & secretly grudge their unselfishness in silence—a bad atmosphere. Our atmosphere decidedly cleared, after this, Tommie [Tomlin] came for the week end, & I am once more full of work, at high pressure, interested, & quite unable, I see, to make plain even to my own eyes, my season of profound despondency.

If I wish to avoid this in future, I recommend, first, incessant brain activity; reading, & planning; second, a methodical system of inviting people here (which is possible, with Nelly obedient & gay); third, increased mobility. For next year, I shall arrange perhaps to go definitely to Ethel Sands. With my motor I shall be more mobile.

But it is always a question whether I wish to avoid these glooms. In part they are the result of getting away by oneself, & have a psychological interest which the usual state of working & enjoying lacks. These 9 weeks give one a plunge into deep waters; which is a little alarming, but full of interest. All the rest of the year one's (I daresay rightly) curbing & controlling this odd immeasurable soul. When it expands, though one is frightened & bored & gloomy, it is as I say to myself, awfully queer. There is an edge to it which I feel of great importance, once in a way. One goes down into the well & nothing protects one from the assault of truth. Down there I cant write or read; I exist however. I am. Then I ask myself what I am? & get a closer though less flattering answer than I should on the surface—where, to tell the truth, I get more praise than is right. But the praise will go; one will be left alone with this queer being in old age. I am glad to find it on the whole so interesting, though so acutely unpleasant. Also, I can, by taking pains, be much more considerate of L.'s feelings; & so keep more steadily at our ordinary level of intimacy & ease: a level, I think, no other couple so long married, reaches, & keeps so constantly.

12. Grizzle, the mongrel fox-terrier the Woolfs acquired in the summer of 1922, became infected with eczema, and was put down on 4 December 1926.

112

Thursday 30 September

I wished to add some remarks to this, on the mystical side of this solitude; how it is not oneself but something in the universe that one's left with. It is this that is frightening & exciting in the midst of my profound gloom, depression, boredom, whatever it is: One sees a fin passing far out. What image can I reach to convey what I mean? Really there is none I think. The interesting thing is that in all my feeling & thinking I have never come up against this before. Life is, soberly & accurately, the oddest affair; has in it the essence of reality. I used to feel this as a child—couldn't step across a puddle once I remember, for thinking, how strange—what am I? &c. But by writing I dont reach anything. All I mean to make is a note of a curious state of mind. I hazard the guess that it may be the impulse behind another book. At present my mind is totally blank & virgin of books.* I want to watch & see how the idea at first occurs. I want to trace my own process.

* Perhaps The Waves or moths (Oct. 1929)

I was depressed again today because Vita did not come (yet relieved at the same time); had to hold L.'s ladder in the garden, when I wanted to write or to try on Nessa's dress; & slightly afraid that this dress is not very successful.

But I am shelving the dress problem on these principles. I am having cheap day clothes; & a good dress from Brooke; & I am being less pernickety about keeping to limits, as I have only to write & stir myself, to make, I wager, quite £50 extra in the year for my own extravagances. No longer shall I let a coat for £3 floor me in the middle of the night, or be afraid to lunch out because "I've no clothes." A broader & bolder grasp is what is wanted. Here I am going into the question of order & so on, like a housekeeper, taking in supplies. Soon, this time next week, I shall have no time for glooming or introspection. It will be "When may I come & see you?" Already Betty Potter has begun.[13]

Now I must scheme a little at my book of criticism.

The Woolfs returned to London on 4 October; there are no entries in VW's diary until 30 October, nor does LW resume his laconic record until 21 October.

13. Betty Potter was the stage name of Elizabeth Meinertzhagen (1892-1948), an ambitious but not very successful actress whom VW had tried to help when she was suicidal a few years earlier. (See *II VW Letters*, 1235.)

Saturday 30 October

It will be when may I come & see you!—too true a prophecy, though made in the damp & solitude of Rodmell. Monday, Ozzie Dickinson, Wednesday, Lady Colefax, Thursday Morgan to meet Abel Chevalley, dine Wells to meet Arnold Bennett, Friday to Monday Long Barn.[1] So the week slips or sticks through my fingers; rage misery joy, dulness elation mix: I am the usual battlefield of emotions; alternately think of buying chairs & clothes; plod with some method revising To the Lighthouse; quarrel with Nelly (who was to catch the afternoon train today because I told a lie about a telephone) & so we go on. Maurice Baring & the Sitwells send me their books;[2] Leonard forges ahead, now doing what he calls "correspondence"; the Press creaks a little at its hinges; Mrs C[artwright]. has absconded with my spectacles: I find Buggers bores; like the normal male; & should now be developing my book for the Press. All these things shoulder each other out across the screen of my brain. At intervals, I begin to think (I note this, as I am going to watch for the advent of a book) of a solitary woman musing[?] a book of ideas about life. This has intruded only once or twice, & very vaguely: it is a dramatisation of my mood at Rodmell. It is to be an endeavour at something mystic, spiritual; the thing that exists when we aren't there.

Among external things, we were at Cambridge for the week end; kept warm at the Bull—& there's a good subject—The Hotel.[3] Many people from Macclesfield talking about motor cars. Mothers, to me pathetic, looking half shyly at their sons, as if deprecating their age. A whole life

1. Oswald Eden Dickinson (1869-1954), brother of VW's old friend Violet whose homes he shared, was secretary to the Home Office Board of Control in Lunacy from 1913-32. Abel Chevalley (1868-1933), French critic of English Literature, was to give a lecture, under the auspices of the P.E.N. Club, on 'Some Tendencies of the French Contemporary Novel' at King's College, Strand, on 4 November; E. M. Forster was presiding. The same day, LW noted that they 'Dined Wells Arnold Bennett & Bernard Shaw'.

2. In addition to *C* (see above, 31 July 1926, n 23), Maurice Baring gave VW his *Punch & Judy and other Essays*, 1924, *Daphne Adeane*, 1926, *Cat's Cradle*, 1926, and *The Glass Mender and other Stories*, 1926 (see *Holleyman*, MH II, pp 5, 6). On 2 October Osbert Sitwell inscribed his *Before the Bombardment*, 1926, 'For dear Virginia Tremblingly from the Author' (*Holleyman*, MH II, p 3); Sacheverell Sitwell presented her with his *All Summer in a Day*, 1926 (sold at Sotheby's on 27 April 1970, lot 93).

3. The Woolfs had stayed at the Bull Hotel, Trumpington Street (now a mere façade concealing new college buildings), on 23 and on 24 October when, after dining with Maynard Keynes, LW read a paper to the Heretics' Club.

opened to me: father, mother, son, daughter. Father alone has wine. An enormous man, like an advertisement of Power: sits in chair. Daddy you'll be miserable in it says girl, herself bovine. Mother a mere wisp; sits with eyes shut; had spent hours driving up writing characters of maids. Shall I remember any of this?

Then Gosse introducing Vita at Royal —— something. I never saw the whole hierarchy of lit. so plainly exposed. Gosse the ornament on the tea pot: beneath him file on file of old stout widows whose husbands had been professors, beetle specialists doubtless, meritorious dons; & these good people, ruminating tea, & reflecting all the depths of the suburbs tinctured with literature, dear Vita told them were "The Hollow Men."[4] Her address was read in sad sulky tones like those of a schoolboy; her pendulous rich society face, glowing out under a black hat at the end of the smoky dismal room, looked very ancestral & like a picture under glass in a gallery. She was fawned upon by the little dapper grocer Gosse, who kept spinning round on his heel to address her compliments & to scarify Bolshevists; in an ironical voice which seemed to ward off what might be said of him; & to be drawing round the lot of them thicker & thicker, the red plush curtains of respectability. There was Vita, who was too innocent to see it, Guedalla, & Drinkwater.[5] I dont regret my wildest, foolishest, utterance, if it gave the least crack to this respectability. But needless to say, no word of mine has had any effect whatever. Gosse will survive us all. Now how does he do it? Yet he seemed to me, with his irony & his scraping, somehow uneasy. A kind of black doormat got up & appeared to be Lady Gosse. So home, with Dotty in a rage, because she was palmed off with Plank. She did contrive to get here though in the end. One night I went in with Vita after the play. She was lying asleep at Mount Street, in a flat at the top of the house: large pale furniture about dimly seen—a dog on her bed. She woke up chattering & hysterical. Virginia Woolf Virginia Woolf My God! Virginia Woolf is in the room. For Gods Sake Vita dont turn the lights on. No light you fool! But I

4. V. Sackville-West gave a lecture at the Royal Society of Literature on the afternoon of 27 October on 'Some Tendencies of Modern English Poetry'. She ended her address with this fragment from T. S. Eliot's poem published in his *Poems 1909-1925*:

> 'Remember us—if at all—not as lost
> Violent souls, but only
> As the hollow men.'

The chair was taken by Sir Edmund Gosse (1849-1928), man of letters, high priest of the literary establishment, and dispenser of a weekly gospel in the *Sunday Times*.

5. Philip Guedalla (1889-1944), historian and biographer; John Drinkwater (1882-1937), playwright and poet.

cant see to get the allella, mumbled Vita.[6] She got it though. We sat & drank. Dusky shapes of glasses & things, a room I had never seen; a woman I scarcely knew; Vita there between us, intimate wi' both; flattery, extravagance, complete inner composure on my part, & so home.

The first three weeks of November, when no diary was written, appear to have been very fully taken up with work on To the Lighthouse, *with Vita (and a visit to her at Long Barn, 6-8 November), with social gatherings and innumerable people. The dinner party on 4 November at the H. G. Wellses', where the Woolfs met the Shaws and Arnold Bennett, was recorded by the latter in his journal; of the Woolfs he wrote: 'Both gloomy, these two . . . But I liked both of them in spite of their naughty treatment of me in the press.'*

Tuesday 23 November

Here I must resolve first of all to find some long solid book to read. What? Tristram Shandy? French memoirs? This is on top of a discussion, at tea about Angus. He dont do, L. says: will never make a manager. So then shall it be another attempt, or Cape, or Secker?[1] These difficulties recur. I should not much like writing for Cape; yet if the Press is sagging on our shoulders, there is little sense in waiting on. Next year L. thinks we could sell to advantage. It gives one a full life: but then life is so full already. Colefax complicates the scene—Colefax is the death of this book. Aren't I always reading her scrawls or answering them. This culminated last week in her dining alone with me, off cold chicken. I found us talking socially, not intimately, she in pearls (shams Vita says) popping up one light after another: like the switch board at the telephone exchange at the mention of names. Geoffrey Scott, Percy Lubbock[,] whoever it might be. Perfectly competent, &, for her purpose, efficient. She is, I maintain, a woman of the world: has all her senses tuned to that pitch. The machine doesn't work in private, though she was very anxious, poor aspiring, slightly suspicious & uneasy woman, that it should. She told me how she had lived till she married running after old ladies with their knitting. So, on marriage, but she was only 19, had kicked her

---

6. VW had been with Vita Sackville-West to the Barnes Theatre on 25 October to the first night of Komisarjevsky's production of *The Three Sisters*. Dorothy Wellesley had a London flat opposite Hyde Park. Alella is a white Catalonian wine.
1. LW noted his conclusion about Angus Davidson in the same words on the same day; see LWP, Sussex, Part II, Q.

heels up: determined to live, like Violet's mother, who leant out of the Palace window at Auckland & said, to an old man selling kippers, Is this life?[2] But now, aged 50, she asks, Is this life? again—rushing round, dining & giving dinners; never able to concentrate in a corner, & secretly, in my opinion, not desiring it but pretending it, as she has the habit of pretence. This is all right in her, but wrong in me. So we don't altogether amalgamate; but I have my reservations, she hers. In came Dadie, to our relief, somewhat; then Sir Arthur, breezy, cheery, competent, patting her, controlling her, petted by her (she reverted to her arch girlish days, when she could eat soup & potatoes without any thought of her figure) sitting on the edge of my shabby dirty down at heels arm chair.[3]

All this rushes on apace. Fame grows. Chances of meeting this person, doing that thing, accumulate. Life is as I've said since I was 10, awfully interesting—if anything, quicker, keener at 44 than 24—more desperate I suppose, as the river shoots to Niagara—my new vision of death; active, positive, like all the rest, exciting; & of great importance—as an experience.

'The one experience I shall never describe' I said to Vita yesterday. She was sitting on the floor in her velvet jacket & red striped silk shirt, I knotting her pearls into heaps of great lustrous eggs. She had come up to see me—so we go on—a spirited, creditable affair, I think, innocent (spiritually) & all gain, I think; rather a bore for Leonard, but not enought to worry him. The truth is one has room for a good many relationships. Then she goes back again to Persia, with Leigh Ashton—that putty faced low voiced rather beaten cur, who is always slinking off with his tail between his legs, but gives, they say, oyster suppers.

I am re-doing six pages of Lighthouse daily. This is not I think, so quick as Mrs D.: but then I find much of it very sketchy, & have to improvise on the typewriter. This I find much easier than re-writing in pen & ink. My present opinion is that it is easily the best of my books, fuller than J.'s R. & less spasmodic, occupied with more interesting things than Mrs D. & not complicated with all that desperate accompaniment of madness. It is freer & subtler I think. Yet I have no idea yet of any other to follow it: which may mean that I have made my method perfect, & it will now stay like this, & serve whatever use I wish to put it to. Before, some development of the method brought fresh subjects in

2. Violet Dickinson's mother had been Emily Dulcibella Eden, third daughter of the 3rd Baron Auckland, Bishop of Bath and Wells from 1854-1869; his Palace was at Wells, not Auckland.

3. Sir Arthur Colefax (1866-1936), KC, was a specialist in patent and trade mark law. The Colefaxes had married in 1901.

view, because I saw the chance of being able to say them. Yet I am now
& then haunted by some semi mystic very profound life of a woman,
which shall all be told on one occasion; & time shall be utterly obliterated;
future shall somehow blossom out of the past. One incident—say the
fall of a flower—might contain it. My theory being that the actual event
practically does not exist—nor time either. But I dont want to force this.
I must make up my Series book.

*On 4 December VW went again to Long Barn to spend the week-end with
Vita Sackville-West; LW, having had Grizzle put down, spent the night
with his brother Herbert at Cookham.*

Saturday 11 December

I have never been able to afford 2/ for a good piece of washleather, yet
I buy a dozen boxes of matches for 1/6.

I am giving up the hope of being well dressed.

Violet Dickinson has just had a third serious operation & I went to
an old Curiosity shop instead of going to see her.[1]

Leonard is lunching with Maynard & a great registered parcel has just
been delivered containing Dadie's dissertation.[2]

It is now close on 3.30.

Some superstition prevents me from reading Yeats' autobiography as
I should like.[3]

I am very happy at the moment: having arranged my week on the
whole well.

But I have been rather unscupulous. I have put off the Stephens, at
Thorpe: & shall probably stay at Knole.

A few thoughts to fill up time waiting for dinner.

An article all about London:

How Vita's inkpot flowered on her table.

Logan's vanity: I write everything 8 times—

(So thats how its done I thought: he thought thats the only way to
produce writing like mine)

1. Violet Dickinson was convalescing in her own home in Manchester Street after a
cancer operation.
2. A slightly revised version of G. H. W. Rylands' Fellowship dissertation was to be
published by the Hogarth Press as *Words and Poetry* in 1928 (*HP Checklist* 175).
3. W. B. Yeats' *Autobiographies: Reveries over Childhood & The Trembling of the Veil*,
first published in 1914 and 1922 respectively, were re-issued in November 1926 in
Macmillan's 6-volume Collected Works of Yeats. The book was discussed by LW
in his 'World of Books' article in the *N & A* on 1 January 1927.

But all my thoughts perish instantly. I make them up so vast. How to blunt the sting of an unpleasant remark: to say it over & over & over again. Walked to Violet's; took her a red carnation & a white one. My feelings quickened as I drew near. I visualised the operation as I stood on the doorstep.

I also have made up a passage for The Lighthouse: on people going away & the effect on one's feeling for them.

But reading Yeats turns my sentences one way: reading Sterne turns them another.

On 22 December the Woolfs went to Cornwall to spend Christmas with Ka and Will Arnold-Forster at Eagle's Nest, Zennor; they returned to London on 28 December.

— 1927 —

1927

The Woolfs returned to Tavistock Square from Cornwall on 28 December, a day earlier than intended, owing to the cold and the colds at Eagle's Nest; they went to Monks House from 4-8 January; and on 17 January VW was taken by Vita Sackville-West to stay with the latter's father at Knole for two nights. VW continued to write her diary in her 1926 book, DIARY XV.

Friday 14 January

This is out of order, but I have no new book, & so must record here (& it was here I recorded the beginning of The Lighthouse) must record here the end. This moment I have finished the final drudgery. It is now complete for Leonard to read on Monday. Thus I have done it some days under the year, & feel thankful to be out of it again. Since October 25th I have been revising & retyping (some parts 3 times over) & no doubt I should work at it again; but I cannot. What I feel is that it is a hard muscular book, which at this age proves that I have something in me. It has not run out & gone flabby, at least such is my feeling before reading it over.

Sunday 23 January

Well Leonard has read To the Lighthouse, & says it is much my best book, & it is a 'masterpiece'. He said this without my asking. I came back from Knole & sat without asking him. He calls it entirely new 'a psychological poem', is his name for it. An improvement upon Dalloway: more interesting. Having won this great relief, my mind dismisses the whole thing, as usual; & I forget it, & shall only wake up & be worried again over proofs & then when it appears.

We went to Cornwall (dare I characterise Will hearing him talk next door—it is Sunday—he is dining with us). He is a water-blooded waspish little man, all on edge, vain, peevish, nervous. Ka is matronly, but substantial. Some views I retain—one of the valley in the evening light—but others were only a dull impression of life suspended & frozen, & the chin sawing of Mervyn: all chapped, becolded.[1] We came home for these

1. William Edward Arnold-Forster (1885-1951) had married VW's old friend Ka Cox in 1918, when he was still in the RNVR. By training and inclination a painter, he now devoted much time to the work of the League of Nations, and in 1926 had

reasons a day early, & next morning I had a letter from the New York H[erald]. & T[ribune] asking me to go there, passage paid, 120 in my pocket &, perhaps, expenses, & write 4 articles. We accepted, on conditions; but have not heard yet. Meanwhile we hesitate, for if Leonard came, we should probably be £150 out of pocket. So it seems. The adventure is tempting. But the grind of moneymaking is scarcely to be endured unnecessarily. We could go to Greece, or Italy for less.

Then Nessa has gone, poor dear creature. I came in two days ago & found her white at the telephone; Elly at the other end saying that Duncan's illness was probably typhoid.[2] I think a left handed marriage makes these moments more devastating: a sense remains, I think of hiding one's anguish; of insecurity. Angus writes the most cautious alarming letters. Anyhow she went yesterday in a snowstorm, & we kissed on the pavement in the snow. We are very intimate—a great solace to me. Vita goes on Saturday.[3] Tomorrow I dine with her at Colefaxes: a brilliant party: no clothes: hair down my back as usual. Does it very much matter? I reached that point of philosophy at Knole the other night, with the bountiful womanly Mrs Rubens & his Lordship the figure of an English nobleman, decayed, dignified, smoothed, effete; respectable I think in his modest way.[4] But I never have enjoyed a party. Balls at Buckingham

---

been appointed a member of the Labour Party Advisory Committee on International Affairs, of which LW was Secretary. At a meeting on 19 January the two of them had been asked to draft a commentary, and presumably it was this they were discussing as VW wrote. Will's younger brother Mervyn Nevil Arnold-Forster (1888-1927), who had fought with the Grenadier Guards and was awarded a MC, was later this year to be considered as manager of the Hogarth Press, but died on 6 May 1927 from pneumonia and the delayed effects of his war service (see below, 16 May 1927).

2. Early in January Duncan Grant had gone to stay with his mother and aunt at Cassis, where they had rented a villa, 'Les Mimosas'; on arrival he collapsed with a fever. Angus Davidson who followed him to Provence for his winter holiday found him very ill and alarmed Vanessa, who had in any case planned to join Duncan and spend several months painting in the south. She left England, with Angelica and her servant Grace Germany, on 22 January; by the time they reached Cassis Duncan was on the mend, and Vanessa installed herself in a flat in the nearby Villa Corsica.

3. Vita in fact left London for Persia on Friday 28 January, after spending most of the morning with VW; Leigh Ashton and Dorothy Wellesley accompanied her.

4. Vita's father, Lionel Edward Sackville-West, 3rd Baron Sackville (1867-1928), was a conscientious JP and member of Kent County Council. In 1919 Lady Sackville had left Knole, to which she never returned, when he installed the singer Olive Rubens (d. 1973) and her husband Walter in the house; but she refused to set him free to marry Mrs Rubens.

Palace are worth looking at. He spends the day sitting on Com[mi]tees at Maidstone; interviews parsons about livings; likes chess & crime. Vita took me over the 4 acres of building, which she loves: too little conscious beauty for my taste: smallish rooms looking on to buildings: no views: yet one or two things remain: Vita stalking in her Turkish dress, attended by small boys, down the gallery, wafting them on like some tall sailing ship—a sort of covey of noble English life: dogs walloping, children crowding, all very free & stately: & [a] cart bringing wood in to be sawn by the great circular saw. How do you see that? I asked Vita. She said she saw it as something that had gone on for hundreds of years. They had brought wood in from the Park to replenish the great fires like this for centuries: & her ancestresses had walked so on the snow with their great dogs bounding by them. All the centuries seemed lit up, the past expressive, articulate; not dumb & forgotten; but a crowd of people stood behind, not dead at all; not remarkable; fair faced, long limbed; affable; & so we reach the days of Elizabeth quite easily. After tea, looking for letters of Dryden's to show me, she tumbled out a love letter of Ld Dorset's (17th century) with a lock of his soft gold tinted hair which I held in my hand a moment.[5] One had a sense of links fished up into the light which are usually submerged. Otherwise no particular awe or any great sense of difference or distinction. They are not a brilliant race. The space & comeliness of it all struck me. I came home to Marjorie Strachey,[6] Tom Eliot, Nessa & Roger. A little constricted our society: no talk of the clergy or of the country; but how lively & agile compared with the

[text ends]

DIARY XVI

Thursday 3 February

Fate always contrives that I begin the new year in February. I ask, why another volume? (but here's an innovation: this is not a book but a block —so lazy am I about making writing books nowadays). What is the purpose of them? L. taking up a volume the other day said Lord save him if I died first & he had to read through these. My handwriting deteriorates. And do I say anything interesting? I can always waste an idle hour reading them; & then, oh yes, I shall write my memoirs out of them, one of these days.

5. In her book *Knole and the Sackvilles* (1947) V. Sackville-West describes Dryden as a constant visitor at Knole, the guest of Charles Sackville, 6th Earl of Dorset (1638-1706); and refers (p 128) to a lock 'of reddish-brown hair of surprising length' enclosed in a love-letter to the Countess of Falmouth.
6. Marjorie ('Gumbo') Strachey (1882-1964), teacher, was Lytton's youngest sister.

That reminds me of the Webbs: those 36 strenuous hours at Liphook, in an emphatic lodging house, with blue books in the passages; & those entirely devoted—by which I mean those entirely integrated people.[1] Their secret is that they have by nature no divisions of soul to fritter them away: their impact is solid & entire. Without eyes & ears (but Mrs Webb listens in & prefers Mozart to Handel, if I may guess) one can come down with more of a weight upon bread & butter or whatever the substance is before one. On a steely watery morning we swiftly tramped over a heathy common talking, talking. In their efficiency & glibness one traces perfectly adjusted machinery; but talk by machinery does not charm, or suggest: it cuts the grass of the mind close at the roots. I'm too hurried to write. Mrs W. is far less ornamental than of old: wispy untidy drab, with a stain on her skirt & a key on her watch chain; as if she had cleared the decks & rolled her sleeves & was waiting for the end, but working.

Saturday 12 February

Exactly what has happened in the Clive Mary affair I cannot say. Did he not sheepishly admit in the kitchen the other night that he was putting it off till March? & then, casually & jauntily tell me as if by chance, the other afternoon, here, that he was going after all. But wont Mary mind? What if she does?—that was practically his answer.[2]

Vita's prose is too fluent. I've been reading it, & it makes my pen run. When I've read a classic, I am curbed &—not castrated: no, the opposite; I cant think of the word at the moment—

Had I been writing P[assenger] to T[eheran] I should have run off whole pools of this coloured water; & then (I think) found my own method of attack. It is my distinction as a writer I think to get this clear & my expression exact. Were I writing travels I should wait till some angle emerged: & go for that. The method of writing smooth narrative

1. The Woolfs stayed Saturday night, 29 January, with Sidney and Beatrice Webb at their Surrey home, Passfield Corner, which Beatrice described (*Diaries 1924-32*, edited by Margaret Cole, 1956, p 32) as a cottage with a comfortable study and delightful loggia; for her reflections on this renewal of relations with 'this exceptionally gifted pair' see *ibid.*, pp 130-31; and for LW's recollection of *her* fervour and appearance on this occasion, see *I LW*, pp 49-50.
2. Clive had announced his decision to break with Mary Hutchinson and to leave England for some months in order to write a book; he changed his mind several times, but eventually set out on 23 February to join Vanessa and Duncan at Cassis. VW's version of the matter at this time is given fully in her letters to Vanessa of 2 and 9 February (*III VW Letters*, nos. 1712, 1715); but the fluctuations of Clive's emotional life were apparent for some considerable time longer.

cant be right; things dont happen in one's mind like that. But she is very skilful & golden voiced.

This makes me think that I have to read To the L. tomorrow & Monday, straight through in print; straight through, owing to my curious methods, for the first time. I want to read largely & freely once: then to niggle over details.

But I am forgetting, after 3 days, the most important event in my life since marriage—so Clive described it: Bobo shingled me. Mr Cizec has bingled me.[3] I am short haired for life. Having no longer, I think, any claims to beauty, the convenience of this alone makes it desirable. Every morning I go to take up brush & twist that old coil round my finger & fix it with hairpins & then with a start of joy, no I needn't. In front there is no change; behind I'm like the rump of a partridge. This robs dining out of half its terrors; in token of which, I'm 'dining out' (the distinction is clear: Roger & Clive & Bloomsbury aint dining out) with Ethel [Sands] & with the [Hubert] Hendersons.

For the rest—its been a gay tropical kind of autumn, with so much Vita & Knole & staying away: we have launched ourselves a little more freely perhaps from work & the Press. But now with Nessa away, Clive away, Duncan away, Vita away, the strenuous time sets in: I'm reading & writing at a great pace; mean to 'do' Morgan;[4] have a fling at my book on fiction; & make all the money we want for Greece & a motor car. I may note that the first symptoms of Lighthouse are unfavourable. Roger, it is clear did not like Time Passes. Harpers & the Forum have refused serial rights; Brace writes, I think, a good deal less enthusiastically than of Mrs D. But these opinions refer to the rough copy, unrevised.[5] And

3. Beatrice ('Bobo') Mayor, *née* Meinertzhagen (1885-1971), wife of an Apostle and sister of the actress Betty Potter; she wrote plays. She and Clive, who were close friends at this time, dined with the Woolfs on 9 February. Charles Cizek was a hairdresser, of 116 Tottenham Court Road.

4. VW 'did' Morgan in her article 'The Novels of E. M. Forster' (Kp C292), not published until November in the *Atlantic Monthly*, though (as he had done with his article on her) she showed him a draft of it in June. Later in the year she also wrote on Forster's *Aspects of the Novel* (the published text of the Clark Lectures he was currently delivering at Cambridge) an article (Kp C288) which, though written considerably later, was published (in the *New York Herald Tribune*) before the one on his novels.

5. The centre section of *To the Lighthouse*, 'Time Passes', translated by Roger Fry's friend Charles Mauron, had been published in Paris in the Winter 1926 issue of *Commerce* (Kp D27). Fry wrote to his wife: 'To tell the truth I do not think this piece is quite of her best vintage' (see *II RF Letters*, no. 590). Both the English and American editions of *To the Lighthouse* were published on 5 May 1927 (Kp A10 a & b). From this diary entry it would appear that several proof copies

anyhow I feel callous: L.'s opinion keeps me steady; I'm neither one thing nor the other.

Yesterday Wells asked us to publish a pamphlet for him.[6] This is a great rise in the world for us; & comes on top of rather a flat talk with Angus. L. says he doesn't "manage". Angus refuses to budge an inch. He can't see the point of it. As he says, too, whats he to do if he leaves? He doesn't want to leave. Though sometimes 'fed up' he likes it better than most work. But I'm persuaded we need, the press needs, a fanatic at the moment; not this quiet easygoing gentlemanliness. I am annoyed at doing cards, & envelopes; & L. does twice the work I do.

Monday 21 February

Why not invent a new kind of play—as for instance
Woman thinks: . . .
He does.
Organ Plays.
She writes.
They say:
She sings:
Night speaks:
They miss

I think it must be something in this line—though I cant now see what. Away from facts: free; yet concentrated; prose yet poetry; a novel & a play.

But today is

Monday 28 February

& I have got into another stream of thought, if thought it can be called.

Let me collect a few logs, drifting in my mind, to represent the past few days.

Clive, standing at the door.

---

had been pulled (by R. & R. Clark, Edinburgh) and that three at least had been sent to America. There are discrepancies between the text of the English and of the American edition (printed for Harcourt Brace by Quinn & Boden Company, N.J.), notably in the section 'Time Passes'. It thus seems likely, particularly in view of Roger Fry's reported opinion, that VW made emendations on her proof which were effected by Clarks but not transmitted to America; and thus that the English edition embodies her final revision.

6. *Democracy Under Revision*, the text of a lecture to be given by H. G. Wells at the Sorbonne on 15 March 1927, was published by the Hogarth Press in March (*HP Checklist* 151).

She cries for the moon.

This was said of Mary. With it he went to Cassis for 3 months.

Again, If Mrs Woolf dont think me worth a penny stamp I said—this being Rose Bartholomew standing at her cottage door on Friday evening. Phrases suddenly seem to me very significant, & then I forget them. My brain is rather stale. Do I like The Lighthouse? I think I was disappointed. But God knows. I have to read it again.

A letter from Vita & Dottie just come. She is not an explicit letter writer. But I must be fond of her, genuinely, to start as I did at the sight of Dottie's hand, thinking she wrote to say V. was ill.

For the rest I think Cowper is a good poet. I'd like to write about him. Shall we go to Greece, Italy or France? I'm glad I didn't dedicate my book to Roger. This I verified in his presence, the other night [*23 February*]. He dined here with Raymond. Raymond is intellectually speaking underbred. Roger a pure aristocrat. Philip [Ritchie] came in, his little green eyes hazed bunged up with drink. So to Rodmell. And now the wind is making the tin screen over the gas fire rattle. How we protect ourselves from the elements! Coming back last night I thought, owing to civilisation, I, who am now cold, wet, & hungry, can be warm & satisfied & listening to a Mozart 4tet in 15 minutes. And so I was.

That ring may be Tom. No. Tom dont run upstairs—only the lower classes do that.

And I dont think I shall go out in the rain, though I am going to spend this week in long romantic London walks. I have successfully broken the neck of that screaming grey goose—society. There's nothing to be afraid of in dining with Ethel or Sibyl—& I'm shingled now. One spins round for a moment & then settles on one's feet. But about the Soul: the soul has sunk to the bottom. I am empty headed tonight, feeling the lack of Nessa rather, & all the prelude of Spring—the vague discomfort & melancholy & a feeling of having come to anchor. But I intend to work harder & harder. If they—the respectables, my friends, advise me against The Lighthouse, I shall write memoirs; have a plan already to get historical manuscripts & write Lives of the Obscure:[7] but why do I pretend I should take advice? After a holiday the old ideas will come to me as usual; seeming fresher, more important than ever; & I shall be off again, feeling that extraordinary exhilaration, that ardour & lust of creation—which is odd, if what I create is, as it well may be, wholly bad.

7. VW had already published two such 'Lives' (reprinted in *The Common Reader*); but her inclination to act as 'a deliverer advancing . . . to the rescue of some stranded ghost' was recurrent.

MARCH 1927

Today I bought a new watch. Last night I crept into L.'s bed to make up a sham quarrel about paying our fares to Rodmell. Now to finish Passage to India.

Saturday 5 March

Both rather headachy & fatigued. This is the last slope up of the year which is always worst. Finishing, correcting the last proofs that is to say, of a book is always a screw. Then I have written rather incessantly, one thing after another. A holiday, without dinner to order, or telephone to answer, or people to talk to, will be a divine miracle. We go to Cassis on the 30th; then to Sicily; so home by Rome. What could be more to my heart. Often I sit & think of looking at things. The greed of my eye is insatiable. To think of seeing a new place fills me with excitement. I now make up pictures of Sicily. Think of the Campagna grey in the evening.

I have been hard pressed about the Eliot fund, & behind the scenes of ladies diplomacy—Chrissie & Sibyl, that is:[1] so much suavity, so much distrust of each other, & so great a desire for compliments. Molly came to tea; could not get her mind off her troubles, first laughing at them— Desmond all right, & so on: then brushing laughter aside, & becoming more & more openly worried. Sibyl had cross examined her about her debts. To such indignities poverty exposes one. So I told her the truth, or what I hope will be the truth: that friends are subscribing enough to send them abroad, Oh how wonderful! she exclaimed, she never having seen Italy or Spain all these years. "I'm afraid Desmond has had rather an unhappy life," she said. "But then think of Lytton . . . Of course I was extravagant about doing the house up . . . but then we can let it." "Rachel goes for long walks at night & reads Coleridge—Oh Desmond's hopeless—he's like a dog who runs out if the door is open." So we laid our heads together over the fire; & felt very sisterly & sympathetic. I distrust though the pleasure one gets in helping one's friends.

Monday 14 March

Although annoyed that I have not heard from Vita by this post nor

1. The winding up of the abortive Eliot Fund (see *II VW Diary*, 19 July 1922, n 13; and *III VW Letters*, separately indexed) of which VW, Lady Ottoline Morrell and Richard Aldington were trustees, was protracted and not finally accomplished until January 1928. Now there was a scheme afoot, in which the prime movers were Christabel McLaren and Lady Colefax, to raise money for the perennially indigent MacCarthys, either to pay their debts, or to enable them to have a holiday abroad. To VW fell the task of transmitting a cheque for £300 to Molly MacCarthy; see *III VW Letters*, no. 1736 of 24 March 1927. See also LWP, Sussex, II D 17f, notebook labelled 'DM Fund March & April 1927'.

yet last week, annoyed sentimentally, & partly from vanity—still I must record the conception last night between 12 & one of a new book. I said I would be on the watch for symptoms of this extremely mysterious process. For some weeks, since finishing The Lighthouse I have thought myself virgin, passive, blank of ideas. I toyed vaguely with some thoughts of a flower whose petals fall; of time all telescoped into one lucid channel through wh. my heroine was to pass at will. The petals falling. But nothing came of it. I shirked the effort—seemed to have no impulse that way, supposed that I had worked out my vein. Faith Henderson came to tea, &, valiantly beating the waters of conversation, I sketched the possibilities which an unattractive woman, penniless, alone, might yet bring into being. I began imagining the position—how she would stop a motor on the Dover road, & so get to Dover: cross the channel: &c. It struck me, vaguely, that I might write a Defoe narrative for fun. Suddenly between twelve & one I conceived a whole fantasy to be called "The Jessamy Brides"—why, I wonder? I have rayed round it several scenes. Two women, poor, solitary at the top of a house. One can see anything (for this is all fantasy) the Tower Bridge, clouds, aeroplanes. Also old men listening in the room over the way. Everything is to be tumbled in pall mall. It is to be written as I write letters at the top of my speed: on the ladies of Llangollen; on Mrs Fladgate; on people passing.[2] No attempt is to be made to realise the character. Sapphism is to be suggested. Satire is to be the main note—satire & wildness. The Ladies are to have Constantinople in view. Dreams of golden domes. My own lyric vein is to be satirised. Everything mocked. And it is to end with three dots . . . so. For the truth is I feel the need of an escapade after these serious poetic

Orlando leading to The Waves. (July 8th 1933)

experimental books whose form is always so closely considered. I want to kick up my heels & be off. I want to embody all those innumerable little ideas & tiny stories which flash into my mind at all seasons. I think this will be great fun to write; & it will rest my head before starting the very serious, mystical poetical work which I want to come next. Meanwhile, before I can touch the Jessamy Brides, I have to write my book on fiction & that wont be done till January, I suppose. I might dash off a page or two now & then by way of experiment. And it is possible that the idea will evaporate. Anyhow this records the odd hurried unexpected way in which these things suddenly create themselves—one thing on top of another in about an

2. Lady Eleanor Butler (1739-1829) and the Hon. Sarah Ponsonby (1755-1831) foreswore matrimony and retreated to Plas Newydd overlooking Llangollen, where they became celebrated as eccentrics. Mrs Fladgate unidentified.

hour. So I made up Jacob's Room looking at the fire at Hogarth House; so I made up The Lighthouse one afternoon in the square here.

Monday 21 March

This is the kind of evening when one seems to be abroad: the window is open; the yellows & greys of the houses seem exposed to the summer; there is that rumour & clamour which reminds one of Italy. Almost in a week now we shall be starting. I dislike the days before going. I went to buy clothes today & was struck by my own ugliness. Like Edith Sitwell I can never look like other people—too broad, tall, flat, with hair hanging. And now my neck is so ugly . . . But I never think of this at home.

How disturbing the summer is! We shall sit reading with the windows open tonight, but my mind will only just touch the page & float off. Something unsettled & melancholy will be in the air. Also it seems the threshold of that vast burning London summer, which alarms me slightly, Vita & Harold will be back; my book will be out. We shall sit in the Square. But I shall not let things worry me much. (so I say—but it is still only March.) We shall have a week at Cassis—a strange resurrection of us all abroad. Many years have gone since Nessa, Clive & I met there. Never with Leonard of course.[3]

My brain is ferociously active. I want to have at my books as if I were conscious of the lapse of time, age & death. Dear me, how lovely some parts of The Lighthouse are! Soft & pliable, & I think deep, & never a word wrong for a page at a time. This I feel about the dinner party, & the children in the boat; but not of Lily on the lawn. That I do not much like. But I like the end.

I get too many letters to answer nowadays. Edith Sitwell came to tea: transparent like some white bone one picks up on a moor, with sea water stones on her long frail hands which slide into yours much narrower than one expects like a folded fan. She has pale gemlike eyes; & is dressed, on a windy March day, in three decker skirts of red spotted cotton. She half shuts her eyes; coos an odd little laugh, reminding me of the Fishers [*VW's cousins*]. All is very tapering & pointed, the nose running on like a mole. She said I was a great writer, which pleased me. So sensitive to everything in people & books she said. She got talking about her mother, blaspheming in the nursery, hysterical, terrible; setting Edith to kill bluebottles. 'But nobody can take a liberty with her' said Edith, who prides herself on Angevin blood. She is a curious product, likable to me:

3. VW had gone to Italy with Clive and Vanessa Bell both in 1908 and 1909.

sensitive, etiolated, affectionate, lonely, having to thread her way (there is something ghostlike & angular about her) home to Bayswater to help cook dinner. She said she would like to attach great bags & balloons of psychology, people having dinner, &c, to her poems, but has no knowledge of human nature, only these sudden intense poems—which by the way she has sent me.[4] In other ages she would have been a cloistered nun; or an eccentric secluded country old maid. It is the oddity of our time that has set her on the music hall stage. She trips out into the Limelight with all the timidity & hauteur of the aristocratic spinster.

On 30 March the Woolfs set out on a month's holiday, travelling via Paris to Cassis, where they again stayed at the Hotel Cendrillon but spent most of their days with the Bells and Duncan Grant at the Villa Corsica. On 6 April they left Toulon by train for Rome, going on next day to Palermo, where they stayed five days before moving on to Syracuse. On the return journey they spent three nights in Naples and a week in Rome, and came home to Tavistock Square late on 28 April. VW's letters give a spirited and detailed account of their travels; see III VW Letters, nos. 1741-7.

Sunday 1 May

We came back on Thursday night from Rome; from that other private life which I mean to have for ever now. There is a complete existence in Italy: apart from this. One is nobody in Italy: one has no name, no calling, no background. And, then, not only is there the beauty, but a different relationship. Altogether I dont think I've ever enjoyed one month so much. What a faculty of enjoyment one has! I liked everything. I wish I were not so ignorant of Italian, art, literature & so on. However, I cannot now write this out, or go into the great mass of feeling which it composed in me. Nelly was found, at 11.30, when we got back, in bed, with some mysterious affection of the kidney. This was a jar; the coffee was a jar; everything was a jar. And then I remember how my book is coming out. People will say I am irreverent—people will say a thousand things. But

4. Edith was the eldest and conspicuously unloved child of Sir George and his tempestuous wife Lady Ida, a daughter of the Earl of Londesborough, whom he had selected for her distinguished pedigree without regard to her character or feelings. After a miserable childhood and youth, Edith managed to leave home in 1914, since when she had lived in a 3-room flat in Pembridge Mansions, Moscow Road, with her ex-governess. (See *Façades: Edith, Osbert & Sacheverell Sitwell* by John Pearson, 1978.) The copy of her just published *Rustic Elegies*, inscribed to VW, was sold at Sotheby's on 27 April 1970, lot 88.

I think, honestly, I care very little this time—even for the opinion of my friends. I am not sure if it is good. I was disappointed when I read it through the first time. Later I liked it. Anyhow it is the best I can do. But would it be a good thing to read my things when they are printed, critically? It is encouraging that, in spite of obscurity, affectation & so on, my sales rise steadily. We have sold, already, 1220 before publication, & I think it will be about 1500, which for a writer like I am is not bad. Yet, to show I am genuine, I find myself thinking of other things with absorption & forgetting that it will be out on Thursday. Leonard never thinks of his book. Vita comes back on Friday. I am angry with Clive for gossiping about my letter to Nessa.[1] It is fine, cold, clear, we dine out, have a char.

Thursday 5 May

Book out. We have sold (I think) 1690 before publication—twice Dalloway. I write however in the shadow of the damp cloud of the Times Lit Sup. review, which is an exact copy of the JsR. Mrs Dalloway review, gentlemanly, kindly, timid & praising beauty, doubting character, & leaving me moderately depressed.[2] I am anxious about Time Passes. Think the whole thing may be pronounced soft, shallow, insipid, sentimental. Yet, honestly, don't much care; want to be let alone to ruminate. Odd how strong this feeling is in me. Now I think we are safe to get our motor car. The next fortnight we shall both be depressed about our books.

Dined with the Wests last night, all solid, shiny, spread & spacious; as if they were settling in; wedding presents; clean covers, carpets, &c. all too handsome for my taste.[3] I'm reverting to squalor as my milieu. And then why did she marry him? He is the type of any other cleverish young journalist, common, glib: uneasy last night, lest we should talk of Angus. But we talked of Madge.

I know why I am depressed: a bad habit of making up the review I should like before reading the review I get. I am excited about my article

1. VW's full and rapturous letters to Vanessa from Sicily and Italy had been read aloud to Clive and Duncan at Cassis, and Clive had retailed their contents to friends met in Paris on his return there. See *III VW Letters*, nos. 1748, 1750.
2. The *TLS* unsigned review of *To the Lighthouse* appeared on 5 May 1927, the day of its publication (*M & M*, p 193); for those of *Jacob's Room* and *Mrs Dalloway*, see also *M & M*, pp 95 and 160.
3. Katherine (Kitty) Leaf had married the journalist Douglas Hammill West on 22 January 1927; they were living at 23 Walpole Street, Chelsea.

on Poetry & Fiction. Writing for an audience always stirs me. I hope to avoid too many jokes.[4] Then Vita will come tomorrow. But I dont want people: I want solitude; Rome.

Nelly away; Pinker [*dog*] away; Clive coming back; Opera in swing; Francis to see me about writing; fine spring weather.

Wednesday 11 May

Vita back; unchanged, though I daresay one's relation changes from day to day. Clive & she together. I think Clive is pretty miserable: his stay at Cassis a failure, so far as writing goes. And then the question rises, has he not gone too far in eating, drinking, love making, to stop dead now? He seemed random & unsettled, much as when he left, only now with no absolute hard arm to cling to, as he fancied when he went to Cassis. He talked (always shifting away from himself yet returning, ambiguously to that centre) about going mad: sometimes thought he was going mad; then how one's life was over; one was spent, played out; this was clear when one saw Julian & Quentin. After all, its an ignominious position to have made the grand refusal, & gone back on it. Mary was at the opera, on a hot evening like this think of listening to Wagner, he said. There's Saxon upstairs, Mary & Sibyl Colefax below. This was all said half enviously, yet doubtfully; as if not knowing what line to take.

My book. What is the use of saying one is indifferent to reviews when positive praise, though mingled with blame, gives one such a start on, that instead of feeling dried up, one feels, on the contrary, flooded with ideas? I gather from vague hints, through Margery Joad, through Clive, that some people say it is my best book. So far Vita praises; Dotty enthuses; an unknown donkey writes. No one has yet read it to the end, I daresay; & I shall hover about, not anxious but worried for 2 more weeks, when it will be over.

Monday 16 May

The book. Now on its feet so far as praise is concerned. It has been out 10 days—Thursday a week ago. Nessa enthusiastic—a sublime, almost upsetting spectacle. She says it is an amazing portrait of mother; a supreme portrait painter; has lived in it; found the rising of the dead almost painful.

4. VW's article, 'Poetry, Fiction and the Future', first given as a lecture at Oxford (see below 6 June 1927, n 1), was published in the *New York Herald Tribune* on 14 and 21 August 1927 (Kp C284), and posthumously in *Granite and Rainbow* as 'The Narrow Bridge of Art'—a title perhaps given by LW.

Then Ottoline, then Vita, then Charlie [Sanger], then Lord Olivier, then Tommie, then Clive:[5] poor Clive—he came in, ostensibly to praise this 'amazing book—far the best you've ever written' but found Eddie who imposed himself resolutely, sharply; & so sat on, but how wandering & unhappy. I have scarcely seen him in this mood ever before—like a person awaked from a sweet dream. But what is it? A disillusionment? A shock? He sees Mary. Has he lost faith? Has the dancing mist of rhapsody failed him—he who was based so solidly on such beef & beer or champagne rather. Suppose one woke & found oneself a fraud? It was part of my madness—that horror. But then as Clive said, you go mad but you bound up again—the inference being that he was to stay mad.

Sold 1802 of The L.: if it makes 3,000 I shall be as they say more than content. Mervyn [Arnold-Forster] dead—did I record; & I haunted for a time by the sight of his prim pinched face, with the nice blue eyes, so suddenly stilled: so unseasonably. The eye plays a large part in these affairs.

This it did on July 13th

Monday 6 June (Whit Monday)

I have been in bed a week with a sudden & very sharp headache, & this is written experimentally to test my brain. It is a horrid dull damp Bank holiday morning—(here L. comes in & we spend fifteen minutes discussing advertisements. The L. has sold 2,200 & we are reprinting). Nessa says its ugly weather when I ring up to offer her half a bottle of turpentine to paint her cupboard with.

But I would like to learn to write a steady plain narrative style. Then perhaps I could catch up with the last few weeks; describe my visit to Oxford;[1] & how I lunched with Clive & dined with Dadie & stood in the basement printing Gottstalk with a great sense of shade & shelter. I like the obscure anonymity of the Press better a good deal than I like Voltaire

5. Vanessa's letter to VW about *To the Lighthouse* is given in the Appendix to *III VW Letters*. Lady Ottoline's letter (14 May 1927) is in MHP, Sussex: 'The Beauty of it is overwhelming—especially to *me* the 2d Part—"Time Passes" . . . All these pages marked & marked, for they seem to me some of the loveliest pages in English prose.' Lord Olivier (see above, 14 May 1925, n 17) was a great admirer of VW's books, but his matter-of-fact comments upon *To the Lighthouse* riled her (see *III VW Letters*, no. 1760).

1. VW had been invited to speak to an audience of undergraduates of both sexes at Oxford on 18 May, and persuaded Vita Sackville-West to accompany her (see *III VW Letters*, no. 1760). Her subject was 'Poetry, Fiction and the Future'. See above, 5 May 1927, n 4.

by Riding.[2] And now, with Morgan's morganatic, evasive, elusive letter this morning, The Lighthouse is behind me:[3] my headache over; & after a week at Rodmell, my freedom from inspection, my deep dive into my own mind will begin.

How odd, it comes into my mind, is Nessa & my jealousy of each other's clothes! I feel her, when I put on my smart black fringed cape, anguished for a second: did I get it from Champco? in the same way I run my eye over her Paris dress, & compare it with my last year's Brooke.[4] Then she says she is going to wear earrings: I say at once that I will; this she resents. Yet, we are both fundamentally sensible, & soon recover from our umbrage.

I think, however, I am now almost an established figure—as a writer. They dont laugh at me any longer. Soon they will take me for granted. Possibly I shall be a celebrated writer. Anyhow, The Lighthouse is much more nearly a success, in the usual sense of the word, than any other book of mine.

A great knot of people came together suddenly last week, or the week before. Tom—so glad to gossip with me off handedly over a cup—no 6 cups—of tea; then he played the gramophone: & Logan, pink & spruce, doing his trick of culture & urbanity & good sense very efficiently.[5] He had been evoking the spirit of Henry James with Desmond in Paris. (Sibyl, by the way, takes to herself all credit for that fund, I observe. Sibyl, Clive & Raymond say, has sold her soul to the devil, & he's now come to fetch it—This phrase is common to them both, & gives the measure of

2. In October 1926 the Woolfs had published a collection of poems called *The Close Chaplet* (*HP Checklist* 91) by Laura Riding Gottschalk (b. 1901), an American poet who had come to England in December 1925, and was associated with Robert Graves. *Voltaire: A Biographical Fantasy*, a long poem written in 1921, was hand-printed at 52 Tavistock Square and published in November 1927 (*HP Checklist* 145). The author's name was printed on the title-page as Laura Riding Gottschalk; but Gottschalk was partially obliterated by overprinting with two 6 pt black rules and did not recur in her subsequent publications.

3. Forster's letter, in MHP, Sussex (copy) is dated from Cambridge on 5 June 1927. 'It is awfully sad, very beautiful . . .; it stirs me much more to questions of whether & why than anything else you have written. . . . I am inclined to think it your best work.'

4. Mme Elspeth Champcommunal (d. 1976), widow of a French painter and a friend of Roger Fry, had been editor of British *Vogue* from 1916 to 1922, when Dorothy Todd succeeded her. Miss Brooke was a dressmaker recommended to VW by the latter the previous year.

5. VW gave tea to T. S. Eliot on Monday 23 May, and the following day to Logan Pearsall Smith, Faith Henderson and Vita and Eddy Sackville-West, after lunching with Clive Bell, Dadie Rylands and Lady Violet Bonham Carter.

smart talk at lunch parties.) Lytton, too, I saw: an invalid after an attack of love, the most desperate since Duncan. We talked, with poor marble eyed Cynthia Noble attentive, as far as she can be, about the O'B. & his life.[6] I often glide into intimacy with Lytton about books. He is enthusiastic, his mind bare, his attention extremely alive, about books; whereas, about love, its more cryptic. Dadie & Douglas were both starched & powdered like pasteboard young men at the ballet;[7] legs quite straight; heads curled; shirts granulated; they were going on to Kitchin's party, to be bored, as they knew; but in perfect trim for it. This Lytton does not quite achieve. We dined ostentatiously rather, it being part of the game to order food from Fortnum & Mason's; part of the pathetic, rather attractive, yet also foolish, showing off, very youthful game of being precisely like other people.

Saturday 18 June

This is a terribly thin diary for some reason: half the year has been spent, & left only these few sheets. Perhaps I have been writing too hard in the morning to write here also. Three weeks wiped out by headache. We had a week at Rodmell, of which I remember various sights, suddenly unfolding before me spontaneously (for example, the village standing out to sea in the June night, houses seeming ships, the marsh a fiery foam) & the immense comfort of lying there lapped in peace. I lay out all day in the new garden, with the terrace. It is already being made. There were blue tits nested in the hollow neck of my Venus.[8] Vita came over one very hot afternoon, & we walked to the river with her. Pinker now swims after

6. For the fluctuations of Lytton Strachey's last great love affair, with Roger Senhouse, see *Holroyd*, ch. 16, 6. Cynthia was the younger daughter of the wealthy Saxton Noble and his cultivated and musical wife, a notable hostess in the world of diplomacy and the arts. Oscar Browning (1837-1923), an Apostle, always known as the 'O.B.', was a lifelong Fellow of King's, to which he returned after fifteen years as an Eton Housemaster; a provocative, stimulating and controversial teacher and educationalist, he was a very prominent Cambridge 'character'. A recently published life of him by H. E. Wortham provided VW's story about Browning and the stable boy in *A Room of One's Own* (p 81).
7. On 24 May, the day of Clive's lunch and VW's own tea-party, the Woolfs, Lytton Strachey and Cynthia Noble had dined at 37 Gordon Square (where they had rented rooms from Vanessa) with Dadie Rylands and Douglas Davidson, Angus's younger brother who, after taking a degree at Cambridge, was now a painter. Fortnum & Mason was and is the grand Piccadilly store specialising in high class provisions. Two days later VW had a headache and was ill for a week before going to Rodmell on 7 June.
8. A headless plaster cast from the antique which stood on a wall in the garden.

Leonard's stick. I read—any trash. Maurice Baring; sporting memoirs. Slowly ideas began trickling in; & then suddenly I rhapsodised (the night L. dined with the apostles) & told over the story of the Moths, which I think I will write very quickly, perhaps in between chapters of that long impending book on fiction.[9] Now the moths will I think fill out the skeleton which I dashed in here: the play-poem idea: the idea of some

The Waves

continuous stream, not solely of human thought, but of the ship, the night&c, all flowing together: intersected by the arrival of the bright moths. A man & a woman are to be sitting at table talking. Or shall they remain silent? It is to be a love story: she is finally to let the last great moth in. The contrasts might be something of this sort: she might talk, or think, about the age of the earth: the death of humanity: then moths keep on coming. Perhaps the man could be left absolutely dim. France: near the sea; at night; a garden under the window. But it needs ripening. I do a little work on it in the evening when the gramophone is playing late Beethoven sonatas. (The windows fidget at their fastenings as if we were at sea.)

We have been to Hyde Park, where the Church boys were marching; officers on horses in their cloaks like equestrian statues.[10] Always this kind of scene gives me the notion of human beings playing a game, greatly, I suppose, to their own satisfaction.

We saw Vita given the Hawthornden.[11] A horrid show up, I thought: not of the gentry on the platform—Squire, Drinkwater, Binyon only—of us all: all of us chattering writers. My word! how insignificant we all looked! How can we pretend that we are interesting, that our works matter? The whole business of writing became infinitely distasteful. There was no one I could care whether he read, liked, or disliked "my writing". And no one could care for my criticism either: the mildness, the conventionality of them all struck me. But there may be a stream of ink in them that matters more than the look of them—so tightly clothed, mild,

9. Vanessa had written on 3 May from the Villa Corsica at Cassis describing how they were beset by moths of a night-time (see *II QB*, p 126); VW was fascinated, and contemplated a story on the theme—the genesis of what was eventually to become *The Waves*. (VW had followed LW back to London on 14 June, the night of the Apostles' dinner.)
10. On the afternoon of Saturday, 18 June, over 6,000 members of the Church Lads' Brigade marched from Wellington and Chelsea Barracks to the parade ground near Marble Arch, where they were inspected by the Prince of Wales.
11. At a ceremony in the Æolian Hall, Bond Street, on 16 June, John Drinkwater presented the Hawthornden Prize for the best literary production of 1926 to V. Sackville-West for her long poem *The Land*; J. C. Squire and Laurence Binyon (1896-1943), poet and art-historian, were also on the selection committee.

& decorous—showed. I felt there was no one full grown mind among us. In truth, it was the thick dull middle class of letters that met; not the aristocracy. Vita cried at night.

Wednesday 22 June

Woman haters depress me, & both Tolstoi & Mrs Asquith hate women. I suppose my depression is a form of vanity. But then so are all strong opinions on both sides. I hate Mrs A.'s hard, dogmatic empty style. But enough: I shall write about her tomorrow:[12] I write every day about something, & have deliberately set apart a few weeks to money making, so that I may put £50 in each of our pockets by September. This will be the first money of my own since I married. I never felt the need of it till lately. And I can get it, if I want it, but shirk writing for money.

Clive's father died yesterday.[13] Harold Nicolson & Duncan dined with us, & Nessa came in afterwards, very silent, inscrutable &, perhaps critical. As a family we distrust anyone outside our set, I think. We too definitely decide that so & so has not the necessary virtues. I daresay Harold has not got them; at the same time, there is a good deal in him I like: he is quick & rash & impulsive; not in our sense, very clever; uneasy; seeming young; on the turn from diplomat to intellectual; not Vita's match; but honest & cordial. L. says he's too commonplace. I liked my little duet with him. He wears a green, or blue, shirt & tie; is sunburnt; chubby, pert[?]; vivacious. Talked of politics, but was flimsy compared with Leonard—I thought. Said it was with L. & me that he felt completely at his ease. Told stories wh. sound rather empty in the bare Bloomsbury rooms.

Thursday 23 June

This diary shall batten on the leanness of my social life. Never have I spent so quiet a London summer. It is perfectly easy to slip out of the crush unobserved. I have set up my standard as an invalid, & no one bothers me. No one asks me to do anything. Vainly, I have the feeling that this is of my choice, not theirs; & there is a luxury in being quiet in the heart of chaos. Directly I talk & exert my wits in talk I get a dull damp rather headachy day. Quiet brings me cool clear quick mornings, in which

12. VW's unsigned review of Margot Asquith (Lady Oxford)'s *Lay Sermons* appeared under the title 'The Governess of Downing Street' in the *N & A* of 30 July 1927 (Kp C283·1).

13. William Heward Bell, colliery owner and a director of the Great Western Railway, died at his Wiltshire home on 21 June, aged 78. Harold Nicolson had finally returned, with Vita, from Persia early in May; and Duncan and Vanessa from France early in June.

I dispose of a good deal of work, & toss my brain into the air when I take a walk. I shall feel some triumph if I skirt a headache this summer.

I sat with Nessa in the Square yesterday. Angelica sends Pinker after a ball. Nessa & I sit on the seat & gossip. She is to see Mary; she is to go to old Bell's funeral. She is learning to motor. She has sold a picture. The point of Clive's affair is that Mary is in love with another. This point was carefully hidden before Easter. His vanity was careful to hide it: her discretion. So I got my version out of proportion. The truth is odd enough though. Unless she will bed with him he is distracted. That she will not do; yet, for lack of him, is distracted herself. The love affair rather increases on her side. It is said to be for someone low in the world. This inclines us to think it Lord Ivor. But the point is one for curiosity only.

Vita's book [*The Land*] verberates & reverberates in the Press. A prize poem—that's my fling at it—for with some relics of jealousy, or it may be of critical sense, I can't quite take the talk of poetry & even great poetry seriously. But the subject & the manner, so smooth, so mild, may be what I dislike; & perhaps I am corrupt. I wonder what I should think if I could get a cool look at some writing of my own.

Oh & Sibyl has dropped me: & I don't feel the fall.

What is then the abiding truth in this phantasmagoria, I ask myself, seeking as I often do some little nugget of pure gold. I think, often, I have the happiest of lives, in having discovered stability. Now one stable moment vanquishes chaos. But this I said in The Lighthouse. We have now sold, I think, 2555 copies.

I am distressed by my failure to make cigarettes. I had a lesson from a man in Francis Street—cant do a thing with my fingers. Angelica is expert with hers already. Nessa says all painters are: this is a perquisite they get thrown in with their gift.

And Adrian came to tea on Sunday, & fairly sparkled. At last I think he has emerged. Even his analysis will be over this year. At the age of 43 he will be educated & ready to start life. I remember Harry Stephen saying that he had his fingers on the gear—the Indian judgeship that is to say—about then.[14] So we Stephens mature late. And our late flowers are rare & splendid. Think of my books, Nessa's pictures—it takes us an age to bring our faculties into play. And now I must write to Ethel Sands, & perhaps, go to the Ballet.[15]

14. Adrian Stephen, on the road to becoming a psychoanalyst, had completed his medical training in 1926; his cousin, Sir Harry Lushington Stephen (1860-1945), was made a judge of the High Court in Calcutta in 1901.

15. VW did write to Ethel Sands (*III VW Letters*, no. 1778), but did not go to the ballet (Diaghileff's season at the Princes Theatre).

Thursday 30 June

Now I must sketch out the Eclipse.[16]

About 10 on Tuesday night several very long trains, accurately filled (ours with civil servants) left King's Cross. In our carriage was Vita & Harold[,] Quentin, L. & I. This is Hatfield I daresay, I said. I was smoking a cigar. Then again, This is Peterborough, L. said. Before it got dark we kept looking at the sky: soft fleecy; but there was one star, over Alexandra Park. Look Vita, that's Alexandra Park, said Harold. The Nicolsons got sleepy: H. curled up with his head on V.'s knee. She looked like Sappho by Leighton, asleep; so we plunged through the midlands; made a very long stay at York. Then at 3 we got out our sandwiches, & I came in from the wc to find Harold being rubbed clean of cream. Then he broke the china sandwich box. Here L. laughed without restraint. Then we had another doze, or the N.'s did; then here was a level crossing, at which were drawn up a long line of motor omnibuses & motors, all burning pale yellow lights. It was getting grey—still a fleecy mottled sky. We got to Richmond about 3.30: it was cold, & the N.'s had a quarrel, Eddie said, about V.'s luggage. We went off in the omnibus, saw a vast castle (who does that belong to said Vita, who is interested in Castles). It had a front window added, & a light I think burning. All the fields were aburn with June grasses & red tasselled plants, none coloured as yet, all pale. Pale & grey too were the little uncompromising Yorkshire farms. As we passed one, the farmer, & his wife & sister came out, all tightly & tidily dressed in black, as if they were going to church. At another ugly square farm, two women were looking out of the upper windows. These had white blinds drawn down half across them. We were a train of 3 vast cars, one stopping to let the others go on; all very low & powerful; taking immensely steep hills. The driver once got out & put a small stone behind our wheel—inadequate. An accident would have been natural. There were also many motor cars. These suddenly increased as we crept up to the top of Bardon Fell. Here were people camping beside their cars. We got out, & found ourselves very high, on a moor, boggy, heathery, with butts for grouse shooting. There were grass tracks here & there, & people had already taken up positions. So we joined them, walking out to what seemed the highest point looking over Richmond. One light burnt down there. Vales & moors stretched, slope after slope, round us. It was like the Haworth country. But over Richmond, where the sun was rising, was a

16. Special trains were run from London to North Yorkshire, which was within the belt of totality for the total eclipse of the sun on 29 June 1927—the first to be visible in Britain for over 200 years. In London bad weather completely obscured the phenomenon.

soft grey cloud. We could see by a gold spot where the sun was. But it was early yet. We had to wait, stamping to keep warm. Ray [Strachey] had wrapped herself in the blue striped blanket off a double bed. She looked incredibly vast & bedroomish. Saxon looked very old. Leonard kept looking at his watch. Four great red setters came leaping over the moor. There were sheep feeding behind us. Vita had tried to buy a guinea pig— Quentin advised a savage[17]—so she observed the animals from time to time. There were thin places in the cloud, & some complete holes. The question was whether the sun would show through a cloud or through one of these hollow places when the time came. We began to get anxious. We saw rays coming through the bottom of the clouds. Then, for a moment we saw the sun, sweeping—it seemed to be sailing at a great pace & clear in a gap; we had out our smoked glasses; we saw it crescent, burning red; next moment it had sailed fast into the cloud again; only the red streamers came from it; then only a golden haze, such as one has often seen. The moments were passing. We thought we were cheated; we looked at the sheep; they showed no fear; the setters were racing round; everyone was standing in long lines, rather dignified, looking out. I thought how we were like very old people, in the birth of the world—druids on Stonehenge: (this idea came more vividly in the first pale light though;) At the back of us were great blue spaces in the cloud. These were still blue. But now the colour was going out. The clouds were turning pale; a reddish black colour. Down in the valley it was an extraordinary scrumble of red & black; there was the one light burning; all was cloud down there, & very beautiful, so delicately tinted. Nothing could be seen through the cloud. The 24 seconds were passing. Then one looked back again at the blue: & rapidly, very very quickly, all the colours faded; it became darker & darker as at the beginning of a violent storm; the light sank & sank: we kept saying this is the shadow; & we thought now it is over—this is the shadow when suddenly the light went out. We had fallen. It was extinct. There was no colour. The earth was dead. That was the astonishing moment: & the next when as if a ball had rebounded, the cloud took colour on itself again, only a sparky aetherial colour & so the light came back. I had very strongly the feeling as the light went out of some vast obeisance; something kneeling down, & low & suddenly raised up, when the colours came. They came back astonishingly lightly & quickly & beautifully in the valley & over the hills The colour for some moments was of the most lovely kind—fresh, various —here blue, & there brown: all new colours, as if washed over & repainted.

17. QB can shed no light on this wild recommendation.

—at first with a miraculous glittering & aetheriality, later normally almost, but with a great sense of relief. It was like recovery. We had been much worse than we had expected. We had seen the world dead. This was within the power of nature. Our greatness had been apparent too. Now we became Ray in a blanket, Saxon in a cap &c. We were bitterly cold. I should say that the cold had increased as the light went down. One felt very livid. Then—it was over till 1999. What remained was a sense of the comfort which we get used to, of plenty of light & colour. This for some time seemed a definitely welcome thing. Yet when it became established all over the country, one rather missed the sense of its being a relief & a respite, which one had had when it came back after the darkness. How can I express the darkness? It was a sudden plunge, when one did not expect it: being at the mercy of the sky: our own nobility: the druids; Stonehenge; & the racing red dogs; all that was in ones mind. Also, to be picked out of ones London drawing room & set down on the wildest moors in England was impressive. For the rest, I remember trying to keep awake in the gardens at York while Eddy talked & falling asleep. Asleep again in the train. It was hot & we were merry. The carriage was full of things. Harold was very kind & attentive: Eddy was peevish. Roast beef & pineapple chunks, he said. We got home at 8.30 perhaps.

Monday 4 July

Back from Long Barn.[1] Thank heaven, I never had to change my dress. Such opulence & freedom, flowers all out, butler, silver, dogs, biscuits, wine, hot water, log fires, Italian cabinets, Persian rugs, books—this was the impression it made: as of stepping into a rolling gay sea, with nicely crested waves: as if the anxious worn life had suddenly been set on springs, & went bounding, springing for the week end. Yet I like this room better perhaps: more effort & life in it, to my mind, unless this is the prejudice one has naturally in favour of the display of one's own character. Vita very opulent, in her brown velvet coat with the baggy pockets, pearl necklace, & slightly furred cheeks. (They are like saviours flannel, of which she picked me a great bunch, in texture[2]) Of its kind this is the best, most representative human life I know: I mean, certain gifts & qualities & good fortunes are here miraculously combined—I liked Harold too.

1. The Woolfs went to stay with the Nicolsons at Long Barn on Saturday, 2 July; LW returned to Tavistock Square on Sunday evening, and VW on Monday.
2. Presumably *Stachys Lanate*, known variously as Saviour's Blanket, Jesus's Blanket, Lamb's, Donkey's or Rabbit's Ears.

He is a spontaneous childlike man, of no great boring power; has a mind that bounces when he drops it; he opens his eyes as he looks at one; has a little immature moustache; curled hair; an air of immaturity which is welcome. I should judge him very generous & kind hearted; an Englishman overlaid with culture; coming of a sunburnt country stock; & not much fined even by diplomacy. After dinner last night we discussed the Empire. "I prefer Sydney to Paris. Australia is more important than France. After all, its our younger sons out there. I feel proud of it. The point is, Raymond, our English genius is for government." "The governed don't seem to enjoy it" said Raymond. Silly ass, said Harold. "We do our job: disinterestedly; we dont think of ourselves, as the French do, as the Germans do. Take the British oil fields. There's a hospital there where they take any one, employee or not. The natives come from all over the place. Don't tell me thats not a good thing. And they trust us." So on to the system of bribery; to the great age of England being the age of colonial expansion. "I grant Shakespeare's a nasty snag." "But why not grow, change?" I said. Also, I said, recalling the aeroplanes that had flown over us, while the portable wireless played dance music on the terrace, "can't you see that nationality is over? All divisions are now rubbed out, or about to be." Raymond vehemently assented. Raymond is all for the triumph of mind. What action matters? Actions matter most of all, said Harold. I was sitting on a carved Italian stool over the log fire; he & Raymond bedded in the soft green sofa. Leonard's injustice to the aristocracy was discussed. Before this, Lord Sackville & Mrs Rubens had come over, partly to protect their respectability, partly to play tennis. (They won't stay at Knole alone if possible; & if they must, sanctify the proceeding by calling on Vita). He is a smooth worn man, inheriting noble nose & chin which he has not put much into himself; a straight, young looking man, save that his face has the lack lustre of a weak man whose life has proved too much for him. No longer does he struggle much for happiness, I imagine; accepts resignedly; & goes to Maidstone almost daily, as part of the routine of his nobility. He plays golf; he plays tennis. He thinks Bernard Darwin must be a man of surpassing brain power.[3] We sat together under a vast goat skin coat of Vita's, watching them play, & I found him smooth & ambling as a blood horse, but obliterated, obfusc, with his great Sackville eyes drooping, & his face all clouded with red & brown. One figured a screw or other tool whose worms & edges have been rubbed smooth, so that though they shine, plaid silver, they no longer grip.

3. Bernard Darwin (1876-1961), son of Sir Francis Darwin and step-son of VW's cousin Florence (Fisher), was golf correspondent of the *Times* and *Country Life* and a prolific writer on a variety of subjects.

Vita very free & easy, always giving me great pleasure to watch, & recalling some image of a ship breasting a sea, nobly, magnificently, with all sails spread, & the gold sunlight on them. As for her poetry, or intelligence, save when canalised in the traditional channels, I can say nothing very certain. She never breaks fresh ground. She picks up what the tide rolls to her feet. For example, she follows, with simple instinct, all the inherited tradition of furnishing, so that her house is gracious, glowing, stately, but without novelty or adventure. So with her poetry, I daresay. Raymond & I travelled up & discussed them. She the most noble character he said; both almost defiantly fortunate, so that Harold touches wood when he reflects on his own life, heaves a sigh & says how, if it were dashed down tomorrow, he would have had his day. But it wont be dashed down at all. It will grow freely & fully round them both; their fruit will ripen, & their leaves golden; & the night will be indigo blue, with a soft gold moon. They lack only what we have—some cutting edge; some invaluable idiosyncracy, intensity, for which I would not have all the sons & all the moons in the world.

Monday 11 July[4]

Waiting for what I do not exactly know. In a mood of random restlessness—Nelly having for 125th time 'given notice' this morning. Shall I go to Ashley Gardens [*Registry Office*] & engage Mrs Collins & her daughter? I am sick of the timid spiteful servant mind; yet perhaps Mrs Collins will be of the same feather. Never mind.

A great storm has torn off one wing of my double windows. But I have never mentioned the absorbing subject—the subject which has filled our thoughts to the exclusion of Clive & Mary & literature & death & life—motor cars. Every evening we go round with Pinker for a game in Gordon Sqre—I talk as if the evenings had been fine—no, we sit there in between the sulphur coloured storms; under the shelter of trees with the rain pattering between the leaves.[5] We talk of nothing but cars. Then, sometimes, word is brought that Mrs Bell is at the door in her car. I rush out, & find her, rather nervously in control of a roomy shabby Renault with Fred beside her. Three times I have been for a little tour with her. And yesterday we commissioned Fred to find us & bring instantly to our door,

---

4. VW has misdated this entry *10 July*; in it she refers to 'Clive's party' which in fact was a dinner party on 11 July (he was at his mother's in Wiltshire on the 10th).
5. The *Times* of 11 July 1927 reported great thunderstorms with consequent heavy flooding and damage in London.

a Singer. We have decided on a Singer.[6] And, the reason why I am distracted now is that Fred is going to ring me up & say if I am to have my first lesson this evening. The sun is shining; the trees dripping. Possibly I may go.

This is a great opening up in our lives. One may go to Bodiam, to Arundel, explore the Chichester downs, expand that curious thing, the map of the world in ones mind. It will I think demolish loneliness, & may of course imperil complete privacy. The Keynes' have one too—a cheap one. Nessa thinks it will break down at once. Nessa takes a very sinister view of the Keynes'. She anticipates ruin of every sort for them, with some pleasure too. Here's Leonard—So then I tell him about the storm, about the telephones, & about Pinker. Then Sibyl who has cut me these 3 months, suddenly writes to say she has been 'unwell', & will I come to tea. No I wont. And now I must quickly dress for Clive's party, where I am to meet Cory & Nessa & Duncan & Christabel: for there's a plethora of parties this week, & tomorrow I'm missing Lydia & Stravinsky;[7] but a kind of philosophy protects me: I shall make out a happy evening somehow; & find a curious pleasure in staying away, imagining. So I must stop & write to Sibyl. With any luck The Lighthouse will reach 3,000 this week.

Saturday 23 July

This is very near the end of the London season. I go to Ethel [Sand]'s at Dieppe (I'm rather proud of crossing the channel again) on Wednesday, then back to Newhaven, where I may be met by my own car. Since making the last entry I have learnt enough to drive a car in the country alone. On the backs of paper I write down instructions for starting cars. We have a nice light little shut up car in which we can travel thousands of miles. It is very dark blue, with a paler line round it. The world gave me this for writing The Lighthouse, I reflect, a book which has now sold 3,160 (perhaps) copies: will sell 3,500 before it dies, & thus far exceeds any other of mine.

The night I did not go to Stravinsky Desmond came, tender & garrulous & confidential. I remember leaning with him out of the window. He

6. The Woolfs acquired their second-hand Singer car for £275 on 15 July. Frederick Pape, husband of Angelica's nurse Louie, was a professional chauffeur who taught Vanessa to drive, and to some extent VW, though she fairly soon gave up. LW had six driving lessons and drove his car alone for the first time on 31 July.

7. L'Histoire du Soldat, a short entertainment with four characters by G. F. Ramuz and music by Igor Stravinsky, first performed in 1918, was being given in an English translation by the Arts Theatre Club; Lydia Lopokova took the part of the Princess. LW (but not VW) dined with the Keyneses before going to it.

was full of love for everyone. He said he loved the way Melinda [*unidenti-fied*] scratched her head or put on her gloves. He said he was now in love with his children. When Dermod asks him for a new perspective for his microscope he feels what he used to feel when he was in love with a woman. He resents his gift of money a little, since he was making £2,000 a year; but then he had 'arrears'; & has now, evidently—£200 to the Bank, £200 for income tax & so on. We talked of love owing to Clive. For that night after I dined with Clive & went through some rather artificial gambols with Christa[bel McLaren] (who has always thought of me as Virginia; & can't quite lose the sense of my being a perfect lady "Look at those hands") Clive walked me round, & standing under the lamp expressed his complete disillusion. "My dear Virginia, life is over. There's no good denying it. We're 45. I'm bored, I'm bored, I'm un-speakably bored. I know my own reactions. I know what I'm going to say. I'm not interested in a thing. Pictures bore me. I take up a book & put it down. No one's interested in what I think any more. I go about thinking about suicide. I admire you for having tried to kill yourself." To think that I should be listening to this in the moonlight from Clive! And he spoke with such dreary good sense too. I could scarcely whip up any ardour of denial. It was all true, it seemed to me. Not, indeed, true of me, but true of him. & so I feebly asked him to come & see me; & I would prove that I was interested in him. He agreed half heartedly, waved his hand, & went off, thinking about suicide. Then we met next night at Raymonds'.[8] Hardly had I come into the room but he started up boasting & professing, perfunctorily a little, but boldly enough. He had had an adventure. Life was changed; had met the loveliest of women, seemed the nicest too, was an aristocrat; she had been kind to him; would Raymond come on to supper on Monday? All this was blustered out, with many a cuff at me (for he always wishes he says to hurt me—even over a motor car) & it was about Valerie Taylor, an actress, whom he had met lunching at the Maclagans.[9] For my own part, I am once more at the stage of thinking Clive 'second rate'. It is all so silly, shallow, & selfish. Granted the charm of his vitality, still one would prefer a finer taste to it. How angry his 'secondrateness' used to make me, in connection with Nessa.

8. In fact, the night after, i.e. 13 July.

9. Valerie Taylor (b. 1902), daughter of an army officer, studied at the Royal Academy of Dramatic Art and first appeared on the London stage in 1924; she was currently appearing in Frederick Lonsdale's *On Approval* at the Fortune Theatre, which ran from April 1927 to June 1928. Eric Robert Dalrymple MacLagan (1879-1951), knighted in 1933, an authority on Italian sculpture, was Director of the Victoria & Albert Museum from 1924-45.

Now I think of it much less often, but I suppose the feeling is there. All this summer he has twanged so persistently on the one string that one gets bored. Love love love—Clive, Clive, Clive—that's the tune of it, thrummed with rather callous persistency; a thick finger & thumb. Now love I dare say nothing against; but it is a feeble passion, I mean a gross dull passion, when it has no part in it of imagination, intellect, poetry. Clive's love is three parts vanity. Now that he can say, or lie, I've been to bed with Valerie, his self love is assuaged. He remains Clive the undaunted lover, the Don Juan of Bloomsbury; & whether its true or not, so long as we think it true, scarcely matters. But I own that he pesters me with his jealousy, or whatever it is, does his best to annoy me, & so I'm not quite the impartial judge I might be. The interesting question remains—why does he always wish to hurt me?

So Desmond & I discussed all this. And The Lighthouse too; & I felt, susceptible as I am, he's doing this partly to thank me for having been generous to him. But I am enough mistress of myself now to let these feelings flow & not disturb my pleasure.

All images are now tinged with driving a motor. Here I think of letting my engine work, with my clutch out.

It has been, on the whole, a fresh well ordered summer. I am not so parched with talk as usual. I have dipped into society more easily. My illness in May was a good thing in some ways; for I got control of society at an early stage, & circumvented my headache, without a complete smash. Thus it has been a free quiet summer: I enjoyed the Eclipse; I enjoyed Long Barn; (where I went twice) I enjoyed sitting with Vita at Kew for 3 or 4 hours under a cloudy sky, & dining at the Petit Riche with her;[10] she refreshes me, & solaces me; I have worked very methodically & done my due of articles, so that with luck, I shall have made £120 *over* my proper sum by September. That is I shall have made £320 by journalism, & I suppose at least £300 by my novel this year. I have thought too much, though on purpose, with my eyes open, of making money; & once we have each a nest egg I should like to let that sink into my sub-consciousness, & earn easily what we need. Bruce Richmond is coming to tea on Monday to discuss an article on Morgan; & I am going to convey to him the fact that I can't always refuse £60 in America for the Times' £10. If I could make easily £350 a year, I would: if I could get some settled job.

At Rodmell I am going, seriously, to begin my book on fiction. With

10. On 21 July the Woolfs had driven in their car to Richmond Park; LW returned home, leaving VW and Vita Sackville-West to visit Kew Gardens and to dine together.

luck I might have this done by January. Then I shall have the Moths full in my brain to pour out. I am keeping it standing a long time, & rather fear that it may lose its freshness. Dadie has involved us (is the word wrong?) with Peter. Dadie dines with Topsy & she pumps him about the Wolves & Peter's book.[11] Dadie wants to crab it & puts it on to us. Leonard says it doesn't do; Virginia thinks it 'Academic'. The result is a long angry letter from Peter, half vanity, half righteous indignation; but we have explained, & all the burden now rests on Dadie. (& partly on me, for Topsy says I wrote her a rude letter about Jane Austen, but this has been explained).

The Press is going on. Novels are the great bloodsuckers. Mary's book will cost us £100; & we shall lose too on The Marionettes. So in the past two days I have rejected Butts & Daglish & Littell; I fancy that we don't do as well as we should with novels.[12] And I'm exposed to the hanging lips & clamorous vanity of Lucy Clifford today: she has an article on George Eliot which she wrote for a special fee (that is where I shall end if I dont take care—talking always of 'fees') for the Nineteenth Century.[13] Gottstalk is finished.

On 27 July LW saw VW off at Victoria on the boat train for Dieppe, when she went to stay with Ethel Sands and Nan Hudson at their Normandy home, the Château d'Auppegard; she returned via Newhaven on 30 July, rejoining LW at Monks House.

RODMELL

Monday 8 August

I was to have written here such a brilliant account of my 3 days at Dieppe. It was to have sprung, suddenly, in a beautiful fountain, out of the table in the window at (name forgotten) overlooking the Seine. The

11. 'Topsy' Lucas (1893-1966), the novelist E. B. C. Jones, was married to 'Peter' (F. L.) Lucas; the book in question was probably his *Tragedy in Relation to Aristotle's POETICS*, which was to be published in the series 'Hogarth Lectures in Literature' early in 1928 (*HP Checklist* 129).

12. Edwin Muir's *The Marionette* and Mary Hutchinson's *Fugitive Pieces* had been published in May and June 1927 respectively (*HP Checklist* 132, 122). The rejected authors were Mary Butts (1893-1937)—possibly her *Armed with Madness* subsequently published by Wishart in 1928; Doris Daglish of Wandsworth (see *III VW Letters*); and probably the American writer Philip Littell (1868-1943), who until 1924 had been editor of the *New Republic* in which a considerable number of VW's articles appeared.

13. Mrs W. K. Clifford (c. 1855-1929), a friend of VW's parents, who had supported herself by her pen after being widowed at twenty-four; the monthly review *Nineteenth Century and After* published no article by her on George Eliot.

Seine there is very broad, & round the bend come constantly steamers,
Norwegian, with petrol, English French; & Nan kept looking to read
their names, showing in all she did a sort of nervous tremulous pride in
France (or do I imagine this?) which hints at the fact that she likes their
life there, alone at Auppegard, better than Ethel.[1] "I'm gregarious" said
Ethel a little waspishly, for she is brittle & acid, the spoilt pet of the more
dour & upstanding Nan. We were, I think, looking over the cliff with the
churchyard on it, the tombstones standing up against the blue sea. But I
was to have written this, & now shall not, I suppose.— It is a very
narrow house, all window, laid with pale bright Samarcand rugs, &
painted greens & blues, with lovely 'pieces', & great pots of carefully
designed flowers arranged by Loomas. A white bull terrier stalks from
room to room, one ear bent over in his fights. Nan, stylishly dressed, sews
dusters of an evening, & Ethel craves talk. Nessa & Duncan say that the
talk skirts & flits & never settles very long; in fact that the house is built
upon the finest silver wood ash: so soft so silver you don't at first notice
how it gets into your throat & makes your skin dry & dusty.

We have motored most days. We opened one little window when we
bought the gramophone; now another/ opens with the motor—I was
going to say, but stopped.

Wednesday 10 August[2]

Yes, the motor is turning out the joy of our lives, an additional life,
free & mobile & airy to live alongside our usual stationary industry. We
spin off to Falmer, ride over the Downs, drop into Rottingdean, then
sweep over to Seaford, call, in pouring rain at Charleston, pass the time
of day with Clive—Nessa is at Bodiam—return for tea, all as light & easy
as a hawk in the air. Soon we shall look back at our pre-motor days as we
do now at our days in the caves. After a week here, Leonard has become
perfectly efficient; I am held back by insufficient lessons, but shall be
expert before September is half through. Various little improvements in
the house keep me on the thrill with hope & despair. Shall I lavish £5
that will be mine on a new spare bed?—alas, I fear I must; then the great
& distasteful operations of furnishing will be over, & next year I shall add
ornament & comfort. Perhaps if I make an extra sum we might build a

1. Anna Hope (Nan) Hudson (1896-1957), an American painter, had met Ethel
   Sands in Paris in 1894, the beginning of their life-long loving companionship.
   Henry Lomas was their butler from 1925-34. Vanessa Bell and Duncan Grant were
   staying at Auppegard, having been commissioned to paint decorations in the loggia.
   See Wendy Baron, *Ethel Sands and her Circle*, 1977, pp 187-90.
2. VW has misdated this entry 'Wednesday Aug. 9th'.

bed sitting room for me in the attic, enlarge L.'s study, & so have a desirable, roomy, light house. For if we had £300 every year to spend, it is difficult to think of anything, except this, travel, & pocket money, to spend it on. Here at the age of 45 are Nessa & I growing little wings again after our lean years. She may rake in another £500; perhaps more.[3] Already she has bought a roll of linoleum & a cupboard. But my state is precarious. With The Lighthouse I may just have climbed to the top of my hill; or again we may wobble back; my journalism may pall on the Americans: no rich father in law will endow me; but Heaven knows, I have not much anxiety. We are flexible, adventurous still I hope.

An odd incident, psychologically as the vanished Kot used to say, has been Morgan's serious concern about my article on him. Did I care a straw what he said about me? Was it more laudatory? Yet here is this self-possessed, aloof man taking every word to heart, cast down to the depths, apparently, because I do not give him superlative rank, & writing again & again to ask about it, or suggest about it, anxious that it shall be published in England, & also that more space shall be given to the Passage to India. Had I been asked, I should have said that of all writers he would be the most indifferent & cool under criticism. And he minds a dozen times more than I do, who have the opposite reputation.[4]

This brings me back to those last days in London when I called on Ottoline, had a shabby easy intimate talk with her, & then, inadvertently as if by touching a button brought on me the whole shower bath of Philip's affection. He came the next day, inconveniently, & the day after when Sibyl was there. Once more I felt the uneasy excitement of 'love', that is of physical desire making someone restless, too restless & emotional to talk simply. But L. came in; Pinker came in, & the amorous Philip, who has lost most of his good looks & is coarse as an old ram, had to leave. But I found a letter at Rodmell, quoting J.'s Room—'Come back to me Darling'—with which I shall make Vita jealous tomorrow. But what course to take, especially now that he is our neighbour, I do not altogether know; nor whether to answer his letter or not.[5]

3. i.e. as a result of her father-in-law's death.
4. Forster's article on VW had 'cheered me very much' (see above, 21 December 1925); his direct response to the draft of her article on him, a letter and a postcard dated 28 June and 10 July respectively, are in MHP, Sussex, where there are also further letters to LW on the subject. 'The vanished Kot', S. S. Koteliansky (1881-1955), had collaborated with both LW and VW in translations from Russian authors published by the Hogarth Press; they had seen a good deal of him while they were still living at Richmond.
5. The Morrells had moved from Garsington to 10 Gower Street, WC1, in May 1927. Philip Morrell's letter of 27 July to VW is in MHP, Sussex. '. . . Yesterday I felt

This, however, is Nelly's first evening back, in the flush of good temper, with Gladys [*a niece?*], & I am beginning to think of my dinner. Since I dined at Auppegard I cannot be said to have dined at all: ham & eggs; cheese & raspberries; once a baked pudding—so we have fed at the hands of poor emaciated Mrs Bartholomew.

Sunday 21 August

Some little scenes I meant to write down.

One was on the flats towards Ripe one blazing hot day. We stopped in a bye road about 3 in the afternoon, & heard hymn singing. It was very lonely & desolate. Here were people singing to themselves, in the hot afternoon. I looked & saw a middle class 'lady' in skirt & coat & ribboned hat, by the cottage door. She was making the daughters of the agricultural labourers sing; it was about three o'clock on a Tuesday perhaps. Later we passed the ladies house; it had a wooden griffin nailed above the door— presumably her crest.

What I like, or one of the things I like, about motoring is the sense it gives one of lighting accidentally, like a voyager who touches another planet with the tip of his toe, upon scenes which would have gone on, have always gone on, will go on, unrecorded, save for this chance glimpse. Then it seems to me I am allowed to see the heart of the world uncovered for a moment. It strikes me that the hymn singing in the flats went on precisely so in Cromwell's time.

That was our only hot day, I think. One day the rain splashed down so fast that it rose again in a fountain, up off the road in our faces.

Sunday 4 September

Many scenes have come & gone unwritten, since it is today the 4th Sept, a cold grey blowy day, made memorable by the sight of a kingfisher, & by my sense, waking early, of being again visited by 'the spirit of delight'. "Rarely rarely comest thou, spirit of delight."[1] That was I singing this time last year; & sang so poignantly that I have never forgotten it, or my vision of a fin rising on a wide blank sea. No biographer could possibly guess this important fact about my life in the late summer of 1926: yet biographers pretend they know people.

A happy summer, this? Well, a striving working splashing social

---

that after all these years of silence I had really begun to talk to you, almost to be friends—yes; I think you are really very different from the writer of the books, but always adorable.'

1. See above, 30 September 1926. The song is Shelley's.

summer. Many meetings; & one or two gaieties.[2] I amuse myself by watching my mind shape scenes. We sat in a field strewn with cut grass at Michelham Priory the other day. It was roasting hot. There was Angus with his pink shirt open; Duncan strolling along with a sketchbook under his arm; the sound of rushing waters; Nessa driving her old blue bonnet with Angelica perched beside her. Nothing much is said on these occasions; but the memory remains: made of what? Of coloured shirts; the pink roof of the Gateway against a greyblue sky; & Pinker; & my being cross about my book on fiction; & Leonard silent; & a great quarrel that hot night; & I coming up here to sit alone in the dark, & L. following me; & sharp hard words; right & wrong on both sides; peace making; sleep; content.

A graveyard scene.

Mr Malthouse's son, a sailor, died of consumption & was buried in the churchyard under the big tree. I went into the churchyard with Angelica that fine afternoon. Avery was digging the grave, throwing up heavy showers of the yellow earth. Mrs Avery, immensely fat & florid, was sprawling on the edge of the grave, with her small children playing about. They were having tea, & dressed in their reds & blue looked more like a picture, by Millais, or some other Victorian, of life & death, youth & the grave, than any real sight. It was quite unconscious; yet the most deliberate picture making; hence, unreal, sentimental, overdone.[3]

The Flying Princess, I forget her name, has been drowned in her purple leather breeches.[4] I suppose so at least. Their petrol gave out about

2. Apart from their frequent meetings with the denizens of Charleston, the Woolfs had a visit from Roger Fry and three from Vita, including one on 27 August when she brought Harold Nicolson, Dorothy Wellesley, and Raymond Mortimer with her; the latter remained to spend two nights at Monks House. On 31 August they picnicked with the Charlestonians at Laughton Place, and drove on to the moated Michelham Priory with its 15th century gatehouse; (Vanessa's Renault was known as 'the Bonnet'). On 2 September the Woolfs and the Charleston party dined with the Keyneses at Tilton and witnessed an 'entertainment' in their new loggia (see *III VW Letters*, no. 1807).

3. Henry Malthouse was the landlord of the Rodmell pub, the Abergavenny Arms; his son Albert John Malthouse died on 28th August 1927. William Avery, the gravedigger, lived in the village. Cf. 'The Third Picture' of 'Three Pictures' in *The Death of the Moth* (Kp A27).

4. Attempting the first westbound transatlantic flight (it was achieved by a German crew in April 1928), Lt-Col. F. F. Minchin and Captain Leslie Hamilton, with Princess Löwenstein-Wertheim as passenger, took off from Upavon Aerodrome near Salisbury on Wednesday, 31 August, to fly the 3,600 miles to Ottawa in a Fokker monoplane named St Raphael; it was sighted the same evening some 800 miles out from the coast of Ireland, and was never seen again.

midnight on Thursday, when the aeroplane must have come gently down upon the long slow Atlantic waves. I suppose they burnt a light which showed streaky on the water for a time. There they rested a moment or two. The pilots, I think, looked back at the broad cheeked desperate eyed vulgar princess in her purple breeches & I suppose made some desperate dry statement—how the game was up: sorry; fortune against them; & she just glared; & then a wave broke over the wing; & the machine tipped. And she said something theatrical I daresay; nobody was sincere; all acted a part; nobody shrieked; Luck against us—something of that kind, they said, & then So long, & first one man was washed off & went under; & then a great wave came & the Princess threw up her arms & went down; & the third man sat saved for a second looking at the rolling waves, so patient so implacable & the moon gravely regarding; & then with a dry snorting sound he too was tumbled off & rolled over, & the aeroplane rocked & rolled—miles from anywhere, off Newfoundland, while I slept at Rodmell, & Leonard was dining with the Craniums in London.[5]

Monday 5 September

Having solidified the vision of the flying Princess into words, I have, strangely enough, laid a phantom which has been very prominent before my eyes. Why should this be so? Some dissatisfaction seems laid to rest. So, gradually, the urgency of the memory dies out too, as in one's own life; in about 48 or 96 hours all trace of the death of the Princess in her purple breeches is smoothed over.

As a matter of fact, we are just in from Brighton, & my mind is agitated by having bought a jersey, which I like; & by having let Leonard bump the back of the car on the gate post. So, to soothe these whirlpools, I write here. We went to Brighton today; & thus added a pounds worth of pleasure to life. Monotony is avoided. Oh, & I thought—but the thought is already escaping—about the enormous activity of the human kind; his feverish runnings about; Brighton & the roads being nothing but a swarm & agitation of human flesh; & yet it is not despicable.

And when I get back here, the same energy is bringing the men back from harvest across the fields; & old Mr Grey, & the poor plodding horse [?]. Now a really comprehensive magnificent statesmanlike mind would take stock of all this human activity & direct it & weld it together. I see this possibility by fits & starts: I see human beings as at the beginning of a vast enterprise, not merely with the usual writers care for the aesthetic

5. The Cranium was an elective dining club started by David Garnett, Francis Birrell, and Stephen Tomlin to enable dispersed friends to keep in touch with each other.

quality. This is a point of view which is more & more forced upon one by places like Peacehaven. All aesthetic quality is there destroyed. Only turning & tumbling energy is left. The mind is like a dog going round & round to make itself a bed. So, give me new & detestable ideas, I will somehow trample a bed out of them.

Tuesday 20 September[6]

A thousand things to be written had I time: had I power. A very little writing uses up my capacity for writing:

Laughton Place & Philip Ritchie's death

These as it happened, synchronised. When Vita was here 10 days ago we drove over to Laughton, & I broke in, & explored the house. It seemed, that sunny morning, so beautiful, so peaceful; & as if it had endless old rooms. So I came home boiling with the idea of buying it; & so fired L. that we wrote to the farmer, Mr Russell, & waited, all on wires, edgy, excited for an answer. He came himself, after some days; & we were to go & see it. This arranged, & our hopes very high, I opened the Morning Post & read the death of Philip Ritchie.[7] "He cant take houses, poor Philip" I thought. And then the usual procession of images went through my mind. Also, I think for the first time, I felt this death leaves me an elderly laggard; makes me feel I have no right to go on; as if my life were at the expense of his. And I had not been kind; not asked him to dinner & so on. So the two feelings—about buying the house & his death—fought each other: & sometimes the house won & sometimes death won; & we went to see the house & it turned out unspeakably dreary; all patched & spoilt; with grained oak & grey paper; a sodden garden & a glaring red cottage at the back. I note the strength & vividness of feelings which suddenly break & foam away. Now I forget to think about Philip Ritchie.

One of these days, though, I shall sketch here, like a grand historical

---

6. VW has misdated this entry 'Tuesday Sept. 18th'.
7. Vita and Harold Nicolson came to tea at Monks House on 8 September, and afterwards the two husbands went up to London together; the following day VW and Vita saw Laughton Place, the remains of an isolated sixteenth-century moated house in the flat country between Ringmer and Ripe; the only surviving portion, a tall and broad brick tower, had been converted in the eighteenth century into a farmhouse. Philip Ritchie died at Winchelsea on 13 September, aged 28, of septic pneumonia following a tonsillectomy. (Despite LW's scorn, VW used to take the arch-Conservative *Morning Post* during the summer months at Rodmell.)

picture, the outlines of all my friends. I was thinking of this in bed last night, & for some reason I thought I would begin with a sketch of Gerald Brenan. There may be something in this idea. It might be a way of writing the memoirs of one's own times during peoples lifetimes. It might be a most amusing book. The question is how to do it. Vita should be Orlando, a young nobleman. There should be Lytton. & it should be truthful; but fantastic. Roger. Duncan. Clive. Adrian. Their lives should be related. But I can think of more books than I shall ever be able to write. How many little stories come into my head! For instance: Ethel Sands not looking at her letters. What this implies. One might write a book of short significant separate scenes. She did not open her letters.

We motored to Long Barn & back yesterday, through suburbs for the most part. All Hampstead, red, sanitary, earnest, view gazing, breeze requiring is lodged in the heights of Ashdown Forest. Now & again one comes on something consciously preserved like the Wren house at Groombridge.[8] One stops the motor & looks. So do other motorists. We found Vita & Dotty sitting over a log fire. Dottie is going to spend £200 a year on poetry: to edit a series of books of unsaleable poetry. This £200 she was giving to the Poetry Bookshop, but deterred by his earnestness & his drunkenness she is crying off: & has laid it at our feet.[9] There will be much comment she says at this. People will say she is buying her way into Bloomsbury. The children were there; Nigel very shabby: Vita dressed him as a Russian boy "Dont. It makes me look like a little girl" he said. There was the French tutor who never spoke.[10] Dotty byronic in her dress, but much improved over the London Dotty. They do not yet know what is to become of Harold, who has refused to go to Buda Pesth.

And Quentin came, & the Keynes's came, & Morgan came. All of this I meant, perhaps, to describe: but then how hard I drive my pen through

8. Groombridge Place, a handsome moated H-plan house on the Kent-East Sussex border near Tunbridge Wells, was built in the third quarter of the seventeenth century in the manner of Inigo Jones rather than Wren.

9. Dorothy Wellesley, herself a poet and anxious to use some of her considerable wealth to encourage poets, became (by arrangement with LW who reserved some rights over choice) the sponsor and editor of the first series of the *Hogarth Living Poets*, in which 24 titles were published between 1928 and 1932. The Poetry Bookshop had been founded in 1913 by the poet and publisher Harold Edward Monro (1879-1932); it survived until his death as a centre for poetry readings and for those interested in poetry.

10. This was Maurice Couve de Murville (b. 1907), a future Prime Minister of France, who in the interval between leaving university and entering the French civil service, spent six summer weeks at the Nicolsons.

one article after another—Hemingway, Morgan, Shelley; & now Biography.[11]

Quentin wont let us play him Wagner: prefers Bach. Nessa's children are terrifyingly sophisticated: so Morgan said when Angelica, rigged up in a long black shawl, acted Lady Cornflax & Lady Ottoline at Charleston. They have grown up without any opposition: nothing to twist or stunt. Hence they have reached stages at 16 or 17 which I reached only at 26 or 27.

But the summer, has never burnt; & is now ashes. Already at half past five the light out here is greyish; the wind swirling; all children indoors; & I shall write a letter or two & go into the house: sit over a fire & read, I think, biography.

But we are very happy—seldom more so, I think. Perhaps things are doing rather well. Theres the motor; Dottie's £200;—& L. said about Laughton Place the other day, "The strange thing is that we always come to the same opinion about things"—which pleased me.

Sunday 25 September

On the opposite page I wrote notes for Shelley, I think by mistake for my writing book.[12]

Now let me become the annalist of Rodmell.

Thirty five years ago, there were 160 families living here where there are now no more than 80. It is a decaying village, which loses its boys to the towns. Not a boy of them, said the Rev. Mr Hawkesford, is being taught to plough. Rich people wanting week end cottages buy up the old peasants houses, for fabulous sums. Monks House was offered to Mr H. for £400: we gave £700. He refused it, saying he didn't wish to own country cottages. Now Mr Allinson will pay £1200 for a couple, & we he said might get £2,000 for this.[13]

11. E. M. Forster stayed the week-end of 10-12 September at Monks House. VW was writing four articles to be published in the *New York Herald Tribune*; they were on Hemingway's *Men Without Women* (see 'An Essay in Criticism', 9 October 1927, Kp C287); on E. M. Forster's *Aspects of the Novel* ('Is Fiction an Art?', 16 October 1927, Kp C288); on *Shelley: His Life and Work* by Walter Edwin Peck ('Not one of Us', 23 October 1927, Kp C289); and on *Some People* by Harold Nicolson ('The New Biography', 30 October 1927, Kp C290).

12. These notes relate to Professor Peck's 2-volume life of Shelley (see note 11 above) and read: '287 1../ Weavers. 2.45/ 2.120 prodigy of crime & pollution/ 2.166 S. shd have lived out of doors/ 167. knocked down for being a d—d atheist./ 172. appreciates the cloud because of an increased knowledge of physiography.'

13. The Rev. James Boen Hawkesford was Rector of Rodmell from 1896 until his death in January 1928. J. M. Allison, see above, 5 September 1926, note 4.

He is an old decaying man, run to seed. His cynicism, & the pleasant turn it gives his simple worn out sayings, amuses me. He is sinking into old age, very shabby, loose limbed, wearing black wool mittens. His life is receding like a tide, slowly; or one figures him as a dying candle, whose wick will soon sink into the warm grease & be extinct. To look at, he is like some aged bird; a little, small featured face, with heavily lidded smoky bright eyes; his complexion is still ruddy; but his beard is like an unweeded garden. Little hairs grow weakly all over his cheeks, & two strands are drawn, like pencil marks, across his bald head. He tumbles into an armchair; & tells over his stock of old village stories, which always have this slightly mocking flavour, as though, completely unambitious, & by no means successful himself, he recouped himself by laughing slyly at the humours of the more energetic. He has a hit at Allinson for building; drily tells us how Capt Stamper won't pay his tithes; how Miss Lucas signs the Captain's cheques for him.[14] The outlay these flashy newcomers make on their field & farms makes him sardonic. But he wont raise a finger either way; likes his cup of Indian tea, which he prefers to China, & doesn't much mind what anybody thinks. He smokes endless cigarettes, & his fingers are not very clean. Talking of his well, he said "It would be a different thing if one wanted baths"—which for some 70 years, presumably, he has done without. Then he likes a little practical talk about Aladdin lamps, for instance, & how the Rector at Iford has a device by which he makes the globe of the Veritas lamp wh. is cheaper serve. It appears that the Aladdin costs 10d & 2/-. But it blackens suddenly & is useless. Leaning over stiles, it is of lamp mantles that the two rectors talk.[15] Or he will advise about making a garage: how Percy shd. cut a trench, & then old Fears should line the walls with cement. That is what he advises; & I fancy many many hours of his life have passed hobnobbing with Percys & Fears, about cement & trenches. Of his clerical character there is little visible. He would not buy Bowen a riding school he said; her sister did that. He didn't believe in it. She has a school at Rottingdean, keeps 12 horses, employs grooms, & has to be at it all day, Sundays

14. Captain Edwin Poulden Fenton Byng-Stamper (1885-1939), late of the Royal Welch Fusiliers, of Northease House, near Rodmell, was one of the principal landowners in the district; he was to marry Miss Frances Byng Lucas, a great-granddaughter of Admiral George Byng, 6th Viscount Torrington.
15. 'Aladdin' and 'Veritas' lamps worked by burning vaporized paraffin oil in a mantle of asbestos filament, which gave a far brighter light than that obtained from a simple wick—though the sudden blackening of the mantle was a hazard of the system. There were Aladdin lamps at Monks House, but VW's summary of the rectors' talk suggests that she did not cope with them. The vicar (since 1909) of Kingston with Iford was the Rev. A. G. Green.

included.[16] But having expressed his opinion in the family conclave, he would leave it at that. Mrs H. would back Bowen. She would get her way. The Rector would slouch off to his study, where he does, heaven knows what. I asked him if he had work to do: a question which amused him a little. Not work he said; but a young woman to see. And then he settled into the armchair again, & so sat out a visit of over an hour & a half.

Wednesday 5 October

I write in the sordid doss house atmosphere of approaching departure. Pinker is asleep in one chair; Leonard is signing cheques at the little deal table under the glare of the lamp. The fire is covered with ashes, since we have been burning it all day, & Mrs B[artholomew]. never cleans. Envelopes lie in the grate. I am writing with a pen which is feeble & wispy; & it is a sharp fine evening with a sunset, I daresay.

We went to Amberley yesterday & think of buying a house there. For it is an astonishing forgotten lovely place, between water meadows & downs. So impulsive we both are, in spite of our years.

But we are not as old as Mrs Gray, who came to thank us for our apples. She won't send to buy, as it looks like begging, since we never take money. Her face is cut into by wrinkles: they make wheals across her. She is 86, & can never remember such a summer. In her youth it was so hot in April often that they couldn't bear a sheet on them. Her youth must have been almost the same time as my fathers. She is 9 years younger, I make out: born in 1841. And what did she see of Victorian England I wonder?[1]

1832
86
___
1918

I can make up situations, but I cannot make up plots. That is: if I pass the lame girl, I can without knowing I do it, instantly make up a scene: (now I cant think of one). This is the germ of such fictitious gift as I have. And by the way I get letter after letter about my books, & they scarcely please me.

Further, we met Mary & Barbara [Hutchinson] in Brighton yesterday; grey, tailor made, elegant, with a touch of pink, & pink silk legs. Yet I fancied some wrinkles about Mary's eyes; & a sharp line or two, made by Clive. We were affable, as people are when they meet after a coolness; we gave them buns. We were extra affable, perhaps; & the shadow of Clive

16. Percy Bartholomew of Park Cottages, Rose's husband, was in 1928 to become LW's gardener and an important figure in his life at Rodmell. The Hawkesfords had two daughters, Olive and Boen; the latter ran the Rottingdean Riding School.
1. Cf. 'Old Mrs Grey' in *The Death of the Moth* (Kp A27). Leslie Stephen was born in 1832.

loomed above us. Going to fetch L.'s hat from Charleston I chanced on one of those evening autumn emotional hours when people want to be intimate, perhaps to boast. And he told me an absurd romantic story—of a girl, lovely, desired, half his age; & how she loved him, & he could not believe it; she must think me a cultivated elderly man, he said; & so "I try I try to control myself" but, wondrously, they went off the other day; had 4 days perfect bliss; & now "the drama begins". That is, it began two days ago, on Monday. Nobody has the least idea who she is. And is it lasting, or genuine, or only a set off against Mary? & will it survive Mary's attacks, & shall we be dragged in, & so on & so on? Those are the thoughts which agitate us this October, which is the birth of the year.

If my pen allowed, I should now try to make out a work table, having done my last article for the Tribune, & now being free again. And instantly the usual exciting devices enter my mind: a biography beginning in the year 1500 & continuing to the present day, called Orlando: Vita; only with a change about from one sex to another. I think, for a treat, I shall let myself dash this in for a week, while   [text ends]

The Woolfs returned to London on Thursday 6 October.

Saturday 22 October

This is a book, I think I have said before, which I write after tea. And my brain was full of ideas, but I have spent them on Mr Ashcroft & Miss Findlater, fervent admirers.[2]

"I shall let myself dash this in for a week"—I have done nothing, nothing, nothing else for a fortnight; & am launched somewhat furtively but with all the more passion upon Orlando: A Biography. It is to be a small book, & written by Christmas. I thought I could combine it with *Fiction*, but once the mind gets hot it cant stop; I walk making up phrases; sit, contriving scenes; am in short in the thick of the greatest rapture known to me; from which I have kept myself since last February, or earlier. Talk of planning a book, or waiting for an idea! This one came in a rush; I said to pacify myself, being bored & stale with criticism & faced with that intolerable dull Fiction, "You shall write a page of a story for a treat: you shall stop sharp at 11.30 & then go on with the Romantics". I had very little idea what the story was to be about. But the relief of

2. Mr Ashcroft, unidentified; Mary Findlater (1865-1963) and her sister Jane (1866-1946) who separately and jointly wrote a number of popular novels, had written appreciatively to VW; her reply, dated 22 October 1927, is published in Eileen MacKenzie, *The Findlater Sisters*, 1964, pp 116-17.

turning my mind that way about was such that I felt happier than for months; as if put in the sun, or laid on cushions; & after two days entirely gave up my time chart & abandoned myself to the pure delight of this farce: which I enjoy as much as I've ever enjoyed anything; & have written myself into half a headache & had to come to a halt, like a tired horse, & take a little sleeping draught last night: which made our break-fast fiery. I did not finish my egg. I am writing Orlando half in a mock style very clear & plain, so that people will understand every word. But the balance between truth & fantasy must be careful. It is based on Vita, Violet Trefusis, Lord Lascelles, Knole &c.[3]

A great many incidents to record. They come always in a rush together, these bright October days, with every one just back, fresh from solitude, cheerful, busy, sociable. Nessa has initiated, informally, Sunday evenings; & there Old Bloomsbury is to gather, after dinner—Helen Clive Roger & so on.

Then I asked the time in the Press a week ago.

"Leonard can tell you" said Angus very huffily.

"Ask Angus. I dont seem to know" said Leonard very grumpy. And I saw Mrs C. lower her head over her typing & laugh. This was the tail of a terrific quarrel about the time between them. Angus was dismissed; but tells Nessa he wants to stay, could tempers be made compatible. A bad year, this, financially, for the Press: yet prospects seem flourishing, if only Marys & Braithwaites didn't eat up all profits. Dottie (who comes to tea with great simplicity, but sits a little long afterwards) is investing her £200 a year in Stella Gibbons &c. & lends me her own poems, which I promptly throw down the W.C.[4] Vita stalks into the press, all red & black (so is Orlando) says Lizzie [a dog?] has been shot by a farmer, no, a publican (she respects farmers, not publicans): comes up here with me, & Harold drops in to say Good bye. We sit very cosy & intimate for all

3. Violet Trefusis, *née* Keppel (1894-1972), with whom Vita, often disguised as a man, had had a passionate and dramatic love affair between 1918-21 (see Nigel Nicolson, *Portrait of a Marriage*, 1973). Henry, Viscount Lascelles (1882-1974), who married the Princess Royal in 1922 and was to succeed his father as 6th Earl of Harewood in 1929, had courted Vita before she engaged herself to Harold Nicolson in 1913. Sasha the Russian Princess and the Archduchess Harriet in *Orlando* were based upon what VW learned of these two from Vita.

4. For the quarrel about the time, cf *II QB*, p 130. R. B. Braithwaite's *The State of Religious Belief* had been published by the Hogarth Press in February 1927 (*HP Checklist* 116); it was based upon the *N & A* Questionnaire (see above, 5 September 1926, n 6). Stella Gibbons (b. 1902), best known for her highly successful first novel *Cold Comfort Farm* (1932), was also a poet; but she was not included in Dorothy Wellesley's series of *Hogarth Living Poets*.

his man about the worldiness, over the gas: he has just been to the Foreign Office & they have been "ever so good. Really they spoil one" he said, being devoted to the Office, which now sends him to Berlin for 3 years.[5] Vita will only go for a short time she says. She likes him. She pets him: wants me to make him a fresh cup of tea.

Then there's Clive. He has laid his stairs with the vividest green, 5 inches thick: has every comfort & convenience. I dine there to meet Harold & Tom: Tom, of course, in white waistcoat, much the man of the world; which sets the key, & off they go telling stories about 'Jean' (Cocteau) about Ada Leverson, Gosse, Valery, &c. &c. & L. & I feel a little Bloomsburyish perhaps; no, I think this sort of talk is hardly up to the scratch. Harold does it best. He was in Petersburg when they blew up Stolypin, or his children; can describe the boom bum bum of a bomb falling from the life: & the Empress with her yellow eye whites; & King George throwing Mr Britling with a violence to the floor. & I 'may be lacking in distinction but I'm damned if I'm an alien' was his comment on some phrase of Wells'.[6]

And that reminds me how we saw the pale dove grey coffin of Mrs Wells slide through the gates at Golders Green. It had tassels like bell pulls on it. Wells sat in bottle blue overcoat by [George Bernard] Shaw, sobbing. One saw his white handkerchief going in & out of his pocket. Mr Page a shaggy shabby old scholar, read some typewritten sheets, by Wells, about "our friend Caroline."[7] "Poor things, poor silly things" she'd say,

5. Harold Nicolson left London for Germany on 25 October to take up his new appointment as First Secretary at the British Embassy.

6. Clive's dinner party was on 20 October. Harold Nicolson retold the story of the 1906 bomb attack by Socialist revolutionaries on the Russian Prime Minister P. A. Stolypin in his life (published 1920) of his father Lord Carnock who, as Sir Arthur Nicolson, was British Ambassador in St Petersburg from 1905-10; Harold himself had been sent by his father to see what had happened. Stolypin escaped unharmed (he was later murdered), but two of his children were among the many injured; the three assassins and twenty-five others were killed. Lord Carnock acted as assistant-secretary to the King in 1917 and was no doubt the source for Harold Nicolson's other story about his reaction to H. G. Wells's wartime novel *Mr Britling Sees It Through*, in which Wells wrote of the sad spectacle of England struggling under an 'alien and uninspiring court'. 'I may be uninspiring,' exclaimed the incensed King, 'but I'll be d---d if I'm an alien.' (See Harold Nicolson, *King George the Fifth. His Life and Reign*, 1952, pp 307-8.)

7. Mrs H. G. Wells, who died on the 6th and was cremated at Golders Green on 10 October, was generally known as 'Jane' although her name was Catherine (*not* Caroline). H. G., wishing to direct attention to a hidden side of her personality, published a memoir of her and several of her stories in *The Book of Catherine Wells* in 1928. Dr Thomas Ethelbert Page (1850-1936) was classical scholar, teacher, and a noted orator.

in their days of ill repute. This colloquialism merged in the burial service; & somehow the whole effect was a little nondescript. The aim was to emphasise life; & generosity & how generous lives continue; one thing touched me. "Some are set on a headland & their lives are a beacon to mankind. Others live retired & are hardly known; but their lives are the most precious" which reminds me of what my father wrote, & meant at the moment, of my mother.[8] Then the coffin slid away "into the furnace of material creation". She had become part of the roses she loved, & of the sun on snow. Poor Jane! It was desperate to see what a dowdy shabby imperfect lot we looked; how feeble; how ugly for the most part. And yet we were doing our best to say something sincere about our great adventure (as Wells almost called it). And he has been adventurous & plunged about in his bath & splashed the waters, to give him his due. Afterwards we stood about congratulating; Lydia sobbed; Shaw said "You mustnt cry. Jane is well—Jane is splendid" & we went off—I to Fortnum & Mason's to buy shoes.

Sunday 20 November

I will now snatch a moment from what Morgan calls 'life' to enter a hurried note. My notes have been few; life a cascade, a glissade, a torrent: all together. I think on the whole this *is* our happiest autumn. So much work; & success now; & life on easy terms: heaven knows what. My morning rushes, pell mell, from 10 to 1. I write so quick I can't get it typed before lunch. This I suppose is the main backbone of my autumn—Orlando. Never do I feel this, except for a morning or two, writing criticism. Today I began the third chapter. Do I learn anything? Too much of a joke perhaps for that; yet I like these plain sentences; & the externality of it for a change. It is too thin of course; splashed over the canvas; but I shall cover the ground by Jan. 7th (I say) & then re-write.

Vita comes; Dottie comes; Clive incessant; Tom; Roger; we have our Bloomsbury evenings; for the first time I have been spending money, on a bed, on a coat (the coat, at the moment, I regret) & had a delicious sense of affluence the other day when at Long Barn I tipped Loune [*the butler*] 5/- for a nights lodging. But the money psychology is odd; & that it doesn't give me enormous pleasure to spend. I doubt that I want anything

8. In October 1895, after the death of his wife, Leslie Stephen gave a lecture upon 'Forgotten Benefactors' at the Ethical Society, which was later published in volume II of his *Social Rights and Duties* (1896); his avowed intention was to 'speak of Julia without mentioning her name', and the text concludes: '. . . the good done by a noble life and character may last far beyond any horizon which can be realised by our imaginations'.

eno'; yet worry about spending wrongly; & must buy an evening dress which worries me too. I have refused Sibyl; accepted Ethel. Fame increases; I think. Young men write about me in their absurd random books. Domestic life, Nelly that is, good as gold.

This is a summary; for I have too many letters to write, & cant catch that cloud which was so heavy in my brain when I sat down.

I made Vita cry the other night; quietly, unself-consciously. "I hate being bored" I said, of her Campbells & Valery Taylors; & this she thought meant I should be tired of her.[1]

Wednesday 30 November

I have just been upstairs & tried on a hat (18/11) which I have just bought at B&H (so they call it) [*Bourne & Hollingsworth, Oxford Street*] to wear at Sibyl's lunch party tomorrow. With that money I could have bought a nightgown. Then I heard a man in a bus talk about quality & state of gentlemaness; & you would call me Sir; as I you Madam. This to a working woman, dowdy pasty plush with a baby. "Had more'n 8" she said to the conductor; whom she called young man; & he called her Ma. This is Dickens; or Shakespeare; or simple English cockney: whichever it is I adore it; & warm the cockles of my heart at it.

A very happy autumn this, I repeat. Nelly raised £5, & for that reason or another in constant spirits & kindness. Offered last night to clear away. She thinks it only fair, as we've raised her. No trouble about people coming. After Xmas discontent will set in no doubt; when I must write criticism; the light languishes; Nessa Vita Clive are all away. But I will steal a march on that depression. Moreover, aren't I proud at the moment. Ruth Draper admires me: I am to meet her on Friday at Elena Richmond's. What an incredible concatenation! So tonight I go to the Pit to see Ruth Draper.[2] Lunch with Sibyl; dine with Ethel; & a new dress, made from one 100 years old. These are the little waves that life makes; which keep us tossing & going up & down on top of them.

1. Vita, dining alone with VW at Tavistock Square on 10 November, had told her of the tribulations of her current affair with Mary Campbell, wife of the South African poet Roy Campbell; the Campbells had returned from his native Durban earlier in the year, and were now living in the gardener's cottage at Long Barn; he, on discovering his wife's liaison with Vita, had reacted violently and threateningly (see below, 7 July 1928). Ignatius Roy Dunnachie Campbell (1902-57) had married Mary Margaret Garman in London in 1922; in 1931 he published his highly disobliging satire on the Nicolsons (and Bloomsbury) *The Georgiad*.
2. Ruth Draper (1884-1956), the already celebrated American character actress, was appearing at the Criterion Theatre for a season of her solo performances.

DECEMBER 1927

[Thursday 1 December]

A rapid note about the lunch party, L. dining at the Cranium.[1]

An art of light talk; about people. Bogey Harris; Maurice Baring. B.H. 'knows' everyone: that is no one. Freddy Fossle? Oh yes I know him; knows Ly So & So; knows everyone: cant admit to not knowing. A polished, burnished diner out. Roman Catholic. In the middle M. Baring says—But Lady Beaverbrook died this morning.[2] Sibyl says Say that again. But BM. [?] was lunching with her yesterday, says Bogey. Well its in the papers: she's dead says M.B. Sibyl says But she was quite young. Lord Ivor asked me to meet the young man her daughter's to marry. I know Lord Ivor says, or wd say Bogey. Well its odd, says Sibyl, giving up the attempt to wrestle with the death of the young at a lunch party. So on to wigs: Lady Charlie used to have hers curled by a sailor on deck before she got up says Bogey. Oh I've known her all my life. Went yatchting with them. Lady . . . eyebrows fell into the soup. Sir John Cook was so fat they had to hike him up. Once he got out of bed in the middle of the night & fell on the floor where he lay 5 hours—couldn't move. BM. sent me a pear by the waiter with a long letter. Talk of houses & periods. All very smooth & surface talk: depends on knowing people: not on saying anything interesting. Bogey's cheeks are polished daily.

Tuesday 20 December

This is almost the shortest day & perhaps the coldest night of the year. We are in the black heart of a terrific frost. I notice that look of black atoms in a clear air, which for some reason I can never describe to my liking. The pavement was white with great powdery flakes the other night, walking back with Roger & Helen; this was from Nessa's last Sunday—last, I fear, for many a month. But I have as usual 'no time': let me count the things I should be doing this deep winters night with Leonard at his last lecture, & Pinker asleep in his chair. I should be reading Bagenal's story; Julian's play; Lord Chesterfield's letters; &

1. LW's Cranium dinner was on 1 December, which must therefore be the date of this entry and of Lady Colefax's lunch party.
2. Henry ('Bogey') Harris (c. 1871-1950), wealthy connoisseur and art collector of 9 Bedford Square, WC1, had been educated at Eton and Christ Church and was a prominent member of Edwardian society; from 1917-21 he was Secretary to the British Legation to the Vatican. Lady Beaverbrook, the somewhat overshadowed wife of the ebullient Press Lord, died of a heart attack at Stornoway House, St. James's, on 1 December.

writing to Hubert [Henderson] (about a cheque from the Nation).[3] There is an irrational scale of values in my mind which puts these duties higher than mere scribbling.

Angus is finally to go: we had another semi-painful interview in the Studio; when he interrupted L.'s dismissal with his own resignation. Not enough money. We think of Francis Birrell as partner; shall ask him tomorrow; & broach the Hogarth Miscellany.[4]

This flashed to my mind at Nessa's children's party last night. The little creatures acting moved my infinitely sentimental throat. Angelica so mature, & composed; all grey & silver; such an epitome of all womanliness; & such an unopened bud of sense & sensibility; wearing a grey wig & a sea coloured dress. And yet oddly enough I scarcely want children of my own now. This insatiable desire to write something before I die, this ravaging sense of the shortness & feverishness of life, make me cling, like a man on a rock, to my one anchor. I don't like the physicalness of having children of one's own. This occurred to me at Rodmell; but I never wrote it down. I can dramatise myself as parent, it is true. And perhaps I have killed the feeling instinctively; as perhaps nature does.

I am still writing the 3rd Chap. of Orlando. I have had of course to give up the fancy of finishing by February & printing this spring. It is drawing out longer than I meant. I have just been thinking over the scene when O. meets a girl (Nell) in the Park & goes with her to a neat room in Gerrard Street. There she will disclose herself. They will talk. This will lead to a diversion or two about women's love. This will bring in O.'s night life; & her clients (thats the word). Then she will see Dr Johnson, & perhaps write (I want somehow to quote it) To all you Ladies.[5] So I shall get some effect of years passing; & then there will be a description of the lights of the 18th Century burning; & the clouds of the 19th Century rising. Then on to the 19th. But I have not considered this. I want to write it all over hastily, & so keep unity of tone, which in this book is

3. Under the auspices of the Union of Democratic Control, LW had been giving a series, which began on 11 October, of six lectures on 'Imperialism and the Problem of Civilization' at Friends House, Euston Road. 'Bagenal's story' is untraced; as is Julian Bell's play: he appears to have sent more than one to VW for her criticism at this period (see *III VW Letters*, nos. 1836, 1865 to Julian Bell, and no. 1843 to Lady Cecil). VW was reading Chesterfield in connection with her review of *The Characters of Lord Chesterfield* edited by Charles Whibley, which was to appear in the *TLS* on 8 March 1928 (Kp C298).

4. Francis Birrell did not join the Press; and nothing ever came of the *Hogarth Miscellany*, or *Annual* as VW elsewhere refers to it.

5. 'To all you Ladies' was written in 1665 by Vita's ancestor Charles Sackville, Earl of Dorset. VW does not quote it in *Orlando*.

very important. It has to be half laughing, half serious: with great splashes of exaggeration.

Perhaps I shall pluck up courage to ask the Times for a rise. But could I write for my Annual I would never write for another paper. How extraordinarily unwilled by me but potent in its own right by the way Orlando was! as if it shoved everything aside to come into existence. Yet I see looking back just now to March that it is almost exactly in spirit, though not in actual facts, the book I planned then as an escapade; the spirit to be satiric, the structure wild. Precisely.

Yes, I repeat, a very happy, a singularly happy autumn.

Facts are: Clive is loved by a lady in Leicestershire: Mary loves (perhaps) Lord A. She wishes to have Clive back on terms. He forgets: has a twinge now & then, but is fancy free. Mary met them walking in Cavendish Square. Raymond will marry Valery. (so we think).

Thursday 22 December

I just open this for a moment, being dull of the head, to enter a severe reprimand of myself to myself. The value of society is that it snubs one. I am meretricious. mediocre; a humbug; am getting into the habit of flashy talk. Tinsel it seemed last night at the Keynes.[6] I was out of humour & so could see the transparency of my own sayings. Dadie said a true thing too: when V. lets her style get on top of her, one thinks only of that; when she uses clichés, one thinks what she means. But, he says, I have no logical power & live & write in an opium dream. And the dream is too often about myself.

Now with middle age drawing on, & age ahead it is important to be severe on such faults. So easily might I become a hare brained egotistic woman, exacting compliments, arrogant, narrow, withered. Nessa's children (I always measure myself against her, & find her much the largest, most humane of the two of us, think of her now with an admiration that has no envy in it: with some trace of the old childish feeling that we were in league together against the world; & how proud I am of her triumphant winning of all our battles: as she [battles?] her way so nonchalantly modestly, almost anonymously past the goal, with her children round her; & only a little added tenderness (a moving thing in her) which shows me that she too feels wonder surprise at having passed so many terrors & sorrows safe—

The dream is too often about myself. To correct this, & to forget one's

6. On 21 December Frankie Birrell and Dadie Rylands dined with the Woolfs before they all went on to the Keyneses' party.

own sharp absurd little personality, reputation & the rest of it, one should read; see outsiders; think more; write more logically; above all be full of work; & practise anonymity. Silence in company; or the quietest statement, not the showiest, is also 'indicated' as the doctors say. It was an empty party, rather, last night. Very nice here, though; & F.B. is I think willing.

On Christmas eve the Woolfs went by train to Lewes where they had left their car, and drove out to Charleston where they spent the next three nights before moving back to Monks House. The Bells were all away spending Christmas with Clive's widowed mother in Wiltshire.

— 1928 —

1928

The Woolfs returned from Monks House to Tavistock Square on Monday 2 January, and for the next two weeks VW saw few people besides her immediate Bloomsbury familiars and Vita Sackville-West, whose father was dying at Knole, and with whom she stayed the night of 14 January at Long Barn. She was absorbed in writing Orlando. *DIARY XVII which follows is written, like the last, on loose-leaf paper.*

Tuesday 17 January

In half an hour or so Nessa & Duncan will look in on their way to Roger's to say good bye. This is the true break in the year: Bloomsbury is dispersed today till May, I suppose. Clive was off to Germany this morning.[1]

Yesterday we went to Hardy's funeral. What did I think of? Of Max Beerbohm's letter, just read; or a lecture to the Newnhamites about women's writing.[2] At intervals some emotion broke in. But I doubt the capacity of the human animal for being dignified in ceremony. One catches a Bishops frown & twitch: sees his polished shiny nose; suspects the rapt spectacled young priest gazing at the cross he carries, of being a humbug; catches Robert Lynd's distracted haggard eye; then thinks of the mediocrity of Squire; next here is the coffin, an overgrown one; like a stage

1. This winter migration, henceforth to be a regular custom for the painters Duncan and Vanessa, was facilitated by their having acquired a secure base in Provence, 'La Bergère', a small house reconstructed from a ruin on his property at Fontcreuse, near Cassis, by Lt. Col. A. S. H. Teed (retd.), late of the Bengal Lancers; this year they were to remain there, with their daughter Angelica, until the end of May. Clive took Quentin to Munich, where he was to spend several months in a family, and then went on with Raymond Mortimer to Dresden, Berlin, and Paris, returning to London on 10 February.
2. Thomas Hardy died at his home on 11 January 1928; by a gruesome historic compromise between his own wishes and those of 'the nation', his heart was interred in his own parish churchyard at Stinsford and his ashes in Poet's Corner, Westminster Abbey; both funeral ceremonies took place at the same hour on 16 January. What appeared to VW an 'overgrown' coffin was in fact the pall-covered bier bearing the casket of ashes. Max Beerbohm had written (30 December 1927, copy MHP, Sussex) that he rated *The Common Reader* 'above any modern book of criticism', but that in her novels VW was 'so hard on us common readers'. VW had agreed to speak to the Newnham Arts Society in May; in the event her talk was postponed until October (see below, headnote before 27 October 1928).

coffin, covered with a white satin cloth: bearers elderly gentlemen rather red & stiff, holding to the corners: pigeons flying outside; insufficient artificial light; procession to poets corner; dramatic "In sure & certain hope of immortality" perhaps melodramatic. After dinner at Clive's Lytton protested that the great man's novels are the poorest of poor stuff; & can't read them. Lytton sitting or lying inert, with his eyes shut, or exasperated with them open. Lady Strachey slowly fading, but it may take years. Over all this broods for me, some uneasy sense, of change, & mortality, & how partings are deaths; & then a sense of my own fame—why should this come over me?—& then of its remoteness; & then the pressure of writing two articles on Meredith & furbishing up the Hardy.[3] And Leonard sitting at home reading. And Max's letter. & a sense of the futility of it all.

Saturday 11 February

I am so cold I can hardly hold the pen. The futility of it all—so I broke off; & have indeed been feeling that rather persistently, or perhaps I should have written here. Hardy & Meredith together sent me torpid to bed with headache. I know the feeling now, when I can't spin a sentence, & sit mumbling & turning; & nothing flits by my brain which is as a blank window. So I shut my studio door, & go to bed, stuffing my ears with rubber; & there I lie a day or two. And what leagues I travel in the time! Such 'sensations' spread over my spine & head directly I give them the chance; such an exaggerated tiredness; such anguishes & despairs; & heavenly relief & rest; & then misery again. Never was anyone so tossed up & down by the body as I am, I think. But it is over: & put away; & Lord Sackville is dead & lies at Withyam, & I passed Knole with Vita yesterday & had to look away from the vast masterless house, without a flag. This is what she minds most. When she left the house behind the old cart horses, she went for ever, she said, after complete rule for three days.[1]

3. Lady Strachey (1840-1928), *née* Jane Maria Grant, Duncan's aunt and mother of ten Stracheys, died in December (see below, 18 December 1928). VW's article on 'The Novels of George Meredith' appeared in the *TLS* of 9 February 1928 (Kp C297). Her tribute to Hardy had long been in preparation; it was begun in December 1921, having been effectively commissioned by Bruce Richmond as early as February 1919 (see *II VW Diary*, 9 August 1921, n 2). It was published, under the title 'Thomas Hardy's Novels', as the leading article in the *TLS*, 19 January 1928 (Kp C294).

1. Vita's father, the 3rd Baron Sackville, died at Knole on 28 January, aged sixty; he was buried, as the Sackvilles have been since the fourteenth century, in the family chapel at Withyham Church, his coffin drawn thither by carthorses. Since he had no son, his titles and estates passed to his brother Charles.

For some reason, I am hacking rather listlessly at the last chapter of Orlando, which was to have been the best. Always always the last chapter slips out of my hands. One gets bored. One whips oneself up. I still hope for a fresh wind, & dont very much bother, except that I miss the fun, which was so tremendously lively all October, November & December. I have my doubts if it is not empty; & too fantastic to write at such length.

For the rest, Bloomsbury today revives. Clive is back: whereupon Mary asks us to lunch: & so we return to some flicker of the snowdrop pallor of very early spring.

My pen protests. This writing is nonsense, it says. And L. is with M[argaret] Ll[ewelyn]. D[avies]. Pinker has the lice. [*Several ink blots.*]

Saturday 18 February

I am happy to say I have still a few pounds in the Bank, & my own cheque book too. This great advance in dignity was made in the autumn. Out of my £60 I have bought a Heal bed; a cupboard, a fur coat, & now a strip of carpet for the hall. This financial revision has been a great success. And I pan out articles so as to write one & earn £30 a month. And I should be revising Lord Chesterfield at this moment, but I'm not. My mind is woolgathering away about Women & Fiction, which I am to read at Newnham in May. The mind is the most capricious of insects— flitting fluttering. I had thought to write the quickest most brilliant pages in Orlando yesterday—not a drop came, all, forsooth, for the usual physical reasons, which declared themselves today. It is the oddest feeling: as if a finger stopped the flow of the ideas in the brain: it is unsealed, & the blood rushes all over the place. Again, instead of writing O. I've been racing up & down the whole field of my lecture. And tomorrow, alas, we motor; for I must get back into the book—which has brightened the last few days satisfactorily. Not that my sensations in writing are an infallible guide.

We dined with Ka.[2] She had unshaded all Nessa's lamps, & somehow commonplaced the house strangely. It was full too of those derelicts whom she collects—the earnest, the ugly, the unhappy. Never have I sat next such driftwood as Mrs Campbell. Garnett was as bad—an over-educated prig. So tired I cant talk—three large committees this afternoon —gave accurate information about cooking eggs.

Before that, there was Todd & Clive—Clive is ubiquitous. Todd like some primeval animal emerging from the swamp, muddy, hirsute. A

2. During her absence in France, Vanessa Bell had let her rooms at 37 Gordon Square to Ka and Will Arnold-Forster. Ka's other guests have not been identified.

woman who is commercial—rather an exception in my world. She spoke of "getting my money back" as Gerald Duckworth might have spoken with the same look of rather hostile & cautious greed, as though the world were banded to rob her. This money-grubbing way is not attractive; but it is lightened by a shimmer of dash & 'chic' even. She stands on her two feet as she expresses it. She is starting a paper—I'm so bored with people starting papers in May! There's Desmond for another.[3] But Todd has none of his bubble & gush. She finds work very dull. She likes life. [*Six words omitted*] flirting with Osbert I presume. She is tapir like, & the creatures nose snuffs pertinaciously after Bloomsbury.

Dadie came in for a moment, rather drawn & white, 'making money' too. We are a little out of that, Leonard & I: L. never makes a penny; I mean tries to: & I could almost wish we were more lavish in our ways. This is occasionally in my thoughts. And what else is? I doubt that I shall ever write another novel after O. I shall invent a new name for them.

Lunch with Mary; lunch with Clive; dinner with Clive; tea with Jane, raised in bed, with her old white head lifted up, on pillows, very aged & rather exalted, able only to talk or listen for 10 minutes or so.[4] Mary & Jack simmering with polished domestic affluence & prettiness: gay bunches everywhere; & paint, & carpets; but not much backing to it. Jack develops, before 3 strikes, the storytelling manner: by 3.30 all the stories are told. Home to shabbiness.

Sunday 18 March

I have lost my writing board; an excuse for the anaemic state of this book. Indeed I only write now, in between letters, to say that Orlando was finished yesterday as the clock struck one. Anyhow the canvas is covered. There will be three months of close work needed, imperatively, before it can be printed; for I have scrambled & splashed, & the canvas shows through in a thousand places. But it is a serene, accomplished

3. Dorothy Todd had been relieved of her editorship of British *Vogue* by its American owners in 1926 as she failed to make it profitable to them; she was now proposing to finance and produce a quarterly of similar quality herself, but did not succeed. Desmond MacCarthy's monthly, *Life and Letters*, subsidised by the Hon. Oliver Brett (later 3rd Viscount Esher), first appeared in June 1928, and he continued to edit it for five years.

4. Jane Ellen Harrison (1850-1928), one-time lecturer and Fellow of Newnham College, Cambridge, was a distinguished classical scholar, archaeologist, and anthropologist. The Hogarth Press had published her *Reminiscences of a Student's Life* in 1925 (*HP Checklist* 64). VW visited her at Mecklenburgh Street, WC1, where she now lived with Hope Mirrlees.

feeling, to write, even provisionally, The End, & we go off on Saturday, with my mind appeased.

I have written this book quicker than any: & it is all a joke; & yet gay & quick reading I think; a writers holiday. I feel more & more sure that I will never write a novel again. Little bits of rhyme come in. So we go motoring across France on Saturday, & shall be back on April 17th for the summer. Time flies—oh yes: that summer should be here again; & I still have the faculty of wonder at it. The world swinging round again & bringing its green & blue close to ones eyes.

Since February I have been a little clouded with headache, had a touch of influenza; & so, with the lights down, & all energy turned to forcing my book along, have not written here. I dislike these months. Shall we try Rome next year? Control of life is what one should learn now: its economic management. I feel cautious, like a poor person, now I am 46. But I may be dead then, I think, & so take my French lessons now, instead of waiting.

Thursday 22 March

There are the last pages at the end of Orlando, & it is twenty five minutes to one; & I have written everything I have to write, & on Saturday we go abroad.

Yes its done—Orlando—begun on 8th October, as a joke; & now rather too long for my liking. It may fall between stools, be too long for a joke, & too frivolous for a serious book. All this I dismiss from a mind avid only of green fields. The sun; wine; sitting doing nothing. I have been for the last 6 weeks rather a bucket than a fountain; sitting to be shot into by one person after another. A rabbit that passes across a shooting gallery, & one's friends go pop-pop. Heaven be praised, Sibyl today puts us off, which leaves Dadie only, & a whole days solitude, please Heaven, tomorrow. But I intend to control this rabbit shooting business when I come back. And money making. I hope to settle in & write one nice little discreet article for £25 each month; & so live; without stress; & so read— what I want to read. At 46 one must be a miser; only have time for essentials.

But I think I have made moral reflections enough, & should describe people, save that, when seen so colourlessly, by duty not wish, one's mind is a little slack in taking notes. Morgan & Desmond were here to tea. Morgan more of the blue butterfly than ever. Unless I talk, he says nothing. And any shadow sends him flitting. Desmond comes in, round as a billiard ball; & this is true of his dear bubbling lazy mind; which has such a glitter & lustre now from mere being at ease in the world that it puts me into a good temper to be with him. He describes, analyses, narrates; does not actually talk. All his blandishments are now active to get articles for "Life & Letters" which comes out in May. I am scarcely flattered now to be asked; yet of course dashed a little when I refuse Mrs van Doren's £120 & she takes no notice.[1] And a little dashed, too, not to get the Femina prize—partly because I've been exhibited as a competitor & people will think me dashed: which I'm not, innately.[2]

Roger & Helen, Ka & Will, the other night. Roger malicious a little, & vain. "I am the most read critic in England, & yet I have nowhere to write." Analysed, this amounts to the fact that The Nation only pays him £5, & Konody gets more, & the pages of the Burlington are more thumbed at his articles than at MacColl's.[3] There is an innocence in this vanity which is likeable; but I am touchy for the reputation of Bloomsbury. I thought I could see Ka & Will comparing us, & being glad we were not impeccable. They compare us with the political world: we them with our own. Will lay with his eyes shut, & I was rather sorry for him. He knows what Roger thinks of his pictures, & what I don't think—for I dont look at them; but he has the generosity to praise my books. We middleaged people now scarcely covet each others good opinion very seriously: are content to be different.

Watery blowy weather; & this time next week we shall be in the middle of France.

The Woolfs spent the week end of 24 March at Monks House, and made the Newhaven-Dieppe channel crossing on Monday 26 March. They drove via Beauvais, Troyes, Beaune, Vienne, Orange and Aix, and reached Cassis on

1. Irita Van Doren (1891-1966), wife of the writer Carl Van Doren, was currently editor of the weekly Book Supplement of the *New York Herald Tribune* and had, since 1925, commissioned a number of articles from VW, including a series of six reviews published in 1927 (Kp C284, 286-90) for which she paid her £120. Presumably she had now offered the same amount for a similar series and been refused; in 1929 she raised her price to £50 an article (see below, 13 April 1929).
2. VW's dejection was premature: on 23 March she read a *Times* report from Paris that she had been awarded the 1927-28 *Prix Femina* for *To the Lighthouse*; official intimation came in a letter from the Honorary Secretary of the British Femina-Vie Heureuse Committee dated 26 March 1928 (LWP, Sussex) by which time VW was in France. The two other final 'competitors' this year were Storm Jameson and Stella Benson.
3. Roger Fry and Ka Arnold-Forster dined with the Woolfs on 20 March; their spouses came in afterwards. Paul G. Konody (1872-1933) was art critic of the *Observer* and *Daily Mail* and author of numerous books on art and artists; D. S. MacColl (1859-1948) an influential administrator and writer upon art.

Sunday 1 April. There they stayed in rooms in the Château de Fontcreuse which belonged to Colonel Teed, taking most of their meals with Vanessa and her family at 'La Bergère'. The return journey, beginning on 9 April, took them, with overnight stops at Tarascon, Florac, Aurillac, Guéret, Blois and Dreux, to Dieppe; after a very rough crossing on 16 April, they left the car in Lewes and took the train to London.

Tuesday 17 April

Home again, as foretold, last night, & to settle the dust in my mind, write here. We have been across France & back—every inch of that fertile field traversed by the admirable Singer. And now towns & spires & scenes begin to rise in my mind as the rest sinks. I see Chartres in particular, the snail, with its head straight, marching across the flat country, the most distinguished of churches. The rose window is like a jewel on black velvet. The outside is very intricate yet simple; elongated; somehow preserved from the fantastic & ornate. Grey weather dashed all over this; & I remember coming in at night in the wet often, & hearing the rain in hotels. Often I was bobbing up & down on my two glasses of vin du pays.

It was rather a rush & a cram—as these jumbled notes testify. Once we were high up on a mountain in a snow storm; & rather afraid of a long tunnel. Twenty miles often cut us off from civilisation. One wet afternoon we punctured in a mountain village & I went in & sat with the family— a nice scrupulous polite woman, a girl who was pretty, shy, had a friend called Daisy at Earlsfield. They caught trout & wild boars. Then on we went to Florac, where I found a book—Girardin's memoirs in the old bookcase that had been sold with the house. Always some good food & hot bottles at night. And there was Nessa & Duncan & Clive (who smacked me in public—curse him for an uneasy little upstart.) Oh & my prize—£40 from the French. And Julian. And one or two hot days & the Pont du Garde in the sun; & Les Beaux (this is where Dante got his idea of Hell Duncan said) & mounting all the time steadily was my desire for words, till I envisaged a sheet of paper & pen & ink as something of miraculous desirability—could even relish the scratch as if it were a divine kind of relief to me— And there was St Remy & the ruins in the sun. I forget now how it all went—how thing fitted to thing; but the eminences now emerge, & I noticed how, talking to Raymond at The Nation this afternoon we had already pitched on the high points. Before that, crossing the graveyard in the bitter windy rain, we saw Hope & a dark cultivated woman. But on they went past us, with the waver of an eye. Next moment

APRIL 1928

I heard Virginia, & turned & there was Hope coming back—"Jane died yesterday" she murmured, half asleep, talking distraught, 'out of herself.' We kissed by Cromwell's daughter's grave, where Shelley used to walk, for Jane's death.[1] She lay dead outside the graveyard in that back room where we saw her lately raised on her pillows, like a very old person, whom life has tossed up, & left; exalted, satisfied, exhausted. Hope the colour of dirty brown paper. Then to the office, then home to work here; & now to work & work, as hard as I can.

Saturday 21 April

A bitter windy rainy day. There is no blue, no red, no green in this detestable spring. Furs are in the shops. I have walked across the Park with Leonard; come home; find the char in the studio; must write here instead of making, as I had meant, some carefully polished sentences—for Orlando is to tell the truth, damned rough.

Life is either too empty or too full. Happily, I never cease to transmit these curious damaging shocks. At 46 I am not callous; suffer considerably; make good resolutions—still feel as experimental & on the verge of getting at the truth as ever. Oh & Vita—to change the subject & take up the burden of facts—has had a stupendous row with her mother—in the course of which she was made to take the pearl necklace from her neck, cut it in two with a pocket knife, deliver over the 12 central pearls, put the relics, all running loose, in an envelope the solicitor gave her. Thief, liar, I hope you'll be killed by an omnibus—so 'my honoured Lady Sackville' addressed her, trembling with rage in the presence of a secretary & a solicitor & a Chauffeur. The woman is said to be mad. Vita very gallant & wild & tossing her head & taking me to the Zoo & saying she was wild & free & wd. make her money now herself by writing.[2]

And I find myself again in the old driving whirlwind of writing against time. Have I ever written with it? But I vow I wont spend longer at Orlando, which is a freak; it shall come out in September, though the

1. Jane Harrison died on 15 April at 11 Mecklenburgh Street; the adjacent graveyard behind the Foundling Hospital, known as St George's Fields, was that of St George the Martyr Church, Queen Square, Bloomsbury. Oliver Cromwell's *grand-daughter* Mrs Gibson was buried there in 1727.
2. The dowager Lady Sackville, *née* Victoria Sackville-West (1862-1936), illegitimate daughter of Lionel Sackville-West (2nd Baron Sackville) and 'Pepita', a Spanish dancer, had married her cousin Lionel Edward Sackville-West (3rd Baron Sackville) in 1890. A woman of abounding vitality, charm, and wealth, she grew increasingly erratic and demanding with age; in 1919 she had left her husband and Knole, and now lived at Brighton. (See V. Sackville-West, *Pepita*, 1937, *HP Checklist* 419.)

perfect artist would revoke & rewrite & polish—infinitely. But hours remain over to be filled with reading something or other—I'm not sure what. What sort of summer do I desire? Now that I have 16 pounds to spend before July 1st (on our new system) I feel freer: can afford a dress or a hat, & so may go about, a little, if I want. And yet the only exciting life is the imaginary one. Once I get the wheels spinning in my head, I dont want money much, or dress, or even a cupboard, a bed at Rodmell or a sofa.

Dined with Lydia & Maynard: two couples, elderly, childless distinguished. He & she both urbane & admirable. Grey comes at Maynard's temples. He is finer looking now: not with us pompous or great: simple, with his mind working always, on Russian, Bolshevists, glands, genealogies; always the proof of a remarkable mind when it overflows thus vigorously into byepaths. There are two royal stocks in England he says from which all intellect descends. He will work this out as if his fortune depended on it. Lydia is composed, & controlled. She says very sensible things.

We went, also, to Jane's funeral, getting 'there' (somewhere out of the world where buses pass only one every 15 minutes), just as the service ended;[3] marching into the church clamorously; but it was only barely full of the dingiest people; cousins I fancy from the North, very drab: the only male relation afflicted, with a bubbly chin, a stubbly beard, & goggly eyes. Distinguished people drag up such queer chains of family when they die. They had hired Daimlers too, which succeeded the coffin at a foots pace. We walked to the grave; the clergyman, a friend, waited for the dismal company to collect; then read some of the lovelier, more rational parts of the Bible; & said, by heart, Abide with me. The gravedigger had given him, surreptitiously, a handful of clay, which he divided into three parts & dropped at the right moments. A bird sang most opportunely; with a gay indifference, & if one liked, hope, that Jane would have enjoyed. Then the incredibly drab female cousins advanced, each with a fat bunch of primroses & dropped them in; & we also advanced & looked down at the coffin at the bottom of a very steep brazen looking grave—But tho' L. almost cried, I felt very little—only the beauty of the Come unto me all ye that are weary; but as usual the obstacle of not believing dulled & bothered me. Who is 'God' & what the Grace of Christ? & what did they mean to Jane?

Raymond to tea—two hours animated admirable light & airy & well

3. Jane Harrison's funeral was at St Marylebone Cemetery, Finchley, on the afternoon of 19 April; it was that evening the Woolfs dined with the Keyneses.

seasoned talk, about facts mostly: ghosts; consciousness; novels: not people much. But he has his shirts made of figured tablecloths, shiny, hard.

And what am I to read? Pinker is back. And Leonard having tea with his mother. And perhaps the old woman has sighed herself through my room, & I can go down & do that typing, & write to the little man who smacks me in public & appeals for my pity—Clive I mean.[4]

Tuesday 24 April

Waiting for Gumbo [Marjorie Strachey]—how I hate waiting for anybody! Can't settle, read, think—so I write: an odd tribute to the uses I put this diary to. And I should be typing O. in the basement. Must now do 10 pages daily till June 1st. Well, I like being an ass on a mill round.

In from the triumph of buying a dress & a coat for about 5.10. What one must do is to face the girl with one's naked kindly searching eye: speak firmly; ask for a looking glass & study effects. Then they quail, under powder & paint. A lovely soaring summer day this: winter sent howling home to his arctic. I was reading Othello last night, & was impressed by the volley & volume & tumble of his words: too many I should say, were I reviewing for the Times. He put them in when tension was slack. In the great scenes, everything fits like a glove. The mind tumbles & splashes among words when it is not being urged on: I mean, the mind of a very great master of words who is writing with one hand. He abounds. The lesser writers stint. As usual, impressed by Shre. But my mind is very bare to words—English words—at the moment: they hit me, hard, I watch them bounce & spring. I've read only French for 4 weeks. An idea comes to me for an article on French; what we know of it.

Friday 4 May

And now theres the Femina prize to record before I go off this brilliant summer day to tea with Miss Jenkins in Doughty Street.[1] I am going dutifully, not to snub the female young. But I shall be overpowering I doubt not. But it is a wonderful day.

4. See *III VW Letters* no. 1885, dated 21 April; Clive was still at Cassis.
1. (Margaret) Elizabeth (Heald) Jenkins (b. 1905) a scholar and graduate of Newnham College, Cambridge, was at this time an unpublished novelist (she was to become a notable biographer). She had been invited to Tavistock Square with John Hayward one evening in March, when she had been the victim of Clive Bell's extravagant gallantries (see *III VW Letters*, no. 1867).

The prize was an affair of dull stupid horror: a function; not alarming; stupefying. Hugh Walpole saying how much he disliked my books; rather, how much he feared for his own. Little Miss Robins, like a red breast, creeping out.[2] I remember your mother—the most beautiful Madonna & at the same time the most complete woman of the world. Used to come & see me in my flat (I see this as a summer visit on a hot day). She never confided. She would suddenly say something so unexpected, from that Madonna face, one thought it *vicious*. This I enjoyed: nothing else made much impression. Afterwards there was the horror of having looked ugly in cheap black clothes. I cannot control this complex. I wake at dawn with a start. Also the 'fame' is becoming vulgar & a nuisance. It means nothing; & yet takes one's time. Americans perpetually. Croly; Gaige; offers:

We have seen an endless number of people—Eddie, Lytton, Miss Ritchie, Francis, Vita,—& now the minute Jenkins.[3]

Thursday 31 May

No I cannot read Proust at the moment—
Leonard is reading Orlando, which goes to the printer tomorrow. It is

2. The Femina-Vie Heureuse Prize (£40) was presented to VW at the Institut Français in South Kensington on 2 May by the popular novelist Hugh (Seymour) Walpole (1884-1941), whom she had once met at luncheon with Lady Colefax (see *II VW Diary*, 16 November 1923); their picture appeared on the back page of the *Times* on 3 May. Elizabeth Robins (1862-1952), actress, author, and feminist, born in Louisville, Kentucky. In 1888 she had settled in London where, in the 'nineties, she pioneered and acted in productions of Ibsen's plays, financed by a subscription fund of which Gerald Duckworth had been treasurer (her *Ibsen and the Actress* (*HP Checklist* 174) was published in the Hogarth Essays series in October 1928). She gave up acting in 1902, but wrote a play *Votes for Women!* (1907), and was a prolific novelist.
3. Herbert David Croly (1869-1930) had since 1914 been one of the editors of the *New Republic*, the New York journal which had published some twenty articles by VW; he and his wife had tea with the Woolfs on 26 April. Crosby Gaige (1882-1949), who came to tea on 5 May, was an American with wide-ranging interests in the theatre, in food and drink, bibliography, and book production; his privately printed $15 edition of *Orlando* was to appear in New York in October, a week before that of the Hogarth Press (see Kp A11; also LWP, Sussex, IID 16a). Alice MacGregor Ritchie (1897-1941), born in Natal, had studied at Newnham College, Cambridge, from 1917-20, and later worked in the League of Nations Secretariat at Geneva; she was now employed partly as traveller for Hogarth Press books, and partly in writing her own: her first novel *The Peacemakers* was published in May 1928 (*HP Checklist* 173).

very quiet at the moment. Whitsun is over. We were at Rodmell & saw
the races, where the marsh used to be. And our field is sold to Allinson—
who is going to build.[4] And what then? I have no brain left over to think
with. And Leonard is arguing in the basement with Dadie. What can it be
about? Pinker is asleep in the chair. Angelica comes back tomorrow. I feel
a kind of drought caused by the lack of Nessa, & ask how shall I manage
if we are apart 6 months, not only 4?[5] But my creed is to batter down
opposition. I have seen—

I daresay a good many people, Rose Macaulay, Rebecca West, Maurois
flash to mind in a bunch last week,[6] & Todd's room; rather to her credit,
workmanlike; Garland pear[l]hung & silken; Todd as buxom as a badger.
Rebecca a hardened old reprobate I daresay, but no fool; & the whole
atmosphere professional; no charm, except the rather excessive charm of
Garland.

Clive's book out—a very superficial one, L. says.[7]

The sun is out again; I have half forgotten Orlando already, since L.
has read it & it has half passed out of my possession. I think it lacks the
sort of hammering I should have given it if I had taken longer: is too
freakish & unequal. Very brilliant now & then. As for the effect of the
whole, that I cant judge. Not, I think 'important' among my works. L.
says a satire.

Gosse is dead, & I am half reconciled to him by they're saying in the
papers that he chose to risk a dangerous operation rather than be an
invalid for life. This kind of vitality always gets me. But—lies otherwise

4. The races held on Whit Monday at Southease inaugurated what the local press
referred to as 'a new Sussex sport' popularly termed 'galloping' or 'flapping'.
'Our field' of some 6½ acres in all consisted of a strip adjoining and level with
Monks House garden to the north, falling away down a steep bank to a larger area
stretching in a wedge shape towards the Ouse Valley 'flats'. The recurrent threat
of this field being built upon was removed when LW finally succeeded in buying
it later this year (see below, 9 August 1928).

5. Angelica, with her friend Judith Bagenal, was brought home from Cassis by train
by Grace Germany; Duncan and Vanessa, who came by car, spent some time in
Paris on the way, and did not reach London until 16 June.

6. André Maurois (1885-1967), French biographer and man of letters. VW had read
and enjoyed his biographies of Shelley (1923) and of Disraeli (1927); he was to
write a preface to the French translation of Mrs Dalloway published in 1929
(Kp D11). She met him (and Arnold Bennett) at a tea party given by Lady Colefax
before Whitsun.

7. *Civilization: An Essay* (1928); LW wrote of it in his weekly page 'The World of
Books' in the *N & A*, 9 June 1928, that both 'Bell's method and his assumptions
are wrong and are bound to lead to wrong conclusions'.

flourish round his grave, & poor dear Desmond with 3 children to keep has to be as profuse of them as anybody.[8]

We met him yesterday in Kingsway, just as I was thinking how I should describe him if I wrote a Memoir, as Molly insists. He loomed up as if my thought had made him visible. He gave me the first number of his paper.

Rose Macaulay says "Yes I won the prize"—rather peevishly.[9] I think at once that she is jealous, & test whatever else she says with a view to finding out whether she is or not. About Colefax: "I'm the only one of all my friends who isn't asked there." About work: 'I've got to work tomorrow' I say, excusing myself for not going to Raymond's party. "So have we all" rather sharply. & so on. This shows through a dozen little phrases, as we're talking of America, articles &c: she is jealous of me; anxious to compare us: but I may imagine it: & it shows my own jealousy no doubt, as suspicions always do. One cdn't know them if one hadn't got them. And now to Angelica with a packet of bulls eyes. I am again beginning to read.

L. takes Orlando more seriously than I had expected. Thinks it in some ways better than The Lighthouse; about more interesting things, & with more attachment to life, & larger. The truth is I expect I began it as a joke, & went on with it seriously. Hence it lacks some unity. He says it is very original. Anyhow I'm glad to be quit this time of writing 'a novel'; & hope never to be accused of it again. Now I want to write some very closely reasoned criticism; book on fiction; an essay of some sort (but not Tolstoy for the Times). Dr Burney's evening party I think for Desmond.[10] And then? I feel anxious to keep the hatch down: not to let too many projects come in. Something abstract poetic next time—I dont know. I rather like the idea of these Biographies of living people. Ottoline suggests herself—but no. And I must tear up all that manuscript, & write a great many notes & adventure out into the world—as I shall do tomorrow, when I go to have my ears pierced with Vita.

8. Sir Edmund Gosse died on 16 May, aged 76. Desmond MacCarthy's tribute to him appeared in the *Sunday Times* of 20 May 1928; its general tenor may be inferred from the opening sentence: ' "How beautifully *he* would do this" must be the first reflection of one who sits down to write a commemorative article in these columns.' MacCarthy was to succeed Gosse as the literary columnist of the *Sunday Times* on 12 August 1928.

9. Rose Macaulay dined alone with VW on 24 May. She had been awarded the *Prix Femina* in 1922 for her eleventh novel, *Dangerous Ages*.

10. For VW's 'book on fiction' see above, 7 December 1925, n 6. 'Dr Burney's Evening Party' was published first in the *New York Herald Tribune*, 21 and 28 July 1929, and reprinted in Desmond MacCarthy's *Life and Letters* in September 1929 (Kp C313).

June weather. Still, bright, fresh. Owing to the Lighthouse (car) I dont feel so shut in London as usual, & can imagine the evening on some moor now, or in France without the envy I used to have, in London on a fine evening. Also London itself perpetually attracts, stimulates, gives me a play & a story & a poem, without any trouble, save that of moving my legs through the streets. I walked Pinker to Grays Inn Gardens this afternoon, & saw—Red Lion Square: Morris'es house; thought of them on winters evenings in the 50ties; thought we are just as interesting;[11] saw the ⟨street⟩ Great Ormond St where a dead girl was found yesterday; saw & heard the Salvation Army making Xtianity gay for the people: a great deal of nudging & joking on the part of very unattractive young men & women; making it lively, I suppose; & yet, to be truthful, when I watch them I never laugh or criticise, but only feel how strange & interesting this is: wonder what they mean by 'Come to the Lord.' I daresay exhibitionism accounts for some of it: the applause of the gallery; this lures boys to sing hymns; & kindles shop boys to announce in a loud voice that they are saved. It is what writing for the Evening Standard is for Rose Macaulay & I was going to say myself: but so far I have not done it.[12]

Wednesday 20 June

So sick of Orlando I can write nothing. I have corrected the proofs in a week; & cannot spin another phrase. I detest my own volubility. Why be always spouting words? Also I have almost lost the power of reading. Correcting proofs 5, 6, or 7 hours a day, writing in this & that meticulously, I have bruised my reading faculty severely. Take up Proust after dinner & put him down. This is the worst time of all. It makes me suicidal. Nothing seems left to do. All seems insipid & worthless. Now I will watch & see how I resurrect. I think I shall read something—say a life of Goethe. Then I shall visit about. Mercifully, Nessa is back. My earth is watered again. I go back to words of one syllable: feel come over me the feathery change: rather true that: as if my physical body put on some soft comfortable, skin. She is a necessity to me—as I am not to her. I run to her as the wallaby runs to the old kangaroo. She is also very cheerful, solid, happy. The trifles that annoy other people, she passes off; as if her

---

11. After leaving Oxford, William Morris and Edward Burne Jones had in 1856-58 shared rooms and a studio at 17 Red Lion Square, which became a rendezvous for their lively circle.
12. In the 1920's Rose Macaulay contributed light articles to the popular press, including the *Evening Standard*, as a means of earning her living.

happiness were a million or two in the bank. And how masterfully she controls her dozen lives; never in a muddle, or desperate, or worried; never spending a pound or a thought needlessly; yet with it all free, careless, airy, indifferent: a very notable achievement.

Julian dines with us tonight to meet Miss Sylva Norman whom I fetched up from complete nonentity on the telephone last night.[1] Another marvel of science. There she was in 10 minutes after we thought of her saying she would LOVE to come. Julian is a vast fat powerful sweet tempered engaging young man, into whose arms I let myself fall, half sister, half mother, & half (but arithmetic denies this) the mocking stirring contemporary friend. Mercifully Julian has his instincts sane & normal: has a wide forehead, & considerable address & competence in the management of life. But my tooth is aching. They will dine with us; & that is what I am ripe for—to go adventuring on the streams of other peoples lives—speculating, adrift

Friday 22 June

So far I wrote & was interrupted—always interrupted; am now off to Ruislip with Pinker to wed her, & it is

Saturday 7 July

& a Saturday morning, very hot & fine.

All last night I dreamt of Katherine Mansfield & wonder what dreams are; often evoke so much more emotion, than thinking does—almost as if she came back in person & was outside one, actively making one feel; instead of a figment called up & recollected, as she is, now, if I think of her. Yet some emotion lingers on the day after a dream; even though I've now almost forgotten what happened in the dream, except that she was lying on a sofa in a room high up, & a great many sad faced women were round her. Yet somehow I got the feel of her, & of her as if alive again, more than by day.

At Long Barn yesterday, a good rather happy visit. I'm interested by the gnawing down of strata in friendship; how one passes unconsciously to different terms; takes things easier; dont mind at all hardly about dress or anything; scarcely feel it an exciting atmosphere, which, too, has its drawback from the "fizzing" point of view: yet is saner, perhaps deeper.

1. Sylva Norman (1901-1971), whose novel *Nature Has No Tune* the Woolfs were to publish in 1929 (*HP Checklist* 203), was a writer and journalist; she reviewed books for the *N & A*, was to become an authority on Shelley and, in 1933, the second wife of Edmund Blunden.

Lay by the black currant bushes lecturing Vita on her floundering habits with the Campbells for instance. Mrs C. beat by her husband, all because V. will come triumphing, with her silver & her coronets & her footmen into the life of a herring-cooker. She cooks herrings on a gas stove, I said, always remembering my own phrases.

But having thus scrambled in a page, I must go—& yet want to stay & write about Sterne.[1]

Monks House
Rodmell.

Wednesday 8 August[1]

Eddy has just gone, leaving me the usual feeling: why is not human intercourse more definite, tangible: why aren't I left holding a small round substance, say of the size of a pea, in my hand; something I can put in a box & look at? There is so little left. Yet these people one sees are fabric only made once in the world; these contacts we have are unique; & if E. were, say killed tonight, nothing definite would happen to me; yet his substance is never again to be repeated. Our meeting is—but the thread of this idea slips perpetually; constantly though it recurs, with sadness, to my mind: how little our relationships matter; & yet they are so important: in him, in me, something to him, to me, infinitely sentient, of the highest vividness, reality. But if I died tonight, he too would continue. Something illusory then enters into all that part of life. I am so important to myself: yet of no importance to other people: like the shadow passing over the downs. I deceive myself into thinking that I am important to other people: that makes part of my extreme vividness to myself: as a matter of fact, I dont matter; & so part of my vividness is unreal; gives me a sense of illusion. Eddy says he thinks "What impression am I making?" constantly & is agitated: as a matter of fact, he is probably making no impression: his agitation is about nothing: he is mistaken.

But, superficially speaking—for fundamentally I was thinking a thousand other thoughts; his presence was only I suppose a light on the surface of my mind—something green or iron-coloured or grey—while the water itself rushed on, in its old fierce way—thoughts about my writing; & about old age; & about buying the field (we bought it this morning) & about the children being noisy; & if I had bought Southease. All this went on sub-cutaneously. Yet his presence somehow checked the

---

1. VW's article on Sterne, 'A Sentimental Journey', was published in the *New York Herald Tribune*, 23 September 1928. Kp C303.
1. VW has written *Wednesday Aug. 9th*. She and LW had come to Rodmell for their summer stay on 24 July.

flow of sub-cutaneous life. I was always having to think what comes next? How am I to break into this other life which is 6 inches off mine in the deck chair in the orchard? So that my own thoughts could not flow deep or rapid, as they are doing now that Eddy is on his way to Tunbridge Wells. And what remains of Eddy is now in some ways more vivid, though more transparent, all of him composing itself in my mind, all I could get of him, & making itself a landscape appropriate to it; making a work of art for itself.

I am, as I write, wherever I come to a stop, looking out of the lodge window, at our field; & the little cottage boys with the cursed shrill voices, playing cricket half way down it; & as usual I am sentimental & worried. Children playing: yes, & interrupting me; yes & I have no children of my own; & Nessa has; & yet I dont want them any more, since my ideas so possess me; & I detest more & more interruption; & the slow heaviness of physical life, & almost dislike peoples bodies, I think, as I grow older; & want always to cut that short, & get my utmost fill of the marrow, of the essence.

I write thus partly in order to slip the burden of writing narrative, as for instance; we came here a fortnight ago. And we lunched at Charleston & Vita came & we were offered the field & we went to see the farm at Lime Kiln. Yet no doubt I shall be more interested, come 10 years, in facts; & shall want, as I do when I read, to be told details, details, so that I may look up from the page & arrange them too, into one of those makings up which seem so much truer done thus, from heaps of non-assorted facts, than now I can make them, when it is almost immediately being done ⟨by me⟩ under my eyes. It was a fine day, last Monday I rather think; & we drove through Ripe; & there was a girl & her feller at the gate in a narrow lane; & we had to interrupt them to turn the motor. I thought how the things they had been saying were dammed, like a river, by our interruption; & they stood there half amused, yet impatient, telling us to go to the left, but the road was up. They were glad when we went; yet gave us a flash of interest. Who are these people in their motor car: where are they going?—& then this sunk beneath the mind, & they forgot us completely. We went on. And then we reached the farm. The oasts had umbrella spokes poking out at the top: all was so ruined & faded. The Tudor farm house was almost blind; very small eyebrowed windows; old Stuart farmers must have peered out over the flat land, very dirty, ill-kempt, like people in slums. But they had dignity: at least thick walls; fireplaces; & solidity whereas now the house is lived in by one old, weedy pink faced man, who flung himself in his armchair. Go where you like— go anywhere, he said, loose jointed, somehow decayed, like the hop oasts;

& damp like the mildewed carpets, & sordid, like the beds with the pots sticking out under them. The walls were sticky; the furniture mid Victorian; little light came through. It was all dying, decaying; & he had been there 50 years, & it will drop to pieces, since there is not enough beauty or strength to make anyone repair it.[2]

Sunday 12 August

Shall I now continue this soliloquy, or shall I imagine an audience, which will make me describe?

This sentence is due to the book on fiction which I am now writing—once more, O once more.[3] It is a hand to mouth book. I scribble down whatever I can think of about Romance, Dickens &c. must hastily [?] gorge on Jane Austen tonight & dish up something tomorrow. All this criticism however may well be dislodged by the desire to write a story. The Moths hovers some where at the back of my brain. Janie & Julian have just gone. Julian a little in the style of Jem, only so much saner: broad browed, wavy haired, vast, fat, powerful, good-tempered.[4] He still laughs a great deal; but perhaps less than he did. Perhaps he is sticking his pitch-fork in the ground. Janie is a little lapdog girl; like those pug faced prominent eyed wrinkled nosed little dogs that women carry about the streets; intelligent, vivacious, opening her mouth wide & snapping it shut; on one side a carpenters granddaughter—on the other a Strachey. Perhaps a little common do I mean? But Clive yesterday at Charleston said that there were no class distinctions. We had tea from bright blue cups under the pink light of the giant hollyhock. We were all a little drugged with the country: a little bucolic I thought. It was lovely enough—made me envious of its country peace: the trees all standing securely—why did my

2. Lime Kiln Farm is about 3½ miles north east of Selmeston; the farmer was appropriately named Deadman. The house was in fact restored, and still exists.

3. VW had been struggling with this 'book on fiction', originally intended for the Hogarth Press 'Lectures on Literature' series, for about two years (see above, 7 December 1925, n 6); it was finally to appear as an extended essay, 'Phases of Fiction', in three parts in *The Bookman*, New York, in April, May, and June 1929 (Kp C312). One of the eight items in MHP, Sussex, connected with this undertaking (95 pages of ms entitled *Phases of Fiction*) is dated 11 August 1928 (MHP/B 6c).

4. James Kenneth ('Jem') Stephen (1859-92), Leslie Stephen's favourite nephew, was both an heroic and alarming figure in VW's childhood; massive, handsome, ebullient, successful and popular, after an accidental blow on the head his behaviour became increasingly excitable and erratic, and he died insane. Jane-Simone ('Janie') Bussy (1906-60), only child of the French painter Simon Bussy and his wife Dorothy, née Strachey, was herself a painter.

eye catch the trees? The look of things has a great power over me. Even now, I have to watch the rooks beating up against the wind, which is high. & still I say to myself instinctively "Whats the phrase for that?" & try to make more & more vivid the roughness of the air current & the tremor of the rooks wing ⟨deep breasting it⟩ slicing—as if the air were full of ridges & ripples & roughnesses; they rise & sink, up & down, as if the exercise ⟨pleased them⟩ rubbed & braced them like swimmers in rough water. But what a little I can get down with my pen of what is so vivid to my eyes, & not only to my eyes: also to some nervous fibre or fan like membrane in my spine.

Janie Julian Leonard & I sat in the orchard till the wind got too strong, & I made them come out on the marsh & was sorry the river was low, or they might have praised it. And (irrelevantly) Miss Ritchie praises Orlando, & I was pleased till I thought, perhaps this is gratitude for our £20. Yet I dont think much either way about Orlando. Odd, how I feel myself under orders; always marching on a definite stage with each book, tho' it is one I set myself. And Duncan at Charleston was a little too aloof & supercilious seeming.

Tuesday 14 August

Just back from Long Barn & Dottie's new house, Penn in the Rocks.[5] Can one really be in love with a house? Is there not something sterile, so that one's mind becomes stringy in these passions? She is too anxious for other people to praise it. And I don't want possessions. I think this is true. I dont want to be Dottie collecting endless settees & arm chairs round myself. But then I have now a pressing sense of the flight of time; & if one is so soon to arrive, why pack all these things? More truthfully, if one is so soon to start, why prepare all these impedimenta. I feel on the verge of the world, about to take flight. Dottie on the other hand feels "I have at least, in spite of every other grudge on the part of fate, 10 or 15 thousand a year; & it is only fair that I should get from my money what I can." Somehow angrily then she sets to work to make her money slave for her. She has bought for ever & ever all these couchant rocks; rocks like kneeling elephants; agonised writhing rocks elongated rocks, rocks with grotesque roots grown into them, & Japanese trees on top. She runs about,

5. Penns-in-the-Rocks (or Penn's Rocks), near Withyham, was a mainly 18th century house of some architectural distinction, remarkable also for the multitude of great natural boulders or rocks of sandstone in the grounds. William Penn, the founder of Pennsylvania, had married the heiress to this property, but it had long since passed out of his family.

defiant strident a little discordant in her top boots with her dogs & says "I'm so tired—so worn out", gesticulates, exaggerates. I like the aristo-cratic tradition of space & a few good things. The house itself is now in sections. Half a ceiling ⟨overhangs⟩ intersects what were & will be dining room & bedroom above. This gives the house a provisional air; it is not a house that has been there 300 years, & housed Penn & other families; it is nothing—which in a house is distressing.

After that country, though, how I adore the emptiness, bareness, air & colour of this! Really. I would not give this view for Dottie's rocks. A relic I think of my fathers feeling for the Alps—this ecstasy of mine over the bare slope of Asheham hill. But then, as I remind myself, half the beauty of a country or a house comes from knowing it. One remembers old lovelinesses: knows that it is now looking ugly; waits to see it light up; knows where to find its beauty; how to ignore the bad things. This one can't do the first time of seeing. But they build with beautiful blocks of grey stone in Kent. D.'s farmhouse was the very house for me, solid, high, with the shape of the stone showing in the wall. This is all thrown in with her rocks. And she ecstasi[s]es over them, fancying them sympathetic to her genius, & makes them into part of her belief in her own genius.

Monks House looked very nice, unexpectedly so, & the great lily in the window has now four flowers. They opened in the night. So I was appeased aesthetically for my disappointment in having no letters—not one. I was going to remark however that Dottie's rocks are powdered pale greys & bright greens; they are grey as elephant backs. There are, too, bunches of scarlet berries hanging against them: only all too verdant, mossy, steamy, & enclosed for my taste. However, in the train it struck me that it is, even from one's own point of view, a great advantage that other people should like trees & so on; Why—I cant at the moment remember.

Friday 31 August

This is the last day of August, & like almost all of them of extraordinary beauty. Each day is fine enough & hot enough for sitting out; but also full of wandering clouds; & that fading & rising of the light which so en-raptures me in the downs: which I am always comparing to the light beneath an alabaster bowl, &c. The corn is now stood about in rows of three for our [*four or*] five solid shaped yellow cakes—rich, it seems, with eggs & spice: good to eat. Sometimes I see the cattle galloping 'like mad' as Dostoevsky would say, in the brooks. The clouds—if I could describe them I would: one yesterday had flowing hair on it like the very fine white hair of an old man. At this moment they are white in a leaden sky; but the sun, behind the house, is making the grass green. I walked to the racecourse today & saw a weasel.

Morgan was here for the week end; timid, touchy, infinitely charming. One night we got drunk, & talked of sodomy, & sapphism, with emotion —so much so that next day he said he had been drunk. This was started by Radclyffe Hall & her meritorious dull book. They wrote articles for Hubert all day, & got up petitions; & then Morgan saw her & she screamed like a herring gull, mad with egotism & vanity. Unless they say her book is good, she wont let them complain of the laws. Morgan said that Dr Head can convert the sodomites.[6] "Would you like to be converted?" Leonard asked. "No" said Morgan, quite definitely. He said he thought Sapphism disgusting: partly from convention, partly because he disliked that women should be independent of men.

Probably the reason why I shall be so much bored this week end by Mrs Woolf is that we shall not be able to say a word we mean.[7] It is like talking to a child; a child, too, with 'feelings': a child with "rights" & a sense of propriety & respectability & what ought to be said & done. Having made up all these principles she is, & they all are, secretly dissatisfied; because they, naturally, get no pleasure from life; are cased in thick wool from any direct contact; & so these people—an immense class—are always uneasy unless they are eating, being flattered, or doing some natural task, like nursing a child. And then, if the child is Leonard, he grows up & is horribly bored by you.

I must now begin Peacock, without attempting to describe the extraordinary primeval appearance of the farm wagons; so laden with the hay in the brooks that they look like some vast shaggy animal moving on very short legs.

We have seen Mr James about the field; & will soon, I hope, sign the agreement, or cheque; & put up a fence, which is my first act as a

6. *The Well of Loneliness*, a novel of Lesbian love by Radclyffe Hall (1886-1943), had been published in July by Jonathan Cape, who had withdrawn it in the face of outraged objections in the popular press and from the Home Secretary. E. M. Forster and LW were united in their opposition, on principle, to such suppression, and organised protests, which included a joint letter from Forster and VW published in the *N & A*, 8 September 1928. (See also P. N. Furbank, *E. M. Forster: A Life*, vol. II (1978), pp 153-5.) Sir Henry Head (1861-1940; knighted 1927), FRS, neurologist. Roger Fry, who had a high opinion of him, had recommended that the Woolfs should consult him when VW was in a suicidal condition in 1913; and they did.

7. Marie Woolf, *née* de Jongh (1850-1939), LW's Dutch-born mother. Widowed in 1892, she had raised a family of six sons and three daughters.

landowner to keep the cottage children out.[8] Nessa, being a mother, &
thus not sentimental about children, says "They can easily play somewhere else."[9]

Monday 3 September

The battle of Dunbar, the Battle of Worcester, & the death of Cromwell
—how often it seems to me I said that to my father ("my" father, not
'father' any more) at St Ives; standing bolt upright in the dining room at
Talland House. And it is a perfect 3rd of September day.[1] Leonard gave
me the blue glass jug today, because he was cross when I slapped his nose
with sweet peas, & because I was nice to his mother; & when I went into
luncheon I saw it on the table. Indeed, I almost cried. He went to Brighton
to get it for me. "I thought of it just as I was getting into the car" he said.
Perhaps I have analysed his motives wrongly.

Seldom have I felt as tired as I did last night. This shaky ramshackle old
lady of 76 wore us out. Her talk—I have written it for Nessa so cannot
repeat[2]—never stops; never follows a line; is always about people; starts
anywhere; at any moment; breaks into a Schubert trio: did you know Len
that Mr Harris lives in Gordon Sqre? So on to his daughters; how she
met one playing bridge &c. What makes it difficult is that she divines
states of feeling to some extent, & would say pointedly "You must often
think of your writing when you are not writing, Virginia", when through
exhaustion I became silent. I had one moment of peculiar & acute discomfort this morning, when she became 'intimate', & said how much she
had been touched when I sat beside her in the car yesterday. Why did I
hate it so? I felt the horror of family life, & the terrible threat to one's
liberty that I used to feel with father, Aunt Mary or George.[3] It is an

8. It would appear that Charles James, a local farmer, had enjoyed grazing rights on
   the field LW was now buying, and negotiations were proceeding for him to
   continue as tenant of the five acres of the lower part, leaving LW to incorporate
   the acre of the upper level (the 'terrace') into his garden.
9. This last sentence, written in a different ink, appears to have been added as an
   afterthought.
1. The historic battles, in 1650 and 1651, between the Parliamentary Army led by
   Oliver Cromwell, and the Scots supporting Charles II in his attempt to gain the
   throne, which were turning points in the Civil War. Cromwell died in 1658.
2. See *III VW Letters*, no. 1919 for this epistolary *tour de force*.
3. Mary Louisa Fisher, *née* Jackson (1841-1916), Julia Stephen's elder sister, had
   regarded it as her duty to supervise her nieces' conduct after their mother's death,
   as did George Duckworth. ('The meddling of aunts and the tyranny of brothers
   exasperated her.' Cf VW's review of Dorothy Osborne's letters which she was
   now reading, Kp C304.)

emotion one never gets from any other human relationship. She had the right to exact this on my part; & would feel pleasure & pain irrationally, & somehow put her claws in me. These feelings are as violent as any. And there was the sentimental, yet very vain & almost insanely selfish discourse about her love for her children; how they—these dull plain serviceable Jews & Jewesses—were all splendid men & women; at which my gorge rose. How strangely she made everything commonplace, ugly, suburban, notwithstanding a charm too: something fresh & vital such as old women have, & not, I think, old men. But to be attached to her as daughter would be so cruel a fate that I can think of nothing worse; & thousands of women might be dying of it in England today: this tyranny of mother over daughter, or father; their right to the due being as powerful as anything in the world. And then, they ask, why women dont write poetry. Short of killing Mrs W. nothing could be done. Day after day one's life would be crumpled up like a bill for 10 pen[ce] 3 farthings. Nothing has ever been said of this.

Monday 10 September

This is written, as 'this' is so often written, to fill up a little jagged piece of time, with Kennedy, the soft duckling boy, with a bill that opens wide & says 'Quack' in the drawing room, & Leonard talking to Mr James about the field.[4] Desmond, who lunched here with Julian has just gone. We spent the afternoon—hour after hour wasting away again, or why not say for once turning to gold & silver—for I should only have been reading Moby Dick otherwise—coining gold & silver talk then—talk very intimate now, more so than ever: a continuation of our talk in Tavistock Sqre the other day: there he said he had now 12 years to live; nine to be exact: & here we talked of his work, money, women, children, & writing; till I took him along the Roman road; & back to tea. I was amused to find that when Rebecca West says "men are snobs" she gets an instant rise out of Desmond; so I retorted on him with the condescending phrase used about women novelists 'limitations' in Life & Letters.[5] But there was no acrimony in this. We talked with fertility;

4. Richard Pitt Kennedy (b. 1910) had left Marlborough, a scholastic failure, at Easter and, thanks to his uncle the architect George Lawrence Kennedy (1882-1954), a fellow-member with LW of the Cranium Club, had started work as an apprentice at the Hogarth Press on 30 April. His illustrated account, *A Boy at the Hogarth Press* (1972), cast in the form of a diary, was written some forty years later and contains minor errors of fact.

5. The Woolfs had driven to London for the day on 5 September, and Desmond MacCarthy had lunched with them at Tavistock Square. In the August number of

never working a seam dry. Do you suppose then that we are now coming like the homing rooks back to the tops of our trees? & that all this cawing is the beginning of settling in for the night? I seem to notice in several of my friends some endearing & affecting cordiality: & a pleasure in intimacy; as if the sun were sinking. Often that image comes to me with some sense of my physical state being colder now, the sun just off one; the old disc of one's being growing cooler—but it is only just beginning: & one will turn cold & silver like the moon.

This has been a very animated summer: a summer lived almost too much in public. Often down here I have entered into a sanctuary; a nunnery; had a religious retreat; of great agony once; & always some terror: so afraid one is of loneliness: of seeing to the bottom of the vessel. That is one of the experiences I have had here in some Augusts; & got then to a consciousness of what I call 'reality': a thing I see before me; something abstract; but residing in the downs or sky; beside which nothing matters; in which I shall rest & continue to exist. Reality I call it. And I fancy sometimes this is the most necessary thing to me: that which I seek. But who knows—once one takes a pen & writes? How difficult not to go making 'reality' this & that, whereas it is one thing. Now perhaps this is my gift; this perhaps is what distinguishes me from other people; I think it may be rare to have so acute a sense of something like that—but again, who knows? I would like to express it too.

Pinker had 4 puppies the day (Friday) we went to the Bagenals & Dotty. Dotty was rust red, shabby, intense a little; she showed us the rocks. Leonard 'took against' her, as nurses say; violently.[6] We drove home very fast. I on the other hand took in favour of Barbara—& wished I had gone up alone with her on to the downs. I—perhaps Leonard interrupted here.

---

his monthly *Life and Letters*, in a review of *Another Country* by H. du Coudray, he had written: 'If, like the reporter, you believe that female novelists should only aspire to excellence by courageously acknowledging the limitations of their sex (Jane Austen and, in our own time, Mrs Virginia Woolf, have demonstrated how gracefully this gesture can be accomplished), Miss du Coudray's first novel may at the outset prove a little disappointing, since here is a writer definitely bent upon the attainment of masculine standards.'

6. The Bagenals, Nicholas Beauchamp (1891-1974) and Barbara, *née* Hiles (b. 1891), had married in 1918 when the former was still in the army and the latter working briefly as an assistant in the Hogarth Press in Richmond (see *I VW Diary*). He had become an expert on fruit trees and, since 1922, had been a lecturer at the East Malling Research Station near Maidstone. The Woolfs called on Dorothy Wellesley at Penn's Rocks on the way home. For LW's virulent reaction to her, see also *III VW Letters*, no. 1922.

Monday 17 September

I have precisely 5 minutes before dinner. Quentin has swallowed those precious two hours in which I was to have read Dorothy Osborne:[7] Quentin grown elegant & self conscious, liking to use French words; very sophisticated, showing in every movement now the shadow of our faults, as a set; uneasy, I doubt not; quick, sensitive; but wanting something of Julian's force & simplicity. So they change parts, growing, changing, turning from fat to thin. The drawing room smells with his paints—the gramophone like Moby Dick is white. Rachel came in with Angelica. She has quicksilver eyes, mended stockings, all the charm & dexterity of a poor clever man's child, whose wits are kept brushed, who mends her stockings, who lives on her adventures.

Desmond was here, talking the other day: intimate again, & yet too urbane, perhaps; or do I think this from the letter that so annoyed me—speaking of my paper's "butterfly lightness"—how angry I was, how depressed I became.[8] Leonard agrees that he has a complex, which leads him to belittle & fondle thus.

Saturday 22 September

This is written on the verge of my alarming holiday in Burgundy. I am alarmed of 7 days alone with Vita: interested; excited, but afraid—she may find me out, I her out. I may (& theres Mabel the Bride in her white dress at the pump. The bridegroom, a carter out of work, wears white socks. Are they pure? I doubt it. They are going to spend their honeymoon near Pevensey. He was 15 minutes late & we saw her come in wearing a wreath. And I felt this is the heart of England—this wedding in the country: history I felt; Cromwell; The Osbornes; Dorothy's shepherdesses singing: of all of whom Mr & Mrs Jarrad seem more the descendants than I am: as if they represented the unconscious breathing of England & L. & I, leaning over the wall, were detached, unconnected.[9] I suppose our

7. VW's review of *The Letters of Dorothy Osborne to William Temple*, edited by G. C. Moore Smith (1928), appeared in the *New Republic*, New York, on 24 October 1928, and in the *TLS*, 25 October 1928 (Kp C304). Quentin Bell was decorating the cabinet of the gramophone at Monks House.
8. Desmond's letter, presumably referring to VW's article 'The Niece of an Earl' (Kp C305) to be published in the October issue of his *Life and Letters*, does not survive.
9. Mabel Mockford, daughter of Mrs Mockford of Briar Cottage, Rodmell, and the late Mr Frank Mockford, married Percy William Jarrett of Northease at Rodmell Parish Church on Saturday, 22 September. The bride was 'prettily dressed in ivory crêpe-de-chine'.

thinking is the cause of this. We dont belong to any 'class'; we thinkers: might as well be French or German. Yet I am English in some way—)

But I was saying I should on the whole be confident about this French journey—that it will turn out well. I'm afraid of the morning most; & 3 o'clock in the afternoon; & wanting something Vita does not want. And I shall spend the money that might have bought a table or a glass. What one buys in foreign travel is a series of scenes; which gradually diminish to one or two, such as I still have of Greece & Venice as I saw them when I was 24 or 5. And I shall love the freedom from hours; & looking about; & the thought of coming back; & sitting talking, & some things I shall read; & one or two views, &—

This has been the finest, & not only finest, but loveliest, summer in the world. Still, though it blows, how clear & bright it is; & the clouds are opalescent; the long barns on my horizon mouse coloured; the stacks pale gold. Owning the field has given a different orient to my feelings about Rodmell. I begin to dig myself in & take part in it. And I shall build another storey to the house if I make money. But the news of Orlando is black. We may sell a third that we sold of The Lighthouse before publication—Not a shop will buy save in 6es & 12es. They say this is inevitable. No one wants biography. But it is a novel, says Miss Ritchie. But it is called a biography on the title page, they say. It will have to go to the Biography shelf. I doubt therefore that we shall do more than cover expenses—a high price to pay for the fun of calling it a biography. And I was so sure it was going to be the one popular book! Also it should be 10/6 or 12/6 not 9/- Lord, lord! Thus I must write some articles this winter, if we are to have nest eggs at the Bank. Down here I have flung myself tooth & nail on my fiction book, & should have finished the first draft but for Dorothy Osborne whom I'm dashing off. It will need entire re-writing but the grind is done—the rushing through book after book & now what shall I read? These novels have hung about me so long. Mercy it is to be quit of them; & shall I read English poetry, French memoirs— shall I read now for a book to be called "The Lives of the Obscure"? And when, I wonder, shall I begin the Moths? Not until I am pressed into it by those insects themselves. Nor have I any notion what it is to be like—a completely new attempt I think. So I always think.

A very gay active summer. Dined with the Keynes' to meet Lord Gage last Wednesday—found him with his flat face & Circassian blood, more of a character than I expected. Clive with inverse snobbery had run him down. We talked about the King, & he snubbed me by saying that he remarked an odd fact—everyone talks to him about the King. Every class, every kind of person, is interested to know what the King has for dinner.

And here was I, the intellectual, the labour woman, doing just the same thing. And there were the Russell Cookes; her I liked; him I hated.[10] A woman is in some ways so much better than a man—more natural, juicy, unfettered. But then he is a bounder, a climber, a shoving young man, who wants to be smart, cultivated, go-ahead & all the rest of it. I must use that cliché because I must do my Osborne article. & it is getting cold out here.

On 24 September VW and Vita Sackville-West sailed from Newhaven to spend a week together in Burgundy (their progress may be followed in III VW Letters, nos. 1926-32 to LW), coming back to England on 1 October. On 4 October the Woolfs returned to Tavistock Square, lunching with Vita at Long Barn on the way. Orlando was published on 11 October. On 20 October, taking Vanessa and Angelica, the Woolfs drove to Cambridge; they stayed the night with Pernel Strachey, the Principal of Newnham, where that evening VW read a paper to the Arts Society, and the next day lunched with George Rylands in his rooms at King's. The following week she again went to Cambridge, this time by train and with Vita, and spoke to the Girton ODTAA Society (26 October). These two papers, on 'Women and Fiction,' were to be expanded and published a year later as A Room of One's Own *(in which Mrs Rylands' lunch party is memorably if extravagantly described).*

Saturday 27 October

A scandal, a scandal, to let so much time slip, & I leaning on the Bridge watching it go. Only leaning has not been my pose: running up & down, irritably, excitedly restlessly. And the stream viciously eddying. Why do I write these metaphors? Because I have written nothing for an age.

Orlando has been published. I went to Burgundy with Vita. We did not find each other out. It flashed by. Yet I was glad to see Leonard again. How disconnected this is! My ambition is from this very moment, 8 minutes to six, on Saturday evening, to attain complete concentration again. When I have written here, I am going to open Fanny Burney's

10. Henry Rainald, 6th Viscount Gage (b. 1895) of Firle Place, Sussex landowner (and Keynes's and Vanessa's landlord); at this period, in addition to being PPS to the Secretary of State for India, he was a Lord-in-Waiting to King George V. The 'Circassian blood' is VW's fantasy. Sidney Russell Cooke (1892-1930), stockbroker, had been a student at King's College, Cambridge, from 1911-14; after war service and an unsuccessful Liberal candidature, he had made a successful career in the City, and the financial pages of the *N & A* had benefited from his advice. In 1930 he was found shot dead, his double-barrelled sporting gun beside him; the verdict was that it was accidental. His wife, *née* Helen Melville Smith, was the daughter of the captain of the ill-fated *Titanic*.

diaries, & work solidly at that article which poor Miss McKay cables about.[1] I am going to read; to think. I gave up reading & thinking on the 24th of Sept when I went to France. I came back, & we plunged into London & publishing. I am a little sick of Orlando. I think I am a little indifferent now what anyone thinks. Joy's life's in the doing—I murder, as usual, a quotation:[2] I mean its the writing, not the being read that excites me. And as I can't write while I'm being read, I am always a little hollow hearted; whipped up; but not so happy as in solitude. The reception, as they say, surpassed expectations. Sales beyond our record for the first week. I was floating rather lazily on praise, when Squire barked in the Observer, but even as I sat reading him on the backs last Sunday in the showering red leaves & their illumination, I felt the rock of self esteem untouched in me. "This doesn't really hurt" I said to myself; even now; & sure enough, before evening I was calm, untouched. And now theres Hugh [Walpole] in the Morning Post to spread the butter again, & Rebecca West—such a trumpet call of praise—thats her way—that I feel a little sheepish & silly. And now no more of that I hope.[3]

Thank God, my long toil at the women's lecture is this moment ended. I am back from speaking at Girton, in floods of rain. Starved but valiant young women—that's my impression. Intelligent eager, poor; & destined to become schoolmistresses in shoals. I blandly told them to drink wine & have a room of their own. Why should all the splendour, all the luxury of life be lavished on the Julians & the Francises, & none on the Phares & the Thomases?[4] There's Julian not much relishing it, perhaps. I fancy

1. Helen MacAfee, not McKay (1884-1956), managing editor and book critic of the *Yale Review* which had already published two articles by VW, had visited her at Tavistock Square at the end of May. VW failed to deliver her intended article on Dr. Burney's party (see *IV VW Letters*, no. 1985).
2.   '. . . Women are angels, wooing:
   Things won are done; joy's soul lies in the doing:
   That she belov'd knows naught that knows not this:
   Men prize the thing ungain'd more than it is:'
          Cressida in *Troilus and Cressida*, I ii
3. J. C. Squire in his review entitled 'Prose-de-Société' in the *Observer*, 21 October 1928, wrote of his impression that 'the author had no gusto in the writing', and concluded that *Orlando* was 'a very pleasant trifle' that would 'entertain the drawing-rooms for an hour'. (See *M & M*, pp 227-9.) Hugh Walpole, 'On a Certain New Book' (*Morning Post*, 25 October 1928) lauded *Orlando* without naming it or its author; Rebecca West (*New York Herald Tribune*, 21 October 1928), called it 'a poetic masterpiece of the first rank'.
4. Elsie Elizabeth Phare (b. 1908), student at Newnham College 1926-29 and later an authority on Gerard Manley Hopkins and Andrew Marvell, was the current secretary of the Newnham Arts Society; Margaret Ellen Thomas (b. 1907) was one

sometimes the world changes. I think I see reason spreading. But I should have liked a closer & thicker knowledge of life. I should have liked to deal with real things sometimes. I get such a sense of tingling & vitality from an evenings talk like that; one's angularities & obscurities are smoothed & lit. How little one counts, I think: how little anyone counts; how fast & furious & masterly life is; & how all these thousands are swimming for dear life. I felt elderly & mature. And nobody respected me. They were very eager, egotistical, or rather not much impressed by age & repute. Very little reverence or that sort of thing about. The corridors of Girton are like vaults in some horrid high church cathedral—on & on they go, cold & shiny—with a light burning. High gothic rooms; acres of bright brown wood; here & there a photograph.

And we saw Trinity & King's this morning. Now to concentrate on English literature—forgetting Mary & Tom & how we went to be read aloud to, & Lady Cunard, & Clive back & Nessa back, & the Well of Loneliness. But Thank God to get back to writing again.[5]

Wednesday 7 November

And this shall be written for my own pleasure,—

But that phrase inhibits me: for if one writes only for one's own pleasure,—I dont know what it is that happens. I suppose the convention of writing is destroyed; therefore one does not write at all. I am rather headachy, & dimly obscured with sleeping draught. This is the aftermath (what does that mean?—Trench, whom I open idly apparently says nothing[1]) of Orlando. Yes, yes, since I wrote here I have become two inches & a half higher in the public view. I think I may say that I am now among the well known writers. I had tea with Lady Cunard—might have

---

of those responsible for inviting VW to speak at Girton, where she was a student from 1926-30. Before the Girton lecture on 26 October VW had seen her nephew Julian Bell, now in his second year at King's, and had then dined with Miss Thomas and another student at the Lion Hotel, Petty Cury (now demolished), where she and V. Sackville-West were staying.

5. The Woolfs had dined with Mary Hutchinson on 17 October and had afterwards gone to T. S. Eliot's house, where he read aloud his unpublished poem *Ash Wednesday*, a draft of which (now in King's College Library, Cambridge) he had previously sent them, inviting criticism. (See *IV LW*, pp 109-10.) Vanessa and Clive Bell had (independently) been in France; the former returned on 18th, the latter on 21st October.

1. *A Select Glossary of English Words used formerly in senses different from their present* (1859), compiled by Richard Chenevix Trench.

lunched or dined any day.[2] I found her in a little cap telephoning. It was not her atmosphere—this of solitary talk. She is too shrewd to expand, & needs society to make her rash & random which is her point. Ridiculous little parrokeet faced woman; but not quite sufficiently ridiculous. I kept wishing for superlatives: could not get the illusion to flap its wings. Flunkeys, yes; but a little drab & friendly. Marble floors, yes; but no glamour; no tune strumming, for me at least. And the two of us sitting there had almost to be conventional & flat—reminds me of Sir Thomas Browne—the greatest book of our times—said a little flatly by a woman of business, to me who don't believe in that kind of thing unless launched with champagne & garlands. Then in came Lord Donegall, a glib Irish youth, dark sallow slick, on the Press.[3] Dont they treat you like a dog? I said. "No, not at all" he replied, astonished that a marquis could be treated like a dog by anyone. And then we went up & up to see pictures on stairs in ballrooms & finally to Lady C.'s bedroom, hung entirely with flower pieces. The bed has its triangular canopy of rose red silk; the windows, looking on the square, are hung with green brocade. Her poudreuse—like mine only painted & gilt stood open with gold brushes looking glasses, & there on her gold slippers were neatly laid gold stockings. All this paraphernalia for one stringy old hop o' my thumb. She set the two great musical boxes playing & I said did she lie in bed & listen to them? But no. She has nothing fantastic in that way about her. Money is important. She told me rather sordid stories of Lady Sackville never visiting her without fobbing something off on her—now a bust, worth £5, for which she paid £100; now a brass knocker. "And then her talk—I didn't care for it . . ." Somehow I saw into these sordid commonplace talks, & could not sprinkle the air with gold dust easily. But no doubt she has her acuity, her sharp peck at life; only how adorable, I thought, as I tiptoed home in my tight shoes, in the fog, in the chill, could one open one of these doors that I still open so venturously, & find a live interesting real person, a Nessa, a Duncan, a Roger. Some one new, whose mind would begin vibrating. Coarse & usual & dull these Cunards & Colefaxes are—for all their astonishing competence in the commerce of life.

And I cannot think what to 'write next'. I mean the situation is, this

2. Maud ('Emerald') Cunard, *née* Burke (1872-1948), American-born widow of the wealthy Sir Bache Cunard of the steamship company, and mother of the rebellious Nancy, was a patroness of the arts and celebrated hostess whose invitations implied a recognition of social, intellectual, or artistic arrival. She lived in Grosvenor Square.
3. Edward Chichester (1903-1975) succeeded his father as 6th Marquess of Donegall the year after his birth. Educated at Eton and Christ Church, Oxford, he was beginning his successful career as a society journalist.

Orlando is of course a very quick brilliant book. Yes, but I did not try to explore. And must I always explore? Yes I think so still. Because my reaction is not the usual. Nor can I even after all these years run it off lightly. Orlando taught me how to write a direct sentence; taught me continuity & narrative, & how to keep the realities at bay. But I purposely avoided of course any other difficulty. I never got down to my depths & made shapes square up, as I did in The Lighthouse.

Well but Orlando was the outcome of a perfectly definite, indeed overmastering impulse. I want fun. I want fantasy. I want (& this was serious) to give things their caricature value. And still this mood hangs about me. I want to write a history, say of Newnham or the womans movement, in the same vein. The vein is deep in me—at least sparkling, urgent. But is it not stimulated by applause? over stimulated? My notion is that there are offices to be discharged by talent for the relief of genius: meaning that one has the play side; the gift when it is mere gift, unapplied gift; & the gift when it is serious, going to business. And one relieves the other.

Yes, but The Moths? That was to be an abstract mystical eyeless book: a playpoem. And there may be affectation in being too mystical, too abstract; saying Nessa & Roger & Duncan & Ethel Sands admire that: it is the uncompromising side of me; therefore I had better win their approval—

Again, one reviewer days that I have come to a crisis in the matter of style: it is now so fluent & fluid that it runs through the mind like water.

That disease began in The Lighthouse. The first part came fluid—how I wrote & wrote!

Shall I now check & consolidate, more in the Dalloway Jacob's Room style?

I rather think the upshot will be books that relieve other books: a variety of styles & subjects: for after all, that is my temperament, I think: to be very little persuaded of the truth of anything—what I say, what people say—always to follow, blindly instinctively with a sense of leaping over a precipice—the call of—the call of— now, if I write The Moths I must come to terms with these mystical feelings.

Desmond destroyed our Saturday walk; he is now mouldy & to me depressing. He is perfectly reasonable & charming. Nothing surprises, nothing shocks him. He has been through it all one feels. He has come out rolled, smoothed, rather sodden rather creased & jumbled, like a man who has sat up all night in a third class railway carriage. His fingers are stained yellow with cigarettes. One tooth in the lower jaw is missing. His hair is dank. His eye more than ever dubious. He has a hole in his blue sock. Yet he is resolute & determined—thats what I find so depressing. He seems to be sure that it is his view that is the right one; ours vagaries, deviations. And if his view is the right one, God knows there is nothing to live for: not a greasy biscuit. And the egotism of men surprises & shocks me even now. Is there a woman of my acquaintance who could sit in my arm chair from 3 to 6.30 without the semblance of a suspicion that I may be busy, or tired, or bored; & so sitting could talk, grumbling & grudging, of her difficulties, worries; then eat chocolates, then read a book, & go at last, apparently self-complacent & wrapped in a kind of blubber of misty self satisfaction? Not the girls at Newnham or Girton. They are far too spry; far too disciplined. None of that self-confidence is their lot.

We paid for our dinner at the Lion. Miss Thomas & Miss ——? were relieved, not to have to part with quite so many half crowns. And they showed us the chocolate coloured corridors of Girton, like convent cells; —

And there was the meeting in Mr Williams Ellises studio—a vast hall in Ebury street, with ostentatiously ragged chair covers.[4] Our raggedness, as a profession, was not ostentatious alas; it is part of our souls; a dowdiness that is not ragged, however; a meticulous respectability which is not my working state; for then I am, I think, almost picturesque. As a crowd together we achieve only dinginess & something egotistic & unreserved in our faces; as for old Garnett, I felt surely someone ought to put that surly shaggy unkempt old monstrosity (certainly his nails want cutting & his coat is matted with mud & burrs) in the lethal chamber. D[itt]o of his mistress: the top half Esquimaux, the bottom Maytime in Hampstead—sprigged muslin, sandals.[5] Vita as usual like a lamp or torch in all this petty bourgeoisdom; a tribute to the breeding of the Sackvilles, for without care of her clothes she appears among them ⟨in all the sanity & strength of a well made body⟩ like a lampost, straight, glowing. None of us have that; or know not how to carry it.

Poor Rose Macaulay—a mere chit; a wafer—& so on to the Hendersons in Hampstead, where my spleen & Frankie's were twin spleens: poor Frankie however kept his rattle & clapper going, hour after hour, sounding alone, while I sank in a tolerable arm chair & could say nothing;

4. Clough Williams-Ellis (1883-1978), already an influential architect, was married to the writer Amabel, daughter of St Loe Strachey; the meeting on 1 November at 22b Ebury Street was held to discuss support for the defence in the forthcoming *Well of Loneliness* case.

5. Edward Garnett (1868-1937), writer, influential publisher's reader, and father of David ('Bunny') Garnett; his mistress was the painter E. M. (Nellie) Heath, who had taken up prison welfare work.

though Mrs Enfield who has read the whole of Balzac made advances with Proust.[6] Faith, I think, saw in this languor, bad manners & conceit. She saw us despising her home & husband. She despised them herself. And she went to bed saying something bitter to Hubert, & looked back into the drawing room, wondering why all the colours were wrong. But then next morning there are the children at breakfast & she recovers somewhat but has to speak severely about Mrs Maypole, the hired help (10/- a night) who dropped the plates, & left Mr Birrell holding the ladle; & the ice was salt. Then she takes up Orlando & says, to Hubert, "This is a greatly over rated book— It is far far worse than The Lighthouse . . .' at the same time, 'What exciting lives these people lead! Bloomsbury . . ."

Thursday 8 November

Just to solace myself before correcting Hardy & Gissing,[7] I will note that we went to Karin's party last night. The truth is the stimulus is too brisk; one rattles; & only a shout can be heard, & one must stand; & one gets caught, like a bramble on a river by some branch; & hooked up out of the eddy. An emerald green Russian talked to me of seals & then gave me a card; I am to lecture 4 times a week for 8 weeks in America—oh yes—& she will arrange most advantageous terms. But won't mention money in a drawing room: so we lapse upon seals again, or Ann [Stephen]'s rabbit—a chinchilla animal lying languidly extended in the midst of the rumpus, exquisite, alien. Ethel Sands, fanning my vanity into a glow: yet she was downright the other night that Orlando isn't a patch on Lighthouse, with talk of luncheon parties where nothing is talked about but &c. &c.

Janet & Angus to dinner.[8] The young man who wants a job is not amiable; poor old Angus cuts up a little rough, & launches into anxious worried explanations about his play. He will never now break through that chrysalis core of gentlemanly reserve, caution, good manners which shells him in. I think he will meditate more & more upon the glories of

6. Doris Edith Enfield, née Hussey (d. 1951). For VW's views on her literary athletics see II VW Diary, 19 July 1922. The Hogarth Press had published her biography of 'L.E.L.' in March (HP Checklist 160).

7. VW's review of The Early Life of Thomas Hardy by Florence Emily Hardy appeared in the N & A of 24 November 1928 (Kp C306). She was also revising an earlier (1927) review of George Gissing's Letters to serve as an introduction to a selection from his writings to be published by Jonathan Cape in 1929 (see Kp C280).

8. Angus Davidson and Janet Vaughan dined at Tavistock Square before the Stephens' party on 7 November. Angus had not been successful in finding a congenial post since leaving the Hogarth Press almost a year earlier.

being a Davidson. Yet he has his scallywag side, the poor man, dancing & dining, which is to his credit. Janet in comparison seemed rapid, decided & lustrous, all in gold for Karin's party with Madge's gold necklace, & something very like Madge now & then; but tempered with the Vaughan decision. She is an attractive woman; competent; disinterested, taking blood tests all day to solve some abstract problem.

... think it

Saturday 10 November

This unexampled fluency here is due to the fact that I should be reading Miss Jewsbury,[9] answering letters (Lady Cunard to dine alone with George Moore) or correcting Hardy & Gissing. All these tasks are unworthy the sacred morning hours. Phrase tossing can only be done then; so I toss them privately here, feeling relieved not to be making money, once in a while. Shall I say that Bennett in the Ev[ening] Standard hurt me less than Squire in the Observer?[10] Not at all, I think;—an odd thing, though, how I am praised & abused: & what a sting I am in the flanks of Squires & Bennetts.

What is more interesting—& Lord knows this is true—I am speaking coolly & faithfully—is the trial yesterday at Bow Street.[11] We were all packed in by 10.30: the door at the top of the court opened; in stepped the debonair distinguished magistrate; we all rose; he bowed; took his seat under the lion & the unicorn, & then proceeded. Something like a Harley St. specialist investigating a case. All black & white, tie pin, clean shaven,

9. VW was reading the novels of Geraldine Jewsbury (1812-1880), the friend of Jane Welsh Carlyle, in preparation for her article 'Geraldine and Jane' to be published in the *TLS*, 28 February 1929 (Kp C309).

10. Arnold Bennett's review of *Orlando*, 'A Woman's High-Brow Lark', appeared in the *Evening Standard*, 8 November 1928. Bennett wrote that VW's 'best novel' *To the Lighthouse* had raised hopes which *Orlando* had now dashed to 'iridiscent fragments' at his feet. See *M & M*, pp 232-3. For Squire's article see above, 27 October 1928, n 3.

11. Jonathan Cape and a London bookseller had been summoned by the Public Prosecutor to show cause why Radclyffe Hall's novel *The Well of Loneliness* should not be destroyed as obscene. The case was heard on 9 November at Bow Street before the Chief Magistrate, Sir Chartres Biron (1863-1940), who ruled that the question of obscenity was one for him alone to determine, and that evidence as to literary merit was inadmissible. His judgement was delivered the following week, on 16 November, when he made an order for the book to be seized and destroyed. An appeal was entered and heard at London Sessions on 14 December when it was dismissed, the court concluding that the book was disgusting and obscene and prejudicial to the morals of the community.

wax coloured, & carved, in that light, like ivory. He was ironical at first: raised his eyebrows & shrugged. Later I was impressed by the reason of the law, its astuteness, its formality. Here have we evolved a very remarkable fence between us & barbarity; something commonly recognised; half humbug & ceremony therefore—when they pulled out calf bound books & read old phrases I thought this; & the bowing & scraping made me think it; but in these banks runs a live stream. What is obscenity? What is literature? What is the difference between the subject & the treatment? In what cases is evidence allowable? This last, to my relief, was decided against us: we could not be called as experts in obscenity, only in art. So Desmond who had got under the palanquin where he looked too indifferent, too calm, too completely at his ease to be natural, was only asked his qualifications & then, not allowed to answer the obscene question, was dismissed. In the hall I talked to Lady Troubridge (who used to sculpt & last time we met was a tea party, as children, in Montpelier Sqre) & John— John lemon yellow, tough, stringy, exacerbated.[12] Their costs run into 4 figures she said. And Leonard thinks this heralds a subscription. After lunch we heard an hour more, & then the magistrate, increasingly deliberate & courteous, said he would read the book again & give judgment next Friday at two, [on] the pale tepid vapid book which lay damp & slab all about the court. And I lost my little Roman brooch, & that is the end of this great day, so far. A curious brown top lighted scene; very stuffy; policemen at the doors; matrons passing through. An atmosphere quite decent & formal, of adult people.

Sunday 25 November

Leonard's 48th birthday. We were at Rodmell, where all has fallen into our hands, rapidly, unexpectedly: on top of the field we get a cottage, & Percy [Bartholomew] is 'our man'. Mrs Percy has inherited from that strange relationship of hers—I suspect her of being the illegitimate child of a circus manager—they travelled—she never speaks of her family— her father died alone—her Auntie left jewels & clothes—she has inherited £330 & some odd shillings. She has bought a set of big white teeth; & now thinks of a gramophone or a wireless set.

12. Una Elena Troubridge (d. 1963), *née* Taylor, was the widow of Admiral Sir Ernest Troubridge (d. 1926) who had obtained a legal separation in 1918 because of her decision to live with Radclyffe Hall—known as 'John'. She was a granddaughter of Sir Henry Taylor, a particular friend of VW's great-aunt Julia Margaret Cameron; her parents' home had been in Montpelier Square, Kensington, and she had studied sculpture at the Royal College of Art.

I took Essex & Eth (Lytton's) down to read, & Lord forgive me!—find it a poor book.[13] I have not finished it; & am keeping it to see if my [*text ends*]

Wednesday 28 November

1928

Father's birthday. He would have been $\dfrac{1832}{96}$ 96, yes, today; & could have been 96, like other people one has known; but mercifully was not. His life would have entirely ended mine. What would have happened? No writing, no books;—inconceivable. I used to think of him & mother daily; but writing The Lighthouse, laid them in my mind. And now he comes back sometimes, but differently. (I believe this to be true—that I was obsessed by them both, unhealthily; & writing of them was a necessary act.) He comes back now more as a contemporary. I must read him some day. I wonder if I can feel again, I hear his voice, I know this by heart?

Last night was one of our evenings—apparently successful; Adrian, Hope, Christa, Clive, Raymond, Bunny, Lytton, Vita & Valery towards the end: & Elizabeth Ponsonby.[14] People enjoyed it. Perhaps I didnt; perhaps I did. Half way through Lytton vanished (he lodges upstairs) brayed out of the room by Clive's vociferation, L. thinks. Clive makes it all very strident, gaslit, band played. I marked a queer change in my feeling when Lytton went. At other times I have felt his silence disapproving; have moderated my folly under it, & tried to keep him from going. But now that man writes Elizabeth & Essex; I kept thinking: well, if he can palm that off on us after years of effort—that lively superficial meretricious book—he can go or stay as he likes. I feel no bite in his disapproval. And though one of my vile vices is jealousy, of other writers' fame, though I am (& I think we all are) secretly pleased to find Lytton's

---

13. *Elizabeth and Essex* was published in December 1928.
14. See Vanessa Bell to Roger Fry, 37 Gordon Square, 19 November 1928 (CH, Camb.): 'Virginia & I have started a most extraordinary series of entertainments on the line of the old Thursday evenings. We are at home here on Tuesday evenings to a most miscellaneous collection. Last week she provided Rose Macaulay . . . & Charlie Sanger, Clive brought Christabel, Raymond & Vita, I produced the Alan Clutton Brocks & a Davidson. It turned out quite amusing as everyone sate & listened while Virginia got wilder & wilder . . . tomorrow night . . . she is going to bring Hugh Walpole! It is an experiment which can be given up at any time . . .' This series of after-dinner At Homes continued until Christmas. The Hon. Elizabeth Ponsonby (1900-40) was a leader of the sophisticated post-war generation of 'bright young people'.

book a bad one, I also feel depressed. If I were to analyse, the truth is I think that the pleasure is mean, & therefore not deep or satisfying; one would, in the depths, have got real pleasure, though superficial pain, had E & E been a masterpiece. Oh yes, I should—for I have a mind that feeds perfectly dispassionately & apart from my vanities & jealousies upon literature; & that would have taken a masterpiece to itself. Mixed last night with my feeling was some curious personal dissatisfaction: that Lytton whom I loved & love should write like that. It is a reflection on my own taste. It is so feeble, so shallow; & yet Lytton in himself is neither. So one next accuses the public; & then the Carringtons & the young men. And one furbishes up a cloistered secluded invalidish Lytton whipping the flanks of the language & putting it to this foaming gallop, when the poor beast is all spavins & sores. And Dadie & Pernel & Janie Bussy & Dorothy [Bussy] all declared with emotion that this book was his best!

So the days pass, & I ask myself sometimes whether one is not hypnotised, as a child by a silver globe, by life; & whether this is living. Its very quick, bright, exciting. But superficial perhaps. I should like to take the globe in my hands & feel it quietly, round, smooth, heavy. & so hold it, day after day. I will read Proust I think. I will go backwards & forwards.

As for my next book, I am going to hold myself from writing till I have it impending in me: grown heavy in my mind like a ripe pear; pendant, gravid, asking to be cut or it will fall. The Moths still haunts me, coming, as they always do, unbidden, between tea & dinner, while L. plays the gramophone. I shape a page or two; & make myself stop. Indeed I am up against some difficulties. Fame to begin with. Orlando has done very well. Now I could go on writing like that—the tug & suck are at me to do it. People say this was so spontaneous, so natural. And I would like to keep those qualities if I could without losing the others. But those qualities were largely the result of ignoring the others. They came of writing exteriorly; & if I dig, must I not lose them? And what is my own position towards the inner & the outer? I think a kind of ease & dash are good;— yes: I think even externality is good; some combination of them ought to be possible. The idea has come to me that what I want now to do is to saturate every atom. I mean to eliminate all waste, deadness, superfluity: to give the moment whole; whatever it includes. Say that the moment is a combination of thought; sensation; the voice of the sea. Waste, deadness, come from the inclusion of things that dont belong to the moment; this appalling narrative business of the realist: getting on from lunch to dinner: it is false, unreal, merely conventional. Why admit any thing to literature that is not poetry—by which I mean saturated? Is that not my grudge against novel[ist]s—that they select nothing? The poets succeeding by simplifying: practically everything is left out. I want to put practically everything in; yet to saturate. That is what I want to do in The Moths. It must include nonsense, fact, sordidity: but made transparent. I think I must read Ibsen & Shakespeare & Racine. And I will write something about them; for that is the best spur, my mind being what it is; then I read with fury & exactness; otherwise I slip & skip: I am a lazy reader. But no: I am surprised & a little disquieted by the remorseless severity of my mind: that it never stops reading & writing; makes me write on Geraldine Jewsbury, on Hardy, on Women—is too professional, too little any longer a dreamy amateur.

Saturday 8 December

Here is a note barely dashed off (10 to one—just finished, very provisionally "Phases of Fiction") after Christabel MacClaren; & her 'winkle' party, as I call it, the other night. I mean she picked me out with a pin—about Lesbianism, & Dotty—(she is not one). My note was about her attitude to men; the adoring, flattering woman's attitude, which I so seldom see so purely. Like a flame leaping up. Clive "the most honourable of men"—yes but said with a devoutness, a radiancy, that made me laugh. Is this the 'natural' attitude between the sexes? What Clive has, the other way round for women? So cordial, so appreciative; I could hear it kindling her voice when she said "The men were bathing or writing letters or talking"—that was at Sherfield.[1] The men, good delightful creatures, were so engaged while that wretched furtive creature D. pursued me. And I can see man after man, Desmond, Clive &c, Wells, Shaw, warming his hands at this natural warmth, & expanding. It amused me. The other thought I had was about the limits of luxury: how far can the human soul stretch into rugs & rooms: at what point they suffocate its force. I have seen several rich people this autumn; & thought them, perhaps, dulled, coarsened by it: Lady Cunard; two days ago Mrs Bowen & Mrs Grenfell at Lydia's.[2]

1. Sherfield Court in Hampshire had been Lady Dorothy Wellesley's previous country house, the centre of her liberal hospitality.
2. Vera (Mrs Harold) Bowen (d. 1967), a friend of Lydia's from the world of music and ballet; her present husband was a wealthy business man. Florence Grenfell, *née* Henderson, was the wife of the banker E. C. Grenfell (later Lord St Just), Conservative MP for the City of London 1922-35.

Sunday 9 December

These reflections are written on a bitter cold evening to get the taste of a sentence into my mouth again. Angelica came this morning, & every time I lifted my pen she,—heavenly little creature that she is, demure, witty fantastic, neatly tipped the cup upside down; like a fool I went on trying to write, & only gave up when I was in a state of exasperation, not with her, but with my book: I was beginning a new beginning to Fiction. Now it is after tea; Angus will be coming to see Leonard about a character; & I am escaped, & can't be got at; & shall read Troilus & Cressida (Chaucer) till dinner. I have again seen too many people, without much intensity. Lydia's foolish tea party; & the Bagenals' lunch, & Christa; & then Long Barn, & being driven up by Dotty; "I cant say I understand Harold—I can't really say I do"—Then Vita, making a sacrifice of her quiet evening, drove up to London & heard her broadcast & went back with her, to save me the solitary drive. This worried me, rather: for whom would I give up this evening? & then Dotty with her pecking exacting ways "Please dear put the window up—put the window down" makes Vita seem to me pathetically gentle & kind. But none of this matters very much I agree, & Lord helping, I shall work all this week—save for the evenings. It is so cold my back is cold now, while the fire roasts my feet; fire is striking & many fire engines have rushed down Southampton Row. The King is dragging along, & the shop assistants are in fear lest they shall lose their Christmas bonus.[3] Christmas impends. And we shall spend it alone here, I think, & go to Rodmell afterwards & plan a new room, with Kennedy. And then to Berlin we say. Meanwhile Nessa & I give our Tuesday evenings, & too many people press to come.

But why I ask "see" people? Whats the point? These isolated occasions which come so often. May I come & see you? And what they get, or I get, save the sense of a slide passing on a screen, I cant say.

Tuesday 18 December

Here I should be pegging away at Fiction; rather an interesting little book I think; but I cannot get my mind down on to it, like a bird of prey firmly attached. I was switched off to write a eulogy of Lady Strachey, burnt yesterday with a bunch of our red & white carnations on top of her.[4]

---

3. George V was suffering from a general blood infection and toxaemia, and there were fears for his life. On 12 December he underwent an operation for the drainage of fluid from his right lung after which he made a slow recovery.

4. Lady Strachey died at 51 Gordon Square, aged 88, on 15 December 1928, and was cremated at Golders Green on 17th. VW's eulogy appeared in the *N & A* on 22 December 1928 (Kp C307; reprinted in VW, *Books and Portraits*, 1977).

It is odd how little her death means to me—for this reason. About a year ago she was said to be dying; & at once (Adrian told me) I made up my usual visualisation; felt the whole emotion of Lady Strachey's passing— her memories & so on—that night; & then she did not die; & now when she does die, not a vision, not an emotion comes my way. These little tricks of psychology amuse me.

L. has just been in to consult about a 3rd edition of Orlando. This has been ordered; we have sold over 6000 copies; & sales are still amazingly brisk—150 today for instance; most days between 50 & 60; always to my surprise. Will they stop or go on? Anyhow my room is secure. For the first time since I married 1912—1928—16 years—I have been spending money. The spending muscle does not work naturally yet. I feel guilty; put off buying, when I know that I should buy; & yet have an agreeable luxurious sense of coins in my pocket beyond my weekly 13/- which was always running out, or being encroached upon. Yesterday I spent 15/- on a steel brooch. I spent £3 on a mother of pearl necklace—& I haven't bought a jewel for 20 years perhaps! I have carpeted the dining room— & so on. I think one's soul is the better for this lubrication; & I am going to spend freely, & then write, & so keep my brain on the boil. All this money making originated in a spasm of black despair one night at Rodmell 2 years ago.[5] I was tossing up & down on those awful waves: when I said that I could find a way out. (For part of my misery was the perpetual limitation of everything; no chairs, or beds, no comfort, no beauty; & no freedom to move: all of which I determined there & then to win). And so came, with some argument, even tears one night (& how seldom I have ever cried!) to an agreement with Leonard about sharing money after a certain sum; & then opened a bank account; & now, at the lowest shall have £200 to put there on Jan. 1st. The important thing is to spend freely, without fuss or anxiety; & to trust to one's power of making more— Indeed, I cannot at this moment very seriously doubt that I shall earn more, this next 5 years, than ever before.

But to return to Max Beerbohm. I met him at Ethel's the other night.[6] As I came in a thick set old man (such was my impression) rose, & I was introduced. No freakishness, no fancy about him. His face is solidified; has a thick moustache; a red veined skin, heavy lines; but then his eyes are perfectly round, very large, & sky blue. His eyes become dreamy & merry when the rest of him is well groomed & decorous in the extreme.

5. See above, 15 September 1926.
6. VW (but not LW, who went to see his sick mother) dined with Ethel Sands on 13 December.

He is brushed, neat, urbane. Halfway through dinner he turned to me & we began a 'nice', interesting, flattering, charming kind of talk; he told me how he had read an article on Addison at Bognor during the war; when literature seemed extinct; & there was his own name. I daresay V.W. catches your eye as M.B. does mine. And nothing has encouraged me more. So I said, as I think, that he is immortal. In a small way, he said; but with complacency. Like a jewel which is hard & flawless, yet always changing. A charming image he said, very kind, approving, & what half flattered half saddened me, *equal*. Am I on that level? Virginia Woolf says—V.W. thinks—how do you write? & so on: I was one of his colleagues & fellows in the art of writing; but not I hoped quite so old. Anyhow he asked me how I wrote. For he hacks every step with his pen, & therefore never alters. He thought I wrote like this. I told him I had to cut out great chunks. I wish you would send them to me, he said; simply; Indeed, he was nothing if not kind; but looked long & steadily. Looked at Lord David [Cecil]—that queer painters look, so matching, so considering apart from human intent; yet with him not entirely. After dinner, he leant on the mantelpiece & Maurice Baring & I flittered round him like a pair of butterflies, praising, laughing, extravagant. And he said he was so pleased by the praise of intelligent people like ourselves. But always he had to be led off to talk politely to this person & that; finally disappeared, very dignified, very discreet in his white waistcoat, pressing my hand in his plump firm one long; & saying what a pleasure &c. I own that I dont find much difference between the great & ourselves—indeed they are like us: I mean they dont have the frills & furbelows of the small; come to terms quickly & simply. But we got, of course, very little way. He talked of Hardy, & said he couldnt bear Jude the Obscure: thought it falsified life, for there is really more happiness than sorrow in life, & Hardy tries to prove the opposite. And his writing is so bad. Then I ran down—but he reads my essays & knows this—Belloc.[7] M.B. said that Belloc, one must remember, poured out ten books a year on history poetry &c. He was one of those full unequal people who were never perfect, as he, M.B., might be called perfect in a small way. But he was glad I didnt like him. Charles Lamb had the most beautiful things in him & then he spoilt them. He had never read a book except Pendennis & Tess of the d'Urbervilles till he left Oxford. And now at last, at Rapallo, he reads. He is taking back Elizabeth & Orlando (pronounced in the French way) to read; treats he looks forward to.

7. See VW's 'The Modern Essay' in *The Common Reader* where she praises Beerbohm, 'the prince of his profession', and disparages Belloc.

Among others were present ... Mrs Hammersley, Lord David, Hutchinsons, &c.[8]

And we dined last night with the Hutchinsons & met George Moor[e] —like an old silver coin now, so white so smooth; with his little flipper hands, like a walruses; & his chubby cheeks, & little knees—yet always saying the thing that comes into his head; fresh, juvenile almost for that reason; & very shrewd. Gave a description of Riceyman Steps[9]—the ferns covered in dust, the man with cancer marrying the woman with fits— Not what one calls a distinguished mind—& what a subject to choose! It seems as if he attaches much importance to subject. He was always praising or altering ways of treating stories. He is writing some Greek novel now, dictating to a charming lady, who has every virtue, save that she is not forthcoming & therefore will not marry. He dictates, & this gives him something to bite upon: then he re-dictates. He never writes. There are no mss of his in existence. Perhaps the dictated style is a true account of his style & H[enry]. J[ames]'s. & accounts for their fluidity, their verbosity.[10] And what it comes to is that the great are very simple; quick to come to terms with; reserved; & dont pay any attention to other peoples books (Moore throws scorn on them all—Shaw—a shriek of vulgarity—poisoned with vulgarity—never wrote a good sentence in his life—Wells—I spare myself Wells—& Galsworthy—) & live in an atmosphere very serene, bright, & fenced off: for all that they are more to the point than ordinary people; go to the heart of things directly. Moore toddled off & got quickly into a cab, Jack said, for all his look of an old silver coin.

8. Violet Mary Hammersley (1878-1964), hostess and patron of the arts, and an old friend of Ethel Sands. Lord David (Gascoyne-) Cecil (b. 1902), younger son of the 4th Marquess of Salisbury; VW had met him at Garsington in 1923 when he was still an undergraduate; he was now a Fellow of Wadham College, Oxford, and writing his life of Cowper. (He also was to write the life of Max Beerbohm, 1964.)

9. *Riceyman Steps* (1923), the novel by Arnold Bennett.

10. George Moore's 'Greek novel' was *Aphrodite in Aulis*, completed in November 1928 and published in 1930. Moore's later work was produced by a method of dictating and re-dictating from what he called 'rigmarole'. Henry James's later works were also dictated.

— 1929 —

1929

The Woolfs had spent Christmas in Bloomsbury, dining with Roger Fry on Christmas day; on 27 December they went to Rodmell, returning to London on 3 January 1929. This is Diary XVIII.

Friday 4 January

How odd to think that I have given the world something that the world enjoys—I refer to the Manchester Guardian—Orlando is recognised for the masterpiece that it is. The Times does not mention Nessa's pictures.[1] Yet, she said last night, I have spent a long time over one of them. Then I think to myself, So I have something, instead of children, & fall comparing our lives. I note my own withdrawal from those desires; my absorption in what I call, inaccurately, ideas: this vision.

We saw Koteliansky on Christmas day. Rather dryer & yellower in the cheeks, like an orange that is old. He was in his shirt sleeves. He had been washing up his Christmas dinner, which was "No, not a very good one . . . Come in Come in". This was Katherine's room he said. It is poverty stricken, tidy, clean—a bed, a table. It looks over back gardens to the trees of Regent's Park. We went straight into the old abuse of Murry; went back ten years, to Richmond, & those long visits; those difficult emphatic ways. He is, one says, the same. Very poor, as definite as ever. Still talking about Lawrence; a very very good writer but his last book DISGUSTING. You must read Counterpoint.[2] Why? Because

1. The third leader in the *Manchester Guardian* of 4 January 1929, headed 'The Year's Novels', developed the theme that 'the novel is the dominant art-form of this age' and said: '. . . a biography which proves on examination to be fiction is sure of a public, while a novel such as Virginia Woolf's "Orlando", which playfully masquerades as biography, is today recognised as the masterpiece it is'. Vanessa Bell and Duncan Grant were both showing with the 26th Exhibition of the London Group at the New Burlington Galleries; Vanessa's big picture was 'The Red Sofa'.

2. Koteliansky lived at 5 Acacia Road, St John's Wood, from 1915 until his death in 1955. The house had been Katherine Mansfield's for a brief happy period until the death of her brother in October 1915 made it unendurable to her. Kot lodged with her Russian successors and when after some years they left, took it over himself. D. H. Lawrence's *Lady Chatterley's Lover* had been published in Florence in the summer of 1928; and Aldous Huxley's *Point Counter Point* in October 1928.

he is a seerious man, a cultivated man. And it is typical of the age. It is a painful book a horrid book but it is that. Still the same seriousness, & concentration upon say 5 objects which he has been staring at these 40 years. Still he gnaws the bone of Katherine & Murry. And all the time some emotion was working in him. He was glad we had come. What could he give us? He gave me a red wooden box, a Russian toy, & stuffed it full of his Russian cigarettes. His voice quivered now & then. He looked at me with emotion. All the linoleum was shining, where he had cleaned it, & he had painted the woodwork with two sorts of Reckitt's blue: so that it shone very bright. He had painted it over & over. There he lives, how heaven knows. People will no longer buy his translations. His dog (a pure Jewish dog) is dead.

Now is life very solid, or very shifting? I am haunted by the two contradictions. This has gone on for ever: will last for ever; goes down to the bottom of the world—this moment I stand on. Also it is transitory, flying, diaphanous. I shall pass like a cloud on the waves. Perhaps it may be that though we change; one flying after another, so quick so quick, yet we are somehow successive, & continuous—we human beings; & show the light through. But what is the light? I am impressed by the transitoriness of human life to such an extent that I am often saying a farewell—after dining with Roger for instance; or reckoning how many more times I shall see Nessa.

Before Christmas Vita Sackville-West had gone to join her husband Harold Nicolson for a ten-week stay in Berlin, where he was Counsellor at the British Embassy. This provided the impulse for the Woolfs to visit Berlin; on 16 January they travelled overnight by Harwich and the Hook of Holland, and stayed at the Prinz Albrecht Hotel, where they were joined on 18 January by Vanessa and Quentin Bell and Duncan Grant who were making a tour of picture galleries in Germany and Austria. They all spent what Vanessa termed 'a very rackety' week in Berlin in the company of the Nicolsons, and the Woolfs returned the way they had come on 21 January; VW reach home in a state of collapse, and for the next six weeks led a virtually invalid life.

Thursday 28 March

It is a disgrace indeed; no diary has been left so late in the year. The truth was that we went to Berlin on the 16th of January, & then I was in bed for three weeks afterwards, & then could not write; perhaps for another three, & have spent my energy since in one of my excited outbursts of composition—writing what I made up in bed, a final version of Women & Fiction.[1]

And as usual, I am bored by narrative. I want only to say how I met Nessa in Tottenham Court Road this afternoon, both of us sunk fathoms deep in that wash of reflection in which we both swim about. She will be gone on Wednesday for 4 months. It is queer how instead of drawing apart, life draws us together. But I was thinking a thousand things as I carried my teapot, gramophone records & stockings under my arm. It is one of those days that I called 'potent' when we lived in Richmond.

Perhaps I ought not to go on repeating what I have always said about the spring. One ought perhaps to be forever finding new things to say, since life draws on. One ought to invent a fine narrative style. Certainly there are many new ideas always forming in my head. For one, that I am going to enter a nunnery these next months; & let myself down into my mind; Bloomsbury being done with. I am going to face certain things. It is going to be a time of adventure & attack, rather lonely & painful I think. But solitude will be good for a new book. Of course, I shall make friends. I shall be external outwardly. I shall buy some good clothes & go out into new houses. All the time I shall attack this angular shape in my mind. I think the Moths (if that is what I shall call it) will be very sharply cornered. I am not satisfied though with the frame. There is this sudden fertility which may be mere fluency. In old days books were so many sentences absolutely struck with an axe out of crystal: & now my mind is so impatient, so quick, in some ways so desperate.

Old age is withering us; Clive, Sibyl, Francis—all wrinkled & dusty; going over the hoops, along the track. Only in myself, I say, forever bubbles this impetuous torrent. So that even if I see ugliness in the glass, I think, very well, inwardly I am more full of shape & colour than ever. I think I am bolder as a writer. I am alarmed by my own cruelty with my friends. Clive, I say, is intolerably dull. Francis is a runaway milk lorry.

I feel on the verge of some strenuous adventure: yes; as if this spring day were the hatching; the portal; the opening through which I shall go upon this experience. So when I wake early, I brace myself out of my terrors by saying that I shall need great courage: after all, I say, I made £1000 all from willing it early one morning. No more poverty I said; & poverty has ceased. I am summoning Philcox next week to plan a room—

1. An interim version of 'Women and Fiction'—based on the lectures VW had given at Cambridge in October—had been sent to New York presumably before she went to Berlin, for it was published there in the *Forum* in March (Kp C310). The 'final version' was to become *A Room of One's Own*.

I have money to build it, money to furnish it. And we have the new car, & we can drive to Edinburgh in June if we like, & go to Cassis.[2]

The new year was threatened with a pumping machine, making this studio a trial; for it pumped every 25 minutes. Now for a fortnight it has not pumped. Am I saved? Now it is so quiet that I only hear sparrows; & a voice singing in the hotel. A perfect room for me. Nessa has taken a studio & will let 37, thus ending, for ever I suppose, her Gordon Square life.[3] How much I admire this handling of life as if it were a thing one could throw about; this handling of circumstance. Angelica will go to school. I have now many admiring letters to answer. Simpkins said today that many great publishers would be proud to have our list. In 10 years we shall be rather celebrated. At anyrate, without any trouble to write well, as there should have been, I have once more launched this diary.

Saturday 13 April

Habits gradually change the face of ones life as time changes one's physical face; & one does not know it. Here am I using this studio to sit in, & with my diary to write down here; almost always after tea I retire here. And then I never print now or address envelopes. So perhaps habit will snuff out this diary one day.

I am sordidly debating within myself the question of Nelly; the perennial question. It is an absurdity, how much time L. & I have wasted in talking about servants. And it can never be done with because the fault lies in the system. How can an uneducated woman let herself in, alone, into our lives? —what happens is that she becomes a mongrel; & has no roots any where. I could put my theory into practice by getting a daily of a civilised kind, who had her baby in Kentish town; & treated me as an employer, not friend. Here is a fine rubbish heap left by our parents to be swept.

It is very quiet & very cold. I walked Pinka through the Saturday streets this afternoon & was woken to the fact that it is April by a primrose on the pavement. I had been thinking I was on one of my January walks, with lights lit at 3.30 in peoples bedrooms. Rodmell was impracticable because of the cold; & until I have a room, I cannot go there meaning to work.

2. In February LW replaced his second-hand Singer car by another with a sunshine roof.
3. The area behind 52 Tavistock Square fronting Woburn Place had been cleared for the construction of an enormous hotel (the *Royal*, 789 rooms)—with the inevitable contamination of the neighbourhood by noise and dirt in the process. Vanessa had acquired a large studio at the back of 8 Fitzroy Street adjacent to Duncan's; now when in London, they lived and worked in these studios until 1940.

We always do mean to work.

I have just agreed to do another 4 articles for Mrs Van Doren, because she has raised her price to £50 an article—so that, whatever the cost, I can have my new room.[1] And all this money is changing my habits. I'm not sure it is not the memorable fact about this spring—for the first time since 1912—16 years that is—I am able to look say at blue lustre cups in a shop & decide, well why not buy them? But they cost £6 ... But then I am making over £1000 a year. I can make as much as I want. This little colloquy still takes place before I can unbend my old penurious muscles. But it is always better to buy than not to buy I think.

$$\frac{\begin{array}{r} 1928 \\ 1912 \end{array}}{16}$$

Hugh Walpole was here the other day, from 4.30 to 7.15 alone, over the fire. The same uneasy talk as usual; brisk & breezy, hating war; & then this morbid egotism & desire to scratch the same place over & over again—his own defects as a writer & how to remedy them, what they spring from; all mixed up with his normal, & usual sense of being prosperous & admired—from which, as he admits when I ask him, he gets great pleasure. He starts indeed to protest that he gives pleasure, does good, but can't bring that out in my presence; which is why he seeks my presence —a scratching stone to rid him of the world's mud. He protests too much. On the other hand, I like these bustling vigour[ous] characters: I like talk of Russia, & war & great doings & famous people— If I don't see them I romanticise them.

Leonard is upstairs finishing the Hogarth Press accounts. Yesterday he gave the three stall hands a bonus: Mrs C. £25; Belcher £20; Kennedy £20.[2] They sent up a bunch of roses later in the day. For the first time we have made over £400 profit. And 7 people now depend on us; & I think with pride that 7 people depend, largely, upon my hand writing on a sheet of paper. That is of course a great solace & pride to me. Its not scribbling; its keeping 7 people fed & housed: a great big man like Percy; a carrot faced woman like Cartwright; they live on my words. They will be feeding off Women & Fiction next year for which I predict some sale. It has considerable conviction. I think that the form, half talk half soliloquy allows me to get more onto the page than any how else. It made itself up & forced itself upon me (in this form—the thinking had been done & the

1. See above, 22 March 1928, n 1. These four commissioned articles, to be published in the autumn in the *New York Herald Tribune* and just previously in the *N & A*, were: 'Cowper and Lady Austen' (Kp C314); 'Beau Brummel' (Kp C315); 'Mary Wollstonecraft' (Kp C316); and 'Dorothy Wordsworth' (Kp C317).

2. Miss Belsher began work as a clerk at the Hogarth Press about two months before Richard Kennedy.

writing stiffly & unsatisfactorily 4 times before) as I lay in bed after Berlin. I used to make it up at such a rate that when I got pen & paper I was like a water bottle turned upside down. The writing was as quick as my hand could write; too quick, for I am now toiling to revise; but this way gives one freedom & lets one leap from back to back of one's thoughts.

Happily, for my health of soul, I am now very little noticed, & so can forget the fictitious self, for it is half so, which fame makes up for one: I can see my famous self tapering about the world. I am more comfortable when shut up, self-contained as now.

The great pleasure of money is to spend a pound—as on a dinner at Richmond—without accounting for it— I dined there with Vita. It was cold. We drove round the Park. I saw a man leading a large cat on a chain. I saw many odd parties in the hotel. How can they come here tonight, I said? There was the old woman gorged like a vulture. The woman with her foot cocked under the table at this ✔ angle, all through dinner: the young spark in grey with the pink carnation; the two prominent-eyed daughters in velvet; & all kinds of emotions, of ridicule & interest crossing the vast room perpetually from one table to another. The waiters, I thought, are only here this one night; everything is unreal & will vanish. But it is going on precisely the same at this moment. Have you had a tiring day Miss ——? says Mrs —— leaning out to speak to her. Oh dreadfully tiring says Miss —— taking her seat at the table with the reserved private bottle of soda water. And in complete desolation she waits for the courses to be brought.

Monday 29 April

And it is pouring. Oh this cold spring! Dry as a bone, though until today, but with never a blue sky. So that my red coat, which is like haws in winter, suits it. I heard the nightingale at Vita's a week or two ago— the one warm night. And we were cold at Rodmell last week, when we went down to see Philcox, who will build two rooms for £320, & take only two months. It was cold; but how silent, how safe from voices & talk! How I resented our coming back; & quickly changed into the social sphere of my soul; & went to lunch with Sibyl; & there had, for my pains, precisely six minutes of tolerable talk with Max Beerbohm. But dear me, how little talk with great men now disturbs me. Are we all chilling & freezing, & do we look into each others old faces as into the craters of the moon? (These I saw silver white & like the spots that are made by water dropping into plaster of paris through Vita's telescope the other day.) I begin to think that youth is the only tolerable thing to look at; & am taking Judy to the Coliseum on Wednesday.[3]

I forgot to say that the pump has begun again & is grinding away at this moment. But I say I shall get used to it—certainly I shall.

This morning I began to revise Phases of Fiction, & with that done, I can see my way clear to a complete imaginative book.

Meanwhile, I am eddying quicker & quicker into the stream, into London: tomorrow Christabel; then Mauron's lecture & Mary & the Keynes' & the Eliots.[4]

Poor Tom—a true poet, I think; what they will call in a hundred years a man of genius: & this is his life. I stand for half an hour listening while he says that Vivien cant walk. Her legs have gone. But whats the matter? No one knows. And so she lies in bed—cant put a shoe on. And they have difficulties, humiliations, with servants. And after endless quibbling about visiting—which he cant do these 8 weeks, owing to moving house & 15 first cousins come to England, suddenly he appears overcome, moved, tragic, unhappy, broken down, because I offer to come to tea on Thursday. Oh but we dont dare ask our friends, he said. We have been deserted. Nobody has been to see us for weeks. Would you really come—all this way? to see us? Yes I said.[5] But what a vision of misery, imagined, but real too. Vivien with her foot on a stool, in bed all day; Tom hurrying back lest she abuse him: this is our man of genius.— This is what I gathered yesterday morning on the telephone.

Sunday 12 May

Here, having just finished what I call the final revision of Women & Fiction so that L. can read it after tea, I stop: surfeited. And the pump, which I was so sanguine as to think ceased, begins again. About W. & F. I am not sure—a brilliant essay?—I daresay; it has much work in it, many opinions boiled down into a kind of jelly, which I have stained red as far as I can. But I am eager to be off—to write without any boundary coming

3. VW's niece Judith (1918-1972) was Adrian and Karin Stephen's younger daughter; the Coliseum was presenting a Variety programme.

4. Charles Mauron (1899-1966), a Provençal intellectual whom Roger Fry had 'discovered' about 1920 and introduced to Bloomsbury. A scientist by training, he was forced by progressive blindness to give up his University research post and, encouraged by Fry, turned to literature and criticism, in which field he produced much original writing, and to translation (he was to translate both *Orlando* and *Flush*). His present lecture (to which VW did not go; see *IV VW Letters*, no. 2025) was on Mallarmé and was given at 37 Gordon Square on 1 May.

5. Eliot wrote on 2 May to postpone VW's visit, saying circumstances were too much for them (copy, MHP, Sussex).

slick in ones eyes: here my public has been too close: facts; getting them malleable, easily yielding to each other.

A wet day, or we should be at Hampton Court with Roger & Mauron. And I am glad of the rain, because I have talked too much. We have seen too many people—Sydney Waterlow perhaps the most notable, as a resurrection. A desperate looking pompous sad respectable elderly man; worldly; but quivering as usual in his shell. Any pin pricks him in the unarmoured skin. I liked him. We met in the dark hall, glad of its darkness. We talked almost too easily, of Lucy Clifford buried with a service; & then his lancers & state at Bangkok—all to his liking. His importance very clear to him. At Oare he is nobody. And so he would like to go back to Bangkok & be important in the East for ever.[1] He can seek the truth no more—has indeed seen through the search for truth, which was in him the search for power. He believes in nothing any more, he said, & is convinced now that nothing will ever change him— So, talking of something else for a moment, he suddenly burst out into a terrific peroration about Spengler; who has changed the world for him—made infinitely more difference than anybody—so fixed & stable & independent is he.[2]

Also we had a party: Roger a little old—to my mind he needs Nessa to fertilise & sweeten him. Some queer rancour often seems to exacerbate him. When his stomach heals his leg aches. And Plomer came—a little rigid, I fear; & too much of a gentleman; & little Blunden, the very image of a London house sparrow, that pecks & cheeps & is starved & dirty.[3] And Julian, to me a very satisfactory young man at present; full of ardour, yet clear, precise; & genial too—with all his apostolic fervour & abstrac-

1. Sydney Waterlow (1878-1944), one-time suitor and old friend of VW (see *VW Diary*, vols. I & II) had rejoined the Diplomatic Service after the war, and had served as British Minister in Bangkok, 1926-28, and then in Addis Ababa, which post he had recently relinquished on grounds of health. His home in England was at Oare, Wiltshire. Mrs Clifford was a figure from VW's even more distant past; she had died on 21st, and was buried at Highgate Cemetery on 24th April. The Woolfs were at Rodmell on that day.

2. Oswald Spengler (1880-1936), German philosopher, whose influential study of the philosophy of history, *The Decline of the West*, had appeared in an English translation in 1926 and 1928.

3. William Plomer (1903-1973), English poet and novelist, was born in South Africa and returned there at the age of fifteen after war-time schooling in England. For the past two years he had been living by teaching in Japan, and had just reached England after a ten years' absence, and met the Woolfs for the first time; in 1925 he had sent them his novel *Turbott Wolfe* from Zululand, and they published it (*HP Checklist* 73) and his other books until 1932. Plomer had known Edmund Blunden in Tokyo where from 1924-27 the latter had been Professor of English Literature at the Imperial University.

tedness a good fellow, warm, kindly; much more apt to see the good than the bad. For example he thought poor little grey mouse Jenkins very nice & very intelligent & sat screwed up on the floor at her feet. He had been consoling Topsy all the afternoon. For Topsy & Peter have separated. Yes they have separated for ever, owing to her flirtatious ways.

Monday 13 May

How odd this is—here I am sitting at 3.10 with nothing much to do—nothing that I need do. I must take up printing again. But we have been to the Singers with the car—its clutch in trouble; & as we started, up came Saxon, on his holiday— Going to the Ring of course, & having a day off. For how many years has he done this—strange methodical character that he is. We dont meet for months, & take up the subject again. He took out his cheque book & said he thought the pattern was changed, with the same interest in that minute detail as he had 30 years ago. He has the same umbrella hanging by a hook on his arm; the same gold watch chain; & his pirouetting attitudes; & sprightly bird-like ways.

What then has life given you, I asked, (myself) looking at the Church at the top of Portland Street.[4] Well, he is free to go to the Opera, to read Plato to play chess. And he will continue doing these things, as if they were the chosen things till he dies. There is a certain dignity in this steady doing of things which seem chosen. Yet—thus one always ends a comparison of lives—I wouldn't for the whole world live yours.

And at 4 I must change & wash & go to the Mauron lecture at Argyll House; & then to Molly & then to dine with Sibyl—which will, I hope finish this lap of my race. Did I say that I still think of life as a series of laps—& still take my fences dutifully & then enjoy nothingness? So if I dine with Sibyl I need not dine with Christabel. I have never got in the frame of mind which makes these fences negligible. Then we go to Rodmell for 6 days; & then home; & then to Cassis; & then home. & then Rodmell; & then the autumn; & then the winter— Oh this pump! I wish I could say I never notice it. Moreover, the idea has come to me that I ought now to be re-reading my own books, for our 'Collected Edition'. L. & Kennedy are working at a dust cover this moment. Shall I run away from my duty & the pump & go & see?[5]

4. Presumably Trinity Church, opposite Great Portland Street Station.
5. The 'Uniform Edition of the Works of Virginia Woolf', printed by photo-litho-offset from the original editions, was initiated with four volumes—*The Voyage Out*, *Jacob's Room*, *The Common Reader*, and *Mrs Dalloway*—issued by the Hogarth Press on 26 September 1929. The typographical design of the dust jacket was improved by Vanessa Bell (see *IV VW Letters*, no. 2040).

MAY 1929

The election draws near, & the Derby.[6] I will go upstairs & read Proust I think, since I am fabricating a few remarks on him for that cursed book —that stone that plunges me deeper & deeper in the water. The reason I dislike dining with Sibyl is that she exacts it: I am to give her a display of intimacy, which she cannot acquire, poor woman, for herself.

Wednesday 15 May

This is written, as many pages in the past used to be written, to try a new pen; for I am vacillating—cant be sure to stick to the old pen any more. And then every gold pen has some fatal draw-back. Never have I met one without. And then one cant be sure till one's written a long screed. And then one's ashamed to go back—& then one does—& then it all begins again, like Mathew Arnold's river, or sea (brings in again &c &c).[7]

I make a note here that I will one of these days read the whole of Matthew Arnold.

I went to Sibyl's dinner; but Heavens, how little real point there is to these meetings—save indeed that the food is good; & there is wine, & a certain atmosphere of luxury & hospitality. This, on the other hand, tends to drug one; one has been given something, for which one has to pay. And I don't like that feeling. The old white haired baby [George Moore] sat propped up in his high chair; his hair now white like flax, like silk; his cheeks tinted a childs pink; his eyes with their marble hardness; his boneless ineffective hands. For some reason, he paid me compliments, indeed referred to me as an authority on English; & even offered, which I daresay was kindly meant, though nothing has happened, to send me one of his books.[8]

What did we discuss? Mostly himself & his books, I think; & how he had known various old dim figures, far away in the past. I told them about Lord Alfred's threat, & this launched him on stories about Robbie

6. Having been in office since October 1924, the Conservatives had called the General Election for 30 May 1929. Derby Day was 5 June.

7. 'Listen! you hear the grating roar
Of pebbles which the waves suck back, and fling,
At their return, up the high strand,
Begin, and cease, and then again begin,
With tremulous cadence slow, and bring
The eternal note of sadness in.'

Dover Beach, published 1867.

8. An uncut presentation copy, inscribed by the author to VW, 1929, of George Moore's *The Making of an Immortal*, was lot 79 in Sotheby's sale on 27 April 1970.

Ross, & his own lawsuits.[9] But he is a detached shrewd old man; without many illusions & not very dependent on anyone, I should say. He wanted to walk back to Ebury Street, but it was raining & they made him take a cab. He talked about Henry James, & a proof sheet which nobody could read; & he said that a sentence ought to form like a cloud at the end of the pen—dont you think so? he said to me. These little compliments were due to my Geraldine & Jane which he said   & references, was an admirable story & should be published as such. It had nothing to do with fact. And I rather think he will die soon—he has to have another operation;[10] but in his detached way. I think these artists are slightly bored by all physical transactions. Let my body die, I can imagine him saying, so long as I can go on forming sentences at the end of my pen—& why not? Save that of course he says he enjoys the pleasures of the body. But that I rather doubt.

And I doubt too if Clive does. Clive is I fancy in bad odour everywhere at the moment, with his silly egotistic ways—writing to me to boast of a 'mystery', which it is clear that I am to impart; but I shant. He is like Lottie *au fond*; & Lottie by the way is dismissed; & is said to owe Karin £8 which she can't pay, & great scenes take place, poor Adrian, as I imagine, moping & glooming in discomfort alone; with Karin savage & violent & competent spasmodically, rushing out to pay bills & put her house in order in ten minutes when she has neglected it all these years: sordid & squalid it all is, & hardly gives me any pleasure, to tell the truth, these sufferings of my friends.

I am depressed. Brace has done it. The oval faced sallow man. They want to keep W. & F., which I like, till the spring, & make P. of F. come out this autumn—a book I hate; & was, as I think, wrongly pressed to undertake.[11] And then Roger wants to come to Rodmell, & I don't like

9. The litigious Lord Alfred Douglas (1870-1945) had threatened to sue the *N & A* and LW for libel unless they published an apology for LW's disparaging review (6 April 1929) of his *Autobiography*. A particular target of Lord Alfred's retributory litigation had been Robert Ross, Oscar Wilde's literary executor, whom LW appeared to him to be defending. In the event the *N & A* published a letter from Lord Alfred (27 April 1929) and no further action ensued. George Moore had won an action for libel brought against him in 1917 by a Louis N. Seymour in respect of his novel *Lewis Seymour and Some Women*.

10. George Moore had undergone preliminary surgery in April 1928, and was anticipating a second, major, operation; but the danger was considered too great, and it was not performed. He lived until 21 January 1933, a month before his eighty-first birthday.

11. In the event Harcourt Brace published *A Room of One's Own* (W[omen] & F[iction]) on the same day as the Hogarth Press, 24 October 1929 (Kp A12); for *Phases of Fiction* see above, 7 December 1925, n 6.

after my protests, to say no; & yet to have to talk & talk—& then Philcox can't get my rooms done, all because of Durrant's long waiting.[12] So my wheel is turning low. & do I like this pen or dont I? Such are my sorrows Mr Wesley, as the man said when the servant put on too many coals.

What Clive says is that he has a mystery; something he cant share; & this annoys me too; the sensation mongering, like Dotty; the desire to be talked of. Oh, I say, if only I could plunge my mind into the delights of pure imagination, & so get some pull on this horrid world of real life!

But I must some how wind up this account of flies in the eye & go up to dinner & try to think of some cause of pleasure with Leonard. Something cheerful. Oh but then I must grind on at Proust, I suppose; & then copy out passages. Never mind, I will try my new pen & see if that doesn't cheer me. Because clearly these miseries are very small trivial miseries, & fundamentally I am the happiest woman in all W.C.1. The happiest wife, the happiest writer, the most liked inhabitant, so I say, in Tavistock Square. When I count up my blessings, they must surely amount to more than my sorrows; even when I have all these flies in my eyes.

Well, what am I going to have for dinner? And I will hastily try my new pen on this last page, making it rapidly describe my complete renovation of domestic life—odd, I didn't do it before: that I order dinner no longer; but write it in a book & thus put glass between me & Nelly.

Oh & George [Duckworth] rang up this morning. A French couple who admire me: could I lunch: & my teeth he says, drop out, while I talk, while I eat; & they preferred Brighton to Penshurst.

Tuesday 28 May

It is an odd summer, this one, unexampled perhaps in our history. We are going off to Cassis on Tuesday for a week. This is a revolution. We have never been abroad so late in the year I think. The Election will be over. We shall be governed by a Tory or a Labour party—Tory, I suppose. For the benefit of posterity I may say that nobody pretends to know, with the exception of the candidates. They are all—even Hubert—confident.[13] And I feel, rather oddly, that this is an important election. Walking down the King's Road with Sidney Waterlow the other night—having been to dine at his club off a mahogany table surrounded by the portraits of statesmen—I had a cocktail, but no wine—& it was a thundery day—

12. G. L. Kennedy had been asked in December 1928 to advise on an extension to Monks House; Durrants were the builders asked to estimate the cost. Philcox's estimate was lower, and the building was entrusted to him in April.

13. Hubert Henderson was standing as Liberal candidate for Cambridge University; he was not elected.

Leonard had a headache—& we sat in the ladies reception room—a ducks egg coloured room with globes of light sending their light up, not down—very cool, smooth solid, something like sitting inside a shape of blanc mange—then said Sidney, feeling that something must be done, shall we go & see the Sangers? It was a thing that one ought to do. It would give them such pleasure. And he bought me 3 bunches of violets at the door from a woman who said it was her 40th wedding day: a tribute to my having once been asked in marriage by Sidney was it?— I held them in my hand all the evening, & we found the Sangers out; only a menial man came up from the basement. So we said we will call on the MacCarthys. And so it was that we walked along the King's Road, talking about the Election.[14] Sidney said that human nature has improved. We are all becoming gentler & wiser. Even the dogs are. One never sees a dog fight now he said, & sure enough the big mongrel trotted across the road very peacefully to sniff at the door of a public house. There the story stops. For I dont think much happened at the MacCarthys. One had to talk. I noticed nothing, I think. The memorable things happen when there is a great space of silence all round them perhaps. I dont know.

Now about this book, The Moths. How am I to begin it? And what is it to be? I feel no great impulse; no fever; only a great pressure of difficulty. Why write it then? Why write at all? Every morning I write a little sketch, to amuse myself.[15]

I am not saying, I might say, that these sketches have any relevance. I am not trying to tell a story. Yet perhaps it might be done in that way. A mind thinking. They might be islands of light—islands in the stream that I am trying to convey: life itself going on. The current of the moths flying strongly this way. A lamp & a flower pot in the centre. The flower can always be changing. But there must be more unity between each scene than I can find at present. Autobiography it might be called. How am I to make one lap, or act, between the coming of the moths, more intense than another; if there are only scenes? One must get the sense that this is the beginning: this the middle; that the climax—when she opens the window & the moth comes in. I shall have the two different currents—the moths flying along; the flower upright in the centre; a perpetual crumbling & renewing of the plant. In its leaves she might see things happen. But who is she? I am very anxious that she should have no name. I dont want a

14. The Woolfs dined with Sydney Waterlow at the United University Club, Suffolk Street, off Pall Mall East; the Sangers lived in Oakley Street, Chelsea, and the MacCarthys in Wellington Square, further east along the King's Road.
15. Professor John Graham, in his monumental edition of the holograph drafts of The Waves (University of Toronto Press, 1976), does not identify these sketches.

Lavinia or a Penelope: I want 'She'. But that becomes arty, Liberty, greenery yallery somehow: symbolic in loose robes. Of course I can make her think backwards & forwards; I can tell stories. But thats not it. Also I shall do away with exact place & time. Anything may be out of the window—a ship—a desert—London.

Friday 31 May

The oculist said to me this afternoon "Perhaps you're not as young as you were". This is the first time that has been said to me; & it seemed to me an astonishing statement. It means that one now seems to a stranger not a woman, but an elderly woman. Yet even so, though I felt wrinkled & aged for an hour, & put on a manner of great wisdom & toleration, buying a coat, even so, I forget it soon; & am 'a woman' again. Another light on my character or appearance— Coming up Southampton Row, a man snapped me & then said stop; & made me pay 6d for a silly little damp film, which I did not want; nor did I want to stay talking politics to a ferrety little rascal, having had little lunch. But my face marked me for his victim.

"We are winning" Nelly said at tea. I was shocked to think that we both desire the Labour party to win—why? partly that I dont want to be ruled by Nelly. I think to be ruled by Nelly & Lottie would be a disaster. It is dribbled out. Last night at Charleston we heard election results spoken very distinctly in the drawing room. Driving home through Lewes there was not a single light downstairs. No one was even listening in. The streets were perfectly empty. One man was pumpshipping against the station wall. I had imagined a crowd, flares, shouts, white sheets—only three black cats, out on business with the mice. So we shall be ruled by labour.[16]

We went down to Worthing to see Leonard's mother, laid like an old rose—rather lovely this time—in a narrow room; with the sea opposite. I watched the porpoises, & some reflections of people walking on the beach. And she cried; & was very dismal; & then rambled off about Caterham 50 years ago; & the Stannards, & how Herbert had rolled all the way down stairs, & drank so much milk that people were astonished. Nothing of life, as we see it, remains to her—only this curious lit up page

16. The Woolfs were registered as voters in the Lewes constituency, so, going *via* Worthing to visit LW's mother, they drove to Rodmell to vote on 30 May, and returned next day to London. Francis Birrell and Raymond Mortimer were living at Charleston in the Bells' absence, and the Woolfs had driven over after dinner on election day. The results of the General Election were: Labour 287; Conservatives 261; Liberals 59; others 8; in consequence, on 5 June Ramsay MacDonald formed his second Labour Government.

of the past, which she turns over & over lying in bed; & cant read or
sleep, yet anxiously demands, does Leonard think she will get well? We
had been saying driving down that one should take poison. She has every
reason; & yet demands more life, more life, at 78. She quarrels; she cant
walk; she is alone; she is looked after by nurses; lives in an hotel, but
demands more life, more life. One odd thing she said was that she had
slept with a governess as a child who had given her a terrible disease, &
been expelled from Holland on that account. I fancy she had never told
anyone this; it was her offering of intimacy to us; a thanksgiving perhaps
for our having come. I was moved by her; could hardly speak. I suppose
human nature, so emotional, so irrational, so instinctive, as it is in her, but
not in me, has this beauty; this what they call 'elemental' quality. One
may get it too, when one is 76. One may lie sobbing, & yet cry does doctor
think I shall recover? One will not perhaps go to the writing table & write
that simple & profound paper upon suicide which I see myself leaving for
my friends. What a day it was—the sea flowing in & out of the bays, all
the way, like the Adriatic, or Pacific; & the sand yellow; & the boats
steaming along; & behind the downs like long waves, gently extending
themselves, to break very quickly; smooth & sloping like the waves. Even
bungalows are all burnt up & made part of this beauty; made of vapour
not zinc. We voted at Rodmell. I saw a white gloved lady helping an old
farm couple out of her Daimler. We have bought a motor lawn mower.
I liked Francis last night. He is so abundant & fertile, so generous & warm
hearted A most divine man—a man I adore—these phrases recur. And then
he amused me with his imitation of Esther talking like Macaulay [*unex-
plained*]. When they read the results he was always talking so loud: & had
to stop short. We called in on Long Barn & left Pinker, & here we are
again after one of these little journeys which seem to have last[ed] 600
years. Everything looks a little strange & symbolical when one comes back.
I was in a queer mood, thinking myself very old: but now I am a woman
again—as I always am when I write. It is scattering & heatening, this
motoring about.

*The Woolfs went to Cassis by train via Folkestone-Boulogne-Paris-Marseilles
on 4 June; they took rooms in Fontcreuse but meals with Vanessa and Duncan
Grant, who drove them to Arles on their homeward journey. They reached
home on 14 June.*

Saturday 15 June

Home last night from Cassis; that is to say from Arles. The hottest
holiday I have ever had. And in some ways different from others; partly

that it was so hot; then that we were alone with Nessa & Duncan; then
that I have become, almost, a landowner. A window owner, anyhow. Yes,
I almost bought La Boudard (& am not sure of the spelling) & have a
contract, to go there at the cost of £2.10 a month.[1] And this means an
infinite number of things—perhaps a complete change; as buying a house
so often does. Already this morning I feel an attachment—say a little
island—floating some way off, but in my possession. And this island means
heat, silence, complete aloofness from London; the sea; eating cakes in
the new hotel at La Ciotat; driving off to Aix; sitting on the harbour dining;
seeing the sardine boats come in; talk with people who have never heard
of me & think me older, uglier than Nessa, & in every way inferior to her;
that odd intimate, yet edgy, happy free yet somehow restrained intercourse
with her & Duncan. It means also buying French books at Toulon &
keeping them in my lovely cool room in the wood; Leonard in his shirt-
sleeves; an Eastern private life for us both; an Indian summer running in &
out of the light of common day; a great deal of cheap wine & cigars; new
alliances, with Currys, Cruthers, & other anomalous oddities[2]—all this
my engagement to make three windows at Boudard means to me.

I forget what the facts of our stay were. We were there for a week,
coming the day before they expected us, oddly enough as we did last year.
There was Duncan in his blue shirt; Angelica & Judith doing lessons on
the terrace. Nessa drove Miss Campbell into the town & brought up the
food every morning. I wrote a little article on Cowper, but lifting the
words with difficulty in the heat, surrounded by black & white butterflies.[3]
And L. & I were very extravagant, for the first time in our lives, buying
desks, tables, sideboards, crockery for Rodmell. This gave me pleasure; &
set my dander up against Nessa's almost overpowering supremacy. My
elder son is coming tomorrow; yes, & he is the most promising young man
in King's; & has been speaking at the Apostles dinner. All I can oppose
that with is, And I made £2,000 out of Orlando & can bring Leonard
here & buy a house if I want. To which she replies (in the same inaudible
way) I am a failure as a painter compared with you, & cant do more than

1. See *IV LW*, p 181: 'we began to buy a villa for ourselves near Fontcreuse; it was
   in fact a small, rather tumbled-down, whitewashed house. But we did not complete
   the purchase.' He saw the practical disadvantages of having three dwellings, and
   the dream evaporated during 1930.
2. English residents at Cassis.
3. Judith, the daughter of Barbara and Nick Bagenal, was born a few weeks before
   Angelica in 1918, and came more than once to Cassis as a companion for her.
   Jean Campbell (d. *c.* 1955?) lived at Fontcreuse with Colonel Teed; they met during
   the war when she had been a nurse. The article was one of those VW was writing
   for the *New York Herald Tribune* (see above, 13 April 1929, n 1).

pay for my models. And so we go on; over the depths of our childhood. Do you remember going down to the town to fetch — which ancient memories Duncan cannot share. He was divinely charming; & praised Nessa too. I put in shred after shred of feeling so that one may compose the salad, & am now running out to get my books from Riley if I can.[4]

VW here begins DIARY XIX.

Saturday 15 June

Against all laws, I am going to make this the first volume of a diary, though as ill luck has it, it is not even the first of the month. But it is the fault of practical life. I can't write any longer in books whose leaves perish. I don't know how to keep them. Here in a bound volume, the year has a chance of life. It can be stood on a shelf.

Pinker has just come home, very fat. And a sense of nothingness rolls about the house; what I call the sense of "Where there is nothing." This is due to the fact that we came back from France last night & are not going round in the mill yet. Time flaps on the mast—my own phrase I think. There are things I ought to do. I ought to correct A Room of one's own: I ought to read & correct the Common Reader. I ought to write several dull silly letters; to gentlemen in Maidstone & Kingston who tell me facts about dahlias; to Sir Philip Sassoon who most unexpectedly sends me, by motor car, his book of travels.[5] But I cant—not for five minutes or so. Time flaps on the mast. And then I see through everything. Perhaps the image ought to have been one that gives an idea of a stream becoming thin: of seeing to the bottom. Lytton once said,—I connect it with a visit to Kew Gardens—that we can only live if we see through illusion. & that reminds me (it is odd by the way, how small a thought is which one cannot express pictorially, as one has been accustomed to thinking it: this saying of Lytton's has always come pictorially, with heat, flowers, grass, summer, & myself walking at Kew) reminds me how the day before we went Lytton came, & we talked about Elizabeth & Essex. This was for the first time. And it was painful, because he minded what we had not said; & we had, to some extent to say it; but it was also a relief, on both sides, because we were glad to say it, & have this reserve over; & glad, I daresay, that Lytton minded; I daresay there was some discreditable element, at least in my

4. R. E. Riley, bookbinder, of 19 Woburn Buildings, Tavistock Square.
5. Sir Philip Sassoon (1888-1939), Under-Secretary of State for Air, 1924-29, in whose company VW had lunched on 25 April as a guest of Sibyl Colefax. His book was *The Third Route. A description of a Voyage to India by Air* (1929).

gladness; yet not much. I daresay, among my disagreeables, is this that I am jealous enough of other writers to be glad when they are made to own their failures; but this was trifling. More important much was the relief that one could say openly that one had disliked E & E for such reasons; & we began to go into them. His suppression of irony; his being tied by the story; the difficulty of using reality imaginatively; a wrong subject for him; could only be treated exactly. He said he had been very doubtful himself; & this is what I liked—that though his surrounders— Carrington Dadie & the rest—all praised, he himself felt, he was not pleased unless we Bloomsbury, praised too. What we said mattered. And I daresay, owing to success, he minds these reservations a great deal more than I should; for I kept thinking of all the criticism I had had. One is pleased when 'after long yea[r]s' such feelings have sway.[6] And I felt, among the discreditable feelings, how I had no longer anything to envy him for; & how, dashing off Orlando I had done better than he had done; & how for the first time I think, he thought of me, as a writer, with some envy. Yet he amused me by protesting that to write like that would be to write like Virginia—a fatal event, it seems.

Now time must not flap on the mast any more. Now I must somehow brew another decoction of illusion. Well, if the human interest flags—if its that that worries me, I must not sit thinking about it here. I must make human illusion—ask someone in tomorrow after dinner; & begin that astonishing adventure with the souls of others again—about which I know so little. Is it affection that prompts?

Sunday 16 June

As I finished those words, in came Leonard to say that Desmond was coming round in two minutes—which he did, so that the sail filled out again & the ship went on. (The reason why I write this is that I cannot go on correcting A Room of one's own. I have read till my own sentences jingle in my ear—& so I begin to make more). Desmond was shabby & baggy in grey. He was bubbling & simmering, off to dine with Crompton Davies at Kettner's, & determined to be punctual.[7] A vein of determination lies in him; & he is the most cooked & saturated of us all. Not an atom remains crude; basted richly over a slow fire—an adorable man, a divine

6. Cf Byron's *When we Two parted*.
7. Crompton Llewelyn Davies (1868-1935), one of Margaret Llewelyn Davies's six brothers, had been at Trinity College, Cambridge, and was an Apostle; he was now a partner in a firm of solicitors, and lived in Gledhow Gardens, South Kensington. Kettner's was (and is) a restaurant in Church (now Romilly) Street, Soho.

man, as Francis would say, for all his power of taking the spine out of me. Happily we did not get on to that—writing that is to say. Julian broke down in his Apostle speech; came dressed as for a ball, & got muddled in his notes & sat down; but with his admirable Stephen solidity did not mind. Also Desmond lost £5 to Lord Rothermere, & another man lost £2,000, over the Election. What circles you live in, said Leonard; & he said that this was only due to the Empire Review. Maynard he said looked as if he were conscious of discord at the Apostle dinner.[8] We talked of Lytton's books. But talk ran into talk; nothing could be spread out; he must not be late for Crompton. He (C.) lives in Gledhow Terrace, with two leather chairs in the dining room; behind it his bedroom; he has his Virgil & a Milton that Desmond gave him. My Milton, said Leonard; & I offered to give Desmond a new despatch box. Off he went talking all the way. And Pinker came back &—

Sunday 23 June

It was very hot that day, driving to Worthing to see Leonard's mother, my throat hurt me. Next morning I had a headache. So we stayed on at Rodmell till today. At Rodmell I read through the Common Reader; & this is very important—I must learn to write more succinctly. Especially in the general idea essays like the last, How it strikes a Contemporary, I am horrified by my own looseness. This is partly that I dont think things out first; partly that I stretch my style to take in crumbs of meaning. But the result is a wobble & diffusity & breathlessness which I detest. One must correct A room of one's own very carefully before printing. And so I pitched into my great lake of melancholy. Lord how deep it is! What a born melancholiac I am! The only way I keep afloat is by working. A note for the summer I must take more work than I can possibly get done. ⟨I am⟩—no, I dont   Aug. 31st This vow I kept

know what it comes from. Directly I stop working I feel that I am sinking down, down. And as usual, I feel that if I sink further I shall reach the truth. That is the only mitigation; a kind of nobility. Solemnity. I shall make myself face the fact that there is nothing—nothing for any of us. Work, reading, writing are all disguises; & relations with people. Yes, even having children would be useless.

We went into the beechwood by the Race Course. I like these woods; & the waters of the greenery closing over one; so shallow, with the sun on

8. The Apostles' dinner had taken place while LW was in France. The April and May issues of the *Empire Review* had predicted a Conservative victory in the General Election of 30 May 1929.

them; then so deep in the shade. And I like the beech boughs, laced about, very intricate; like many arms; & the trunks, like the stone pillars in a church. But if I were Mrs Bartholomew I should certainly do something violent. This thought kept coming to me. What though could one do, at the bottom of that weight[?]; with that incubus of injustice on top of one? Annie Thompsett & her baby live on 15/ a week. I throw away 13/- on cigarettes, chocolates, & bus fares. She was eating rice pudding by the baby's cradle when I came in.[9]

However, I now begin to see the Moths rather too clearly, or at least strenuously, for my comfort. I think it will begin like this: dawn; the shells on a beach; I dont know—voices of cock & nightingale; & then all the children at a long table—lessons. The beginning. Well, all sorts of characters are to be there. Then the person who is at the table can call out any one of them at any moment; & build up by that person the mood, tell a story; for instance about dogs or nurses; or some adventure of a childs kind; all to be very Arabian nights; & so on: this shall be Childhood; but it must not be my childhood; & boats on the pond; the sense of children; unreality; things oddly proportioned. Then another person or figure must be selected. The unreal world must be round all this—the phantom waves. The Moth must come in: the beautiful single moth. There must be a flower growing.

Could one not get the waves to be heard all through? Or the farmyard noises? Some odd irrelevant noises. She might have a book—one book to read in—another to write in—old letters.

Early morning light—but this need not be insisted on; because there must be great freedom from 'reality'. Yet everything must have relevance.

Well all this is of course the 'real' life; & nothingness only comes in the absence of this. I have proved this quite certainly in the past half hour. Everything becomes green & vivified in me when I begin to think of the Moths. Also, I think, one is much better able to enter into other's—

Sunday 30 June

I broke off; somebody I imagine interrupted. My melancholy has been broken, like a lake by oars, since I wrote. I have been so active. We have seen so many people. Last night we dined with Roger, tonight with Clive; Lytton came; Vita came; we had a party. I brought a dress in Shaftesbury Avenue. It was very hot, I think; & is now cold, indeed, for the first time for weeks, it is, or has been raining. I am writing idly, to solace my eyes

9. Annie, who was to become the Woolfs' cook and domestic at Monks House, was a daughter of the Mrs Thomsett who had sometimes worked for them in earlier years.

after two hours of intense correction—that much corrected book, Women
& Fiction. It shall go to the printer tomorrow I swear. And then I can
bask entirely in the light of some fiction. But I have written myself out of
that mood, & find it difficult to get back to it. This last half year I made
over £1800; almost at the rate of £4000 a year; the salary almost of a
Cabinet minister; & time was, two years ago, when I toiled to make £200.
Now I am overpaid I think for my little articles— And I still think that
the great pleasure of prosperity is to be able to go into a shop & buy a
pocket knife. Well, after tomorrow I shall close down article writing, &
give way to fiction for six or seven months—till next March perhaps. And
I here record my intention to see to the writing of this new book much
more carefully; to strike out redundancies. Now that I have, I think,
gained the free use of my pen, I must begin to curb it. Hitherto my freedom has had to be fought for.

Helen Anrep last night was distracted & worried, like a wet overblown
Rose. Baba got out of her bed & went on the roof & fell asleep there. So
Miss Cox proposes to put her down into a lower class for a year. And
Roger had news that her Hampstead House was falling down; would need
£500 spent on it. And how could she live on the income of £3,000 if she
sold it to the Hampstead Hospital?[10] The other day in Paris she thought
she was going to have a child by Roger. "And I've failed utterly with the
children I have—And I feel a hundred." So she plained & crooned, sitting
beside Roger, with her hand on the arm of his chair. Sometimes he put his
hand on hers. They were affectionate & private; this is Roger's private
life. And it keeps him happy, while superficially he whirls from doctor to
doctor; & springs & spins, & looks out places on the map—unable not
to verify & track down any statement, however pointless. He told us how
in some great French cave, there is a patch of green vegetation wherever
the torchlight has fallen. And Mauron ran his hand along a ledge & thought
it was moss. But it was bats dung. The bats fly up into the air.

Desmond is being very brilliant about the Byron letters & the Boswell
papers. Think! There are 18 volumes of Boswell's diaries now to be
published. With any luck I shall live to read them. I feel as if some dead

10. Anastasia (Baba) Anrep was the elder of Boris and Helen Anrep's two children;
she was a boarder at Hayes Court School, near Bromley, of which Miss Catherine
Cox was headmistress. (It was at this school that VW had given a lecture on 30
January 1926 (see Headnote, 1926), when she was driven there by Mary Hutchinson
whose daughter was also a pupil.) Baba's punishment was commuted from a year
to a term. Helen had left her husband and her house in Pond Street (adjacent to
the then Hampstead General Hospital) to live with Roger Fry at 42 Bernard
Street, WC1.

person were said to be living after all—an odd effect, this disinterment of a mass more of Boswell when one had thought all was known, all settled. And father never knew; & Sir Edmund Gosse is dead. These papers were in a cabinet in Ireland.[11]

And now it is almost time for lunch; & after lunch I must again read my book; with a view, if possible, to shortening & condensing the last pages.

The Woolfs spent each week-end in July at Rodmell, and on 27th moved there for ten weeks' respite from the metropolitan 'helter skelter'. VW had been suffering intermittently from headaches and depression. Ka Arnold-Foster came to Monks House for the night of 4 August.

Monday 5 August

Yes that is the date, & the last was June 30th—a tribute to the helter skelter random rackety summer I spent. Far the pleasantest memories, standing out like green weed on some civet grey pond, were the week ends here: the divine fresh week ends, with the hay cutting & the lights lambent; Leonard's new room, Hedgehog Hall a-building, & my lodge being made into the palace of comfort which it now is. For I am now sitting here, oppressed by the Bank holiday atmosphere which gets into the wild country air, the lonely marshes, & makes the village seem smug & suburban. The girls & men are playing stool ball; Leonard & Percy are making a pipe conduct water into the Pond. It is a chocolate brown, & lived in by small fish. Yes it was a scattered summer; I felt as if the telephone were strung to my arm & anybody could jerk me who liked. A sense of interruption bothered me. And then these people one 'sees'—how blurred the image becomes! What damp blotting paper my mind was, as I left Ottoline's on Thursday afternoon, & determined not to speak to another soul. There is a sort of irreverence in treating thus the venerable soul of man: one curses it, & bites it & gets embittered by it. More pleasure is to be had from one nights talk with old dunderheaded Ka than from these flittering &

11. Desmond MacCarthy, in reviewing a new edition of James Boswell's *The Hypo-chondriak* in his 'World of Books' column in the *Sunday Times* of 30 June, wrote: 'I used to think that when the Great Book was opened in the Valley of Jehoshaphat, it would be the entries under the head "Byron" which would contain fewest surprises for us, but apparently it is Boswell who after all has succeeded most triumphantly in anticipating the Day of Judgment.' Boswell's private papers discovered at Malahide Castle, near Dublin, in 1925-26, were issued in a privately printed and costly limited edition in eighteen volumes between 1928-34—the first six edited by Geoffrey Scott.

glitterings. In London I should only have girded at her. Here, spreading herself out in her slow heavy footed way one took in an easy half critical, half appreciative impression—the chief element being amusement at her protestations. When the story was not to her credit as a social centre, it was to his as a speaker, politician, gardener, artist, husband, thinker— everything. Indeed I cut her short this morning, as she exalted his brain, by saying we all live on illusion; Will's brain is one of them. Thus pulled up she jibbed a moment, & then recovered, & saw the sense; not quite, perhaps; but in her slow way, larded over with these shams & gentilities & politics & appearances, she is honest too. And we talked about Rupert. But my reflection—every visit leaves one with a reflection—was this, about talking in protest, to impress, its futility, its universality: only she is more open & insistent, for some reason, than we are—or so I hope. Take away that motive from one's talk, & how much would be left? How often don't I vaguely feel blessing my sentence, the face of my own vanity, which de- mands that I shall pay it this tribute.

And then I'm cross with Vita: she never told me she was going abroad for a fortnight—didnt dare; till the last moment, when she said it was a sudden plan.[1] Lord Lord! I am half amused though; why do I mind? what do I mind? how much do I mind? I shall fire up & accuse her, & see to the bottom of her vessel. One of the facts is that these Hildas are a chronic case; & as this one won't disappear & is unattached, she may be permanent. And, like the damned intellectual snob I am, I hate to be linked, even by an arm, with Hilda. Her earnest aspiring competent wooden face appears before me, seeking guidance in the grave question of who's to broadcast. A queer trait in Vita—her passion for the earnest middle-class intellectual, however drab & dreary. And why do I write this down? I have not even told Leonard; & whom do I tell when I tell a blank page? The truth is, I get nearer feelings in writing than in walking [*sic*]—I think: graze the bone; enjoy the expression; have them out of me; make them a little creditable to myself; I daresay suppress something, so that after all I'm doing what amounts to confiding. Why did Pepys write his diary after all?

I should be tackling Mary Wollstonecraft. I am in the thick of my four Herald articles,[2] thus cutting into my Moths (but I had proofs of A Room to correct) & hope to be quit of it all by August 14th & then go down step by step into that queer region. I must make a great try for it—for this

1. On 16 July Vita had gone for a walking holiday in the Val d'Isère with Hilda Matheson (1888-1940), first Director of Talks for the BBC, who had become one of her intimate friends.
2. The articles commissioned by the *New York Herald Tribune*; see above, 13 April 1929, n 1.

difficult book—& after that? Always adventure: with that sense to guide me, I shant stagnate anyhow.

You can choose between us, I say, stopping writing; & get some satisfaction from making up caustic phrases. Yet I'm not very caustic, only by starts.

Thursday 8 August

This is written to while away one of those stupendous moments—one of those painful, ridiculous, agitating moments which make one half sick & yet I dont know—I'm excited too; & feel free & then sordid; & unsettled; & so on—I've told Nelly to go; after a series of scenes which I wont bore myself to describe. And in the midst of the usual anger, I looked into her little shifting greedy eyes, & saw nothing but malice & spite there, & felt that that had come to be the reality now: she doesn't care for me, or for anything: has been eaten up by her poor timid servants fears & cares & respectabilities. And so at lunch L. & I settled it; & I spoke two words, which she almost pulled out of my mouth in her eagerness to show herself delighted & eager & hard & untouched—a sordid painful scene after 15 years; but then how many I have had, & how degrading they are. & if we dont break now we drift on endlessly—oh but all these old arguments I know by heart. Whats new & strange is to have made an end of it, for though we only speak of her staying away till October, I dont think we shall ever begin again. This is an occasion for some of the small virtues of life—cheerfulness, & decision, & the determination to start fresh & better. In truth we never should have gone on, I daresay, if it hadn't been for the war; I dont know: I'm confirmed in my wish to have no resident servants ever again. That is the evil which rots the relationship. But now I must go to Annie Thomsett again.

(margin) Another scene, Aug. 30th; but these reflections stood me in good stead—& I laughed. But what a confounded bore it is

Saturday 10 August[3]

Well, Heaven be praised; it is all over & calm & settled. Nelly—how long ago that seems!—is staying—Yes, we found we cdnt get Mrs Thomsett; & I had two minutes of energetic courage; & so, Nelly saying, she thought—but I'm too bored. And I'm too deliciously relieved to have seen Vita this moment & find that her story to me was precisely true—& she brought documents to prove it—& was very upset—& had gone

3. VW has mis-dated this entry *Saturday Aug 9th.*

like a donkey & telephoned to Hilda—who is also very upset, & was altogether so simple & sincere & saw that my position was reasonable—oh yes, she could not have stood it a moment—but why, I ask myself, does it bore me so insufferably to write down what is so acutely exciting at the moment? My own lack of narrative power. Indeed I was more worried & angry & hurt & caustic about this affair than I let on, even to the blank page; yet afraid too of exaggeration. Of course, one is right about Nelly—right that she is, in bad moods almost insufferably mean, selfish & spiteful; but—& this is an interesting psychological remark, she is in a state of nature; untrained; uneducated, to me almost incredibly without the power of analysis or logic; so that one sees a human mind wriggling undressed—which is interesting; & then, in the midst of one's horror at the loathesome spectacle, one is surprised by the goodness of human nature, undressed; & it is more impressive because of its undress. For example, she thought I had given her notice permanently; but instead of giving way, —& yet she had nowhere to go to—to rage or spite, she bicycled into Lewes to get us cream for dinner: the motive being genuine I think; we must not suffer; & how could she leave us without a cook? It is this mixture that one can't understand; & that makes one always plunge so heavily in dealing with her. She said too that she would find it very difficult to get a place; since it is all the fashion now to engage cooks only who will live out (& this sentence is another example of my inability to write narrative). And it will happen again, her spite & meanness; but we shan't part now, I think. And I'm half pleased to find that it is harder to part after 15 years than I thought. And I'm pleased—oh very pleased—about Vita.

Thursday 15 August

These tumults over, then I had a headache. And two ideas come to me—to break my rule & write about the soul for once; & to write some exact dialogue: I just note this, it being dinner time.

We are back from Brighton where I brought a corner cupboard. And if I had time, I would here dissect a curious little spotted fruit: this melancholy. It comes with headache, of course. And I had come to the blind alley —the cul de-sac. Writing this compressed article, where every word is like a step cut in the rock—hard work, if ever writing was; & done largely for money; & whats money, compared with Nessa's children; & then the—

Monday 19 August

I suppose dinner interrupted. And I opened this book in another train of mind—to record the blessed fact that for good or bad I have just set the

last correction to Women & Fiction, or a Room of One's Own. I shall
never read it again I suppose. Good or bad? Has an uneasy life in it I think:
you feel the creature arching its back & galloping on, though as usual much
is watery & flimsy & pitched in too high a voice.

William Plomer has been for the week end & gone. A compressed
inarticulate young man, thickly coated with a universal manner fit for all
weather & people: tells a nice dry prim story; but has the wild eyes which
I once noted in Tom, & take to be the true index of what goes on within.
Once or twice he almost cracked his crust—sitting on the stones this
morning for instance.

I dont suppose you know how separate I feel myself from all my con-
temporaries. I am afraid I was very inadequate last night (at Charleston).
I apologised for the family party. No that was delightful; except that
Clive Bell seemed inharmonious. What d'you think of Wyndham Lewis,
of Joyce ?[4] (V.) I dont like scolds. It spoils the voice. I like old men of 80
like Moore & Yeats who have kept their minds working. "Exactly. That's
the precise point" (these are William's words). And fathers are difficult.
Mine has no interest in anything. But I dont live at Pinner for choice.
I dislike Roy Campbell's pose.[5] He used to fly a kite at the end of a fishing
rod. William (he said the Mr was awkward) is notably trying to be like
other people: to justify his life among natives & colonels, which has given
him this composure. Beside him Julian seemed a mere child, & Duncan
a contemporary. May he bring Butts to see us?[6] He is a very self-contained
independent young man, determined not to be rushed in any way, &
having no money at all, he gave Nelly 5/ for a tip. I think he shows up
well against the Raymonds & the Frankies—is somehow solid; to their
pinchbeck lustre.

I have now written myself out of a writing mood; & cannot attack
melancholy, save only to note that it was much diminished by hearing
Nessa say she was often melancholy & often envied me—a statement I

4. The Woolfs took Plomer to dine at Charleston on Sunday. The family party felt
   inclined to apologise to Plomer on VW's behalf: by declaring that this shy and
   modest poet claimed descent from both Shakespeare and William Blake she made
   everyone feel ill at ease. (See II QB, p 149.) Percy Wyndham Lewis (1882-1957)
   the aggressive, contentious writer and artist; and James Joyce (1882-1941) were
   both VW's exact coevals.
5. William Plomer had known the poet Roy Campbell and his wife Mary in South
   Africa; he and Campbell had collaborated in the production of Voorslag, a magazine
   intended to serve as a lash or goad to the 'mental hindquarters' of South Africa's
   'bovine citizenry'; see Chapter 17, The Autobiography of William Plomer (1975).
6. Anthony Butts (1900-1941), an old-Etonian painter with whom Plomer formed a
   deep and close friendship.

thought incredible. I have spilt myself among too many stools she said (we were sitting in her bedroom before dinner). Other peoples melancholy certainly cheers one. And now, having written my four little brief hard articles, I must think of that book again, & go down step by step into the well. These are the great events & revolutions in one's life—& then people talk of war & politics. I shall grind very hard; all my brakes will be stiff; my springs rusty. But I have now earned the right to some months of fiction. & my melancholy is brushed away, so soon as I can get my mind forging ahead, not circling round.

Wednesday 21 August

Geoffrey Scott died last week of pneumonia in New York. Let me think what I can remember of him. I met him first in 1909 at Florence at Mrs Berenson's. We went out for lunch, & he was there; & they discussed Francis Thompson. Afterwards we went to a party at Mrs Ross's: Mary came in with a brother, both disguised as Barnes, & had to reveal themselves as Stracheys before Mrs Ross would take any interest. Then she emphasised the fact that she was Meredith's mistress, leading us all down a lawn; —a terrace I suppose, overlooking Fiesole. I was unhappy that summer, & bitter in all my judgments; & cannot remember anything of Geoffrey Scott save that he was part of that unnatural Florentine society; & therefore in my mood, rather contemptible—long & familiar & aesthetic & at his ease, where I was rustic, provincial & badly dressed.[7] This impression then waits without a second till that summer evening, in 1925, I think, at Long Barn.[8] I had motored down with Dotty & Vita for my first visit & had sat shyly in the motor observing their endearments rather awkwardly, & how they stopped the Rolls Royce to buy great baskets of strawberries; & again I felt, not provincial, but ill-dressed, under-equipped; & so stepped on to the terrace at Long Barn; & forth came Geoffrey, smiling a little superciliously, as of old; & shook hands. Harold [Nicolson] was behind him, much more downright & burly & to my taste. That night we sat in

7. Geoffrey Scott, who died on 16 August, aged 46, had once been assistant to Bernard Berenson, the authority on Italian painting, at his villa *i Tatti* outside Florence; Berenson's neighbour, and a close friend of his wife Mary (*née* Pearsall Smith, the mother of Rachel and Karin Costelloe), was the formidable Janet Ross, *née* Duff-Gordon (1842-1927), who had lived in Italy since 1867; she was the model for more than one of Meredith's heroines, and wrote many books herself. (See Appendix II for VW's description of her.) Mary Hutchinson's mother, a cousin of Lytton Strachey's, married Sir Hugh Barnes; the brother was James Strachey Barnes. Francis Thompson (1859-1907), poet.
8. The year was in fact 1924. See *II VW Diary*, 5 July 1924.

the long room, & after Harold had grown sleepy sitting on the fender
knocking his head against the fringe of the Italian cover on the mantelpice,
Geoffrey sat with us, & was drawn by Dotty into telling stories for my
amusement. He did this very well; I remember, though I dont remember
what the stories were about. He was a very clever man, I thought; & I
tried to place him, & concluded that he had some grudge against me as
member of a circle he somehow respected but was not of; told me, I
remember, that he could not distinguish an article by me in the Nation
from one by Morgan or Lytton—we all wrote the same ironic style—&
that I felt was said by way of showing me—& we were the two scallywags
at that particular party—that he was up to our little ways & had no respect
for them. Then next day we went over Knole, where again, as at Florence,
he was very much at his ease, & knew every piece of furniture or silver &
called Lord Sackville Lionel as if he had known him & Vita familiarly
many years, just as he had known the Rosses & the Berensons. And he
was tall, & dark & had the distinguished face of a failure; reminded me a
little of Bernard Holland & other 'brilliant' young men,[9] who remain
'brilliant' & young well into the 40ties & never do anything to prove it.
Harold walked back through the Park to think out some speech about
Byron, simply & straightforwardly, rather to my & I think Geoffrey's
amusement. The others—Dotty Vita & Geoffrey—took me to the station;
& I said goodbye to him there, & never spoke to him again. I had the
feeling that he & Dotty & Vita & Harold were all a set; very intimate &
familiar, & indeed said so, when they challenged me, as usual, with Bloomsbury & its closed walls. "But you are the same—you make me feel that
you are all very intimate" I said, & they half denied it; but only half.
For, as I learnt later, I had broken in upon the height of his affair with
Vita. It was flaming very strongly that particular month, or week; it was
the time when she returned his passion, for a moment; when he was
swearing that she must leave Harold & live with him. After that, my
intercourse with him was only by hearsay—through messages—Karin
said her mother wished her to arrange a meeting between Geoffrey & me
—& then through Vita's explanations, later, when she told me how he
was waiting for her, had left his Villa Medici & Lady Sybil on her account;[10]
& was now fuming in a mews off Regent's Park expecting her while she
sat at Tavistock Square talking to me. One night, she said, he almost
strangled her—seized her by the throat; & she turned black & he was

9. See below, note 12.
10. Geoffrey Scott had in 1918 married the widowed Lady Sibyl Cutting who owned
the Villa Medici, Fiesole; his love affair with Vita Sackville-West began in the
autumn of 1923 and lasted with considerable intensity for a little less than a year.

frightened. And I heard how furious he was on the downs above Rodmell that summer, late at night, when they were driving home, from Lady Sackville I suppose. Vita saw lights in the valley & said that I was down there asleep. Whereupon he flew into another rage—they were calling the dogs who had gone hunting, & the wind blew his hat off. He called me 'that woman'. And I saw him, in full evening dress, at the ballet with Sybil [Colefax]. And then never again.

He is dead in New York, & all those papers about Boswell—what will become of them; & the life that was to have made him immortal will never be written; & he remains the brilliant young man for ever.[11]   I was offered £2000 to write it

And I have turned over two pages by mistake. Perhaps I can think of some other figure to write in there, going backwards, before I need go in: & it is a lovely evening; & I want to stay out here writing, & trying my new pen.

Nobody has died, to my knowledge, of much interest. And if it comes to putting down talk, the truth is that, except in novels, people don't talk.

Well, Bernard Holland, as I have mentioned him.[12] But I cannot put my hand on any first meeting or even second. I believe I first heard him mentioned when I was say ten years old; & he had just become engaged to Helen Duckworth. Stella said to mother, "But can they know what he thinks then?"—or words which made me surmise that there was something dark & queer about this young man; something that to Stella seemed incongruous with the rusticity & conventionality of her Duckworth aunt & uncle. Then that little light, revealing as it was, goes out; & there is only hearsay about Bernard till, in 1902 or 3 perhaps, Dorothea took me uninvited to stay at Canterbury with Canon Holland;[13] & there was Bernard; & he was saturnine, with his great eyebrows almost meeting; & his sunk cheeks; & his gloom; & his height; & about him there hung, now more authentically, that reputation for brilliance & strangeness that was his, years ago, at Cambridge. Poor old Bernard—he's a genius, I once

11. At the time of his death Geoffrey Scott had been engaged in editing the Boswell papers, see above 30 June 1929, n 11. For the offer in the marginal postscript, see below, 1 March 1930.

12. Bernard Henry Holland (1856-1926), son of Rev. F. J. Holland, Canon of Canterbury, and his wife Mary Sibylla, née Lyall; educated at Eton and Trinity College, Cambridge, called to the Bar in 1882. He was private secretary to the Duke of Devonshire 1892-94 and to the Secretary of State for the Colonies 1903-8 and served as secretary to various Royal Commissions 1891-1908. In 1895 he married Florence Helen Duckworth, a cousin of VW's half-sister Stella Duckworth.

13. Dorothea Jane Stephen (1871-1965), youngest child of Sir James Fitzjames Stephen, and VW's cousin.

heard Harry Stephen say. He interested me because I imputed to him 'imagination'—the quality I most admired & missed most in my father & his agnostic friends. Bernard had edited his mother's letters, & I liked them in a sentimental way, seeing in them something imaginative, too; something that was coloured & pensive & intimate, unlike anything the Stephen family produced.[14] So that I looked at Bernard in the low room under the Cathedral with interest, & even hoped he might think me clever or imaginative or something. But I doubt that he detached me from the shadow of Dorothea. He was occupied & mysterious, in touch with politics & Cabinet ministers; highly thought of by the Lytteltons, & vaguely credited with being himself much more able & capable than they were; but he was too much of a genius, too queer & individual, so people said, to do anything for himself. And Helen played up to this version of Bernard very femininely; wandering about vague eyed, cherry cheeked, ecstatic, religious; like some woman I thought in a novel by Charlotte Yonge.[15] We were taken to see a sister of Mary Sibylla's, & she said, clasping her tea cup, that whenever she heard thunder she imagined that someone had been killed by it. There was all that kind of imagination afloat. Bernard stalked about in it, aloof, intellectual, silent; appreciative perhaps, but never said so. Helen played little melancholy scraps of Beethoven; which moved me; but Bernard snapped "Whats that? Gilbert & Sullivan?" to snub her sentimentality I suppose. And then, when there was talk of going back in the train together, he stopped it. He said that he must be alone & work. So I suppose I made no impression; & received one that was not altogether favourable. A sort of false gloom was his I thought; unless indeed he were tremendously imaginative. I read a book he wrote anonymously about becoming a Roman Catholic & got a faint seductive whiff of a world where people were very brilliant & thought about their souls; a semi-worldly world it seemed; rather fluent; rather too clear & plausible & pensive, but still attractive & unfamiliar. And then again I met him at Ottoline's; & then I was older, & he was more pronounced. That is he was still sardonic; cavernous; but no longer so lean, or so silent. He flirted, even I could see, with Ottoline; & had become one of those distinguished young men who are very brilliant when they dine out—like Herbert Paul perhaps;[16] they appear without

14. *Letters of Mary Sibylla*. Selected and edited by her son, Bernard Holland (1898).
15. The Lytteltons were a large aristocratic family with influence and connections in Church and State—part in fact of the Ruling Class. Charlotte M. Yonge (1823-1901), the prolific writer whose popular romances purvey a highly religious view of life.
16. Herbert Woodfield Paul (1853-1935) had been President of the Oxford Union, a Liberal MP, and then settled down as a Civil Service Commissioner and a writer

their wives, who are deaf or mad; influence politics; write unsigned articles; & flirt with ladies of title. Ottoline told me that Bernard had written her a sonnet, after another dinner party. And then he turned Roman Catholic. He wrote a vast life of the Duke of Devonshire; he wrote a vast history of the Holland family;[17] but that was all that came of his gloom & his imagination & his genius, & when he died, a year or two ago, even his friends never wrote to the Times about him.

Thursday 22 August

And so I might fill up the half hour before dinner writing.

I thought, on my walk that I would begin at the beginning: I get up at half past eight & walk across the garden. Today it was misty & I had been dreaming of Edith Sitwell. I wash & go into breakfast which is laid on the check table cloth. With luck I may have an interesting letter; today there was none. And then bath & dress; & come out here & write or correct for three hours, broken at 11 by Leonard with Milk, & perhaps newspapers. At one luncheon—rissoles today & chocolate custard. A brief reading & smoking after lunch; & at about two I change into thick shoes, take Pinker's lead & go out—up to Asheham hill this afternoon, where I sat a minute or two, & then home again, along the river. Tea at four, about; & then I come out here & write several letters, interrupted by the Post, with another invitation to lecture; & then I read one book of the Prelude. And soon the bell will ring, & we shall dine & then we shall have some music, & I shall smoke a cigar; & then we shall read—La Fontaine I think tonight & the papers—& so to bed. Here I will copy some lines I want to remember,

> The matter that detains us now may seem,
> To many, neither dignified enough
> Nor arduous, yet will not be scorned by them,
> Who, looking inward, have observed the ties
> That bind the perishable hours of life
> Each to the other, & the curious props
> By which the world of memory & thought
> Exists & is sustained.

---

of biography and history. He was married to a sister-in-law of Lady Ritchie, VW's 'Aunt Anny'.

17. *The Life of Spencer Compton, 8th Duke of Devonshire* (2 vols. 1911), and *The Lancashire Hollands . . . With illustrations and pedigrees* (1917). In 1923 he published *Belief and Freedom*, a popular argument on behalf of Roman Catholicism.

They are from the 7th book of the Prelude.[18] A very good quotation I think.

But my skeleton day needs reviving with all sorts of different colours. Today it was grey & windy on the walk; yesterday generous & open; a yellow sun on the corn; & heat in the valley. Both days differ greatly; both are among the happiest of my life—I mean among the happy undistinguished days, ripe & sweet & sound; the daily bread; for nothing strange or exalted has happened; only the day has gone rightly & harmoniously; a pattern of the best part of life which is in the country like this; & makes me wish to command more of them—months of them.

Now my little tugging & distressing book & articles are off my mind my brain seems to fill & expand & grow physically light & peaceful. I begin to feel it filling quietly after all the wringing & squeezing it has had since we came here. And so the unconscious part now expands; & walking I notice the red corn, & the blue of the plain & an infinite number of things without naming them; because I am not thinking of any special thing. Now & again I feel my mind take shape, like a cloud with the sun on it, as some idea, plan, or image wells up, but they travel on, over the horizon, like clouds, & I wait peacefully for another to form, or nothing—it matters not which.

One picture I saw—Phil Burne Jones sitting in the square of St Mark's, in evening dress, alone one August night in 1912—for we were on our honeymoon. He looked dissipated & lonely, like a pierrot who had grown old & rather peevish. He wore a light overcoat & sat, his foolish nervous white face looking aged & set unhappy & eager & disillusioned, alone at a little marble table, while everyone else paraded or chattered & the band played—he had no companion—none of his smart ladies—nobody to chatter to, in his affected exaggerated voice; paying astonishing compliments, using dears & darlings & going into that once fashionable whinny of laughter which must I think have come down from Burne Jones himself —& Phil was a kind of dissipated degenerate, spending all the thousands that were paid for those wan women on staircases, on love affairs, on luxuries, on being a fashionable bachelor & fairy God father to the Trees & Taylors & other fashionable young ladies—a very timid conventional man at bottom, with a horrid taste in pictures, presumably, but a way with children. Lowell noticed that at St Ives. And I am still grateful for pictures that he drew for us. He belongs to the gallery of brilliant young men of 50, for he died a year or two ago.[19]

18. Wordsworth's *Prelude* (1850 version) Book VII, 458-466.
19. Philip Burne-Jones (1861-1926) succeeded his father Edward, the pre-Raphaelite artist, as 2nd Baronet in 1898; an un-serious painter with a gift for caricature, he

The best part of my walk this afternoon was certainly on the top of the down leading to Juggs Corner.

Yes, yes, but that is days ago. I saw a woman in white sitting against soft snow banks of blue & white sky; & a child in blue: I saw all the downs glooming & brightening. But it is now

Monday 2 September

& I am writing these words because Lyn (yes, she is Lyn) is reading in the garden, & I am talk-dried, & cant begin the Moths as I should, or patch up finally those old articles.[1] A long day it was yesterday—rather exhausting —hard work talking to someone one hardly knows in the orchard. A very nice young woman, with that essential bareness—I cant think of the word—that young women so often have—without illusions, about herself; an honesty bred of poverty. Keeping going on £200 a year in London which she earns. Pays her way week by week on articles; & her father has £600 as a presbyterian minister in Aberdeen, & will have £400 to retire on, & has 5 children. So that she will never have a penny of her own. All this breeds a kind of veracity & clear sightedness & austerity which I prefer, perhaps, to the lush undergrowth which surrounds Dotty. One gardener more or less, one persian pot more or less, what does it matter— her life is crowded & otiose; but Lyn knows every object in her room, & has saved up & bought them by saving so that they are exact & polished. Well, but of her? Oh I'm so sick of talk, & analysis.

This book would form in me could I let my mind lie asleep, calm like a tideless sea; but all this time I'm breaking my mind up; destroying the growth underneath. Never mind, after tomorrow when I go to Vita, solitude begins.* I shall ruminate for a month. Lyn has this austerity.

* This was a sanguine guess—not fulfilled

She is direct & sensible; goes to the W.C. frankly; but is not sexually

---

led a frivolous social life as a man about town. The 'wan women on staircases' is an allusion to his father's painting of 1872-80 in the Tate Gallery, 'The Golden Stairs'. The Trees were the three vivacious daughters of Sir Herbert Beerbohm Tree; and the Taylors, Viola and Una, the granddaughters of Sir Henry Taylor (see above, 10 November 1928, n 12). James Russell Lowell (1819-1891), poet and man of letters, was American Ambassador in London, 1880-85, and in effect, VW's godfather.

1. Lyn Lloyd Irvine (1901-1973) had got to know the Woolfs as a result of her submitting poetry to the *N & A* and a novel to the Hogarth Press; though he did not publish it, LW thought well enough of her writing to invite her to contribute reviews to the *N & A*. Enid Welsford (below), a lecturer in English at Newnham, was a friend of hers.

advanced I should say; has had no indulgences with young men or wine; has something cool headed & sensible about her, derived from her theological father, her Scots farmer birth no doubt. She has been trained in English literature & is, what young women so seldom are, or were, a trained critic. She gives her opinion precisely & methodically, rather as Janet Vaughan would do on a case. (Janet was here last week end, by the way.) This trained mind is new & rather strange. It seems to eliminate enthusiasm, perhaps too drastically. Its odd to find everything weighed & criticised. & words of sobriety & insight issuing from this innocent round pink face; these candid blue eyes. She will spend money on face powder—went to buy a special brand & bought a cactus instead. Oh & she told a story about the dead man on the sands. She & Enid Welsford were motoring. One night they came to a bay & Enid wanted to walk to a long stretch of sand. So they went; & Lyn saw a coat & a pair of boots in the sand; & found it was a dead man. She stopped & went back, giving Enid the slip, not thinking that children might find it; absolutely horrified; her first sight of a dead person. This was made vivid to me. Enid came back. Did you see something? Yes I saw it. So they told the villagers. The man had been unhappily married & had seemed depressed & so killed himself, to be found that sad grey night—his boots sticking out of the sand, the face I suppose very ghastly.

I have just read a page or two of Samuel Butler's notebooks to take the taste of Alice Meynell's life out of my mouth.[2] One rather craves brilliance & cantankerousness. Yet I am interested; a little teased by the tight airless Meynell style; & then I think what they had that we had not—some suavity & grace, certainly. They believed in things & we didn't; & she had 7 children & wrote about 5 paragraphs a day for society papers & so on—all the time looking like a crucified saint; & was also very merry & witty perhaps—anyhow absolutely steeped in various sorts of adventure & life—went to America lecturing & made £15 a lecture, which she sent back to help Wilfrid. But it is not exactly this that I mean. When one reads a life one often compares one's own life with it. And doing this I was aware of some sweetness & dignity in those lives compared with ours—even with ours at this moment. Yet in fact their lives would be intolerable—so insincere, so elaborate; so I think—all this word paring &

2. *The Notebooks of Samuel Butler*, a selection edited by Henry Festing Jones, was first published in 1912. *Alice Meynell. A Memoir*, by her daughter, Viola Meynell, 1929. Alice Meynell, *née* Thompson (1847-1922), poet and essayist, had married the journalist and editor Wilfred Meynell in 1877; they had three sons and four daughters, many of whom, as they grew up, were accommodated in cottages in the grounds of the large farmhouse the Meynells owned at Greatham in Sussex.

sweetness & charity. Viola cant help dropping in lump after lump of sugar
—only two sharp & therefore memorable things survive—her mother
failed as a friend. She never gave enough. Old Coventry Patmore, whom
she thought the equal of Sh[akespea]re, complained that he had lost the
primacy among her friends & dropped out; whereupon she went alone
into the drawing room, for she hated to express her feelings, & also hated
long accounts of illness & death in biographies, turning her face away
from her son in her last illness, & letting him only kiss her hand. Secondly
there was the oddity of her admiration for Chesterton. Had I been a man &
very big I could have been Chesterton. That is, her views were all peculiar
& angular, & stuck to pedantically. She had a line of her own. But it would
be a wonderful relief if Viola would give up being pointed & precise &
tell us something casual & familiar—only she cant: her mind in stays.
Katherine Mansfield described a visit to the house in Sussex—All the Ms.
in barns & cottages; & the daughters singing long monotonous ballads, &
then, by way of contrast & to surprise a scallywag I daresay with their
liveliness breaking into music hall songs taught them by their brothers in
law. Katherine described them like so many B[urne]. J[ones]. mermaids
with long lush hair, plucking at mediaeval instruments & intoning those
verses. Mrs M. sat by. And I saw her in 1910 (?) at Mrs Ross's, & heard
her say that saying about the climate & then there she was ecstatic in an
omnibus.—I recorded my regret that one ever saw poetesses in the flesh.[3]
For she was a poetess too—it strikes me that one or two little poems will
survive all that my father ever wrote. But its odd—this comparing that
goes on as one reads a life—I kept thinking how little good could be said
of me.

Wednesday I think the *4 September*

I am just back from Long Barn, that is from Ashdown forest, where L.
fetched me; & I have just eaten a pear warm from the sun with the juice
running out of it, & I have thought of this device: to put

The Lonely Mind

separately in The Moths, as if it were a person. I don't know—it seems
possible. And these notes show that I am very happy.
I daresay it is the hottest day this year—the hottest September day

3. VW described having tea with Mrs Ross at Poggio Gherardi during her visit to
Florence in 1909, and her impression of Alice Meynell, in her *Greece/Italy Notebook,
1906-09* (Copy, MHP Sussex, A7): see Appendix II.

these twenty years. So the papers may say tomorrow. Really it was too hot in the garden at Long Barn. The children were querulous—Nigel riding round in between the flower beds on his bicycle, & Ben stretched on the seat saying in a reasonable sad voice, Nigel you aren't well—you dont look well. Boski says you dont. Mummy he ought to wash his feet. Vita (from the window) but he has washed his feet. Ben. Well they're dirty again. Boski came in with the time table. The buses dont fit. They cant get back from Fairlawn before 8. Vita. Then ring up Mrs Cazalet & say they cant come. I must tell them they must put it off. She went to Harold's room where they sat working with Mr O'Connor, & told them. Nigel began arguing. She was firm, & strode away. All this happened in blazing heat.[4] The car was very hot. George brought a bottle of soda water. We lunched among some pine trees in Ashdown Forest, & lay full length afterwards, I with my straw hat over my face. Then L. met us, punctually at 4, at Duddimans (no—not that name) & we sat on some prickly holly leaves on the heath & talked to Vita about Harold's letter. He says her poems aren't worth publishing. She is very calm & modest, & seems not to mind much—a less touchy poet never was. But then can a real poet be an un-touchy poet?[5]

She was very much as usual [?]; striding; silk stockings; shirt & skirt; opulent; easy; absent; talking spaciously & serenely to the Eton tutor, an admirable young man, with straight nose & white teeth who went to bed, or to his room, early, leaving us alone. I remarked the boys calling him Sir & bending with salaams over his hand & then kissing Vita—how English—how summery & how upper class—how pleasant—how without accent. This has been going on a thousand years I felt; at least, I can remember summers like this—white flannels & tennis, mothers, & tutors & English houses & dinner with moths getting in the candles & talk of tennis tournaments & ladies asking one to tea all my life—so pleasant, so without accent. And the tutor was the eternal tutor of young men— joking, affectionate, stern: watching Nigel with a sort of amusement & tenderness "There spoke the real Nigel" when N. said he hoped he had

4. For the past year Boski—Audrey le Bosquet—had been Vita's secretary. Fairlawne, the Cazalet's home, was at Tonbridge. Vincent Mansfield O'Connor (1904-1930), a junior classical master at Eton, was acting as the Nicolson boys' tutor during the summer holidays.

5. George Thomsett was the Nicolson's butler. The meeting place was probably Duddleswell, roughly half way between Monks House and Long Barn. Harold Nicolson had written to advise Vita against the publication of *King's Daughter*, a collection of her poems which included some of a lesbian character; it was due to appear in the 'Hogarth Living Poets' series, and was in fact published in October 1929 (*HP Checklist* 207).

spilt the gravy on his trousers:—like a stream flowing deep & correct & unruffled through narrow banks. This kind of thing we now do to perfection. It is not interesting, but from its admirable completeness & sameness makes one tender towards it.

Nelly has been out this afternoon & picked, I think, 7 lbs of blackberries to make into jam. Please remember this as her way of thanking me for having Lottie—after all, she has no other. And one tends to forget it.

Monday 16 September

Leonard is having a picnic at Charleston & I am here—'tired'. But why am I tired? Well I am never alone. This is the beginning of my complaint. I am not physically tired so much as psychologically. I have strained & wrung at journalism & proof correction; & underneath has been forming my Moths book. Yes, but it forms very slowly; & what I want is not to write it, but to think it for two or three weeks say—to get into the same current of thought & let that submerge everything, writing perhaps a few phrases here at my window in the morning. (And they've gone to some lovely place—Hurstmonceux perhaps, in this strange misty evening;—& yet when the time came to go, all I wanted was to walk off into the hills by myself. I am now feeling a little lonely & deserted & defrauded, inevitably). And every time I get into my current of thought I am jerked out of it. We have the Keynes's: then Vita came; then Angelica & Eve; then we went to Worthing, then my head begins throbbing—so here I am, not writing—that does not matter, but not thinking, feeling or seeing—& seizing an afternoon alone as a treasure—Leonard appeared at the glass door at this moment; & they didn't go to H[urstmonceu]x or anywhere; & Sprott was there & a miner, so I missed nothing—one's first egotistical pleasure.[6]

Really these premonitions of a book—states of soul in creating—are very queer & little apprehended.

Another reflection—nothing is so tiring as a change of atmosphere. I am more shattered & dissipated by an hour with Leonard's mother than by 6 hours—no, 6 days, of Vita. (Nessa doesn't count). The tremendous gear changing that has to take place grinds one's machinery to bits. And

6. Walter John Herbert ('Sebastian') Sprott (1897-1971), a Cambridge Apostle, had been appointed Lecturer in Psychology at Nottingham University College in 1925. On 13 September, on one of LW's regular filial visits to his mother, ensconced in a Worthing hotel for the summer, the Woolfs took Nelly Boxall and Angelica and her friend Eve Younger with them; the little girls then stayed the night at Monks House.

I have done this constantly—& what is more than doing it, I've foreboded doing it—I've counted up the days & felt Worthing brooding over me. & then, psychologically again, having Nelly in the car is to me a strain—imposes another forced atmosphere. None of these things would matter much if one's engine were going at full speed—how I tossed off every interruption when I was writing Orlando!—but it is as if they got in to the spokes—clogged the wheels—always just prevented me from getting the machine swinging round. And then I am 47: yes: & my infirmities will of course increase. To begin with my eyes. Last year, I think, I could read without spectacles; wd. pick up a paper & read it in a tube; gradually I found I needed spectacles in bed; & now I can't read a line (unless held at a very odd angle) without them. My new spectacles are much stronger than the old, & when I take them off, I am blinded for a moment. What other infirmities? I can hear, I think, perfectly: I think I could walk as well as ever. But then will there not be the change of life? And may that not be a difficult & even dangerous time? Obviously one can get over it by facing it with common sense—that it is a natural process; that one can lie out here & read; that one's faculties will be the same afterwards; that one has nothing to worry about in one sense— I've written some interesting books, can make money, can afford a holiday—Oh no; one has nothing to bother about; & these curious intervals in life—I've had many—are the most fruitful artistically—one becomes fertilised—think of my madness at Hogarth—& all the little illnesses—that before I wrote To The Lighthouse for instance. Six weeks in bed now would make a masterpiece of Moths. But that wont be the name. Moths, I suddenly remember, dont fly by day. And there cant be a lighted candle. Altogether, the shape of the book wants considering—& with time I could do it.

Here I broke off.

Saturday 21 September

Angelica goes to school for the first time today I think;[7] & I daresay Nessa is crying to herself—one of the emotions I shall never know—a child, one's last child—going to school, & so ending the 21 years of Nessa's children—a great stretch of life; how much fuller than I can guess —imagine all the private scenes, the quarrels, the happinesses, the moments of excitement & change, as they grew up. And now, rather sublimely she

7. Hitherto, when Vanessa had been in London, Angelica had had lessons from Miss Rose Paul in Mecklenburgh Square; now she was sent as a boarder to a small private girls' school, Langford Grove, near Chelmsford, of which the headmistress was Mrs Curtis.

ends her childhood years in a studio alone, going back, perhaps rather sadly to the life she would have liked best of all once, to be a painter on her own. So we have made out our lives, she & I, propelled into them by some queer force; for me, I always think of those curious long autumn walks with which we ended a summer holiday, talking of what we were going to do—'autumn plans' we called them. They always had reference to painting & writing & how to arrange social life & domestic life better. Often we thought about changing a room, so as to have somewhere to see our own friends. They were always connected with autumn, leaves falling, the country getting pale & wintry, our minds excited at the prospect of lights & streets & a new season of activity beginning—October the dawn of the year. But I am rambling off like an old woman into the past, when as I sat down, waiting for tea, I said to myself I have so many things to write in my diary.

Another of those curious plums, things falling unexpectedly in our way, has just happened. Annie the large eyed sad young woman has been to ask us to buy her a cottage, & let her do for us always, in fact be our servant here. She & her baby, aged two, have been turned out at a fortnights notice to make room for two spinster dog breeders. Humanity says we ought to buy her her cottage, & take no rent—let her work it off. Another £350, & repairs—more articles. She would make an ideal servant, I believe; she would be a great standby; one could come here as long as one liked—& poor dear Nelly could be left in London,—for she gave notice again this morning, to Leonard this time, about his coal scuttle. It seems we are settling & rooting almost daily. I should have to dismiss poor spindly Bartholomew. It needs some thinking—meanwhile Annie is up against this terrific high black prison wall of poverty—has to manage with a child on 15/- a week.

These reflections, which branch off down so many paths make me linger, over the two other records—Peter, & my future, which I thought I was going to write; but it is tea time, & then I want to wander off up the downs or along the river, straightening my ideas.

Please God nobody comes to tea. Yet Lytton & Antony Blunt & Peter are all at Charleston.[8] Please God I say these delightful & divine people dont come & make me concentrate again all in my face & brain. I want to swim about in the dark green depths. By the way last night in the Evening Standard James Laver called me a great writer "nobody need seek to

8. Peter Lucas had stayed at Monks House on 18 and 19 September, before going on to Charleston. Anthony Frederick Blunt (b. 1907), later to become an eminent art historian, was at Trinity College, Cambridge, an Apostle, and a friend of Julian Bell.

qualify the greatness of Miss Virginia Woolf"—hah! I hope Arnold Bennett sees that.[9]

Sunday 22 September

And it is ten minutes past ten in the morning, & I am not going to write a word. I have resolved to shut down my fiction for the present. My head aches too easily at the moment; I feel The Moths a prodigious weight which I can't lift yet. And yet, so odd a thing is the mind, I am never easy, at this early hour, merely reading or writing letters. Those occupations seem too light & diffused. Hence, though write letters I will & must— to Dotty, to Gerald Brenan, to peevish Eddy, I will canter here a moment. It is a fine September morning; the rooks cawing, the shadows very long & shallow on the terrace. The body has gone out of the air. It is thinning itself for winter. It is becoming pale & pure like the eyes of an old man. An exacting & rather exhausting summer this has been. What with going to London, going to Worthing & having people here, I have never settled in; I feel I should like to stay on & avoid London for a time. The car makes us almost too movable. On the other hand, this is the best appointed summer we have ever had. Never has the garden been so lovely—all ablaze even now; dazzling one's eyes with reds & pinks & purples & mauves: the carnations in great bunches, the roses lit like lamps. Often we go out after dinner to see these sights. And at last I like looking about the drawing room. I like my rug; my carpet; my painted beams. And for some odd reason I have found lovelier walks this year than ever—up into the downs behind Telscombe. Partly it is the weather, perhaps; we have had day after day of cloudless warm sun; the sky has been blue day after day; the sun has gone down clean, clear, leaving no feathers or battlements in the west. And lying out here I have seen the sun rise, & the moon shining one night like a slice of looking glass, with all the stars rippling & shining; & one night I had that curious feeling of being very young, travelling abroad, & seeing the leaves from a train window, in Italy—I cant get the feeling right now. All was adventure & excitement.

As for Peter, how right how charming how good he is!—but damn it

9. LW went to London for the day on 20 September and presumably brought back the *Evening Standard* which contained James Laver's article headed 'Supreme Gift Denied to Women'. Though expressing the view that in general women had failed to reach the front rank in the creative arts, he conceded that the novel was today almost a feminine preserve: 'Who would wish to deny the quality of greatness to Miss Virginia Woolf, for example, . . .' James Laver (1899-1975), an assistant-keeper in the Victoria and Albert Museum since 1922, was also a fertile writer and journalist. Arnold Bennett contributed an article each week to the *Evening Standard*.

all, what an uninteresting mind, intellectually. I cant put my finger on it, but nothing remains in one's mind after seeing him, nothing interesting, no suggestion. Incessant similes, perpetual quotation; he sees life with great ardour through books. And then he is now all agog to copulate, which makes his stories centre round that fascinating subject too inevitably —copulation & King's College Cambridge. He went through the war, & has had 4 years of battle & blood & wounds, & yet his mind keeps the virginal simplicity of a girls; he has the rigidity, at 36, of a crusted college character. I suppose the mixture is not very rich in him—thats all: father a schoolmaster, mother a housekeeper, life in the suburbs, scholarships &c: that was his upbringing; & then coming out of his shell, he deliberately vowed to be pagan, to be individual, to enjoy life, to explore his own sensations when there wasn't much matter to go on. Hence the repetition, the egotism, the absence of depth or character; but I feel all this far more when he writes than in talk. In talk his charm & niceness, his integrity, his brightness, all make him a very nice, dear, delightful, memorable (yes, but not interesting) human being. He will marry; he will become Prof. of Engl. Lit. at Camb.

Wednesday 25 September

But what interests me is of course my oil stove.[10] We found it here last night on coming back from Worthing. At this moment it is cooking my dinner in the glass dishes perfectly I hope, without smell, waste, or confusion: one turns handles, there is a thermometer. And so I see myself freer, more independent—& all one's life is a struggle for freedom— able to come down here with a chop in a bag & live on my own. I go over the dishes I shall cook—the rich stews, the sauces. The adventurous strange dishes with dashes of wine in them. Of course Leonard puts a drag on, & I must be very cautious, like a child, not to make too much noise playing. Nelly goes on Friday & so I shall [have] a whole week to experiment in—to become free in.

Yesterday morning I made another start on The Moths, but that wont be its title. & several problems cry out at once to be solved. Who thinks it? And am I outside the thinker? One wants some device which is not a trick.

The greenhouse began to be built yesterday. We are watering the earth with money. Next week my room will begin to rise. It strikes me that one is absurd to expect good temper or magnanimity from servants, considering what crowded small rooms they live in, with their work all about them.

10. Cooking at Monks House had hitherto been done on a solid fuel range.

Then, old Mrs. Woolf—(I mean I am making a few notes, heaven knows why, but one always thinks there is a reason.) She has come to wear a charm & dignity to me, unknown before, now her old age is crumbling down all the cheerful sentimental small talk—she becomes curiously more humane & wise, as old women are; so pliable, so steeped in life that they seem to become philosophic, & more mistress of the art of living than much cleverer people. So many many things have happened before her; illnesses, births, quarrels, troubles—nothing much surprises her, or long upsets her. True she is peevish & bored as a child; but has attained some carelessness of show & pomp & respectability, as if she had washed her hands of most things & were playing on a beach, rather an enviable old age in many ways, though intolerable too. Always take opportunities I heard her murmuring to Pinka who had eaten all our soup. And then the long stories about her cooks, & how she had taught them cooking when she was rich. 'Now you are poor & plain' one of them wrote 'after my great sorrow' here she sighs, & would cry, but is easily diverted & presses a tin of toffee on me.

I must go into the kitchen to see my stove cooking ham now

Wednesday 2 October

We have just been over Annie's cottage—so I suppose it is. & we therefore own another fair sized house; but the arrangement with Annie seems another of those plums which since this time, or August, last year, have dropped into our hands here. She will cook; my oil stove makes hot meals practicable at all hours; but I am dazed with the Brighton conference; hearing Henderson orate & seeing him get red slowly like a lobster; we went on Monday too (how my days of reflection have dwindled! one must give it all up now) & heard a good, interesting, debate.[1] The audience makes an extraordinary baaing noise; not talk, not footsteps—& I thought how politics was no longer an affair of great nobles & mystery & diplomacy, but of commonsense, issuing from ordinary men & women of business—not very exalted, but straight forward, like any other business affair.

The light is dying; I hear the village boys kicking footballs; & all those reflections, comments, that occur to me walking are died out—the atmosphere, winter, change, London's imminence, scatter, finally, my poor efforts at solid concentration. Yet I have, these last days, set my book

1. The Labour Party annual conference opened in the Dome, Brighton, on Monday, 30 September, when the main debate was on Family Allowances. On Wednesday, 2 October, the Foreign Secretary Arthur Henderson gave a survey of Government policy in foreign affairs.

alight I think—got it going; but at a rate like that of Jacob's Room
Mrs Dalloway days—a page at most, & long sitting sucking my pen.
And all the Americans write & cable for articles. And I shall go in & read
Phedre, having picked some apples. Leonard in the cold windy road is
cleaning the car.

*LW packed up and drove to London on Thursday 3 October, leaving VW
at Monks House; he returned on Saturday, when Maynard and Lydia Keynes
came to tea, and they both drove back to Tavistock Square on Sunday afternoon, 6 October.*

Friday 11 October

And I snatch at the idea of writing here in order not to write Waves
or Moths or whatever it is to be called. One thinks one has learnt to write
quickly; & one hasn't. And what is odd, I'm not writing with gusto or
pleasure: because of the concentration. I am not reeling it off; but sticking
it down. Also, never, in my life, did I attack such a vague yet elaborate
design; whenever I make a mark I have to think of its relation to a dozen
others. And though I could go on ahead easily enough, I am always stopping
to consider the whole effect. In particular is there some radical fault in
my scheme? I am not quite satisfied with this method of picking out things
in the room & being reminded by them of other things. Yet I cant at the
moment devise anything which keeps so close to the original design &
admits of movement.

Hence, perhaps, these October days are to me a little strained & surrounded with silence. What I mean by this last word I dont quite know,
since I have never stopped 'seeing' people—Nessa & Roger, the Jeffers',
Charles Buxton, & should have seen Lord David & am to see the Eliots—
oh & there was Vita too.[2] No; its not physical silence; its some inner
loneliness—interesting to analyse if one could. To give an example—I
was walking up Bedford Place is it—the straight street with all the boarding
houses this afternoon, & I said to myself spontaneously, something like
this. How I suffer, & no one knows how I suffer, walking up this street,

2. Charles Roden Buxton (1875-1942), whom LW described as a 'nineteenth-century
non-conformist Liberal of the best type' (*IV LW*, p 245); disillusioned with the
Liberal Party he joined the Labour Party and was at this time an MP. He and LW
were respectively Chairman and Secretary of the Labour Party Advisory Committees on International and Imperial Affairs. Robinson Jeffers (1888-1962), the
American poet, and his wife Una had tea with the Woolfs on 7 October; the
Hogarth Press published three books of his poems in their 'Hogarth Living Poets'
series (*HP Checklist* 167, 196, 226).

engaged with my anguish, as I was after Thoby died—alone; fighting something alone. But then I had the devil to fight, & now nothing. And when I come indoors, it is all so silent—I am not carrying a great rush of wheels in my head— Yet I am writing—oh & we are very successful—& there is—what I most love—change ahead. Yes, that last evening at Rodmell when Leonard came down against his will to fetch me, the Keynes's came over. And Maynard is giving up the Nation, & so is Hubert, & so no doubt shall we.[3] And it is autumn; & the lights are going up; & Nessa is in Fitzroy Street—in a great misty room, with flaring gas & unsorted plates & glasses on the floor,—& the Press is booming—& this celebrity business is quite chronic—& I am richer than I have ever been— & bought a pair of earrings today—& for all this, there is vacancy & silence somewhere in the machine. On the whole, I do not much mind; because, what I like is to flash & dash from side to side, goaded on by what I call reality. If I never felt these extraordinarily pervasive strains— of unrest, or rest, or happiness, or discomfort—I should float down into acquiescence. Here is something to fight: & when I wake early I say to myself, Fight, fight. If I could catch the feeling, I would: the feeling of the singing of the real world, as one is driven by loneliness & silence from the habitable world; the sense that comes to me of being bound on an adventure; of being strangely free now, with money & so on, to do anything. I go to take theatre tickets (The Matriarch) & see a list of cheap excursions hanging there, & at once think that I will go to Stratford on Avon Mob fair tomorrow—why not?—or to Ireland, or to Edinburgh for a week end.[4] I daresay I shant. But anything is possible. And this curious steed, life; is genuine— Does any of this convey what I want to say?—But I have not really laid hands on the emptiness after all.

Its odd, now I come to think of it—I miss Clive.

It occurs to me that Arthur Studd was another of the brilliant young men.[5] But there was something innocent about him, compared with

3. Since April 1923, when Maynard Keynes and his associates had acquired control of it, Hubert Henderson had edited the *N & A*; he was now leaving at the end of the year to take up an appointment as joint secretary to the newly-formed Economic Advisory Council. Keynes, as chairman of the *N & A* board, was seeking an amalgamation with the *New Statesman*—which was eventually effected in 1931.
4. Stratford-on-Avon's ancient 'mop' or fair was held each year on 12 October; on this date the Woolfs went to the Royalty Theatre to see Mrs Patrick Campbell in *The Matriarch* by G. B. Stern.
5. Arthur Haythorne Studd (1863-1919), educated at Eton and King's College, Cambridge; then studied painting at the Slade School and in Paris. He became obsessed by Whistler, three of whose paintings he bequeathed to the National Gallery.

Bernard & Geoffrey: he spoke through his nose, & had a soft guttural voice; & a bald forehead, & rather handsome brown eyes, like a dogs: he was canine, in some ways; travelled, distinguished, rich; with a stout mother he disliked, & thus won my mother's sympathy. He had thick red hands, but painted in the manner of Whistler—gesticulating over the canvas, & then producing some little pleasing melodious still life, with which, rather mystically, he was very pleased. It was 'being an artist' that took his fancy. He had lovely rooms in Cheyne Walk; & the white girls & pink clouds & rivers & fireworks of Whistler hung in them. He went to Samoa, to paint Whistlers perhaps, & came back when Stella was dead & grieved for her I think. He had loved her, in his fumbling ineffective way. Then he wrote little poems, about Eton, which he loved, & hoped to be buried there— But why should he think of being buried, with all his advantages? There was something ineffective about him—he could not do anything; but had, to us as children, a kind of romance; was supposed to do extravagant impossible things—like hiring a cab & taking us all off suddenly to play cricket at Lords—that I remember. I suppose he was the flower of Eton & the 90ties, getting itself varnished with art & Paris & studio life, & Chelsea. He sent me a post card from St Ives once, & a poem about Eton—& then—clap came the war; & being endlessly kind & generous & inefficient, no doubt he did great things for refugees, & died, without any notice being taken, that I am aware of—a rich bachelor; not much over 50 I suppose. Another 'young man'—not brilliant exactly, but congenial in my memory, modest, fresh, unexpected, & always so nasal.

Sunday 13 October

It comes to me to ask, how far could I live at this moment in Nessa being with Angelica at school? Can one supplement one's life? I think a little. Julian has driven her over from Cambridge, this still soft grey morning. It is sunny & misty in the country. She got into the car in the King's Parade, where the paper sellers are & the young men are hurrying I suppose along to breakfast. Then they drive, with a map on their knees; Julian rather tense, staring through his spectacles. Some very intimate things are hinted at—of wh. I know nothing—or rather he grunts & half says things, which she understands. She is very excited, at the same time practical. Julian is excited too. They are both very anxious to see Angelica. How will they see her first? She will come running down the stairs into the private room, on the left; with the Adams fireplace. And then? She will 'fly into Nessa's arms'. Nessa will hold her very tight to get the sensation of her child's body again. Julian will call her "dear". They will go out together into the park. Angelica will like to show off her knowledge of rules & ways & the best places to sit in; other girls will smile, & she will say 'Thats Claudia' or Annie. Thats Miss Colly—Thats Mrs Curtis. And all the time they will be feeling the comfort & excitement of being together—of having only just broached their time together. Nessa will get at ever so many things: questions of happiness, teaching, liking, loneliness—change. They will be very proud of each other & aloof. & Julian will peer about, through his glasses, liking Nessa & Angelica better than anybody I daresay; the simple crude boy—whom I shall now never know, I daresay. For—as I am going to say to Nessa on Wednesday— you are a jealous woman, & dont want me to know your sons, dont want to take, but always to give; are afraid of the givers. What will she answer?

But Leonard will go on moving the apples, & so I cannot write anything except my—what I am pleased to call—my diary. I wish I could write more succinctly, by the way, & with less use of the present participle. My carelessness shocks me. Nature is having her revenge, & is now making me write one word an hour.

Wednesday 23 October

As it is true—I write only for an hour—then sink back feeling I cannot keep my brain on that spin any more—then typewrite, & am done by 12— I will here sum up my impressions before publishing a Room of One's Own.[6] It is a little ominous that Morgan wont review it.* It makes me suspect that there is a shrill feminine tone in it which my intimate friends will dislike. I forecast, then, that I shall get no criticism, except of the evasive jocular kind, from Lytton, Roger & Morgan; that the press will be kind & talk of its charm, & sprightiness; also I shall be attacked for a feminist & hinted at for a sapphist; Sibyl will ask me to luncheon; I shall get a good many letters from young women. I am afraid it will not be taken seriously. Mrs Woolf is so accomplished a writer that all she says makes easy reading . . . this very feminine logic . . . a book to be put in the hands of girls. I doubt that I mind very much. The Moths; but I think it is to be waves, is trudging along; & I have that to refer to, if I am damped by the other. It is a trifle, I shall say; so it is, but I wrote it with ardour & conviction.

We dined last night with the Webbs, & I had Eddy & Dottie to tea.

* He wrote yesterday 3rd Dec. & said he very much liked it

6. It was published on 24 October 1929 in both England and America, though a small limited edition was issued three days previously in the United States (see Kp A12).

As for these mature dinner parties one has some friendly easy talk with one man—Hugh Macmillan—about the Buchans & his own career;—the Webbs are friendly but can't be influenced about Kenya:[7] we sit in two lodging house rooms (the dining room had a brass bedstead behind a screen) eat hunks of red beef; & are offered whisky. It is the same enlightened, impersonal, perfectly aware of itself atmosphere. "My little boy shall have his toy"—but dont let that go any further "—that's what my wife says about my being in the Cabinet". No they have no illusions. And I compared them with L. & myself, & felt (I daresay for this reason) the pathos, the symbolical quality of the childless couple; standing for something, united.

As for 'seeing' Eddy & Dottie, there is not much to it; an occasional phrase one remembers—Eddy's being in love with two people: Dotty's rational account of a bore whom she helps: Eddy wishes me to read his diary, but some, nameless, friend objects; but he agreed, before long: it is a gratification to him. And so $1\frac{1}{2}$ hours passed. Dotty deplored Vita's too early fame. Yet I suppose she loves her; is devoted; queer things lodge in people's souls;

I am very carefully & cautiously becoming a reader & a thinker again. Since I have been back I have read Virginia Water (a sweet white grape); God; —all founded, & teased & spun out upon one quite simple & usual psychological experience; but the man's no poet & cant make one see; all his sentences are like steel lines on an engraving;[8] I am reading Racine, have bought La Fontaine, & so intend to make my sidelong approach to French literature, circling & brooding—

Saturday 2 November

It takes precisely 10 days for anything to happen to a book—It is now Saturday 2nd. Nov: & the R. of ones O. has sold, I think 100 copies

7. Hugh Pattison Macmillan (1873-1952), created Lord Macmillan of Aberfeldy in 1930, was a Scottish lawyer who became Lord Advocate in the Labour administration of 1924, and served as chairman on innumerable committees and commissions. John Buchan, the author (later, as Lord Tweedsmuir, governor-general of Canada), was married to Susan Grosvenor, one of the aristocratic circle VW had known through Violet Dickinson in her youth. LW, who as secretary of the Labour Party Advisory Committee on Imperial Affairs had played a significant part in formulating the party's policy, was urging Sidney Webb, now Secretary of State for Colonial Affairs, to implement Labour's promises to finance the provision of education and roads for the native population of Kenya.

8. *Virginia Water* (1929), a first novel by Elizabeth Jenkins. *God: an Introduction to the Science of Metabiology* (1929), by John Middleton Murry.

this morning; none before, or scarcely any, this largely due to Vita's flamboyant broadcast. And I cant remember all the things I was intending to
say,— like Renard—the man who kept a diary of the things that occur to
one.[1]

I dreamt last night that I had a disease of the heart that would kill me
in 6 months. Leonard, after some persuasion, told me. My instincts were
all such as I should have, in order, & some very strong: quite unexpected,
I mean voluntary, as they are in dreams, & have thus an authenticity which
makes an immense, & pervading impression. First, relief—well I've done
with life anyhow (I was lying in bed) then horror; then desire to live; then
fear of insanity; then (no this came earlier) regret about my writing, &
leaving this book unfinished; then a luxurious dwelling upon my friends
sorrow; then a sense of death & being done with at my age; then telling
Leonard that he must marry again; seeing our life together; & facing the
conviction of going, when other people went on living. Then I woke,
coming to the top with all this hanging about me; & found I had sold a
great many copies of my book; & was asked to lunch by Madame Kallas[2]
—the odd feeling of these two states of life & death mingling as I ate
my breakfast feeling drowsy & heavy.

[Tuesday 5 November]

Oh but I have done quite well so far with R. of one's Own: & it sells,
I think; & I get unexpected letters. But I am more concerned with my
Waves. I've just typed out my mornings work; & can't feel altogether
sure. There is *something* there (as I felt about Mrs Dalloway) but I can't
get at it, squarely; nothing like the speed & certainty of The Lighthouse:
Orlando mere childs play. Is there some falsity, of method, somewhere?
Something tricky?—so that the interesting things aren't firmly based? I
am in an odd state; feel a cleavage; here's my interesting thing; & there's
no quite solid table on which to put it. It might come in a flash, on re-reading
—some solvent. I am convinced that I am right to seek for a station whence
I can set my people against time & the sea—but Lord, the difficulty of
digging oneself in there, with conviction. Yesterday I had conviction; it
has gone today. Yet I have written 66 pages in the past month.

1. Vita Sackville-West spoke of *A Room of One's Own* on 31 October in her bi-
monthly talk on books for the BBC; it was printed in *The Listener* on 6 November
1929 (see *M & M*, p 257). Jules Renard (1864-1910), author of *Poil de carotte*
(1894); his *Journal* was published in 17 volumes in 1925-27.
2. Mme Kallas was the wife of Dr Oskar Kallas, the Estonian Minister in London.

Yesterday Sibyl came; & I told her that she was like a bird holding a stinking mouse in its claws—& the mouse was life. She admitted it. She said she had to go through an unpleasant business; was going to Paris this morning; would tell me of it afterwards. Then she bemoaned her lot, guardedly; how she had grown up so late, & only now began to see what it was she wanted. I gather that it is intimacy, simplicity, & friendship that she wants; & it is a little late in life to demand them; & how can she get them now, needing £20,000 a year too? So Arthur cant retire; they must sit there & see the season through; she cant, at the moment, master life; it is not a dead mouse after all; but wriggles. She looked ringeyed, puckered—I saw her in a flash, quite old. Her eyes were very tragic.

The unpleasant business was that she lost her nest egg—said to be £50,000, in America. Now gives tea parties only

And today Stephen Tennant comes to tea.[3] & Arthur Waley. On Sunday we were at Rodmell; & my room is now about three feet of brick, with the window frames in; rather an eyesore, for it cuts off the garage roof & the downs—both pleasanter sights than I had thought. They have driven a small hole through the little room, for the passage; so that by this time, no doubt, that is in being. & things fall & rise & disappear & re-appear. And most of my joy was turned to rage because I let Southease sale of furniture slip, & could have furnished my room perfectly for £20 I daresay. Such is one's life—yes, such: (a convenient phrase;) And I am asked daily to lecture; & L.'s freedom draws near. Wright will inherit, & is making his dispositions.[4] I keep saying "We shall be able to do that when you have left the Nation". Still, you see what with oil stoves & Annie, battling my way to freedom. Jan. 1st is the day. We have had the Nation for nearly seven years, without making it blood & bone of ours, as once I thought possible. A tepid paper; neither this nor that, with the perpetual drag of Hubert & Harold, Hubert kindly incompetent, Harold competent but to me, all wood, red apple, sawdust, plausibility, respectability, hesitation & compromise.

3. The Hon. Stephen James Napier Tennant (b. 1906), the fourth son of 1st Baron Glenconner, was a painter and an aesthete.
4. LW's previous attempts to throw off the shackles of the literary editorship of the N & A had been subverted by Maynard Keynes; now with the impending change of editor (see above, 11 October 1929, n 3), he re-asserted his resolve to resign on 31 December (see also letters to Keynes and Henderson, LWP Sussex, 14 December 1929). Henderson was to be succeeded by his assistant-editor Harold Wright (1883-1934), and LW by Edmund Blunden; but as the latter was not free until mid-February, in the event LW continued his work until then.

Sunday 17 November

A horrid date. Yes, I am feeling a little sick, a little shivery; I cant settle to anything; I am in a twitter; I try to read Mauron—to write—& my lips begin forming words; I begin muttering long conversations between myself & Vita about Dotty on the telephone; about Miss Matheson: I act parts: I find myself talking aloud; I say things over & over again like this "I want to know if after what happened the other morning you want to give me notice? . . . Well, then, as you wont answer, I am afraid I must now give you notice . . . But I want to explain exactly why it is. After you told me to leave your room I went to Mr Woolf & said that I could not keep you as my maid any longer. But I haven't made up my mind in a hurry. I have been thinking about it since June. I tried to arrange not to order dinner so that we might avoid scenes. But the scenes at Rodmell were worse than ever. And now this is the last. I am afraid I can't go on with it. This is the 17th of Nov. I shall expect you to go on the 17th Dec." Yes, this is what I have to say to Nelly at 9.30 tomorrow, & then I go to Mrs Hunt's [*Domestic Agency*]. And I am almost trembling with this nervous anticipation as I write. But it must be done.

Monday 18 November

Well it is over, & much better than I expected—at least for the present. To my question Do you want to give me notice? she replied "I have given you notice— . ." Further argument was attempted & cut short by me. "Then you wish to go at the end of your month—12th December." "As we refused her an hours extra help when she was ill, yes." But this was said without conviction. I clinched it by looking at the calendar (which I could not see, blind as I am) & then left her, in the calmest flattest way possible—which means I'm afraid that she has no more intention of going on Dec. 12th than I have of taking ship to Siberia. So be it. My mind is like a gum when an aching tooth has been drawn. I am having a holiday— reading old Birrell[5], & shall hope that the dust will be settled now for a week or two. The Horsham tiles are being put on my roof, so Percy writes this morning; which means that my rooms must be almost done. And now I have an extra room there—Nelly's—yes; & no servant in the house

5. Augustine Birrell (1850-1933), the author and Liberal statesman, and Frankie's father, had been at Charleston when the Woolfs had tea there with Frankie and Raymond Mortimer on 7 July; on 13 July, old Birrell sent VW the three volumes of his *Collected Essays, 1880-1920* (1922), with an inscription and a note. See *Holleyman*, VS II 1.

here—thank God—two friends to come in one early t'other late; no more Bloomsbury gossip—no more Lottie barging in & out; no more fear of having people to lunch & tea & dinner; no more pains in the back, swollen ankles, & ups & downs of passion & effusion. And so, what with the oil stove, Annie, giving up the Nation, new rooms new servants, the new year will be one of the most interesting—a great advance towards freedom which is the ideal state of the soul. Yet it must not be thought that I have suffered acutely from servitude. My one claim on my own gratitude is that, directly I feel a chain, I throw it off: think of leaving Fitzroy; leaving Hogarth—leaving Hyde Park Gate I was going to say to round the sentence & indeed I think I have been an old struggler after my fashion— not so valiant I daresay as Nessa, but tenacious too & bold.

Monday 25 November

I merely add idly (ought I not to be correcting To the Lighthouse[6]) that the difficulties with Nelly are to avoid an apology. She has weakened, & is now all out to catch us weakening. She wished L. many happy returns this morning. She came to me on Friday & asked me why I did not speak. I had some difficulty in being stiff & angry & saying that after her behaviour & accusations it was impossible. Mrs Hunt promises an abundance of permanent dailies, & so I think the die is cast. I have no doubt difficulties will begin, again; but not the old intolerable difficulties, no, no, never again.

I broadcast; & poured my rage hot as lava over Vita. She appeared innocent—I mean of telling H[ilda] M[atheson]. that I could easily cut my Brummell to bits.[7] And then I discussed her friends, Vita's friends, & said that here, in their secondrateness, was the beginning of my alienation. I cant have it said "Vita's great friends—Dottie, Hilda & Virginia". I detest the 2ndrate schoolgirl atmosphere. She sat silent for the most part, & only said I was right. Harold had said the same. The thing to do is to check it. She cant stop what she's begun. And then in a hurry to Rodmell, where the roof is on, & the floor stretched with planks. The bedroom will be a lovely wonderful room what I've always hoped for.

6. *To the Lighthouse* was the fifth volume in 'The Uniform Edition of the Works of Virginia Woolf' (see above, 13 May 1929, n 5); it was published by the Hogarth Press on 19 February 1930 (Kp A10c).
7. VW broadcast her piece about Beau Brummell on the BBC on 20 November; Hilda Matheson, the Talks Director, insisted on alterations to VW's script—'made me castrate Brummell'. (See *IV VW Letters*, no. 2100 to T. S. Eliot; also no. 2099).

Saturday 30 November

I fill in this page, nefariously; at the end of a morning's work. I have begun the second part of Waves—I dont know, I dont know. I feel that I am only accumulating notes for a book—whether I shall ever face the labour of writing it, God Knows. From some higher station I may be able to pull it together—at Rodmell, in my new room. Reading The Lighthouse does not make it easier to write; nor these impending final interviews with Nelly & new servants. We had a party—dining out at the Red Lion—last night; Julian & Rachel; Lyn, Hope, Plomer, Brian Howard, Nessa afterwards. Too many people, Leonard said. I dont know. I dislike B. Howard; I dislike his decadence, & protruding eyes, & unbuttoned waistcoat & floating tie.[8] On the make, Leonard says. Plomer, on the other hand, was very plump & vigorous, fresh from the Bayswater murder; the details of which he said—how he had cleaned scraps of brain from the carpet apparently—could not be told.[9] The young Jewess was attacked in bed at 4 last Sunday morning by a mad husband with a razor. First he locked the door, so that she banged & kicked, with the razor slashing her all the time in vain: at last burst out, with her head hanging by the skin to die on the landing. If William had not been away that week end the Chinese man would have come to him; & he thinks, killed him too. But this is not his line, he says as a novelist; & the psychic ladies who invest the house, like the coarser kind of bug & beetle, disgust him with their sea-ants. They table turn, & hear the voice of Mrs Frip—(not her name) from the other side; one, very fat with curled hair, said, "And it all happened a million years ago." Disgusting, William said. His eyes—the representative part of him—flashed & goggled.

It is said that Hope has become a Roman Catholic on the sly. Certainly she has grown very fat—too fat for a woman in middle age who uses her brains, & so I suspect the rumour is true. She has sat herself down under the shade. It is strange to see beauty—she had something elegant & individual—go out, like a candle flame. Julian, for instance, could not see,

8. Brian Howard (1905-1958), of American parentage, had been educated at Eton and Oxford, where he achieved notoriety as an extravagant dandy and aesthete. He was presumably brought to the after-dinner gathering at Tavistock Square by William Plomer.

9. Plomer's landlady, Sybil Sarah de Costa, known as Mrs Sybil Starr, was brutally murdered by her putative husband James Achew, alias James Starr, on Sunday 24 November, at Pembridge Villas, Bayswater. Achew, an American citizen said to have Red Indian blood, was sentenced to death at the Old Bailey on 17 January, but reprieved on grounds of insanity and committed to Broadmoor. Plomer's novel *The Case is Altered* (1932, *HP Checklist* 302) is based on this drama.

I think, that Hope had ever been a young & attractive woman. She has some vigour of mind though. Lyn has less than I could wish. When she has written her review, there is not much left. And her 'niceness'—housekeeping & nursing her sister who is ill—take the edge off. Had she £100, she would insure against illness, she said; because illness means that one cant work; this week, neither she nor her sister has made a penny. On that foundation it is hard to rear any very robust character; she is fretted & anxious.

Certainly it is true that if one writes a thing down one has done with it.

Saturday 30 November

It is still Saturday the 30th November, & we have been to Greenwich, leaving Nessa & Duncan to paint Dottie's tables in Mr James' shed.[10] Mr James is one of the Morris craftsmen; & has a tile making works near the river. He wears striped trousers & spats & will sit up all night, indulging himself with cups of tea, when the tiles are firing. Now & then you take out a tile to test it. He has three Kilns, the most expensive costing £300: & the Rotherhithe tunnel is near at hand. Leonard & I walked under the river (I thinking of the pressure of grey water round it; & of the absurd sublimity of errand boys & nursemaids walking on dry land under the river) & we came up in Greenwich & walked there on the parade where I walked a year or two ago in a temper. A man in a jersey was sitting in a glass shelter. How odd—to sit there, with nothing to do! And we saw the hospital, yellow & pink; & then it rained, & we went back & talked to Mr James about his tiles & then drove through the East End to the garage. I bought two crumpets for a penny; & we came home. Duncan began telling me the story of the London artists; & how Roger is so much hated by the critics that they wont notice the London artists. This is said to mean that Keith Baynes doesn't sell. And so Nessa is having a tea party tomorrow to discuss the matter with Porter & Keith Baynes. For this she bought some cakes. And they are having Angus to dinner. So am I not thank God.[11]

10. Mr L. J. James had his works at Wharf (now Saunders Ness) Road on the Isle of Dogs; Vanessa and Duncan were decorating tiles destined for the dining room at Penns-in-the-Rocks. It was not the Rotherhithe but the Millwall-Greenwich foot tunnel which was near at hand.

11. With the backing of Maynard Keynes, the London Artists Association had been founded in 1925 on co-operative principles to enable a small group of artists to work in relative freedom from financial anxiety. There were seven original members, including Vanessa, Duncan, Roger Fry, Keith Baynes (1887-1977), and the New Zealander Frederick J. Porter (1883-1944). Angus Davidson had become the LAA's secretary in the summer.

Sunday 8 December

Dear me; last Monday, as L. advised, I asked Nelly if she wished to go: & so (as I foreboded) she said reasonably no; & proposed solutions; we were landed; not emotionally, rather weariedly, & disillusionedly on my part, in a compromise: to try Mansfield for a month,—(here is L. to ask about alterations—that is a 2nd E.C. & new lavatory basin which being settled—& its a roaring wind) we ⟨then⟩ if the trial is unsatisfactory then to part without further discussion for ever.[1]

Just back from Rodmell. The roof is on; the floors are made; the windows in; giving, it seemed vast sweeping views of flooded meadows; but there was only a blink of light even at midday; we were engulfed in whirling wet; working up to such a storm on Friday night as I have, I think, never been in. It went round & round; & there was thunder in the crash of the wind; & great zigzags of lightning; & hail drumming on the iron roof outside my room; & such a fury of noise one could not sleep. So at one I went up to L. & looked at the lighted windows in the village; & thought, really with some fear, of being out alone that moment. Suppose the tree crashed, or the slates came off? We were not very securely sheltered, there under our slate roof; still better than being at sea. Dreams were all blown about, elongated, distorted, that night. A tree down in the churchyard. Trees down all the way up today. A curious sense of community brought by the storm. A man killed at Chailey sleeping in a shed; a woman at Eastbourne; a boy at Worthing. However, the mind was very still & happy. I read & read & finished I daresay 3 foot thick of MS read carefully too; much of it on the border, & so needing thought. Now, with this load despatched, I am free to begin reading Elizabethans—the little unknown writers, whom I, so ignorant am I, have never heard of, Puttenham, Webb, Harvey.[2] This thought fills me with joy—no overstatement. To begin reading with a pen in my hand, discovering, pouncing, thinking of theories, when the ground is new, remains one of my great excitements. Oh but L.

1. The plan was to employ Mrs Mansfield, who lived in the basement of 37 Gordon Square, to relieve the discontented Nelly of some of the burden of housework at 52 Tavistock Square.

2. VW made notes (see Holograph Reading Notes, vols XI and XII in the Berg Collection) on George Puttenham's *The Arte of English Poesie* (1589); on William Webbe's *A Discourse of English Poetrie* (1586)—both in Constable's English Reprint editions of 1895; and on Gabriel Harvey's *Works*, ed. A. B. Grosart, 1884; his Commonplace Book, ed. G. C. Moore Smith, 1913; and his *Letter Book*, *1573-1580*, ed. E. J. L. Scott, 1884. Cf 'The Strange Elizabethans' in *The Common Reader, Second Series*, 1932 (Kp A18).

will sort apples, & the little noise upsets me; I cant think what I was going to say.

So I stopped writing, by which no great harm was done; & made out a list of Elizabethan poets.

And I have, with great happiness, refused to write Rhoda Broughton & Ouida for de la Mare. That vein, popular as it is, witness Jane & Geraldine, is soon worked out in me. I want to write criticism. Yes, & one might make out an obscure figure or two. It was the Elizabethan prose writers I loved first & most wildly, stirred by Hakluyt, which father lugged home for me—I think of it with some sentiment—father tramping over the Library with his little girl sitting at HPG in mind. He must have been 65; I 15 or 16, then; & why I dont know, but I became enraptured, though not exactly interested, but the sight of the large yellow page entranced me. I used to read it & dream of those obscure adventurers, & no doubt practised their style in my copy books. I was then writing a long picturesque essay upon the Christian religion, I think; called Religio Laici, I believe, proving that man has need of a God; but the God was described in process of change; & I also wrote a history of Women; & a history of my own family—all very longwinded & El[izabe]than in style.[3]

Tuesday 10 December

A bad day yesterday, because I had Vita to lunch, which I hate, & lost one of my green leather gloves. We had tea with Leonard's mother, who, sitting in a new room, fairly flabbergasted us by her accident. The hotel was struck by lightning on Friday; a chimney stack fell; her room was filled with soot & sparks—& there she was, dramatising it, shivering, shocked, yet buoyant & secretly pleased to be the centre of catastrophe again. As usual she had behaved with perfect calm—"but I feel these things so much afterwards" & was anxious to give pounds of tobacco to the workmen engaged in mending the roof. "What right, I said to myself, have we to sit here & see those poor fellows carrying bricks? Oh their lives—carrying bricks to the roof in this gale—& I sitting here" (in a pink hotel bedroom). This is her fluid imagination—pounds of tobacco, as Harold [Woolf] said, wdn't do much to cure the social system.[4]

It is I think a proof of the pressure at which we live that I have said

3. Nothing remains of these juvenile works.
4. LW's mother lived in hotels, moving from London to Worthing for the summer months. Her present abode was in Earls Court. Harold (1882-1967) was her third son.

nothing of our lawsuit—or have I? against the hotel, against the jazz band.[5]
Rachel, William Plomer & ourselves go to court on Friday. Why are the
facts so intolerably dull? I shrink from writing them. I rather liked Scadding
& Bodkin's office; & swearing by almighty God; but Rachel & Wm. enjoy
it more than I do. It is more unexpected. Rachel will tell her friends about
it—as I should have done. But whole days knocked out of the week bore
me. I feel that my greatest triumph is to achieve a quiet evening—in which
to read El[izabe]thans. And Charlie Sanger is very ill—I figure him lying
worn out, worn out & without much solid happiness to show for it; like
some old gold link—so good, so genuine; affectionate; honourable; but a
worn disappointed man I think: no natural happiness: a conscience; &
then Dora.

Thursday 12 December

Here, just back from Rodmell, & some rather forced conversation with
Mr Philcox (the wife & I went to America—I dont like America—you
pay separate for breakfast—room, double 24 dollars). I will rapidly note
my evidence for tomorrow though Pritchard now says we shall be postponed—for the hotel cant get a witness. What I shall say—(I have the
pump all right,) is this about the autumn.

We came back early in October & the music was very bad. My husband

Case settled; expenses
paid: 15th Jan. (about)

wrote to the Secretary who wrote & assured him
that everything wd. be done. Next night the music
was so bad that my husband rang up the hotel;
but they said they could do nothing. The music slightly improved, & we
waited till the end of Nov. when it became so bad we were unable to sit
in the room. The party was on 29th: on the 30th it was intolerable.

How easily facts escape me!

Saturday 14 December

No I am too tired to write; have been rushed, what with the lawsuit
&c; have had toothache: & so sit passive, hoping that some drops will
form in my mind. By the way, the sales of A Room are unprecedented—
have beaten Orlando; feels like a line running through ones fingers; orders

5. Since the opening of the Royal Hotel (see above, 28 March 1929, n 3), the Woolfs
had been disturbed in the evenings by the noise of dance music from its ballroom.
LW's complaints proving ineffective, he took legal action against the hotel
company, and eventually won his case (see *IV LW*, pp 124-7). Scadding and
Bodkin were solicitors of 2 Endsleigh Street, Tavistock Square.

for 100 taken as coolly as 12's used to be. We have sold, I think 5500; & our next years income is made.

Had I married Lytton I should never have written anything. So I thought at dinner the other night. He checks & inhibits in the most curious way. L. may be severe; but he stimulates. Anything is possible with him. Lytton was mild & damp, like a wet autumnal leaf. Lonely, & growing elderly; so he compares notes with Clive apparently. Our case stands over till next Thursday, & will probably be settled in the interval—some compromise made. Yesterday they screwed down some windows—the law had that instant effect. The law was sad-coloured, impressive. We saw Mr Preston at 10; he was in a black court coat, with dirty white bands; a self confident sandy, polite man. What a pugnacious chap you are! I heard another K.C. say to him in court. An admirable manly atmosphere—schoolboys come to responsibility they seemed; all so aquiline & definite under their frizzled grey wigs. Then the Judge (Farwell) came in. We rose. He bowed. He looked superhumanly sage, dignified, sad; the wig again cutting his forehead off & accentuating the deep reflective eyes—a sallow, sodden wearied face; so intent that he was monosyllabic—could not afford to open his mouth unnecessarily; merely nodded. All was over in 10 minutes I suppose. I felt the stress of it all; that man sitting there intent under his canopy in the small crowded court, never dropping a word, till 4 in the afternoon.[6]

Sunday 15 December

Tooth better, but not what I call a vigorous head; an idling, unconcentrated head—too much doing in Tavistock Sqre these last days. Last night we went to The Calendar (by Edgar Wallace) with Ann; & there was a cheer, & behold a great golden Queen bowing in a very small bow windowed box.[7] Also, when the lights went up, the King, red, grumpy, fidgeting with his hands; well groomed, bluff; heavy looking, with one white flower in his buttonhole, resenting the need, perhaps, of sitting to be looked at between one of the acts—his duty to be done; & then not

6. LW's case against the Imperial Hotel Company was heard before Mr Justice Farwell (Sir Christopher Farwell, 1877-1943) in the Chancery Division of the High Court on Friday 13 December; Herbert Sansome Preston, KC (d. 1935), appeared for the Woolfs. The case was several times adjourned, and finally settled out of court in LW's favour on 31st, not 15th, January 1930 (according to LW's diary).
7. Ann (b. 1916) was the elder of Adrian and Karin Stephen's two daughters; the play was at Wyndham's Theatre. The Duchess of York, daughter-in-law of King George V and Queen Mary, is now better known as Queen Elizabeth the Queen Mother.

much liking the little remarks cast at him, to minimise his labour, by the Queen. Once the D[uche]ss of York sat with the Queen; a simple, chattering, sweethearted little roundfaced young woman in pink: but her wrist twinkling with diamonds, her dress held on the shoulder with diamonds. The Queen also like a lit up street with diamonds. An odd feeling came to me of the shop window decorated for the public: these our exhibits, our show pieces. Not very impressive—no romance or mystery—the very best goods. Yet he descends, I daresay, from Hengist; goes straight back, this heavy bluff grumpy looking man, to Elizabeth & the rest;[8] will have his face forever in our history. He took spectacles out of a bright red case.

I thought (as I so often think things) of many comments to be written. One remains. If I were reading this diary, if it were a book that came my way, I think I should seize with greed upon the portrait of Nelly, & make a story—perhaps make the whole story revolve round that—it would amuse me. Her character—our efforts to be rid of her—our reconciliations.

The Woolfs drove to Rodmell for two weeks' Christmas break on Saturday 21 December. It rained heavily; the Bells were at Seend; LW pruned the fruit trees.

[*Thursday 26 December*]

Rodmell. Boxing day

And I am sitting in my new room—bedroom, not sitting room; with curtains fire table; & two great views; sometimes sun over the brooks & storm over the church. A violent Christmas; a brilliant serene Boxing day; & both very happy—completely, were it not for the damnable Byng-Stamper & his power to sell the down to a syndicate to exploit. That this is his intention comes through Percy; & I am wrought up to protest; indeed I must write to Ottoline & ask her the name of the little man who protects downs. This place is always being risked & saved; & so perhaps will be again. Cutting down trees & spoiling downs are my two great iniquities—what the Armenians were to Mrs Cole.[9] I find it almost

8. This suggests a rather inattentive reading of *Elizabeth and Essex* by VW.
9. Percy's story was that the landowner Captain Byng-Stamper was to sell a forty-acre field on Rodmell Hill for building. LW made various moves to avert this, including writing to the Prime Minister (see LWP, Sussex, II Ia), but failed to prevent the erection of several houses and bungalows in the following years. VW wrote to Ottoline, but not until February 1930 (*IV VW Letters* no. 2141). Mrs Cole was headmistress of the girls' school in Kensington where LW had attended the Kindergarten; she had been 'obsessed with the horrors and barbarism of the Armenian massacres' (*V LW*, pp 22-3; see also *I LW*, p 52).

incredibly soothing—a fortnight alone—almost impossible to let oneself have it. Relentlessly we have crushed visitors—Morgan, Roger, Adrian. We will be alone this once, we say; & really, it seems possible. Then Annie is to me very sympathetic; my bread bakes well. All is rather rapt, simple, quick effective—except for my blundering on at The Waves. I write two pages of arrant nonsense, after straining; I write variations of every sentence; compromises; bad shots; possibilities; till my writing book is like a lunatic's dream. Then I trust to some inspiration on re-reading; & pencil them into some sense. Still I am not satisfied. I think there is something lacking. I sacrifice nothing to seemliness. I press to my centre. I dont care if it all is scratched out. And there is something there. I incline now to try violent shots—at London—at talk—shouldering my way ruthlessly—& then, if nothing comes of it—anyhow I have examined the possibilities. But I wish I enjoyed it more. I dont have it in my head all day like The Lighthouse & Orlando.

Before I went Clive came to tea; sat alone for an hour or two. He asked me if I had been told that he had criticised A Room? I said no. He was a little rasped; said the jokes were lecture jokes. "Girls come round me"— too much of that—little ideas—nothing to compare with Orlando. And then, inconsistently, he praised O. above L[ighthouse]. against what he said at the time. But his criticism is founded upon the theory that I cant feel sex: have the purple light cut off; & *therefore* must write Orlando's not Lighthouses. I daresay there's some truth—especially in his saying that my soliloquies, trains of thought, are better than my silhouettes. But, as always, his own axe wants grinding: that Love is enough—or if love fails, down one goes for ever. For we got on Mary of course; & again he protested that no one could have acted other than he did—& then he vaguely threatened an alliance, in France, with his loved—or the lady who loves. But does she love? Does she take him to Egypt? All trembles now on some unreality. Everything has been shifted by Mary; no fundament left. And I always feel, how jolly, how much hunting, & talking & carousing there is in you! How long we have known each other—& then Thoby's form looms behind—that queer ghost. I think of death sometimes as the end of an excursion which I went on when he died. As if I should come in & say well, here you are. And yet I am not familiar with him now, perhaps. Those letters Clive read made him strange & external.[10]

But a dog barks, & my lamp flickers—even in my perfect room. So down to Leonard, to read Elizabethans & put our glass dish on the fire.

10. There was a proposal in the air at this time that the Hogarth Press should publish a collection of Thoby Stephen's letters, but nothing came of it. See *IV VW Letters*, no. 2118, to Vanessa.

Saturday 28 December

Bernard Shaw said the other night at the Keynes'[11]—& the Keynes's have just wrecked my perfect fortnight of silence, have been over in their Rolls Royce—& L. made them stay, & is a little inclined to think me absurd for not wishing it—but then Clive is his bugbear at present—Bernard Shaw said to me, I have never written anything except poetry. A man has written a book showing how by altering a word or two a whole act of the D[octo]rs Dilemma is in rhythm. In fact my rhythm is so strong that when I had to copy a page of Wells the other day in the midst of my own writing my pen couldnt do it. I was wanting to write my own rhythm —yet I hadn't known till then that I had so strong a rhythm. Heartbreak House is the best of my plays. I wrote it after staying with you at the Webbs in Sussex—perhaps you inspired it.[12] And Lydia is making the Lady into Queen Victoria. No I never saw Stevenson—Mrs Stevenson thought I had a cold.

You write Irish Mr Shaw. So does Mr Moore. Moore's an odd man— a very small talent cultivated with the utmost patience. We used to laugh at him in the old days. He was our butt. He was always telling us stories about himself & a lady—a grand lady—& she was always throwing something at his head & just missing it—& he used to say "Wait wait, there's a good passage coming". Nobody was better tempered. But he was our laughing stock. And one day Zola said to me I've discovered your great English novelist! Who's that said I. His name is George Moore. And I burst out laughing not our little George Moore, with his stories about himself? But it was. A lesson, you see, not to be too quick in judging ones friends.

But all his stories are autobiographic, I said.

Yes, they are all about George Moore & the lady who throws something at his head. —is writing a life of Moore & has asked me to tell the story of his early days. I am collecting my works. I find that I wrote a million words about the theatre. I dont know what to do with it. My wife wants me to leave out. But I think it gives a curious picture of the time. I am ashamed to think that I could ever have written so badly. The collection is limited

11. VW had talked to Shaw at an evening party given by the Keyneses on 19 December at 46 Gordon Square.
12. The Woolfs had spent the weekend of 17-19 June 1916 with the Sidney Webbs at Turner's Hill in Sussex; the Bernard Shaws were fellow-guests. Shaw was to repeat his compliment associating VW with *Heartbreak House* in a letter to her of 10 May 1940 (see *III LW*, p 126); he had in fact been occupied with the play some years before meeting her.

to 21 volumes. Theyre going to be sold in different bindings in America—
some in leather very expensive—others quite cheap—hawked about all
over America by peddlars. Im not a modest man but even I blushed at the
stuff I've had to write for my publishers. Essential to every home & so on.
I say out of twelve people, there will always be 3 women as clever as the
men. What I've always told them is go for the governing bodies—dont
mind about the vote. Insist upon representation. Now women are far more
enthusiastic about business than men. They get things done. Men gossip
in clubs. Oh but youve done more for us than anyone, Mr Shaw. My
generation, & Francis Birrell's (he was sitting behind) we might be nice
people, but we're different owing to you.

Happier said Francis.

Then Lydia came & broke in, with Mrs Shaw.

— 1930 —

1930

1930

Saturday 4 January

This is the new year, & I shall continue this book—from economy. I am having a holiday; it is fine; & so inveterate an habitual am I, I find it easier to walk after lunch than before. Far from doing nothing, I intend to write some letters, & have been pondering the early works of Miss Easedale.[1]

The idea has come to us that we will live here from April onwards. And merely because of that idea, the view from my window looks different. It becomes usual[?], something for a long unstressed time; hitherto I have always seen it as an interlude; a breathing space. I note, for that Portrait of Nelly that I should write, if I were editing these pages, that her letter to me began Dear Madam—which I hold to be as Carlyle used to say "Significant of much". But these are notes merely; for some reason it bores me to enlarge.

Vita came yesterday with a green glass tank in which Japanese flowers expand in water. Here my mind would expand like that—the advent of the Keynes' made it shrivel.[2] And we wasted our fine day, that should have been spent at Rye, talking in their very ugly room. But I am not saying that *they* are ugly: that would be blasphemous. This perpetual denigration of human nature & adoration of solitude is suspect. Only, here I'm bound to the board, like an insect, for another three months; & my one fine day I grudge to society. Tonight we dine at Charleston & so home tomorrow to the pump, to the dance music; to Braithewaite, Goldie, Ottoline, Sprott & so on—to be 'seen' to 'see'. A little music though—the opera—that I shall like. And now I must answer letters & so start London free from that anyhow.

The Woolfs returned to Tavistock Square on 5 January.

1. Joan Adeney Easdale, a sixteen-year-old girl from Kent, had sent her 'piles of dirty copy books written in a scrawl without any spelling', in which VW discerned real merit. Her *A Collection of Poems (written between the ages of 14 and 17)* was published as no. 19 in the Hogarth Living Poets series (*HP Checklist* 253) in February 1931, and a further volume *Clemence and Clare* as no. 23 in 1932 (*HP Checklist* 287).
2. The Keyneses had turned up at Monks House in a chauffeur-driven car on the 28th, and persuaded the Woolfs to lunch with them at Tilton on 31 December.

JANUARY 1930

Thursday 9 January

I merely note that I am going to try to keep next week entirely free from 'seeing' people, bating my dinner at Bogy Harrises to meet the Prime Minister, & Angelica's party. I am going to see if I can keep 7 days out of the clutch of the seers. I have arranged to do my seeing all this week, & have plodded along faithfully, & industriously: Braithewait & Miss Matthews, Dottie, Ottoline, Goldie, Sprot, Quentin, Miss Matheson & Plomer last night & Eddy to tea today, Vita tomorrow, Quentin on Saturday; & then nobody I swear on Sunday.[3]

Sunday 12 January

Sunday it is. And I have just exclaimed, And now I can think of nothing else. Thanks to my pertinacity & industry, I can now hardly stop making up The Waves. The sense of this came acutely about a week ago on beginning to write the Phantom party: now I feel that I can rush on, after 6 months hacking, & finish: but without the least certainty how its to achieve any form. Much will have to be discarded: what is essential is to write fast & not break the mood—no holiday, no interval if possible, till it is done. Then rest. Then re-write.

As for keeping a week free—I am now going to visit L.'s mother: then to the Frys after dinner. Marjorie Strachey to tea tomorrow: Duncan, I think, on Tuesday; Vita on Friday; Angelica on Saturday; Bogey Harris Wednesday: one day remains entire—Thursday—& thats the end of my week.

Thursday 16 January

A page of real life. Last night at Bogey Harrises. I came in, flung into the room in my red coat. A very painted raddled tall, pink woman (Mrs Graham Murray [*unidentified*]); & the rest, in an oval room, with painted ceiling, & books—"given me by Horne with Ben Johnson's autograph—

---

3. For Bogey Harris's dinner, see below, 16 January; Angelica's party was to be a fancy-dress one in Vanessa's studio on 18 January (see *II QB*, p 150); the Woolfs gave dinner to Richard Braithwaite and his friend Marjorie Matthews (1903-1972, Newnham 1922-25) at Boulestin on 6 January; on 8th, G. L. Dickinson, Sebastian Sprott and Hilda Matheson dined with them at Tavistock Square, and Lady Ottoline, William Plomer, and Quentin Bell came in afterwards; on the evening of the 9th, the Woolfs went to a performance of Mozart's early opera, *La Finta Giardiniera*, at the Scala Theatre.

the first edition of Dante— Lady Londonderry will be late; but we wont wait".[4] I have forgotten the prime minister—an unimpressive man; eyes disappointing; rather heavy; middle class; no son of the people; sunk; grumpy; self-important; wore a black waistcoat; had some mediocrity of personality. In came Lady L. very late; in ruby velvet, cut to the middle of the back, small, running, quick, current, energised. All went in to dinner, & I was too blind to read Sir Robert Vansittart on the man's card, so had to jumble for my neighbours pursuit.[5] Never mind. They all called each other Van, Bogey, Ramsay, Eadie, across the table; engaged in governing England: A mazer bowl fingered by Roger, drew Ramsay for two minutes, rather heavily into the open; took it; looked at it, laying his shabby drab spectacle case on the table; said he had never signed any authority for the sale of the mazer to America;[6] then lapsed into tete à tête with the ladies—murmuring, unresonant. And so upstairs, Ly L. running ahead, opening doors, taking us into little rooms to look at Majolica, at altarpieces. Then round the fire she started off, fluent, agreeable, hard hitting, like a rider, or Captain, without an ounce of spare flesh, telling stories—old men who had operations & were then mad—left their money in a muddle—her own father mad for two years—Farquhar muddling up the Fife Settlements & the Liberal Party fund[7]—all indiscreet, open, apparently; the chat of a perfectly equipped, un nonsensical, well fed, athletic woman, riding her horse at every fence. We discussed Birth

4. 'Bogey' Harris had been greatly influenced by the scholar and collector Herbert Horne (1864-1916) who spent his later years in Florence, to which city he bequeathed his palazzo and his collection (that of Harris was sold at auction after his death). Lady Londonderry, née Edith (Edie) Helen Chaplin (1878-1959), wife of the 7th Marquess of Londonderry and daughter of the 1st Viscount Chaplin (1840-1923) whose life (Henry Chaplin. A Memoir, 1926) she wrote, was a Conservative political hostess who had charmed the Labour Prime Minister, Ramsay MacDonald.
5. Sir Robert Gilbert Vansittart (1881-1957), civil servant and diplomatist, and like his host an old Etonian. He had risen steadily in the Foreign Office until in 1928 he was appointed Principal Private Secretary to the Prime Minister—a post he retained temporarily under Ramsay MacDonald. On 1 January 1930 he had returned to the Foreign Office as Permanent Under-Secretary.
6. The 'Pepys' or Saffron Walden mazer, hallmarked 1507, was sold at Christie's in July 1929 and, through Harris, was acquired by J. Pierpont Morgan. At that time the export of works of art was unrestricted.
7. The first Earl Farquhar (1844-1923), Master of the Household to Edward VII, had been Treasurer of the Unionist (Tory) Party; after the war he refused to relinquish to them funds collected while the party had been in coalition with the Liberals. At his death he made lavish bequests, in particular to King Edward's niece Princess Arthur of Connaught, Duchess of Fife, who was both his executor and principal beneficiary.

Control. 'Dear Edie, you wont let me convert you. But when you see your miners, with those terrible illegitimate children—

Eight in a room. One bed. What can you expect? They speak straight out to me, the old fashioned ones. Cant do anything else. What would you do? What should we do, if we lived like that? But we're not beasts. We can control ourselves. I detest Prohibition for that reason.'

Swept on, energetically, confidently, to the Webbs (woman sprung up beside me like a cobra) "Our class & yours can never meet. What difference is there? But these clever people! Yeats & Lady Gregory on a committee are hopeless—but both very clever people. Cant do anything."[8]

Ly L. can do whatever she wishes. She looked like an early Victorian picture—a Lawrence, I thought; a small pinched well cut face; healthy; without paint; very pink, pearls knotted about her wrists. The other woman garish, like a ruined almond tree. The rooms all set out with cases, chests, pictures objects. "I never give more than £10: I hunt about in rag & bone shops." Bogy has the glazed stuffed look of the well fed bachelor. Is evidently one of those elderly comfortable men of taste & leisure who make a profession of society; a perfectly instinctive snob. Knows everyone; lunches with Lord Lascelles; has taken the measure of it all exactly; nothing to say; proficient; surly; adept; an unattractive type, with all his talk of Lords & ladies, his belief in great houses; something of a gorged look, which connoisseurs have; as if he had always just swallowed a bargain. Something airless & too tidy in the house; a plethora of altar pieces. He pads about, gorged, without anything to seek for, save in old rag & bone shops; at the crest (I suppose) of his world. I suppose that this centre to one's mind—an altarpiece—is a bad one; too still & capable of acquisition. He never wants anything unattainable, I daresay: & so has feathered his nest. Roger says he has 'flair'; Roger who looks like a ravaged scavenger & lives with sardine tins & linoleum; yes, but Roger's house seems alive, with a living hand in it, manipulated, stretched. Why do interesting people never fix them down among objects (beautiful) & Duchesses (desirable). I tried, sitting on a priceless settee, picked up in Whitechapel for £10 (I never give more) to analyse my sensations. The ladies showed a perfect commercial grasp of the situation. Ramsay was tossed between them like a fish among cormorants. I had the impression that they did not rate this acquisition high; but took it as part of the days work. Ly L. had him to herself in a shaded room for an hour. Failing this, she had her claims written down to hand him.

Angelica said at the pantomime, as we watched the spangled lady dance,

8. Lady Gregory (1852-1932) was co-founder in 1902 with the poet W. B. Yeats of the Irish National Theatre.

"I shall never be able to dance like that but I may be able to paint like she dances."[9]

Sunday 26 January

I am 48: we have been at Rodmell—a wet, windy day again; but on my birthday we walked among the downs, like the folded wings of grey birds; & saw first one fox, very long with his brush stretched; then a second; which had been barking, for the sun was hot over us; it leapt lightly over a fence & entered the furze—a very rare sight. How many foxes are there in England? At night I read Lord Chaplin's life. I cannot yet write naturally in my new room, because the table is not the right height, & I must stoop to warm my hands. Everything must be absolutely what I am used to.

I forgot to say that when we made up our 6 months accounts, we found I had made about £3,020 last year—the salary of a civil servant: a surprise to me, who was content with £200 for so many years. But I shall drop very heavily I think. The Waves wont sell more than 2,000 copies. I am stuck fast in that book—I mean, glued to it, like a fly on gummed paper. Sometimes I am out of touch; but go on; then again feel that I have at last, by violent [It has sold about 6,500 today, Oct. 30th 1931—after 3 weeks. But will stop now I suppose.] measures—like breaking through gorse—set my hands on something central. Perhaps I can now say something quite straight out; & at length; & need not be always casting a line to make my book the right shape. But how to pull it together, how to compost it—press it into one—I do not know; nor can I guess the end—it might be a gigantic conversation. The interludes are very difficult, yet I think essential; so as to bridge & also give a background—the sea; insensitive nature—I dont know. But I think, when I feel this sudden directness, that it must be right: anyhow no other form of fiction suggests itself except as a repetition at the moment.

Lord Buckmaster sat next me. I was talking to Desmond about Irene. Suddenly Ethel said leaning across,

But did you ever know Lord Tennyson? & my evening was ruined. Typical of these parties.[10]

9. As the Woolfs took Angelica to the Pantomime (*Puss in Boots* at the *Lyceum*) on 20 January, the above entry cannot all have been written on 16 January.
10. VW dined with Ethel Sands on 21 January (LW went to his mother). Stanley Owen Buckmaster, 1st Viscount Buckmaster (1861-1934), Law Lord, appellate judge and member of the Judicial Committee of the Privy Council, had been a Liberal MP and became Lord Chancellor in Asquith's government, 1915-16. Ethel's ill-judged enquiry is later ascribed by VW to Lord Buckmaster (see *IV VW Letters*, nos. 2128, 2133).

Monday 10 February

Charlie Sanger died yesterday,[1] the very fine cold day, when we were driving up. I feel sorry in gusts. I wish we had dined there. I shall miss some peculiar thing—loyal, worn, romantic; flowing with affection. He knew us when Thoby died; had always clasped my hand warmly, sat sparking, glittering, elfish; very sympathetic, very serious, in the right way. He had a stern view, I think; had found life hard; & envisaged its hardness for others. Yes; I have a peculiar feeling for him—can one say more? And this is the sorrow for him—feeling one will never again have that. (I cant analyse—have indeed a slight temperature, & am in two minds if it is influenza, & whether to tell Leonard, who has had it—to put off Ethel Smyth, & Nessa—to go to bed—what is the sensible thing to do?[2]

Sunday 16 February

To lie on the sofa for a week. I am sitting up today, in the usual state of unequal animation. Below normal, with spasmodic desire to write, then to doze. It is a fine cold day & if my energy & sense of duty persist, I shall drive up to Hampstead.[3] But I doubt that I can write to any purpose. A cloud swims in my head. One is too conscious of the body & jolted out of the rut of life to get back to fiction. Once or twice I have felt that odd whirr of wings in the head which comes when I am ill so often—last year for example, at this time I lay in bed constructing A Room of One's Own (which sold 10,000 two days ago). If I could stay in bed another fortnight (but there is no chance of that) I believe I should see the whole of The Waves. Or of course I might go off on something different. As it is I half

1. C. P. Sanger died on the 8th not the 9th of February.
2. Dame Ethel Smyth (1858-1944), composer, author and feminist; daughter of an army general, she had to fight for a musical career and became an inveterate campaigner. She studied music in the circle of Brahms in Leipzig, wrote many operas (VW saw the first production of *The Wreckers* at His Majesty's Theatre in 1909), was a militant (and imprisoned) suffragist, and published a sequence of books of recollections; VW recorded her views of *Impressions that Remained* in the year of its publication (see *I VW Diary*, 28 November 1919), and reviewed her *Streaks of Life* in 1921 (Kp C218). Dame Ethel had now written in praise of *A Room of One's Own* and proposed a meeting; owing to VW's health this was several times postponed (see *IV VW Letters*, nos. 2136, 2138, 2140, 2143), but took place on 20 February.
3. The Woolfs *did* drive to Hampstead, and LW took a walk; he too had been ill and in bed with a temperature the previous week, but as usual recovered more quickly than VW.

incline to insist upon a dash to Cassis; but perhaps this needs more determination than I possess; & we shall dwindle on here. Pinker is walking about the room looking for the bright patch—a sign of spring. I believe these illnesses are in my case—how shall I express it?—partly mystical. Something happens in my mind. It refuses to go on registering impressions. It shuts itself up. It becomes chrysalis. I lie quite torpid, often with acute physical pain—as last year; only discomfort this. Then suddenly something springs. Two nights ago, Vita was here; & when she went, I began to feel the quality of the evening—how it was spring coming: a silver light; mixing with the early lamps; the cabs all rushing through the streets; I had a tremendous sense of life beginning; mixed with that emotion, which is the essence of my feeling, but escapes description—(I keep on making up the Hampton Court scene in The Waves —Lord how I wonder if I shall pull this book off! It is a litter of fragments so far). Well, as I was saying, between these long pauses (for I am swimmy in the head, & write rather to stabilise myself than to make a correct statement), I felt the spring beginning, & Vita's life so full & flush; & all the doors opening; & this is I believe the moth shaking its wings in me. I then begin to make up my story whatever it is; ideas rush in me; often though this is before I can control my mind or pen. It is no use trying to write at this stage. And I doubt if I can fill this white monster. I would like to lie down & sleep, but feel ashamed. Leonard brushed off his influenza in one day & went about his business feeling ill. Here am I still loafing, undressed, with Elly coming tomorrow. But as I was saying my mind works in idleness. To do nothing is often my most profitable way.

I am reading Byron: Maurois: which sends me to Childe Harold; makes me speculate.[4] How odd a mixture: the weakest sentimental Mrs Hemans combined with trenchant bare vigour. How did they combine? And sometimes the descriptions in C.H. are "beautiful"; like a great poet.

There are the three elements in Byron:

1 The romantic dark haired lady singing drawing room melodies to the guitar.

> "Tambourgi! Tambourgi! thy 'larum afar
> Gives hope to the valiant, & promise of war;

. . . . . .

4. André Maurois' *Byron*, 1930. VW had the French edition in 2 volumes. The quotations which follow are from *Childe Harold's Pilgrimage*: 1: Canto II, lxxii, from verses i and ii of the Albanians' song; 2: Canto II, lxxvi; 3: Canto II, xxxvii; 4: i.e. Canto I, lxix, lxx, 'two Stanzas of a buffooning cast (on London's Sunday)' (Byron to Dallas, 21 August 1811); 5: Canto II, xcvi.

> Oh! who is more brave than a dark Suliote,
>> In his snowy camese & his shaggy Capote"
> —something manufactured: a pose; silliness.

2 Then there is the vigorous rhetorical, like his prose, & good as prose.

> Hereditary Bondsmen! Know ye not
>> *Who* would be free *themselves* must strike the blow?
>> By their right arms the conquest must be wrought?
>> Will Gaul or Muscovite redress ye? No! . . .

3 Then what rings to me truer, & is almost poetry.

> Dear Nature is the kindest mother still!
>> Though always changing, in her aspect mild;

(all in Canto 11 of C H.)

>> From her bare bosom let me take my fill,
>> Her never-weaned, though not her favoured child.

* * *

> To me by day or night she ever smiled,
>> Though I have marked her when none other hath,
>> And sought her more & more, & loved her best in wrath.

4 And then there is of course the pure satiric, as in the description of
5 a London Sunday; & finally (but this makes more than three) the inevitable half assumed half genuine tragic note, which comes as a refrain, about death & the loss of friends.

> All thou could have of mine, stern Death! thou hast;
>> The parent, Friend, & now the more than Friend:
>> Ne'er yet for one thine arrows flew so fast,
>> And grief with grief continuing still to blend,
>> Hath snatched the little joy that life had yet to lend.

These I think make him up; & make much that is spurious, vapid, yet very changeable, & then rich & with greater range than the other poets, could he have got the whole into order. A novelist, he might have been. It is odd however to read in his letters his prose an apparently genuine feeling about Athens: & to compare it with the convention he adopted in verse. (There is some sneer about the Acropolis). But then the sneer may have been a pose too. The truth may be that if you are charged at such high voltage you cant fit any of the ordinary human feelings; must pose; must rhapsodise; don't fit in. He wrote in the Inn Album that his age was 100. And this is true, measuring life by feeling.

Monday 17 February

And this temperature is up;
but it has now gone down; & now

[*Thursday 20 February*]

Feb. 20th, I must canter my wits if I can. Perhaps some character sketches.

Snow:[5]

She came in wrapped in a dark fur coat; which being taken off, she appeared in nondescript grey stockinette & jay blue stripes. Her eyes too are jay blue, but have an anguished starved look, as of a cat that has climbed on to a chimney piece & looks down at a dog. Her face is pale, & very small; indeed, has a curious preserved innocency which makes it hard to think that she is 50. However, her neck is very loose skinned; & there are the dewlaps of middle age. The preserved look seems to indicate lack of experience; as if life had put her in a refrigerator. And we talked— She brought me a parcel, & this was a book from Ethel Smyth, with a letter, which to veil the embarrassment which I supposed her to feel, I read aloud. Her comment was "What miles away all this is from Cheltenham!" Then we talked—but it was her starved & anguished look that remains & the attitude of mind. She seemed to be saying inwardly "I have missed everything. There are Vanessa & Virginia, They have lives full of novels & husbands & exhibitions. I am fifty & it has all slipped by." I gathered this from the jocose pertinacity with which she kept referring to herself. She said the climate of Cheltenham is so sleepy that she often cant paint; & after lunch they put on the gramophone; & then she goes most days to her mother at Bockhampton, where she likes meeting the village people. Farmers wives shake hands. After her mothers death—but she is only 80 & as firm as a rock—she & Lily who is political, but of course that doesn't take up all her time exactly, are going to live at Harrogate, where the climate is not so sleepy, & they know more people. Nothing long distracted her from her central concern—I have had no life & life is over. Even clothes suggested the same old theme. A dressmaker had told her that one enjoyed life more if one was well dressed. So she was

5. Margaret (Margery) Kemplay Snowden (1878-1966?), daughter of a Yorkshire vicar, had been a fellow-student of Vanessa's at the Royal Academy Schools at the beginning of the century; she remained her faithful friend and correspondent, living in Cheltenham, with her sister and near her mother. She came to tea with VW on 18 February.

trying this specific, to the tune of £8.8 at Pomeroy's in Old Burlington Street. But this worried & fretted her too. In fact I have seldom got a more dismal impression of suffering—too ignoble & petty to be called suffering: call it rather frustration, non-entity; being lifted on a shelf, & seeing things pass; "but then I am very lazy—thats what it is—I lapse into comfort." I should call it lapsing into despair. "What can three women do alone in the country?" Lord, how I praise God that I had a bent strong enough to coerce every minute of my life since I was born! This fiddling & drifting & not impressing oneself upon anything—this always refraining & fingering & cutting things up into little jokes & facetiousness—thats whats so annihilating. Yet given little money, little looks, no special gift, but only enough to make her devastatingly aware that other people have more gift, so that she sees her still lives against the superior still lives of Margaret Gere & the Cotswold school,—what can one do?[6] How could one battle? How could one leap on the back of life & wring its scruff? One would joke, bitterly; & become egotistical & anxious to explain & excuse; & plaintive. What I thought most pathetic was the fact that about 5.30 she began to fidget (she never does anything boldly & directly) with her gloves, & say she must be going. But where? I asked. To the Polytechnic to hear a lecture upon French literature. But why? "Oh one never hears French talked in Cheltenham." Dear dear, but I could tell you all about French literature, I said. However, she shillied shallied; & whether she wanted to go or to stay, I don't know. And when I asked her what she was going to do that night, Well that depends how long the lecture lasts, she said, feebly laughing. Wont you go to a play? No I think I shall have what is called a snack at the Temperance hotel;—Lord Lord, I repeat again. And it isn't as if she were unconscious & oblivious: no, she knows that the dog is there, & arches her back & puts out her paw, but ever so feebly & fussily.

Friday 21 February

No two women could be more extravagantly contraposed than Marjorie Snowden & Ethel Smyth. I was lying here at four yesterday when I heard the bell ring then a brisk tramp up the stairs; & then behold a bluff, military old woman (older than I expected), bounced into the room, a little glazed flyaway & abrupt; in a three cornered hat & tailor made suit. "Let me look at you".

6. Margaret Gere (1878-1965) studied painting at Birmingham and at the Slade; she lived at Painswick in Gloucestershire and was, like Margery Snowden, a member of the Cheltenham Group of Artists. She was primarily a figure painter.

That over, Now I have brought a book & pencil. I want to ask.

Here there was a ring at the bell. I went to look over. Then we went to tea.

First I want to make out the genealogy of your mothers family. Old Pattle—have you a picture? No. Well now—the names of his daughters. This lasted out tea. Afterwards, on the sofa, with Ethel stretching her legs out on Pinker's basket, we talked ceaselessly till 7—when L. came in. We talked—she talked considerably more than I. (On the stairs going up to tea I had asked to be Virginia; about ten minutes after tea she asked to be Ethel: all was settled; the basis of an undying friendship made in 15 minutes:—how sensible; how rapid;) & she got off; oh about music—"I am said to be an egoist. I am a fighter. I feel for the underdog. I rang up Hugh Allen & suggested lunch.[7] My dear Sir Hugh—my dear Ethel—there are facts you dont know about your sex. Believe me I have to go on coming to London, bullying, badgering—at last, they promise me 14 women in the orchestra. I go & find 2. So I begin ringing up." She has a vein, like a large worm, in her temple which swells. Her cheeks redden. Her faded eyes flash. She has a broad rounded forehead. She recurred to dress. I have to go to Bath to hear dear Maurice Baring's little plays; & then we go to (here Elly interrupted) Rottingdean.[8] And I must take an evening suit. Thats what worries me. I'm only happy in this—I have one gown I wear for conducting. And then I have to pack (here is a pineapple from Leonard's mother who waits outside). "My maid? But she's only a general—an Irish woman. "Dr (she calls me Dr) Mrs Woolf doesn't mean to see you. Heres another letter from her—to put you off." But I've come. And dont it show that my appetite for life is still great? I've thought of nothing but seeing you for 10 days. And this friendship has come to me now." So sincere & abrupt is she, & discriminating withal—judging Vita & her secondrate women   Enid Bagnold friends shrewdly—that perhaps something gritty & not the usual expansive fluff, may come of it. I like to hear her talk of music. She has written a piece—on Brewster's Prisoner; & will have the gorgeous fun of orchestrating it this summer.[9] She says writing music is like

7. Sir Hugh Percy Allen (1869-1946), Professor of Music in the University of Oxford from 1918 until his death and Director of the Royal College of Music, 1918-37.

8. Maurice Baring, since 1893 one of Ethel Smyth's closest friends, had a house at Rottingdean, near Brighton. He had published two volumes of *Diminutive Dramas*, 1910 and 1919.

9. Henry Bennet Brewster (1859-1908), a cosmopolitan Anglo-American philosopher and writer whom Ethel Smyth had met in Florence when she was twenty-five. He was the only man with whom she was ever to be in love; he was married, a fact

writing novels. One thinks of the sea—naturally one gets a phrase for it. Orchestration is colouring. And one has to be very careful with one's 'technique'. Rhapsodises about A Room; about Miss Williamson;[10] about the end of some book of Maurice Baring's. "I'm in the street. I belong to the crowd. I say the crowd is right." Perhaps she is right to belong to the crowd. There is something fine & tried & experienced about her besides the rant & the riot & the egotism—& I'm not sure that she is the egotist that people make out. She said she never had anybody to admire her, & therefore might write good music to the end. Has to live in the country because of her passion for games. Plays golf, rides a bicycle; was thrown hunting two years ago. Then fell on her arm & was in despair, because life wd. be over if she could not play games. 'I am very strong' which she proved by talking till 7.30; then eating a biscuit & drinking a glass of vermouth & going off to eat a supper of maccaroni when she got to Woking at 9.

"I'll tell you all about it" she grinned at her maid, who asked if I was a nice woman. A fine old creature, certainly, Ethel. She talks French 'méringues' with a highly French accent.

Saturday 22 February

I had meant to write a sketch of George—Sir George Duck-worth[11]—as he announced himself to Nelly—& of Lytton; both unexpected visitors yesterday—for I'm not to go down to the studio till Monday; & so must canter my pen amateurishly here; but ten minutes ago the idea came to me of a possible broadsheet; which I wd. like to adumbrate, before discussing with L. My notion is a single sheet, containing say 2,000 or if printed back & front 4,000 words. Art, politics, Lit., music: an essay by a single writer to be printed at irregular intervals; sent to subscribers; costing 6d. Sometimes only a reproduction. It should be a statement about life: something somebody wants to say; not a regular comment. Very little

---

which complicated an already intense relationship. Brewster had written the libretto, based on his own drama, for her opera *The Wreckers*, and her last large-scale work, the oratorio *The Prison*, took its inspiration from his metaphysical work *The Prison: A Dialogue* (1891), republished with a memoir by Ethel Smyth in 1930.

10. Elizabeth Williamson (b. 1903), a great-niece of Ethel Smyth, was an astronomer and a mathematician who taught at University College, London.

11. George Duckworth had been knighted in 1927; in 1924-7 he had served as English Trustee and chairman of the Irish Land Trust for the provision of houses and land for ex-servicemen in Ireland under the Act of Settlement.

expense wd. be involved. It would have a spring & an urgency about it wh. the regular sheets lack. Sometimes only a picture. To be closely under L. & my thumbs, so as to give character & uniformity. To lapse for a month if necessary. No incubus of regular appearance. A circular signed by L. & me to be sent round. Young writers enlisted. Signed articles. Everything of the humblest, least ostentatious. The Hogarth News. The Broadsheet.—name to be decided. You see I wd. like to write on Scott this week, & cant, because Richmond has sent the book already.[13] L. wd. do politics. Roger art. The young would have their fling. Possibly, if expenses were kept down, they could get £5 or so, & have their names. But they must not be essays—always—must be topical to some extent.

And in June, I was offered the Editorship of a 4ly; by ⟨the Graphic⟩ Mr Bott & Mr Turner of the Book Club: L. is refusing it at this moment (30th June)[12]

That being enough to go upon in talk after lunch—& it is a fine still day & perhaps we may drive to Richmond & try my legs walking—I will obediently, like a student in the art school—sketch Sir George. First his jowl: it is of the finest semi-transparent flesh; so that one longs to slice it, as it rests, infinitely tender, upon his collar. Otherwise he is as tight as a drum. One expects his trousers to split as he sits down. This he does slowly & rises with difficulty. Still some sentiment begins to form misty between us. He speaks of 'Mother'. I daresay finds in me some shadowy likeness—well—& then he is not now in a position to do me harm. His conventions amuse me. I suppose these family affections are somehow self-protection. He preserves a grain or two of what is me—my unknown past; my self; so that if George died, I should feel something of myself buried. He is endlessly self-complacent. His stories, once started, roll comfortably—he is immensely comfortable—into the pocket of his solid self esteem. I ask, What about the hogs (the Chesterfield hogs) & he replies that the cowman's wife has had a very long labour. Margaret has been very worried. Dalingridge was lit up all night. They had to use the

See Sir George Duckworth on 'Pigs' in todays Times. Pigs are the most intelligent of animals. I own a small herd of white pedigree hogs."[14]

12. No further details of this offer have been found.
13. The book VW hoped for must have been Stephen Gwynne's recently published *The Life of Sir Walter Scott*; a review of it appeared in the *TLS* on 27 February. But see below, 1 May 1930, when Bruce Richmond *did* send her a book on Scott.
14. This marginal note was added on 30 June 1930; that day's *Times* had published a letter from Sir George Duckworth of Dalingridge Place, Sussex, 'Owner of a small herd of pedigree Middle White pigs'; it was a response to a speech by Lloyd

telephone—to send for the dr. The womans mother slept in the house—
& so it goes on, singing cosily & contentedly the praises of the good
master & mistress—which I have no doubt they are. And he trots out his
little compliments—asked to be Sheriff. And he wishes to know if I am
making fabulous sums—& he chuckles & dimples & respects me for
being asked to a party by the Lord Mayor. And he twits Eddy Marsh for
being fond of the society of the great. And he deplores the nudity of
Nessa's pictures—& so prattles & chortles & gives me turtle soup &
advises about the preparation & so takes himself off, to meet Henry &
return to Dalingridge & the cowman & the hogs—a very incestuous
race—& his cook Janet & his Bronnie, home on leave from the Navy—
well, it does appear as if human life were perfectly tolerable; his voltage
is absolutely normal. The world has been made for him.[15]

Lytton came in after dinner. Very twinkly, lustrous, easy & even warm.
Leonard made cigarettes. I lay on the sofa in the twilight of cushions.
Lytton had been sent a book about Columbus & told us the story making
it into a fantastic amusing Lytton book[16]—Columbus a mad religious
fanatic who sailed west & west because he had read in Isaiah a prophesy;
his crew being convicts let out from prison; & they came to Cuba & he
made them sign a statement that this was India, because it was too large
to be an island; & they picked up gold & gems & went back to Spain &
the King & Queen rose as he came in. Here are all the elements of a Lytton
concoction, told with great gusto; irony; a sense of the incongruous &
dramatic. Then we warbled melodiously about Dadie, & Cambridge; &
Charlie; & so on. He has a new gramophone. He is editing Greville.[17]
He is very content too—not for George's reasons; & very well equipped,
& buys books; & likes us; & is going to Cambridge this week end. Its

---

George who was reported as saying he was 'not surprised that Mr Baldwin has
always expressed a preference for the society of pigs'. Sir George wrote that
whereas townsmen were apt to speak of both farm labourers and pigs as the last
word in stupidity, his considerable experience led him to conclude that the skill
of the former ranked well above all other labourers', 'while the "pig" is markedly
superior to all other farm animals in general intelligence'.

15. George Duckworth had three sons; Auberon and Henry were the two eldest.
16. Lives of Columbus by André de Hevesy and Jacob Wasserman had recently been
   issued in translation. Lytton published nothing on this subject.
17. An expurgated edition of the memoirs of Charles Greville had been published in
   1888 and Lytton, who had been engaged in a long campaign for the publication
   of the complete text, had for the past six months been working on the manuscripts
   in the British Museum, helped by Ralph Partridge and Frances Marshall. His
   edition of *The Greville Memoirs from 1814-1860* eventually appeared in 8 volumes
   in 1938, the editorial work completed by Roger Fulford.

odd how little one remembers what is actually said. I am thinking of the new paper.

Saturday 1 March

And then I went for a walk & brought on a headache, & so lay down again till today, Saturday—a fine day—when we propose to drive off—oh Thank God a thousand times—to Rodmell & there be at rest. This
To Hampstead Garden suburb [*on 22 February*]
little affair has taken 3 weeks, & will land me in 4, of non-writing inexpressiveness. Yet I'm not sure that this is not the very thing for The Waves. It was dragging too much out of my head— If ever a book drained me, this one does. If I had wisdom, no doubt I should potter at Rodmell for a fortnight, not writing. I shall take a look at it one of these mornings in my sunny room.

One evening here I had the odd experience of perfect rest & satisfaction. All the bayonets that prod me sank. There I lay (I daresay for an hour) happy. And the quality was odd. Not an anxiety, not a stir, anywhere. No one coming. Nothing to do. All strain ceased. A
[*word illegible*]
supreme sailing with . . . through the dominion (I am quoting—I think Shelley—& it makes nonsense.) This is the rarest of all my moods. I cant recall another. Perhaps at Rodmell sometimes. Everything is shut off. It depends upon having been in the stir of London for some time. Not to have to get up & see Sibyl or Ethel or anybody—what a supreme relief! And now I have a chance to brew a little quiet thought. Yesterday I was offered £2,000 to write a life of Boswell by Doran Heinemann. L. is writing my polite refusal this moment.[1] I have bought my freedom. A queer thought that I have actually paid for the power to go to Rodmell & only think of The Waves by refusing this offer. If I accepted I would buy houses, tables & go to Italy; not worth it. Yesterday we went over 57 Russell Sqre wh. we may take. But I rather dread the noise & the size—I dont know. A lovely view.

Monday 3 March

Rodmell again. My new bedroom again. Children playing in the school. A thick pearl grey blue day; water drops on the window. Suppose health were shown on a thermometer I have gone up 10 degrees since yesterday,

1. LW's diary, 28 February 1930: 'Reeves came fr Doubleday Doran ask V write Boswell'. A. S. Frere Reeves was a director of William Heinemann Ltd, which at this time was owned by Doubleday Doran of New York.

when I lay, mumbling the bones of Dodo: if it had bones;[2] now I sit up, but cannot face going down & bringing an MS to read. Curiosity begins to stir all the same. Such is the effect of 24 hours here, & one ramble for 30 minutes on the flats. The sun wells up, like a pulse, behind the clouds. Tremendous shoals of birds are flying,—& the flop eared trains meeting as usual under Caburn.[3]

Molly Hamilton writes a d—d bad novel.[4] She has the wits to construct a method of telling a story; & then heaps it with the dreariest, most confused litter of old clothes. When I stop to read a page attentively I am shocked by the dishabille of her English. It is like hearing cooks & scullions chattering; she scarcely articulates, dashes it off, I imagine, on blocks of paper, on her knee, at the House of Commons perhaps; or in the Tube. And the quality of the emotion is so thick & squab, the emotions of secondrate women painters, of spotted & pimpled young men: I dont know how she conveys such a sense of the secondrate without gift: the soft pedal too, & the highminded pedal; & no wit; & not precision; & no word standing alone, but each flopping on to the shoulder of another— Lord what a style! What a mind. It has energy & some ability—chiefly shown in the method; but that breaks down; & that too is laboriously lifted. Now being still flabby in the march of the mind, I must read Sea Air—a good manuscript.[5]

Tuesday 11 March

all because I have to buy myself a dress this afternoon, & cant think what I want, I cannot read. I have written, fairly well—but it is a difficult book—at Waves; but cant keep on after 12; & now shall write here, for 20 minutes.

My impressions of Margaret [Llewelyn Davies] & Lilian [Harris] at Monks House were of great lumps of grey coat; straggling wisps of hair; hats floppy & home made; thick woollen stockings; black shoes, many

2. *Dodo* (1893) was a once celebrated novel by E. F. Benson in which the eponymous heroine is based on Margot Tennant (Mrs Asquith), and her candid friend Edith Staines on Ethel Smyth.

3. This train image occurs in *II VW Diary*, 7 January 1920, and in *The Waves*, p 204; but the word used is *lop* not *flop*.

4. Mary Agnes (Molly) Hamilton (1882-1966), a vigorous and able writer and journalist, of whom VW had seen a good deal in the years after the war. She had been elected Labour MP for Blackburn in 1929. Her latest novel was *Special Providence* (1930).

5. Author unidentified; *Sea Air* was the title of a book by the popular romantic novelist Isobel C. Clarke published in 1932—but it seems unlikely that it was submitted to the Hogarth Press.

wraps, shabby handbags, & shapelessness, & shabbiness & dreariness & drabness unspeakable. A tragedy in its way. Margaret at any rate deserved better of life than this dishevelled & undistinguished end. They are in lodgings—as usual. Have, as usual, a wonderful Xtian Scientist landlady; are somehow rejected by active life; sit knitting perhaps & smoking cigarettes, in the parlour where they have their meals, where there is always left a dish of oranges & bananas. I doubt if they have enough to eat. They seemed to me flabby & bloodless, spread into rather toneless chunks of flesh; having lost any commerce with looking glasses. So we showed them the garden, gave them tea (& I dont think an iced cake had come Lilian's way this 6 weeks) & then—oh the dismal sense of people stranded, wanting to be energised; drifting—all woollen & hairy. (It is odd how the visual impression dominates.) There is a jay blue spark in Margaret's eye, now & then, But she had not been out of the lodging for 5 weeks because of the East wind. Her mind has softened & wrinkled, sitting indoors with the oranges & cigarettes. Lilian is almost stone deaf, & mumbles & crumbles, emerging clearly only once, to discuss politics. Something has blunted Margaret's edge, rusted it, worn it, long before its time. Must old age be so shapeless? The only escape is to work the mind. I shall write a history of English literature, I think, in those days. And I shall walk. And I shall buy clothes, & keep my hair tidy, & make myself dine out. But perhaps life becomes repetitious, & one takes no trouble; is glad to be shovelled about in motor cars. M. has her tragic past. She is pathetic to me now—conciliatory & nervous where she used to be trenchant & severe. Janet she says writes endless notes; has sisters for ever staying with her to convalesce; & Emphie caught up their little white dog the other day from a wild herd of racing greyhounds, & had it bitten to death in her arms.[6] This is the sort of adventure that only befalls elderly unmarried women, on whom it makes a tremendous & very painful impression—so defence-less are they, so unable to throw off the damp blanket that surrounds them. What I miss is colour, energy, any clear reflection of the moment. I see those thick stockings & grey hairy wraps everywhere.

Monday 17 March

The test of a book (to a writer) [is] if it makes a space in which, quite naturally, you can say what you want to say. As this morning I could say

6. Janet Case lived with her sister Emphie at Minstead in the New Forest; she was the youngest of six sisters. From 1925-37 she contributed a weekly 'Country Diary' to the *Manchester Guardian*.

what Rhoda said. This proves that the book itself is alive: because it has not crushed the thing I wanted to say, but allowed me to slip it in, without any compression or alteration.

Friday 28 March

Yes, but this book is a very queer business. I had a day of intoxication when I said Children are nothing to this: when I sat surveying the whole book complete, & quarrelled with L. (about Ethel Smyth) & walked it off, felt the pressure of the form—the splendour & the greatness—as—perhaps, I have never felt them. But I shan't race it off in intoxication. I keep pegging away; & find it the most complex, & difficult of all my books. How to end, save by a tremendous discussion, in which every life shall have its voice—a mosaic—a——. I do not know. The difficulty is that it is all at high pressure. I have not yet mastered the speaking voice. Yet I think something is there; & I propose to go on pegging it down, arduously, & then re-write, reading much of it aloud, like poetry. It will bear expansion. It is compressed I think. It is—whatever I make of it—a large & potential theme—wh. Orlando was not perhaps. At any rate, I have taken my fence.

Home from tea with Nessa & Angelica. A fine spring day. I walked along Oxford St. The buses are strung on a chain. People fight & struggle. Knocking each other off the pavement. Old bareheaded men; a motor car accident; &c. To walk alone in London is the greatest rest.

Tuesday 1 April

And we have got to go & dine with Raymond now, this very potent, astonishingly exciting warm evening. I sit with my window open & hear the humming see a yellow window open in the hotel: I walked back from Leicester Square. What queer memories have got themselves mixed into this evening I asked. Something from a very soft, rather mystic evening; not feverish & fretful; no; by the sea; blue; gentle. And I dropped in at the dressmaker. She has no teeth. She was stitching. She said like a friend Mrs Woolf we are going to move. And I thought you wdnt mind if I left out the stitching as my eyes ached. All that is said tonight is gentle & happy & seems to thrust into some soft tide. I cant get it right, naturally.

Nessa is at Charleston. They will have the windows open; perhaps even sit by the pond. She will think This is what I have made by years of unknown work—my sons, my daughter. She will be perfectly content (as I suppose) Quentin fetching bottles; Clive immensely good tempered.

They will think of London with dislike. Yet it is very exciting; I shall sip my wine at Raymond's, & try & elicit something from Lytton. And so must change.

Friday 4 April

I am trying to sketch my last chapter—unsuccessfully; so will use 10 minutes to note my observations at Raymond's. Chiefly upon the atmosphere of buggery. Lytton's face lit up with love & rapture when I deserted the delightful women, with all their gifts, for Mr Williamson, brilliant & beautiful, but unknown, of Oxford. Raymond sat on the arm of Lytton's chair. Morgan came in from Meleager. And I went to see Ronnie behind the scenes. He was looking very nice in shorts. Eddy came in from Cochran's latest.[1] He had had to stand & was (I am making up The Waves) peevish. (humour is what it lacks). Anyhow, he said, Ensor (I forget) looked very pretty in a white suit—the rest oh so hideous. At this the other buggers pricked their ears & became somehow silly. I mean rather giggly & coy. An atmosphere entirely secluded, intimate, & set on one object; all agreed upon the things they liked. Raymond barked once or twice rudely (he is underbred, in voice anyhow) his feeling that I was noting, scoffing. Told me how Gerbault loathed women; then protested that I was not to believe all the stories of D'Annunzio & Duse: there was another side; *she* had maltreated him.[2] A protest; raucous, & obtrusive. A photograph of Stephen Tennant (Siegfried Sassoon goes to the same dressmaker) in a tunic, in an attitude was shown about; also little boys at a private school. Morgan became unfamiliar, discussing the beauties of Hilton Young's stepson.[3] "His skating is magnificent" (then in an undertone deploring some woman's behaviour). This all made on me a tinkling, private, giggling, impression. As if I had gone in to a men's urinal.

1. Mr Williamson, still unknown. R. C. Trevelyan's verse tragedy *Meleager* was being performed by the Players Company at the Rudolf Steiner Hall. *Cochran's 1930 Revue* at the London Pavilion was the latest in the succession of spectacular entertainments put on by the showman C. B. Cochran (1872-1951).
2. Alain Gerbault (1893-1941), French navigator and former international tennis player, had sailed round the world single-handed in 1925-9. Gabriele D'Annunzio (1863-1938), Italian poet, novelist and playwright whose liaison with the celebrated Italian actress Eleonora Duse (1859-1924) was in every sense a theatrical one.
3. (Edward) Hilton Young (1879-1960), whom VW had once thought of as a possible husband (see *I QB*, p 131), was now a Conservative MP: he had married in 1922 the widow of Captain R. F. Scott ('Scott of the Antarctic') and his stepson was Peter Scott (b. 1909) the artist and naturalist.

Wednesday 9 April

What I now think (about the Waves) is that I can give in a very few strokes the essentials of a person's character. It should be done boldly, almost as caricature. I have yesterday entered what may be the last lap. Like every piece of the book it goes by fits & starts. I never get away with it; but am tugged back. I hope this makes for solidity; & must look to my sentences. The abandonment of Orlando & Lighthouse is much checked by the extreme difficulty of the form—as it was in Jacob's Room. I think this is the furthest development so far; but of course it may miss fire somewhere. I think I have kept stoically to the original conception. What I fear is that the re-writing will have to be so drastic that I may entirely muddle it somehow. It is bound to be very imperfect. But I think it possible that I have got my statues against the sky.

Friday 11 April

Yesterday walked through the Waddesdon Greenhouses with Mr Johnson.[4] There were single red lines taking root in sand. Cyclamen by the hundred gross. Azaleas massed like military bands. Carnations at different stages. Vines being picked thin by sedulous men. Nothing older than 40 years, but now ready made in perfection. A fig tree that had a thousand lean regular branches. The statues tied up, like dead horses, in sheets. The whole thing dead. Made, planted, put into position in the year 1880 or thereabouts. One flower wd. have given more pleasure than those dozens of grosses. And the heat, & the tidiness & the accuracy & the organisation. Mr Johnson like a nectarine, hard, red, ripe. He was taught all he knew by Miss Alice, & accepted admiration as his income. Sir he called us.

Sunday 13 April

I read Shakespeare *directly* I have finished writing, when my mind is agape & red & hot. Then it is astonishing. I never yet knew how amazing his stretch & speed & word coining power is, until I felt it utterly outpace & outrace my own, seeming to start equal & then I see him draw ahead & do things I could not in my wildest tumult & utmost press of mind

4. The Woolfs lunched with LW's brother Philip at his home at Upper Winchendon, and in the afternoon were shown over the Waddesdon greenhouses by Mr Johnson, the head gardener. Miss Alice de Rothschild (d. 1922) had inherited the Waddesdon estate from her brother Baron Ferdinand in 1898; at her death her heir, James de Rothschild, had appointed Philip Woolf, a relation by marriage, estate manager.

imagine. Even the less known & worser plays are written at a speed that is quicker than anybody else's quickest; & the words drop so fast one can't pick them up. Look at this, Upon a gather'd lily almost wither'd (that is a pure accident: I happen to light on it.)[5] Evidently the pliancy of his mind was so complete that he could furbish out any train of thought; &, relaxing lets fall a shower of such unregarded flowers. Why then should anyone else attempt to write. This is not 'writing' at all. Indeed, I could say that Shre surpasses literature altogether, if I knew what I meant.

I meant to make this note of Waddesdon greenhouses. There were rows of hydrangeas, mostly a deep blue. Yes, said Mr Johnson, Lord Kitchener came here & asked how we blued them . . .[6] I said you put things in the earth. He said he did too. But sometimes with all one's care, they shot a bit pink. Miss Alice wouldn't have that. If there was a trace of pink there, it wouldnt do. And he showed us a metallic petalled hydrangea. No that wouldnt do for Miss Alice. It struck me, what madness, & how easy to pin ones mind down to the blueness of hydrangeas, & to hypnotise Mr Johnson into thinking only of the blueness of hydrangeas. He used to go to her every evening, for she scarcely saw anyone, & they would talk for two hours about the plants & politics. How easy to go mad over the blueness of hydrangeas & think of nothing else.

The Woolfs drove to Rodmell on 16 April for Easter and did not return to London until 27th.

Wednesday 23 April

This is a very important morning in the history of The Waves, because I think I have turned the corner & see the last lap straight ahead. I think I have got Bernard into the final stride. He will go straight on now, & then stand at the door; & then there will be a last picture of the waves. We are at Rodmell, & I daresay I shall stay on a day or two (if I dare) so as not to break the current & finish it. O Lord & then a rest; & then an article; & then back again to this hideous shaping & moulding. There may be some joys in it all the same.

5. 'When I did name her brothers, then fresh tears
    Stood on her cheeks, as doth the honey-dew
    Upon a gather'd lily almost wither'd.'
                                    Titus Andronicus, III, i.

6. Horatio Herbert Kitchener, 1st Earl of Khartoum and Broome (1850-1916), Field-Marshal and popular military hero.

MAY 1930

Saturday 26 April

Having had no letters for 3 days I feel my balloon shrink. All that semi-transparent globe wh. my fame attaches to me is pricked; & I am a mere stick. This is very wholesome; & grey; & not altogether displeasing though flat.

Sunday 27 April

A queer adventure, to come back & find Lottie in the house (her great box under the kitchen table) having been dismissed by Karin for stealing. She was sent with a policeman to the station. She is to sleep here tonight. And I am to see Karin.

Tuesday 29 April

And I have just finished, with this very nib-full of ink, the last sentence of The Waves. I think I should record this for my own information. Yes, it was the greatest stretch of mind I ever knew; certainly the last pages; I dont think they flop as much as usual. And I think I have kept starkly & ascetically to the plan. So much I will say in self-congratulation. But I have never written a book so full of holes & patches; that will need re-building, yes, not only re-modelling. I suspect the structure is wrong. Never mind. I might have done something easy & fluent; & this is a reach after that vision I had, the unhappy summer—or three weeks—at Rodmell, after finishing The Lighthouse. (And that reminds me—I must hastily provide my mind with something else, or it will again become pecking & wretched, —something imaginative, if possible, & light; for I shall tire of Hazlitt & criticism after the first divine relief—. & I feel pleasantly aware of various adumbrations in the back of my head; a life of Duncan: no, something about canvases glowing in a studio: but that can wait.)

I must run upstairs & peep in & tell Leonard & ask about Lottie, who has been after a place; & by the way injured yesterdays lap I am afraid with her vicissitudes.

Pm. And, I think to myself as I walk down Southampton Row "And I have given you a new book."

Thursday 1 May

And I have completely ruined my morning. Yes that is literally true. They sent a book from The Times, as if advised by Heaven of my liberty; & feeling my liberty wild upon me, I rushed to the cable & told Van

302

Doren I would write on Scott. And now having read Scott, or the perky & impertinent editor whom Hugh provides to dish up tasty fragments, I wont & cant:[1] & have got into a fret trying to read it, & writing to Richmond to say I cant; & have wasted the brilliant first of May which makes my skylight blue & gold; have only a rubbish heap in my head; cant read, & cant write, & cant think. The truth is, of course, I want to be back at The Waves. Yes that is the truth. Unlike all my other books in every way, it is unlike them in this, that I begin to re-write it, & conceive it again with ardour, directly I have done. I begin to see what I had in my mind; & want to begin cutting out masses of irrelevance, & clearing, sharpening & making the good phrases shine. One wave after another. No room. & so on. But then we are going touring Devon & Cornwall on Sunday which means a week off; & then I shall perhaps make my critical brain do a months work, for exercise. What could it be set to? Or a story?—no, not another story now. Perhaps Miss Burney's half sister's story,[2]

On Sunday 4 May the Woolfs set out on a week's tour by car of South-Western England, travelling Hogarth Press books in Bath, Bristol, Exeter, Truro and Penzance, and staying in hotels; they lunched at St Ives on 7 May, and then turned homewards, driving via Exeter, Shaftesbury, Salisbury and Winchester to Lewes, spending two nights at Monks House before returning to London on 11 May.

Sunday 18 May

The thing is now to live with energy & mastery, desperately. To despatch each day high handedly. To make much shorter work of the day than one used. To feel each like a wave slapping up against one. So not to dawdle & dwindle, contemplating this & that. To do what ever comes along with decision; going to the Hawthornden prize giving rapidly & lightheartedly; to buy a coat; to Long Barn; to Angelica's School;

---

1. Irita van Doren was anxious to publish further articles by VW in the Book Supplement of the *New York Herald Tribune*. *The Private Letter-Books of Sir Walter Scott*, edited by Wilfred Partington, was reviewed in the *TLS* on 15 May 1930; but not by VW. The book has an introductory letter by Hugh Walpole.
2. Probably written for Mrs van Doren (who paid well), 'Fanny Burney's Half-Sister' was first published in the *TLS* of 28 August 1930; it appeared in two parts under the more legitimate title of ' "Evelina's" Step Sister' in the *New York Herald Tribune* on 14 and 21 September 1930 (Kp C324).

thrusting through the mornings work (Hazlitt now) then adventuring.[3] And when one has cleared a way, then to go directly to a shop & buy a desk, a book case. No more regrets & indecisions. That is the right way to deal with life now that I am 48: & to make it more & more important & vivid as one grows old.

This is all very well; but what if Nelly then gets taken ill with her kidneys, must have an operation. Soberly & seriously a whole fortnight has been blown from my life; because I have had to hang about to see Elly, to buy food, to arrange with Taupin, to arrange with the hospital; to go there in an ambulance. My mind in order to work needs to be stretched tight & flat. It has been broken into shivers. With great plodding I have managed to write about the Women's Guild. And I consider setting to work on The Waves. I have had over 6 weeks holiday from it. Only again, this morning is ruined because I sit waiting a char, who does not come. And we have Lyn & Sir R. Storrs to tea.[4]

VW stayed the night of 23 May at Long Barn, after being taken by V. Sackville-West to see her prospective home, the ruined Sissinghurst Castle; the following day LW drove her, Vanessa and Duncan to visit Angelica at her school near Colchester. Nelly Boxall went into hospital on 28 May, and was operated on 3 June. On 29 May the Hogarth Press installed a new printing machine; the old one was given to Vita Sackville-West, and is still at Sissinghurst Castle. From 5-10 June the Woolfs were at Rodmell for Whitsun; on 11th they went to see Paul Robeson, Sibyl Thorndike and Peggy Ashcroft in Othello *at the Savoy Theatre.*

Sunday 15 June

How many skips there are here! Nothing said of our tour through the West; nothing said of N.'s operation; of Taupin, who lost my key broke

3. The 1930 Hawthornden Prize was presented by Stanley Baldwin to Lord David Cecil for his biography of Cowper, *The Stricken Deer* (1929), at the Æolian Hall on 22 May. VW's article on William Hazlitt was being written for the *New York Herald Tribune*, in which it appeared on 7 September 1930 (Kp C325).
4. This paragraph, undated, appears to have been added late in May. Mrs Tauplin was an elderly and incompetent Frenchwoman recommended by Vanessa and Helen Anrep as a temporary domestic in Nelly Boxall's absence. Margaret Llewelyn Davies had persuaded VW to write an introductory letter to a collection of letters by Co-operative working women which she was editing; *Life as We have Known It* was published by the Hogarth Press in March 1931 (*HP Checklist* 250; see also Kp B11). Sir Ronald Henry Amherst Storrs (1881-1955), diplomat, linguist, connoisseur of the arts and writer, was a friend of Ethel Smyth's; at this period he was Governor of Cyprus.

tumblers & cooked with the faded inspiration of one who had been a good cook; & nothing said of the divine relief of my quiet evenings, without servants; & how we dine out at the Cock; & how we say, can't this last? & then how I rang up Mrs Walters; & that experiment, an arduous one, begins tomorrow.[1] Leonard is not apt at a crisis. I mean his caution sticks his back up. He foresees obstacles. He has a philanthropic side too, which I distrust. Must be good to dependants. I am too hurried to spread these notes wider. At anyrate, Mrs W. an American who wishes to work, has been a journalist, is an intellectual, comes into our service tomorrow; being, as it were, Miss Ritchie, or Lyn Eirven. I have to give her orders; & she has to empty the slops. Will it work? will it last? Anyhow—every sentence begins anyhow—an interesting experience.

Monday 16 June

Mrs Walters is now here. And she says "What do you want with a Char?" But then new brooms &c. She is not new in one sense; rather old & lined; no, younger than I am; but a hard face, I think; but I forbear to crack her kernel. The interest will be to get a new light on housekeeping. My books are now my idol. Can I manage on less? How many pints? How many pounds of butter? Oh to be rid of servants—for all the emotions they breed—trust, suspicion, benevolence, gratitude, philanthropy, are necessarily bad.

And Nellie is now deposited on us for a day; turned out of hospital at a moments notice. I am amused to witness the conflict between L. & me. I hold a brief (hiddenly) for Walters; he (hiddenly) for Nelly. If the books are high, he secretly rejoices. If the food is good, I secretly denigrate Nelly's cooking. It is odd how those old scenes rankle in my mind—how unwilling I am to have her back. Partly the silence is so grateful; & partly the absence of lower classes. I think with real shrinking of having her in control again. Yet she is obliging friendly affectionate; & I cannot bring myself to talk to her as I should. I am always seeing myself told to "leave my room".

But enough—a useful phrase.

I dont know why, but I have stinted this book. The summer is in full swing. Its elements this year are Nessa & Duncan, Ethel Smyth, Vita & re-writing The Waves. We are very prosperous. On making up half yearly accounts, we find that we each get £425: & next year is sure, owing

1. Mrs Karl Walter, *née* Margaret Hardy, acted as cook-housekeeper to the Woolfs for six weeks—until they went to Rodmell for the summer.

to the gigantic sale of The Edwardians—it verges on the 20,000. And it is not a very good book. Ethel Smyth drops in; dropped in yesterday for instance, when I was so methodically devoting my morning to finishing the last page of type setting: On Being Ill;[2] I heard a ring, went up, & saw an old char in her white alpaca coat; sat her down; disburdened her of cardboard boxes; full of white pinks; & looked at her rather monumental old colonel's face (girt round with an inappropriate necklace, for she was going to lunch with Beecham.[3]) I get, generally, two letters daily. I daresay the old fires of Sapphism are blazing for the last time. In her heyday she must have been formidable—ruthless, tenacious, exacting, lightning quick, confident; with something of the directness & [single-?] ness of genius, though they say she writes music like an old dryasdust German music master. Her style in writing memoirs though is to her credit—indeed she has ridden post haste through life; & accumulated an astonishing number of observations, with which she qualifies her conversation so as to drive L. almost frantic. One speech of hers lasted 20 minutes unbroken, he says, the other night. We were starting for a picnic at Ken Wood with Nessa & Duncan. Their sublime ineptitude made me laugh & made Ethel laugh & made Eddy peevish. There we sat in the garage, heaving, rotating, stinking. Then we stuck in Gower Street. The night drew on & the wind rose. A spot of rain descended. We heaved our way up to Hampstead. The house was cadaverous; the rhododendrons blanched. Where should we dine? Better go back to Fitzroy St—which we did, & dined off sandwiches & strawberries about 10 o'clock in the highest glee. She is a game old bird—an old age entirely superior in vitality to Margaret's.

[Sunday 6 July]

And to tell the truth in the 15 minutes that remain before I go up to Mrs Walter's cold & exquisite but rather expensive lunch—to tell the truth I am slightly annoyed, both with Margaret & with Mr Birrell. Those were two kind acts of mine: the Women's Guild article & the article on

2. The sales of The Edwardians by Vita Sackville-West published on 29 May 1930 (HP Checklist 235) quite outstripped all expectations; the initial printing had been 3,030; by 19 June it had sold 18,000 copies. A special limited edition of 250 numbered and signed copies of VW's On Being Ill was published in November 1930 (HP Checklist 245).

3. Sir Thomas Beecham, Bt (1879-1961), conductor and impresario, was a staunch champion of Ethel Smyth's music and did much—though never as much as she would have liked—to bring her work before the public.

B.[1] Neither has thanked me. M. sent a postcard. Yet I spent two or even 3 weeks on that Letter; & worked & worked. Never—this is the moral—do a kindness in writing. Never agree to use one's art as an act of friendship. And therefore refuse to write about Maurice Baring, as he wishes.

We came into Ethel's drawing room last Thursday & found a row standing against the window—the D[uche]ss of Sermoneta, M. Baring, & Joyce Wethered.[2] Can I tell the story? I said to Maurice as we plodded after Joyce—Ethel running helter skelter after her great fuzzy dog—I said "This is like a party in literature—like Jane Austen's box hill party." There was a space & a formality & a definiteness about it that made it a real entertainment—with longueurs, with crises, with lapses, with culminations. We all had to wash. We all had to do this, to do that. Ethel's home is better than I expected. She has more beauty & even comfort about than I expected from her alpaca coat. The red & pink roses were thick on the walls. The flowers were lush in the beds. All was glowing & bright. She has white rough cast walls; & no furniture that has cost more than a pound or two—much is old schoolroom furniture endeared to her by her intense egotistic imagination. "It was there I sat, when Mary played the piano . . . And I said Mary couldn't you play G. sharp instead of G. natural . . . Thats the bed—Virginia you will have this room when you come to stay—where Sargent used to sleep, lying across: (because it is an old iron bed). And thats my father & mother—*she* was the artist . . ."[3]

1. In response to the persistence of Miss MacAfee, VW had offered her (*IV VW Letters*, no. 2166) an article based on Augustine Birrell's *Collected Essays* (see above, 18 November 1929, n 5) which was duly published in the June 1930 number of the *Yale Review* (Kp C323). For the Women's Guild article, see above 18 May 1930, n 4.
2. The Woolfs drove to Woking on the afternoon of 3 July for a party at Ethel Smyth's house, Coign (and did not get home until 11.30 p.m.). The Roman Duchess of Sermoneta, *née* Vittoria Colonna (1880-1954), wife of the 15th Duke (who lived in Canada), a lady-in-waiting to the Queen of Italy and an energetic member of international high society, contributed frequent articles to the *Daily Mail*; she was initially an admirer of Mussolini. Joyce Wethered (b. 1901) was British Ladies Open Golf champion in 1922, 1924, 1925 and 1929; she encouraged Ethel's passion for the game.
3. Mary (1857-1933) was the second (Ethel was the third) of the six daughters of Major-General J. H. Smyth, Royal Artillery, and his wife Nina, *née* Struth. Her preference for G natural is recalled in Ethel Smyth's memoirs, *Impressions that Remained* (1919), vol. I, p 83. Mary married Charles E. Hunter (d. 1916), and dissipated his immense fortune on lavish entertainment, on writers, musicians, and painters; she had been a particular friend of the American painter John Singer Sargent (1856-1925), who had achieved a unique position in English society with his portraits of the rich and fashionable.

But I got the impression of a very genuine, breeze blown mind; a free, entirely energised character—no impediments no inhibitions—the freest talk with Maurice. "I met a nephew of yours Ethel, with two names". "Well you might have—with two names". No, I cant give the sense of her largeness, & space & ease & good breeding & character. She is, oddly, much more expert as a hostess than as a guest; doesn't talk too much; is penetrating & quick, & has this delicious ease in summoning, conjuring up, people, like Lady Balfour & Mrs Lyttelton from the neighbourhood.[4] They sat on the sofa while I, sipping champagne, talked fast & furious to Maurice B. who turned lobster colour & trembled, & chattered about his books. There were 5 people who used to help me: all are now dead. He has had his sorrows: I dont know what: loved ladies, I daresay.

[*Monday 21 July*]

And I went down again to Woking on Tuesday (this is written waiting for Vita, on a very wet cold afternoon. She is going to drive us round to look at a wardrobe. I am going to buy a gilt wardrobe I think. Well, it is very wet, & I am rather discomposed, with making 2 articles into one & so on.[5] And I am not dining (here)

Wednesday 23 July

Edith Sitwell has grown very fat, powders herself thickly, gilds her nails with silver paint, wears a turban & looks like an ivory elephant, like the Emperor Heliogabalus.[6] I have never seen such a change. She is mature, majestical. She is monumental. Her fingers are crusted with white coral. She is altogether composed. A great many people were there—& she presided. But though thus composed, her eyes are sidelong & humorous. The old Empress remembers her Scallywag days. We all sat at her feet—cased in slender black slippers, the only remnants of her slipperiness & slenderness. Who was she like? Pope in a nightcap? No; the imperial majesty must be included. We hardly talked together, & I

4. Lady Betty Balfour (1867-1942), whose husband had just succeeded his brother as 2nd Earl of Balfour, lived at Fishers Hill, Woking; Dame Edith Lyttelton, *née* Balfour (d. 1948), was the widow of the Rt. Hon Alfred Lyttelton, PC, MP.
5. VW was converting the two parts of ' "Evelina's" Step Sister' (Kp C324) for publication as a single article in the *TLS* (see above 1 May 1930, n 2).
6. VW went to one of Edith Sitwell's tea-parties at Pembridge Mansions on 22 July. Heliogabalus, real name Varius Avitus, Roman Emperor (AD 218-222); his profligacy was so great as to shock even the Romans.

felt myself gone there rather mistakenly, had she not asked me very affectionately if she might come & see me alone. Her room was crowded with odds & ends of foreigners: the uncrowned King of Barcelona; Gerald's partner; Osbert; Lady Lavery &c.[7] Lady L. discussed the air crash. She said le Bon Dieu had taken them all at the right time. They had all done with life. Once too she would have been glad to die . . . This refers to the deaths of Lord Dufferin Lady Ednam &c.[8] I was driving down to the Temple with Vita, & we bought a Standard in the gateway. 'Titled victims' she said. Well it cant be Harold I said. Then I read out Lady Ednam, Marquis Dusserre (for so they reported him) & then in the stop press Lord Dufferin— What Lady Ednam? Dufferin? she cried. There was Harold on the pavement before their house.[9] "Yes, he said, Its Lady Ednam" "But its Freddy too" cried Vita (no she spoke composedly). God said Harold & read the stop press. Now what are we to do? I cant broadcast said Vita. I must tell my mother said Harold. First I'll get the paper though. Good Lord—Yes its Dufferin & Lady Ednam. "Is that Lady Carnock. Darling I have some bad news for you. Have you seen the paper? Freddy's been in a smash. He's killed, they think. Could you tell Aunt Lal?" What did your mother say Harold? Just 'Oh'. Now we cant dine with Lady Cunard. Oh yes dear we must. Perhaps I shall have to go down & see them— It was, as one says, like a scene in a play. The newspaper: the telephoning. The extreme simplicity & composure of it all: Boski typing; the man cleaning shoes; Harold telephoning, like a man in a play. So they drove off that wet grey evening to Lady Cunard's: dinner at 9. 30 people; & I did not go. (& I hear the whole party waited for me for half an hour)[10]

7. Thomas Balston (1883-1967) was a partner in Duckworth & Co, publishers, from 1921-34. Hazel Lavery (d. 1935), the beautiful Irish-American second wife of the painter Sir John Lavery, was a prominent figure in London society. The 'uncrowned king of Barcelona' was possibly Antonio de Ganderillas (1886-1970), wealthy international man of the world and friend of artists, who was attached to the Chilean Embassy in London.

8. On 21 July a private Junker monoplane flying from Le Touquet to Croydon crashed at Meopham, Kent; the crew of two and the four passengers—the Marquess of Dufferin and Ava, Viscountess Ednam, Sir Edward Ward, and Mrs Hennik Loeffler, wife of a company director of Grosvenor Square—were all killed.

9. Since leaving the Diplomatic Service at the end of 1929 to join the *Evening Standard*, Harold Nicolson had rented a flat at 4 King's Bench Walk, Inner Temple. Lady Carnock was his mother.

10. '. . . to dinner at Lady Cunard's. A very large party. Some of the young women did not see fit to turn up so that I found myself with an empty chair on one side . . .' (see *The Diaries of Evelyn Waugh*, edited by Michael Davie, 1976, p 323, 21 July 1930).

Saturday 26 July

Just back from a night at Long Barn, where I retrieved that fact about Emerald's party, waiting half an hour, all in the sulks too for the smash of their best friends. And Lady E. & Mrs S. strewed Kent with £62,000 worth of jewels.[11] Jewels in their hats, round their necks: somehow this makes me less sorry for them; undemocratic though I am. I rather like thinking of pearls pendant from oak trees.

I have 15—no 12—minutes before lunch; & am all of a quiver with home coming to L., to 2 newts in the bathroom, Letters (from Ethel, & flowers) books &c. A very nice homecoming; & I daresay a sample of my life, picked out of the mass (as it is, when one comes back) makes me a little amazed at my own happiness. I daresay few women are happier—not that I am consistently anything; but feel that I have had a good draught of human life, & find much champagne in it. It has not been dull—my marriage; not at all.

I liked rambling over Vita's new fields,[12] & talking to Mrs Page about the haycrop; & then champagne for dinner—an extravagance of Harold's; sleep in the sitting room; a log fire; dogs; aeroplanes at night; dogs again; & breakfast in bed—mushroom & peach & hot bath, & so home, as I say, to the newts & Leonard. Clive will come to tea. Perhaps we may go to the play.[13] And perhaps I might decide to have a new educated woman as servant. This comes on top of a day of Nelly Lottie & Mrs Mansfield. Their jokes their presence their familiarity, wh. rouse the usual reflections.

Passing the public House this Sunday afternoon, the buzz of voices through the door was exactly the same as at an evening party. My first thought was censorious: people in public houses. But this was soon corrected. I dont see much difference between the Marchmont Arms & Argyle [Argyll] House; or 3 Albert Road if it comes to that; except that we drink champagne & wear satin, & I sit between Lord Gage & Bernstorf.[14]

11. VW has definitely, if mistakenly, written *Mrs S* in place of *Mrs L*.
12. In March, before she had seen Sissinghurst, Vita had bought four fields at Long Barn.
13. The Woolfs went with Vanessa and Quentin Bell to a production of *The Importance of Being Earnest* at the Lyric Theatre, Hammersmith, on 28 July. John Gielgud took the part of John Worthing.
14. Albrecht Bernstorff (1890-1945), diplomatist, was on the staff of the German Embassy in London from 1922 to 1933, when he was recalled, and later murdered, by the Nazis.

Monday 28 July

A queer inconclusive but possibly fruitful conversation with Mrs Walter this morning. I think she would like to stay, if we could offer more wages. The truth is her husband has mistresses; or flirts. And she wishes to devote herself to us entirely—to do everything—that I should never have to order coffee. But she is going to think it out in August in Italy with Karl. I rather suspect (in my private mind) that we shall make a break here with Nelly, & take her—a great risk; rather fun: I feel 10 years younger instantly at the thought of a change. Anyhow, my constant relief at the absence of Nelly seems to prove that the system is as wrong as I've always said. Rooms empty of servants; to sit quietly; to have no jag [?], no unreal condescending talk. Other drawbacks suggest themselves —still anything for experiment—anything.

The Woolfs went to Rodmell for their summer break on 21 July.

Wednesday 6 August

This is written at Rodmell; oh yes, & it is the best, the freest, the comfortablest summer we have ever had. Figure to yourself feet swollen in boots. One takes them off—that is my state without poor dear Nelly; with nice bright Annie. The rain pelts—look at it (as the people in The Waves are always saying) now. My dinner is cooking. I have so many rooms to sit in, I scarcely know which to choose. And new chairs. And comfort everywhere, & some beginnings of beauty. But it is the freedom from servants that is the groundwork & bedrock of all this expansion. After lunch we are alone till Breakfast. I say, as I walk the downs, never again never again. Cost what it may, I will never put my head into that noose again.

I walk; I read; I write, without terrors & constrictions. I make bread. I cook mushrooms. I wander in & out of the kitchen. I have a resource besides reading. Why we ever suffered that discomfort so long, that presence always grumbling, always anyhow (for thats unfair) at a different angle from ours, needing gramo [*text ends*]

Wednesday 20 August

Last night was Quentin's birthday. "Another Quentin birthday over" said Maynard, at the gate after the fireworks, counting perhaps the remaining years. The rockets went roaring up & scattered their gold grain. That is an old phrase; but I always think of grain when I see them.

I can never find another. The willows were lit grey over the pond. The bonfire was forked, like branches in a wind. Nessa, in red, threw on a screen. Angelica, whirring & twirling like an old screaming witch, danced round it. "Childhood—true childhood" said Lydia. For some minutes everything that was said had the quality of sayings in a Tchekhov play.

I am writing while my potatoes boil. It has been a hot heavy ugly crusty[?] day; still, sulphurous; & the dogs have barked all round the village, one starting another. And the men have hammered on the spire. And I have been driven out & in. I have slept here, over an article by Vernon Lee, sent me in Ethel's daily letter. Ethel's letters are daily: for we have so much to make up. Time is short. "I would like to see Italy before I die" she says in todays letter. Should I curtail her & curb them? I think not. If one adventures, adventure wholly. And she is so courageous, remarkable shrewd, that it would be mere poltroonery for me to hold off for fear of ridicule (still they hammer, at 6.45.) So I let that old bonfire rage red & perhaps throw a screen on it. It is a very happy free, & indeed to me occasionally sublime summer. Yes, I think I have decided against Nelly: but dont let me rub that sore. I think I am on the back of The Waves now. Then my walks. How lovely it was exploring yesterday to the Hump! How strange that in almost 20 years I have never been that way—out along the marsh road beyond Sutton house. I see a line I might make to Lewes. I fell in & twisted my ankle. I saw an astonishing assortment of cones & angles of grey & gold down, back against back. I was very happy. I like the still, the profound slow happiness best. One day I walked to Firle, in a shower & found a 4 bladed pocket knife.

The Waves is I think resolving itself (I am at page 100) into a series of dramatic soliloquies. The thing is to keep them running homogeneously in & out, in the rhythm of the waves. Can they be read consecutively? I know nothing about that. I think this is the greatest opportunity I have yet been able to give myself: therefore I suppose the most complete failure. Yet I respect myself for writing this book. Yes—even though it exhibits my congenital faults.

Janet Vaughan is engaged, & Gerald Brenan married.[1]

Barbara [Bagenal] last night was aged, out of her element, peevish, & very red & beaky.

Julian silent. Clive undoubtedly on a fresh tack which does not allow of intimacy with me. I make these notes waiting in vain for that very

1. Janet Vaughan's engagement to David Gourlay was announced in *The Times* on 13 August 1930. Gerald Brenan and Gamel (Elizabeth Gammell) Woolsey (1899-1968), an American poetess, were ostensibly but not legally married from August 1930. See Gerald Brenan, *Personal Record, 1920-72* (1974), pp 220-29.

interesting remark to occur wh. was on the tip of my tongue; & will not now emerge, though I bait & wait. If one writes little notes, suddenly one thinks of something profound. I am reading Dante, & I say, yes, this makes all writing unnecessary. This surpasses 'writing' as I say about Shre. I read the Inferno for half an hour at the end of my own page: & that is the place of honour; that is to put the page into the furnace—if I have a furnace. Now to mash the potatoes. & L. has laid my carpet.

Monday 25 August

Ethel came for a night on Friday, & in order to drown Percy's mowing I will write here; for the friction of writing is a protection; & the dogs & the spire have been bad today. But they are bad because I am re-writing Hazlitt; having stopped The Waves at the break; & I am happy; & it is a very hot day; & we have been into Lewes, & I walked home part of the way. This is the only really hot day we have had. But I wish if I can to describe Ethel. At least let me pelt in a few notes of this curious unnatural friendship. I say unnatural because she is so old, & everything is incongruous. Her head is an enormous size over the temples. Music is there, she said, tapping her temples. That way lies insanity. What Walter said; what Wach (or someone) said—she cannot refrain from repeating what I guess to be very worn compliments, often repeated to herself at dead of night.[2] For she cannot get over unfortunately her own ill-treatment. A refrain occurs; & it is all the more marked for being in contrast with the generosity, sense, balance, & shrewdness of all else. Off her own music, & the conspiracy against her—for the Press are determined to burke her, though she fills every hall—thats the line of it—she is an admirable guest. Oh yes & more. I went through some odd vicissitudes, in the way of emotion. Lying in my chair in the firelight she looked 18; she looked a young vigorous handsome woman. Suddenly this vanishes; then there is the old crag that has been beaten on by the waves: the humane battered face that makes one respect human nature: or rather feel that it is indomitable & persistent. Then, she is worldly; by which I mean something I like; unembarrassed, aired, sunned, acquainted with this way of life & that; lived in many societies; taken her own way in shirt & tie vigorously unimpeded; then I am conscious, I suppose, of the compliment she pays me. But then she is over 70. And (oh the dogs—oh Percy!—& I had

2. The conductor Bruno Walter (1878-1962) was a loyal admirer of Ethel Smyth's music; the Prussian Adolf Wach (d. 1926), Professor of Jurisprudence at Leipzig University, and his wife Lili, who was Mendelssohn's daughter, were close friends from her student days in Germany.

marked off such a lovely evening—what am I to do?) She is sometimes
startlingly quick. She has a lightning speed of perception which I liken to
my own. But she is more robust; better grounded on fact than I am. She
takes in a situation in one word. I told her about Margaret & my difficulties with the paper. No woman of 30 could have seen so swiftly or put
the matter more succinctly in a nutshell. (her fault as a talker is diffusity).
I had some interesting moments. About jealousy for instance. "D'you
know Virginia, I dont like other women being fond of you." "Then you
must be in love with me Ethel". "I have never loved anyone so much" (Is
there something senile in this? I dont know). "Ever since I saw you I
have thought of nothing else &c. I had not meant to tell you." But I want
affection. "You may take advantage of this". No. Well, this, so far as I can
boil it down, is Ethel's state. But what I like in her is not I think her love
for how difficult it is to make that intelligible—it is compact of so many
things—she exaggerates—I am sensitive to exaggeration—what I like is
the indomitable old crag; & a certain smile, very wide & benignant. But
dear me I am not in love with Ethel. And oh yes—her experience.

Thursday 28 August

It is the hottest day of the year: & so it was last year, almost on this day;
& I was at Long Barn, & there was the Eton tutor, a nice young man with
blue eyes white teeth & straight nose—& he now lies at the bottom of a
crevasse in Switzerland—this very hot evening—lies crushed beside his
Mary Irving: there are the two bodies for ever. I suppose some ice drips,
or shifts: the light is blue, green; or wholly black; nothing stirs round
them. Frozen, near together, in their tweeds & hobnail boots there they
lie.[3] And I am here; writing in my lodge, looking over the harvest fields.

I suppose they felt whirled, like hoops; battered; senseless, after the
first horror of feeling out of control.

A very violent summer.

So I said to Janie Bussy Julian & Quentin on the terrace last Sunday.
The church was finished today & the scaffolding taken down. I am
reading R. Lehmann, with some interest & admiration[4]—she has a clear
hard mind, beating up now & again to poetry; but I am as usual appalled
by the machinery of fiction: its much work for little result. Yet I see no
other outlet for her gifts. And these books dont matter—they flash a clear

3. Vincent O'Connor, the junior classical master at Eton who had tutored the
Nicolson boys the previous summer, and his fiancée Mary Irving died in a climbing
accident in the Swiss Alps on 21 August.
4. *A Note in Music* (1930), Rosamund Lehmann's second novel.

light here & there; but I suppose no more. But she has all the gifts (I suppose) that I lack; can give story & development & character & so on.

Annie offered me a paper weight of Strahn [? *Strachan*] in Scotland today in return for our paying her oculists bill.

Tuesday 2 September

I was walking down the path with Lydia. If this dont stop, I said, referring to the bitter taste in my mouth & the pressure like a wire cage of sound over my head, then I am ill: yes, very likely I am destroyed, diseased, dead. Damn it! Here I fell down—saying "How strange—flowers". In scraps I felt & knew myself carried into the sitting room by Maynard, saw L. look very frightened; said I will go upstairs; the drumming of my heart, the pain, the effort got violent at the doorstep; overcame me; like gas; I was unconscious; then the wall & the picture returned to my eyes; I saw life again. Strange I said, & so lay, gradually recovering till 11 when I crept up to bed. Today, Tuesday, I am in the lodge & Ethel comes—valiant old woman!

But this brush with death was instructive & odd. Had I woken in the divine presence it wd. have been with fists clenched & fury on my lips. "I dont want to come here at all!" So I should have exclaimed. I wonder if this is the general state of people who die violently. If so figure the condition of Heaven after a battle.

I think one might write a fantasia called Reflections on the sight of a daddy long legs. There was one just now (I have moved in from the lodge, thus disturbing both L. & Annie) crawling over the handmade paper on wh. I have to sign my name 600 times.[1] This bright sunny patch was his only pleasure. Yes, & then one dislikes daddies because they eat one's plants. One has some kindness for their very few pleasures. What is one's relation to insects?

It suddenly comes over me how I used to hook a piece of paper to me out of the nurse's eye in other illnesses—what a tremendous desire to write I had.

I will use these last pages to sum up our circumstances. A map of the world.

Leaving out the subject of Nelly, which bores me, we are now much freer & richer than we have ever been. For years I never had a pound

1. An exaggeration: the edition of *On Being Ill*, typeset by VW herself, was limited to 250 copies (Kp A14). See above, 16 June 1930.

extra; a comfortable bed, or a chair that did not want stuffing. This morning Hammond [*Lewes furnishers*] delivered 4 perfectly comfortable arm chairs—& we think very little of it.

I seldom see Lytton; that is true. The reason is that we dont fit in, I imagine, to his parties nor he to ours; but that if we can meet in solitude, all goes as usual. Yet what do one's friends mean to one, if one only sees them 8 times a year? Morgan I keep up with in our chronically spasmodic way. We are all very much aware of life, & seldom do anything we do not want to. My Bell family relations are young, fertile & intimate. Julian & Quentin change so much. This year Q. is shabby easy natural & gifted; last year he was foppish, finicky & affected. Julian is publishing with Chatto & Windus.[2] As for Nessa & Duncan I am persuaded that nothing can be now destructive of that easy relationship, because it is based on Bohemianism. My bent that way increases—in spite of the prodigious fame (it has faded out since July 15th: I am going through a phase of obscurity; I am not a writer: I am nothing: but I am quite content) I am more & more attracted by looseness, freedom, & eating one's dinner off a table anywhere, having cooked it previously. This rhythm (I say I am writing The Waves to a rhythm not to a plot[3]) is in harmony with the painters'. Ease & shabbiness & content therefore are all ensured. Adrian I never see. I keep constant with Maynard. I never see Saxon. I am slightly repelled by his lack of generosity; yet would like to write to him. Perhaps I will. George Duckworth, feeling the grave gape, wishes to lunch with Nessa; wishes to feel again the old sentimental emotions. After all, Nessa & I are his only women relations. A queer cawing of homing rooks this is. I daresay the delights of snobbishness somewhat fail in later life—& we have done—'made good'—that is his expression.

My map of the world lacks rotundity. There is Vita. Yes—She was here the other day, after her Italian tour, with 2 boys; a dusty car, sand-shoes & Florentine candlepieces, novels & so on tumbling about on the seats. I use my friends rather as giglamps: Theres another field I see: by your light. Over there's a hill. I widen my landscape.

Diary XX. The first page is inscribed:

September 8th 1930

Monks House

Rodmell

2. *Winter Movement* was published in October 1930.
3. Cf *IV VW Letters*, no. 2224 of 28 August to Ethel Smyth.

Monday 8 September

I will signalise my return to life—that is writing—by beginning a new book, & it happens to be Thoby's birthday, I remark. He would have been, I think, 50 today.

After coming out here I had the usual—oh how usual—headache; & lay, like a fibre of tired muscle on my bed in the sitting room, till yesterday. Now up again & on again; with one new picture in my mind; my defiance of death in the garden.

But the sentence with which this book was to open ran "Nobody has ever worked so hard as I do"—exclaimed in driving a paper fastener through the 14 pages of my Hazlitt just now. Time was when I dashed off these things all in the days work. Now, partly because I must do them for America & make arrangements far ahead, I spend I daresay a ridiculous amount of time, more of trouble on them. I began reading Hazlitt in January I think. And I am not sure that I have speared that little eel in the middle—that marrow—which is one's object in criticism. A very difficult business no doubt to find it, in all these essays; so many; so short; & on all subjects. Never mind; it shall go today; & my appetite for criticism is, oddly, whettened. I have some gift that way, were it not for the grind & the screw & the torture—

Vita comes tomorrow; we go to Sissinghurst on Wednesday; I shall attack The Waves on Thursday. So this illness has meant two weeks break—but as I often think, seasons of silence, & brooding, & making up much more than one can use, are fertilising. I was raking my brain too hard.

Anyhow, this is the happiest summer since we had Monks House; the most satisfactory. We hope on Percy's evidence—P. was tidying old Hawkesworth's grave—that the Byng Stamper farm has been bought by a horsebreeder, & all the land is to be under grass—not bungalows. And Annie surprises one daily with her amenity, dexterity & sympathy—the most convincing argument in favour of living out that I know. Yesterday I sent an advertisement to Time & Tide—but hush! Profound secrecy is essential.[4] The weather is September weather, bright, sunny, cool. We have a project of making my bedroom the sitting room—for the view. To let it waste, day after day, seems a crime: elderly eyes cannot waste. No, I would like to have another life, & live it in action. So I thought.

4. *Time and Tide*, 13 September 1930: 'Woman of intelligence and initiative wanted to do entire work of flat, WC1, for two writers. Live out. Good cooking essential. Might suit two friends half-day each. Wages by arrangement. Long summer holidays, also at Easter and Christmas. Box 8415.'

looking at Caburn, & imagining the feelings of a strong young man, who was walking up it, with wife & children, & a career in the City . . . I think. No he was a politician; & I think he was also an Indian civil servant. He was not a writer: These are the stories one invents. And this: "At the age of 50 Priestley will be saying "Why don't the highbrows admire me? It isn't true that I only write for money." He will be enormously rich; but there will be that thorn in his shoe—or so I hope. Yet I have not read, & I daresay shall never read, a book by Priestley. And I (to solace myself) get a letter from a Mr Spender saying he cares for my praise more than for that of any critic—& he sends me his poems.[5] And I invent this phrase for Bennett & Priestley "the tradesmen of letters".

Wednesday 24 September[6]

I have taken up my staff again; I wish I could say that my book was my staff; but oh dear, how many people I have seen—dashing that support from my hand! It must have been the afternoon I wrote this—yes, because L. & Percy were in the middle of moving the furniture into the sitting room—that Mary & Barbara [Hutchinson]'s little medicine bottle heads appeared at the window. How I scowled! And then there was Alice Ritchie, then the Wolves, then Morgan, then a party at Charleston then London, & then those curious women, Miss Ibbotson & Mrs Starr.[7]

"I am a cousin of Florence Nightingale" said Mrs Starr. When I said I was also related, her rather shifty eyes became shiftier. "I cant make

5. J. B. Priestley (b. 1894), whose best-selling books *The Good Companions* and *Angel Pavement* were published in 1929 and 1930 respectively. Stephen Spender (b. 1909) had recently left Oxford, where his passion for poetry and his ambition to be a poet had intensified. (See his autobiography, *World Within World*, 1951.)

6. The following calculation appears on the opposite page:

280	
120	(the length of
116	the Waves at this
280	moment—a 3rd
29,160	done, I suppose)

7. LW's mother, his sister Bella and her husband Thomas Southorn, on leave from Hong Kong, came to tea at Monks House on 12th (and again, with Harold Woolf, on 26th) September; Alice Ritchie came for the night on 17 September; E. M. Forster for the weekend of 20-22 September. On 23rd the Woolfs drove to London for the day to interview applicants who had responded to VW's advertisement in *Time and Tide* (see above, 8 September, n 4)—Miss Ibbotson, Mrs Starr, and Miss Rivett-Carnac. On 25th Ka Arnold-Forster came to lunch at Monks House, and Dorothy Bussy with her niece and nephew, Ellie and Dick Rendel, to tea.

omelettes" said Miss Ibbotson, addressing herself plaintively & at the same time peevishly to Mrs Starr. "It would be a great disaster of course if you sent in your dishes all burnt" said Mrs Starr. "You would give me notice, I suppose" said Miss Ibbotson. Miss Ibbotson was bankrupt; "Beggars can't be choosers" she said, "& so thats why I'm back again at *this*". Miss Ibbotson had once owned two motor cars & driven them for hire in London, but competition with the men had been too much. She had also been ill. She was skinny, raddled; wore a small corduroy jacket, & a rather dirty white shirt; had a red pocket-handkerchief; thick mended stockings & thick shoes. Mrs Starr was dressed in blue Liberty silk & a straw hat. She reproved Miss I. for being too diffident. "If I could have a trial" Miss I. repeated. But you will soon pick it up" said Mrs S. "I cant do fancy cooking" said Miss I. "And I would like to do some of the cleaning." "I shall do the cleaning" said Mrs S. "& you will do the kitchen." These remarks were shot at each other, & plainly represented much previous argument, though why Mrs S., so compact, if sly, had come into touch with Miss I., so wild, with her staring blue eyes & her wideawake, I could not say. An indefinable aroma of sordidity, instability, shadiness, shiftiness pervaded them. They were sure, I think almost at once, that we had seen through them, & that the place was not for them. "We live on Salads" said Mrs S. "though I am not a vegetarian." Sure enough the brown holland bag which they left behind them contained a number of lettuces wrapped in paper.

Miss Rivett-Carnac is the scion of a great Indian family who let her live in Wimbledon with her mother on a pound a week.[8] She has been through a good deal: social work; hostels; running clubs. She is about 35; a perfect lady, enough to be careless of being one; only anxious for shelter, & wages, & a little time to herself. She might do—she might be a superior Walter. She has, oh dear, suffered much. And is perhaps, vengeful, acid, worn, trusty, starved of happiness.

Could anything be done to make us less popular? we ask. For instance if I pied Leonard's hair—would that make his mother, Bella, Tom [Southorn], Harold [Woolf], Dorothy Bussy, Ellie Rendel & Ka Cox refuse to invite themselves to see us?

When I offered Miss Rivett-Carnac £50 yesterday it seemed to me nothing, because I was thinking that I can make that by writing 2,000 words. But 5 years ago, £50 was a substantial sum. How money has

8. The Rivett-Carnacs were an old Derbyshire family, a great number of whose sons served in the army or civil administration in India. VW engaged Miss Rivett-Carnac as a temporary replacement for the still convalescent Nelly; she came to Tavistock Square on 13 October and stayed until Christmas.

shrunk in my mind! This is one of the most curious things in my existence
—the shrinkage of money.

A perfect September day, after some very imperfect November days;
the swallows skimming the terrace; Percy asking if it will be fine tomorrow;
if so, he will mow the lawn. The bees are suspected to have been busy. In
that case we shall take honey tonight. L. & P. spent the afternoon—
Trim & Uncle Toby—mending the fence;[9] I spent it walking the downs.
I still have in spite of building a perfect stretch, & by juggling a little,
can convert distant houses into haystacks.

I am reading Dante; & my present view of reading is to elongate
immensely. I take a week over one canto. No hurry.

Our friends work us very hard. Heres Tom Eliot: when are you back?
Here's Miss Bartlett [unidentified], may we come to tea. Heres— & my
two months' respite nibbled at by all who choose. I think I will spend
August next year in Northumberland.

Monday 29 September

So all those days were completely ruined by the assiduity of our friends.
When one has to tidy the table, pick fresh flowers, collect chairs & be
ready, at 4, or at one, to welcome, & all the rest of it the circumjacent
parts of the day are ruined. On the whole L.'s family do the trick most
thoroughly. Everything is such an effort; so unreal; what I say is so
remote from what I feel; their standards are so different from mine; I
strain myself perpetually with trying to provide the right cakes, the right
jokes, the right affection & inquiries. Naturally it often goes wrong, as on
Friday. Harold, who is to me the most sympathetic of them, told a story
of the Woolf temper; how Philip had broken down the servants bedroom
door in a rage, because they had put a bottle, unfastened, into Bab's bed,
& refused to come & make it. Mrs W. who is the vainest of women (poor
old lady—yes, ones feeling of poor old woman churns[?] & muddles all
one's feelings of her egotism, her vanity) took this as a slur upon herself;
& began querulously & peevishly to defend her methods of education, &
to pay herself the usual compliments upon her wonderful management of
so many fatherless & penniless children. And then of course she requires
to have these praises corroborated, & will not be satisfied until I have also
wondered & exclaimed at her amazing unselfishness & courage & agreed
that the Woolf temper is merely a proof of their intelligence. Here of
course, I begin to see very plainly how ugly, how nosey, how irreparably
middle class they all are. Indeed, my aesthetic sense is the one that protests

9. See Sterne's Tristram Shandy.

most obstinately—how they cheapen the house & garden— How they bring in an atmosphere of Earls Court & hotels, how impossibly out of place, & stuffy & towny & dressy & dowdy they look on the terrace, among apple trees & vegetables & flowers! But there I am pinned down, as firmly as Prometheus on his rock, to have my day, Friday 26th of September 1930, picked to pieces, & made cheap & ugly & commonplace; for the sting of it is that there is no possible escape—no escape that wont make old Mrs Woolf begin to dab her eyes & feel that she is not being welcomed—she who is so "painfully sensitive"—so fond of cakes, so incapable of amusing herself, so entirely without any interest in my feelings or friends; so vampire like & vast in her demand for my entire attention & sympathy, while she sits over the fire, in her dreary furs & ugly bonnet & large boots, with her pendulous cheeks & red nose & cheap earrings, talking about Worthing & the charms of Dr Watson & the niceness of everybody, & how she will come to Worthing every year, & will expect to come to tea with us. Lord Lord! how many daughters have been murdered by women like this! What a net of falsity they spread over life. How it rots beneath their sweetness—goes brown & soft like a bad pear!

At the same time I cannot make out a case for myself as a maltreated person. No, because I have an interest beyond my own nose. But let me note that old age can only be made tolerable by having a firm anchor outside gossip, cakes, & sympathy. Think of imposing even one afternoon of such a burden upon Quentin Julian & Angelica! I shall spend my day at the British Museum. (This is one of those visual images, without meaning when written down, that conveys a whole state of mind to me)

Rodmell is full of incident, drama, &, sometimes I think, coming home over the flats, of beauty & solemnity. Mr Fears the epileptic died on Thursday. He had been locked in his room for weeks; but escaped, made off to Southease, & called on the Thomases to present his grievance to the Rector.[10] One of his grievances was that Mrs Dedman had stolen part of his garden—& it is said—& I can believe it—that this was no figment. There she stands in the street, ominous, glum, predatory, grasping, complaining. Then a doctor taps at the window: someone has been taken ill in the street & carried into a cottage. It was the mother of Miss Emery the dog breeder.[11] She now lies dying perhaps, & her husband must be taken for a motor drive while they are burying Mr Fears to distract him

10. The Rev. Walter Webb Thomas, Rector of Southease since 1904. For a description of this eccentric clergyman see *III LW*, pp 66-7.
11. Miss Emery was now the Woolfs immediate neighbour at Charnes Cottage.

from the thought of death. It is the most miserable of days, cold & drizzling, the leaves falling; the apples fallen; the flowers sodden; mist hiding Caburn. Yet I have written well, & cannot make out a case for myself as a maltreated person.

The great game of diplomacy is begun with Nelly. I have told Dr McGlashan that we will pay her wages, but not have her back till she is well.[12]

The Woolfs went to Charleston on 1st October whither, at his suggestion, George Duckworth brought his wife and one son to a family luncheon party. On 4th October the Woolfs returned to Tavistock Square.

Saturday 11 October

The fifty coffins have just trundled by, in lorries, spread rather skimpily with Union Jacks—an unbecoming pall—& stuck about with red & yellow wreaths. The only impressive sight was the rhythmical bending backward slow march of the Guards: for the rest, the human face is often pock marked & ignoble; poor gunners[?] look bored & twitch their noses; the crowd smells; the sun makes it all too like birthday cakes & crackers; & the coffins conceal too much. One bone, one charred hand, wd. have done what no ceremony can do: & the heap of a ceremony on ones little coal of feeling presses uneasily. I refer to the burial this morning of the 48 'heroes' of the R101.[1] But why 'heroes'? A shifty & unpleasant man, Lord Thomson by all accounts, goes for a joy ride with other notables, & has the misfortune to be burnt at Beauvais. That being so, we have every reason to say Good God how very painful—how very unlucky—but why all the shops in Oxford St & Southampton Row shd. display black dresses only & run up black bars; why the Nation should be requested to think of nothing else; why the people should line the streets & parade through Westminster Hall, why every paper should be filled

12. Nelly was staying with her relations at Peaslake, Shamley Green, Surrey, while recuperating from her operation; Dr Alan McGlashan was her doctor there.

1. The experimental flight of the R101 from Britain to India ended in disaster when the airship crashed near Beauvais in the early hours of Sunday 5 October. Of the 54 passengers 48 were killed, among them the Secretary of State for Air, Lord Thomson of Cardington. On the day of burial at Cardington churchyard crowds lined the route taken by the funeral procession from Westminster Hall, where the coffins had lain, to Euston. In addition to this show of public mourning there had been a memorial service at St Paul's on 10 October attended by heads of state, ministers and ambassadors.

with nobility & lamentation & praise, why the Germans should muffle their wireless & the French ordain a day of mourning & the footballers stop for two minutes' silence—beats me & Leonard & Miss Strachan.[2]

Wednesday 15 October

I say to myself "But I cannot write another word". I say "I will cut adrift—I will go to Roger in France—I will sit on pavements & drink coffee—I will see the Southern hills; I will dream; I will take my mind out of its iron cage & let it swim—this fine October". I say all this; with energy: but shall I do it? Shant I peter out here, till the fountain fills again? Oh dear oh dear—for the lassitude of the spirit! Rarely rarely comest thou now, spirit of delight. You hide yourself up there behind the hotel windows & the grey clouds. (I am writing this with a steel pen which I dip in the ink, so as to forestall the day when my German pens are extinct). It is dismal to broach October so languidly. I rather think the same thing happened last year. I need solitude. I need space. I need air. I need the empty fields round me; & my legs pounding along roads; & sleep; & animal existence. My brain is too energetic; it works; it throws off an article on Christina Rossetti; & girds itself up to deal with this & that.

Rivett is installed. And she cooks like a freehanded lady. Light sketchy dishes arrive. This is only our second day, & Annie, infinitely happy garrulous & anxious to stay—how can I put up with Rodmell now, she says. I shall feel shut up inside something—Annie goes today. A curious little interlude this. Alas, one day last week Nelly appeared—of course on her best behaviour—very much the old & trusted servant, with, I think, a dash of suspicion. Why did I not have her back & give her help, seeing that she had been with us 15 years?—that I think was in her mind. But we kept it down; & she is off to Colchester for 10 days & then—oh dear, I say again, oh dear. Nessa & Duncan are at Cassis, which brings the delicious vision of France too near me—Oh to walk among vineyards I cry again. And lots of people are on the buzz: dined last night with Raymond, a shabby & diminished Raymond, whom I like better than the dashing. Not much wine & so on. He has given up parties & takes Wyndham Lewis much to heart "A middle aged man-milliner" said Lewis in that pamphlet which is like the gossip & spite & bickering of a

2. Miss Strachan was one of the clerks at the Hogarth Press. The following page—that between the entries for 11 and 15 October—is given up to part of a draft of 'I am Christina Rossetti' (Kp C328) which VW has crossed through, noting in the margin: 'Written here by mistake'.

suburban housemaid who has been given notice & is getting a bit of her own back.[3]

Saturday 18 October

But behold, I think the spirit of delight is hovering over me, after 2 days at Rodmell, in spite of Ethel Smyth, in spite of Emmie Fisher.[4] Two teasing & tormenting letters from them were, of course, forwarded. But we walked to Lewes over the fields—yes, reached our goal, came out under that tunnel; now I have planned this walk for almost 20 years & never taken it. Home now, & find another letter, shaken & remorseful from Ethel, & Tom's new edition of Johnson,[5] & ever so many flowers.

Wednesday 22 October

Just back from headache cheating—there should be a name for these peregrinations—at Hampton Court. My misery at the sere & yellow leaves,[6] & the ships coming in & I not there & I not there—drove me to take a day off; indeed to plan 2 days off; but no: it rains now; & I'm for the fire.

My misery is Leonard's. Rivett cant cook. Poor woman! Bowed down with a sense of the failure of her life, creeping broken winged, arid, deprecatory, diffident, she sends in meagre savourless dishes & attempts nervous combinations of tapioca & orange. No, no: go she must. And then I think Annie—for ever. But the misery of these trifles can be devastating. Brown sole, brown sauce, & nothing else. And when I make a joke she laughs, as she laughed once in some tennis court to some subaltern I imagine, vainly. She is inve[r]tebrate; crushed; & what, I ask, is to become of her? And how am I to detach her seaweed clinging from my kitchen? For naturally this was a chance, a new start for her; something

3. Wyndham Lewis's satire *The Apes of God* had been published by him in a limited edition in June 1930; Mortimer reviewed it under the heading 'Mr Gossip' in the *N & A* of 12 July. A favourable review by Roy Campbell had been rejected by the incoming editor of the *New Statesman*, upon which, in September, Lewis brought out a pamphlet entitled *Satire & Fiction* incorporating Campbell's review, laudatory letters of support, and fighting comments by Lewis himself.

4. Emmeline (1868-1941) was the fourth of VW's eleven Fisher cousins; in 1915 she had married the musician R. O. Morris. VW did not preserve her letter, and the nature of the tease and torment is unknown.

5. T. S. Eliot had written an introductory essay to a reprint of *London: A Poem/ and/ The Vanity of Human Wishes/ by Samuel Johnson Ll.D*, produced in a limited edition, Autumn 1930 (see Gallup, *T. S. Eliot: A Bibliography*, 1969, B15).

6. 'my way of life/ is fall'n into the sear, the yellow leaf;' *Macbeth* V iii.

untried. And when I say No you can't cook, she will see her hope go bang like a rabbit in a shooting gallery. And I detest these dislodgments. Nelly again yesterday: apprehensive & suspicious; though I think not shaken seriously in her belief that she will come back to her [*sic*]. Thank the Lord, it rains, & I can bring myself to heel easily now. Winter has set in; draw the curtains; light the fire; & so to work.

Thursday 23 October

Behold, the rather familiar experiment—a new pen, new ink. "I'm afraid ma'am", said the youth at Partridge & Cooper's, "that the Penkala's are extinct." A voice on the telephone had spoken their doom. I went along Faringdon market this afternoon looking for the man with the barrow. I saw the grey towers of, I suppose, Smithfield. I almost went into St Paul's & saw Dr Donne, now uncovered again;[7] but being as I say to myself, pressed for time, I walked on, down the Strand.

Ethel came in yesterday evening; rather battered in an old moleskin coat; in the triangular hat which the hotel proprietor at Bath has made into its shape with a few pins. Well, I begin to make note of her, because, among other things—how many others—she said would I like her to leave me some of her letters—the Maggie Benson & Mrs Benson & Lady Ponsonby letters in her will?[8] Would you like me to write something about you? I said. Oh yes; what fun! But I should try some experiments. Oh what fun! How I should enjoy it! But I should get it all wrong. Yes, of course; or tear them up. Do just as you like. H. B.'s letters I'm leaving to Maurice Baring; but he'll do nothing. He'll tear them up.

So I am to some extent Ethel's literary executor, a post I have always vaguely desired; & so I now make a few notes as she talks, for a portrait. One would have to bring out her enormous eagerness. She was telling me how she reads Travel books; & her eyes—her blue, rather prominent eyes, positively glitter. And this is not talk about herself, or her music— simply about how people climb—their adventures. Her cheeks burn too. But she looks now & then aged: she said that she was a very brave woman.

7. Extensive restoration work had just been completed at St Paul's; the monument representing Donne in his shroud by Nicolas Stone, 1631, stands in the south choir aisle.
8. Mary Benson, *née* Sidgwick (1842-1918), wife of an Archbishop of Canterbury; her elder daughter Margaret (1865-1916); and Lady Ponsonby, wife of the private secretary to Queen Victoria and herself a sometime Maid of Honour—three ladies who had been deeply involved in Ethel's tempestuous emotional life and correspondence.

It is a quality I adore. And I have it. One of the bravest things I ever did

This she copied from Mrs Pankhurst

was to tell people my age. My vivacity &c—Everyone thinks I'm 20 or 30 years younger. *Well* —(a characteristic word, indicating what really becomes necessary—a break—a new paragraph—a wedge inserted in the flood) Well—when I wanted people to realise how long I'd waited for recognition—& have never really had it—I did that—though I hated it: I told them my age, so that they couldn't go on saying Oh but she came into her own—she was recognised. This referred I think, but it is difficult to insert one's own wedges, to the Jubilee Concert at Berlin, on which occasion Lady Jones behaved so badly.[9] She was on her way—is now I suppose in the train or on the ship, this cold grey day—to Belfast, to conduct her Sea Songs[10] (one of my best things) & then, directly thats done, back she comes, across the Irish channel, & returns to Woking & goes on writing about H.B.: that looming imponderable figure: who has so queer an existence; for if I ask about him Logan, Ottoline &c. say Oh a petit maitre; a drawing room philosopher; to which Logan adds the son of a dentist, & Ottoline adds, he made love to me, & I found him intolerable. This was the man who dominated Ethel's life, this wraith who wanders about in Logan's & Ethel's lives. What a strange job then to write, as I may one day, the life of a woman whose past is thus nebulous. And I have only come in time to hear about the past. Everything is past. She hopes not to live another seven years; gives me to understand that now that her last barren years have been fructified by knowing me, she can sing her nunc dimittis. Since all the fiery years of desire are over. Yet I doubt if they are quite over. Yet it is a fine spectacle, & a curious one, this old woman summing up her experience & hymning her love for H.B. as a swan song (& people say an ugly song, for they say, her musical genius is another delusion—all her life then has been based on illusions; & that as I perceive when I talk to her is manifestly untrue). I must now write to the living Ethel—so one's perspective shifts.

Monday 27 October

How comfortless & uneasy my room is,—a table all choked with papers. &c. I'm now grinding out Waves again, & have perhaps an hour & a half to spend: a short time on Dante; a short time on MSS: a short time here—

9. Occasion unidentified; Ethel Smyth wrote several autobiographical books: *Impressions that Remained*, 2 vols. 1919; *Streaks of Life*, 1921; *A Final Burning of Boats*, 1928; *As Time Went On*, 1936; *What Happened Next*, 1940.
10. Presumably her 'Three Moods of the Sea', 1913.

with another pen. Yesterday we went to Warlingham & sat in a gravel pit, like a Cezanne. I made this comparison, to appease myself for not being in France. And we walked along a bridle path; & saw old quiet farms, & rabbits, & downs, all preserved as by a magic ring from Croydon. Never was the division between London & country so sharp. Home, & made dinner; & read MSS: But rather casually & unanimously we have decided within the last week to stop the Press. Yes; it is to come to an end. That is we are to go on only with my books & Ls. & Dotty perhaps; & what we print ourselves. In short, we shall revert next October to what we were in the Hogarth House days—an odd reversal, seeing that we are now financially successful. But what's money if you sell freedom? we say. And what's the point of publishing these innocuous novels & pamphlets that are neither good nor bad? So we make this decision, casually, walking round the Square after lunch & thus slip another shackle from our shoulders. This is what I call living with a pilot in the ship—not mere drifting ahead.

Sunday 2 November

And tonight the final letter to Nelly is to be sent; there it rests in my red bag, but I have great reluctance to read it over, as I had to write it. Yet I don't suppose she will mind acutely. For one thing, she has been prepared, I think, by our readiness to do without her; & then since the famous scene last November I think she has been aware of a change. These 5 months at any rate have proved that we are freer, easier & no less comfortable, indeed more comfortable, without her, for all her good humour, sense & niceness; which now that I have written the letter, I see once more in their true proportions. And I am vague & in the air, because I doubt that Annie will come—doubt if she should—wish indeed to have livers out in future. Oh never again to have scenes with servants—that is my ambition. How we used to walk round the Sqre considering Nelly's ultimatums; what hours we have spent & should still spend. No: this is a wholesome break, & takes 10 years off my shoulders. Oh, but I shall have to see her—

[? *Wednesday 5 November*]

These are further notes about Nelly, since it is a queer little bit of life broken off; servant psychology & so on. To my long, explicit & affectionate letter she has returned one word: Dear Mr & Mrs Woolf. Thank you for your cheque: Yrs truly.

But yesterday evening, an embittered, frightened angry voice, this is

Rivett's description, & by the sound she identified Nelly, was heard on the telephone. She asked for me; but I was, happily, out or down here. We conjecture that after launching her snub, she came up to consult Lottie, perhaps see Mrs Hunt, & for some reason they decided upon an interview. I imagine she has now gone back. And the sense of freedom spreads wider & wider. The letter is sent; the shock over. And I come in & find the house empty & silent.

A slight inaccuracy, if applied to the past few days. Ethel Lyn & Hugh Walpole to tea on Monday; Vita Clive & Hilda Matheson to dine; Hugh again later, & his piteous, writhing & wincing & ridiculous & flaying alive story of Willie Maugham's portrait.[1] Indeed it was a clever piece of torture; Hugh palpably exposed as the hypocritical booming thick skinned popular novelist, who lectures on young novelists & makes his own books sell: who is thick fingered & insensitive in every department. But said Hugh, turning round on his bed of thorns again & yet again, & pressing them further & further in, Thats not what I mind so much. What I mind are a few little things—little things Willie & I had together—only he & I knew—those he has put into print. Thats what I cant get over. For instance I cant tell you all the meanings there are to me in his saying I was like a man in love with a duchess—(the meaning is that Hugh is in love with a male opera singer[2]). Would you mind Virginia? (this said past midnight, Vita & I alone) And I said I should. "And he wrote to me & said he could not believe that I could be hurt. He said he had written without a thought of me. But that letter is almost worse than the book."

Clive is home blind of one eye & much in need of society. I thought him, why heaven knows, rather admirable & touching; determined not to be a burden on his friends, yet very grateful for our kindness (& I must ask him to come in tonight). So much instructed somehow in the little graces & also the inevitable lonelinesses, without his Mary, but then I think he has his Joan. And he cant read or write, & has hired a reader. Its the evenings that will be bad he said. Nessa characteristically writes from Cassis that she doesn't think much of it, & supposes that spectacles, 'which we all wear' will put it right.

And Julian's poems are out, & I am relieved—but why, vanity of my own critical powers? jealousy of his fame?—to hear that Vita agrees with me that for all his admirable good sense & observation & love of country life, he is no poet. People who treat words as he does rather afflict me—

1. The character of Alroy Kear in W. Somerset Maugham's novel *Cakes and Ale* was closely based upon that of his old friend Hugh Walpole.
2. This was Lauritz Melchoir (1890-1973), the Danish *Heldentenor*, whom for some years Walpole regarded as his 'perfect friend'.

I say this to discharge me partially of vanity & jealousy. Common sense & Cambridge are not enough, whatever Bunny may say.

Saturday 8 November

I pressed his hand when we said goodbye with some emotion: thinking This is to press a famous hand: It was Yeats, at Ottoline's last night. He was born in 1865 so that he is now a man of 65—& I am 48: & thus he has a right to be so much more vital, supple, high charged & altogether seasoned & generous. I was very much impressed by all this in action. He has grown very thick (Last time I met him—& I may note that he had never heard of me & I was slightly embarrassed by O.'s painstaking efforts to bring me to his notice, was in 1907—or 8 I suppose, at dinner at 46).[3] He is very broad; very thick; like a solid wedge of oak. His face is too fat; but it has its hatchet forehead in profile, under a tangle of grey & brown hair; the eyes are luminous, direct, but obscured under glasses; they have however seen close, the vigilant & yet wondering look of his early portraits. I interrupted a long dream story of de la Mares when I came in: about seeing Napoleon with ruby eyes & so on. Yeats was off, with vehemence even, kindling & stumbling a little, on dreams; those which have colour are rare & mean—I forget what. De la Mare told another very cryptic dream about a book with circles in it; the outermost ring black, the inner blue & so on. Yeats identified this dream at once as the dream of the soul in some particular state—I forget what. Tagore had told him he said that he had dreamed once as a young man; & if he could find the dream again it would become permanent.[4] And so on to dreaming states, & soul states; as others talk of Beaverbrook & free trade—as if matters of common knowledge. So familiar was he, that I perceived that he had worked out a complete psychology, which I could only catch on to momentarily in my alarming ignorance. De la M. had just been to the National Gallery, & had got no pleasure from the pictures. I said this flow & ebb of consciousness made all criticism unstable. He said one must go by the plus's always. Yeats said he could get nothing from Rembrandt, nothing from El Greco. He then explained our pleasure in pictures, or other works of art, by an elaborate metaphor, taken from his psychology; about the sharp edges of things being brought into contact; & the same

3. William Butler Yeats lived to be seventy-three; he died early in 1939. From 1895-1919 he had a London foothold at 18 Woburn Buildings (now Woburn Walk), Bloomsbury. He knew Clive slightly, and must have accepted an invitation to dine with the Bells at 46 Gordon Square early in their married life there.
4. Rabindranath Tagore (1861-1941), the Bengali poet and mystic.

order then coming in our consciousness: & thus our closest contact results from some sudden clicking to of edges, which—I have lost the metaphor now completely. Then, discussing what poems we could come back to unsated, I said Lycidas; De la M. said no. Not Milton for him: he could never recognise his own emotions there. Milton's woodbine was not his woodbine, nor M.'s Eve his Eve. Yeats said he could not get satisfaction from Milton; it was Latinised poetry (as somebody said, Milton had (in some way irreparably) damaged the English language). This attached itself to a cosmology evidently, in which Latins & Romans play their part. And so to modern poetry, & the question of the spade. Yeats said that "we", de la M. & himself, wrote 'thumbnail' poems only because we are at the end of an era. Here was another system of thought, of which I could only snatch fragments. He said that the spade has been embalmed by 30 centuries of association; not so the steam roller. The great age of poetry, Shakespeare's age, was subjective; ours is objective; civilisations end when they become objectified. Poets can only write when they have symbols. And steam rollers are not covered in symbolism —perhaps they may be after 30 generations. He & de la M. can only write small fireside poems. Most of emotion is outside their scope. All left to the novelists I said—but how crude & jaunty my own theories were beside his: indeed I got a tremendous sense of the intricacy of the art; also of its meanings, its seriousness, its importance, which wholly engrosses this large active minded immensely vitalised man. Wherever one cut him, with a little question, he poured, spurted fountains of ideas. And I was impressed by his directness, his terseness. No fluff & dreaminess. Letters he said must be answered. He seemed to live in the centre of an immensely intricate briar bush; from wh. he could issue at any moment; & then withdraw again. And every twig was real to him. He also spoke about the necessity of tragedy. It is necessary to attempt the impossible; but it must be possible. All creation is the result of conflict. James Stephens, some of whose poems he much admires, & I have never read, was so poor as a boy that he used to pick up the bread thrown to the ducks & eat it.[5] There must be tragedy in order to bring out the reverse of the soul. (This belongs to another theory about the soul & its antitype, which I vaguely remember in his poems). He said that Tom very cleverly made use of mythologies, for instance the Fisher King in the Waste Land; & mythologies are necessary. Ezra Pound writes beautifully when he uses them. Then suddenly must speak of—some common object—& at once his

5. James Stephens (1880?-1950), Irish writer, author of *The Crock of Gold* (1912), had been brought up in an orphanage and at times had gone so hungry as to have 'fought with swans for a piece of bread' (*DNB*).

rhythm breaks. I said we did not talk enough, not easily & equally. He told us of men he had met in trains. I liked his transitions to dialect & humour. With men perhaps he might be coarse. He had been staying with Masefield who, to celebrate the 30th year of their friendship, had got young women to recite Yeatses lyrics at Boars Hill. Their voices had been too small for the theatre; but Yeats had been greatly touched.[6] Judith M. is nice & good but not pretty. Hence she will have to marry a man she knows; not at first sight. And Mrs M. seemed simple & he liked her better than usual. Indeed, he seemed very cordial, very generous; having been warmed up by his 65 years; & being in command of all his systems, philosophies, poetics & humanities; not tentative any more. Hence no doubt his urbanity & generosity. Compare him with Tom for instance, who came to tea the day before, & may be, for anything I know, as good a poet. Poor Tom is all suspicion, hesitation & reserve. His face has grown heavier fatter & whiter. There is a leaden sinister look about him. But oh—Vivienne! Was there ever such a torture since life began!—to bear her on ones shoulders, biting, wriggling, raving, scratching, unwholesome, powdered, insane, yet sane to the point of insanity, reading his letters, thrusting herself on us, coming in wavering trembling—Does your dog do that to frighten me? Have you visitors? Yes we have moved again. Tell me, Mrs Woolf, why do we move so often? Is it accident? Thats what I want to know (all this suspiciously, cryptically, taking hidden meanings). Have some honey, made by our bees, I say. Have you any bees? (& as I say it, I know I am awaking suspicion). Not bees. Hornets. But where? Under the bed. And so on, until worn out with half an hour of it, we gladly see them go. Vivienne remarked that I had made a signal that they should go. This bag of ferrets is what Tom wears round his neck.

6. John Masefield (1878-1967), who in May 1930 had been appointed Poet Laureate, had built a small theatre, the Music Room, beside Hill Crest, his home at Boar's Hill, and it was there that the recital attended by Yeats had been given on 5 November. In a letter to his wife, dated 8 November, Yeats wrote of this occasion and of his visit to Lady Ottoline's: 'I had a rather moving experience at Masefield's. At his little theatre he made a long eulogy on my work & myself—very embarrassing—& then five girls with beautiful voices recited my lyrics for three quarters of an hour. I do not think the whole audience could hear but to me it was strangely overwhelming ... Yesterday I met De la Mare & Virginia Wolf [sic] at Lady Ottoline's and here is the upshot of my talks and a metaphor of Lady Ottoline's

> We that had such thought;
> That such deeds have done,
> Must ramble on—thinned out,
> Like milk on a flat stone.'

On second thoughts, Yeats & de la Mare talk too much about dreams to be quite satisfactory. This is what makes de la Mare's stories (lent me by Ottoline) wobbly.[7]

[? *Tuesday 11 November*]

Now what will happen next, when The Waves is done? I think some book of criticism; (Mrs Stiles to take away wastepaper) But I am dissatisfied with my own smart endings. I must get on to a peak & survey the question. These are our stages.

I thought, to give this book continuity, I would copy every day the headlines in the paper. But I cant remember them.

Mr Scullin & Labour. Armistice day celebrations. The Blazing Car murder. Prince of Wales's next Expedition.—at a shot.[8]

William Plomer is back.[9] Nessa returns, wifely ready to read or sit with Clive, on Thursday. Roger too. And I cry O Solitude—& look towards Rodmell. And the weather goes on blue & balmy. And I go to the dentist, & so does Leonard. And Rivett is a nervous but clean cook. And Nelly has appealed to Dr McGlashan. And we await development.

The other night, sitting on the floor by my side, Vita suffered considerably from jealousy of Ethel. She praised her, stoutly, but bitterly. She has all the abandonment that I, living in this age of subtlety & reserve, have lost. She claims you; rushes in where I force myself to hold back. When Hugh was here he said casually that he had met Ethel at tea. Such agony went through her she could not speak. And I noticed nothing; & in my usual blind way, made my usual mocking joke. This V. took seriously & brought out my letter for me to read.

[*Wednesday 12 November*]

Alas, too numb brained to go on with Bernard's soliloquy this morning. A very little weight on me brings me low. And Clive has been a little

7. De la Mare's most recently published collection of stories was *On the Edge* (1930).
8. James Scullin, prime minister of Australia, was currently visiting Britain and Europe; during his absence a schism had broken out in the Australian Labour Party as to how to deal with the country's financial crisis. Alfred A. Rouse was to be executed on 10 March 1931 for the murder of an unknown man whose remains had been found in a burnt-out car in a village near Northampton on 6 November. The Prince of Wales was due to sail on 15 January to South America where he would open the British Empire Trade Exhibition in Buenos Aires on 14 March 1931.
9. Since the beginning of the year Plomer had been wandering in Europe with his friend Anthony Butts.

weight, added to the usual round; the dentist, shops & callers &c. So I cant write. And last night we sat through a sticky valiant evening at Hope's. Hope liberated from all restraint by [*illegible*] was it? Hope school girlish, voluble, excited, the first time I have seen it since Jane's death. Mrs Plunket Greene there (20 years added since we met at Savage's dinner party) now she is grey, pendulous; with the oddest bird technique of the head & eyes I have ever seen—for ever craning, peering, advancing, exactly like a lively arch bird of some kind. A Roman Catholic—not, unless you remembered her 20 years ago, a very nice or clever woman— something too insinuating.[10]

Wednesday 12 November

And I had my talk with Nelly last night. Going up to sit still for an hour, & read perhaps Dotty's poem I heard a shop bell, I thought, looked down the stairs & saw Nelly. So we sat for two hours. An odd meandering contradictory, mainly affectionate & even intimate talk. One of her pre-occupations to establish her own hard lot & innocence of all offence among the servants of the click.[11] We had treated her badly, turning her off because of ill-health. Confronted by me, she advanced this more as an excuse, almost a joke than anything. "Still I can't understand why you won't have me back . . ." But Nelly, you gave me notice 10 times in the past 6 years—& more . . . But I always took it back. Yes, but that sort of thing gets on the nerves. Oh ma'am I never meant to tire you—dont go on talking now if it tires you—but you wouldnt give me any help. Now Grace had all the help she wants—Well, I says, this is long service. But then Nelly you forgot that when you were with us. But then for 3 years I've been ill. And I shall never like any mistress as much as I like you . . . & so on & so on—all the old tunes, some so moving; so pathetic, some (I'm glad to say) so irrational hysterical & with that curious senseless reiteration of grievances which used to drive me frantic. The truth—but I could never tell her this—is that that kind of dependence & intimacy, with its exactness, & jealousy & its infinite minuteness wears one down; is a psychological strain. And then the gossip. Oh I wont say how I've

10. Mrs Plunkett Greene was one of the two daughters of Sir Hubert Parry, the composer and director of the Royal College of Music, 1894-1918; they had been Kensington neighbours of the Stephen family. Gwen had married the baritone Harry Plunkett Greene (d. 1936) in 1899. Sir George Savage (1842-1921), consulting physician and a specialist in mental illness who had been both friend and medical adviser to the Stephens, particularly on VW's problems.

11. The Bloomsbury servants referred to themselves as a clique.

heard, but I've heard—. You say——& so at last, after every variety of feeling, I was left with the one feeling No I could not have you sleeping here again. To be free of this inspection this frying in greasy pans, at all costs. None of this can be said, & the situation, if far less stormy than I feared, has its sharp edges. Poor old Nelly one thinks, finding a place—packing up—going to Registrys—after 15 years.

[*Added later*] And then I let her come back, for 3 months, from Jan. 1st. How am I ever to apologise to myself sufficiently?

Sunday 23 November

Ethel yesterday in a state of wonderment at her own genius. "Cant think how I happened" she says, putting on my hat, & bidding me observe what a nutshell it is on top of her gigantic brow.

Another observation, based on parties at Rhondda's & lunch with Harold:[12] given clothes I could soon dine & lunch every day & get so easily the hang of it that it mattered nothing. And so would have no point.

Sunday 30 November

"Oh I have had so much unhappiness in my life" said Mary, sobbing "It has been so dangerous, so difficult. How I envy you!"

Tuesday 2 December

No I cannot write that very difficult passage in The Waves this morning (how their lives hang lit up against the Palace) all because of Arnold Bennett & Ethel [Sands]'s party.[1] I can hardly set one word after another. There I was for 2 hours, so it seemed, alone with B. in Ethel's little back room. And this meeting I am convinced was engineered by B. to 'get on good terms with Mrs Woolf'—when heaven knows I don't care a rap if I'm on terms with B. or not. B. I say;

Soon after this A B. went to France, drank a glass of water, & died of typhoid. (March 30th, his funeral today)

12. Margaret Haig Thomas, Viscountess Rhondda (1883-1958), feminist, founder and editor (from 1926) of the weekly *Time and Tide*. The Woolfs had dined with her on 20 November and the following day went to a luncheon at the Garrick Club in celebration of Harold Nicolson's 44th birthday before going to Long Barn for the night.

1. Ethel Sands' dinner party, for fourteen guests, was on 1 December. Arnold Bennett died in London on 27 March 1931.

because he can't say B. He ceases—shuts his eyes—leans back. One waits. "*be*gin" he at last articulates quietly, without any fluster. But the method lengthens out intolerably a rather uninspired discourse. Its true, I like the old creature: I do my best, as a writer, to detect signs of genius in his smoky brown eye: I see certain sensuality, power, I suppose: but O as he cackled out "what a blundering fool I am—what a baby—compared with Desmond McCarthy—how clumsy—how could I attack professors?" This innocence is engaging; but wd. be more so if I felt him, as he infers, a "creative artist". He said that George Moore in The Mummer's Wife had shown him the Five Towns: taught him what to see there: has a profound admiration for G.M.: but despises him for boasting of his sexual triumphs. "He told me that a young girl had come to see him. And he asked her, as she sat on the sofa, to undress. And he said, she took of[f] all her clothes & let him look at her— Now that I dont believe . . . But he is a prodigious writer—he lives for words. Now he's ill. Now he's an awful bore—he tells the same stories over & over. And soon people will say of me "He's dead"." I rashly said "Of your books?" No, of me—he replied, attaching, I suppose, a longer life than I do to his books.

"Its the only life" he said (this incessant scribbling, one novel after another, one thousand words daily) I dont want anything else. I think of nothing but writing. Some people are bored. "You have all the clothes you want, I suppose" I said. "And baths—And beds. And a yacht." "Oh yes, my clothes cdnt be better cut."

And at last I drew Lord David in. And we taunted the old creature with thinking us refined. He said the gates of Hatfield were shut "shut away from life". 'But open on Thursdays' said Lord D. "I dont want to go on Thursdays" said B. "And you drop your aitches on purpose" I said "thinking that you possess more 'life' than we do." "I sometimes tease" said B. "But I dont think I possess more life than you do. Now I must go home. I have to write one thousand words tomorrow morning".

And this left only the scrag end of the evening: & this left me in a state where I can hardly drive my pen across the page.

Question: Why does Desmond like talking to Lord Esher?[2]

Reflection: it is presumably a bad thing to look through articles, reviews &c. to find one's own name. Yet I often do.

Resolution: To say to Ethel one day—How can you attach this importance to everything you do when you call yourself a Christian (inspired by this mornings letter & its emphasis about the score of the Prison)

2. Oliver Brett (1881-1963), who provided both financial and editorial support for Desmond's monthly *Life and Letters*, had succeeded as 3rd Viscount Esher on the death of his father in January 1930.

Thursday 4 December

One word of slight snub in the Lit. Sup. today makes me determine, first, to alter the whole of The Waves; second, to put my back up against the public—one word of slight snub.[3]

Friday 12 December

This, I think, is the last days breathing space I allow myself before I tackle the last lap of The Waves. I have had a week off—that is to say I have written three little sketches; & dawdled, & spent a morning shopping, & a morning, this morning arranging my new table & doing odds & ends —but I think I have got my breath again & must be off for 3 or perhaps 4 weeks more. Then, as I think, I shall make one consecutive writing of the waves &c—the interludes—so as to work it into one—& then—oh dear, some must be written again; & then, corrections; & then send to Mabel; & then correct the type; & then give to Leonard. Leonard perhaps shall get it some time late in March. Then put away; then print, perhaps in June.[4]

Meanwhile we dine with Mary on Sunday to meet Mr Hart Davis who may come to the press—but in what capacity?[5] And two days ago we saw over 25 T[avistock]. S[quare]. to which we may move, if we decide to leave this, & can let it. But there too are obstacles; an hotel building alongside, & fewer rooms, & more expense.

Paper headlines. Spanish Revolution. Russian timber yard scandal. Burst water main in Cambridge Circus.[6]

---

3. A half-column review of the limited edition of *On Being Ill* appeared in the *TLS*, 4 December 1930. The reviewer approved of the theme but thought that the reader was led away from it: 'The subject has shown a new, precipitous face for an instant, and once more vanished into the mist. The essay with its vellum and green covers, beautiful end-papers and fine type, remains placidly on the table.'
4. *The Waves* was to be published on 8 October 1931.
5. Rupert Hart Davis (b. 1907), educated at Eton and Oxford and who was later to found his own publishing firm, was at this time what he calls an office boy at William Heinemann Ltd.
6. It had been reported from Madrid on 12 December that the garrison at Jaca in the Spanish province of Huesca had revolted under the rumoured leadership of Major Franco. Evidence from three 'escaped Russian prisoners' as to the conditions under which the timber industry was currently being conducted at Archangel and in other Soviet prison camps had recently been published in the newspapers; Sir Edward Hilton Young MP had called on the Government to take action to put a stop to 'a trade stamped with the worst features of servile labour'.

Tuesday 16 December

I will never dine out again. I will burn my evening dress. I have gone through this door. Nothing exists beyond. I have taken my fence: & now need never whip myself to dine with Colefax, Ethel, Mary again.

These reflections were hammered in indelibly last night at Argyll House. The same party: same dresses; same food. To talk to Sir Arthur about Q. V.'s letters, & the dyestuff bill, & I forget⁷—I sacrificed an evening alone with Vita, an evening alone by myself—an evening of pleasure. And so it goes on perpetually. Lord & Lady Esher, Arnold Bennett—old Birrell. Forced, dry, sterile, infantile conversation. And I am not even excited at going. So the fence is not only leapt, but fallen. Why jump?

Thursday 18 December

Spain strikes. Illness of M. Poincaré. Suicide of Peter Warlock. Dyestuff Bill.⁸

Lord David, Lytton & Clive last night. Told them how I had burnt my evening dress in the gas fire—general agreement that parties are a folly. Clive specially emphatic. Talk about the riddle of the universe (Jeans' book) whether it will be known; not by us; found out suddenly: about rhythm in prose; Lytton is bringing out a new book of essays; what shall it be called; on living abroad; Clive says we (L. & I) are provincial. I say no mud abroad & fireflies in one's hair; Blenheim discussed; Lytton against it; Clive in favour; I say no sense of human personality; Lord David's aunt perpetually tears up her life of Ld Salisbury; feels the cause of the lunatics; no Cecils like dogs; Q.V. discussed; Bitter tea; A Lion

7. *The Letters of Queen Victoria (Third Series)*, Vol. I, 1886-1890, edited by G. E. Buckle, had recently been published. The Dyestuffs Act was due to lapse in January 1931 but under the Expiring Laws Continuance Bill the Conservative majority in the House of Lords secured a prolongation of the Act for a further twelve months. In 'Am I a Snob?' (*Moments of Being*, p 190) VW asserts that she was once 'the second leading authority in England on the Dyestuffs question'.

8. Martial law had been proclaimed in Spain on 15 December and labour unrest was widespread. Raymond Poincaré, the French statesman, was reported from Paris on 15 December as being seriously ill with congestion of the lungs and uraemia. Philip Heseltine (1894-1930), musicologist and under the pseudonym Peter Warlock a composer, had died of gas poisoning at his home in Chelsea on 17 December. The inquest concluded that there was insufficient evidence to decide whether his death was the result of suicide or an accident.

rages; Clive's eyes; Ld D. sneezed across the table; my bag came; fog all day.[9]

[*Friday 19 December*]

Spanish Rising. Prince of Wales' Chill. Carnera beats M.[10]

"Violet so delighted me", said Ethel, "by saying precisely what I wished her to say. I was so struck by the terrific strength & gentleness of V. & by her nose". Now I dont like this: I dont like that Ethel should know that I like compliments; I dont like liking them; I dont like Mrs Woodhouse fabricating them on the telephone.[11]

Saturday 20 December

W. H. D. Douglas drowned: six English lost: New motor regulation. Lord Willingdon appointed Viceroy of India.[12]

And Kingsley Martin lunched with us (sweeping up turkey as a char sweeps feathers) & said that the Nation & the N.S. are to amalgamate; & he is to be editor (highly secret, like all nonsense) & would L. be literary editor? No; L. wd. not.[13]

9. James Jeans' Rede Lecture, *The Mysterious Universe*, had been published in November. Strachey's *Portraits in Miniature and other Essays* appeared in May 1931. *Blenheim* (1930) was by G. M. Trevelyan. Lady Gwendolen Cecil published three volumes (1922, 1924, 1932) of her *Life* of her father the third Marquess of Salisbury, but never completed it. *Bitter Tea* by the American novelist Grace Zaring Stone had recently been published by Cobden Sanderson; 'A Lion rages', unidentified.

10. The rising in Spain had been declared a 'Republican failure' in the newspapers. The Prince of Wales had a 'slight' chill which prevented him visiting Windsor Great Park and caused him to miss a dinner at the Savoy. The Italian heavyweight Primo Carnera beat Reggie Meen of Britain in Round 2 at the Albert Hall on Thursday 18 December.

11. Violet Kate Eglinton Gordon-Woodhouse, *née* Gwynne (1872-1948), an amateur but outstanding harpsichordist and clavecinist, a pioneer of the revival of early music, whom Ethel regarded as the most musical of all her musical friends.

12. The English cricketer J. W. H. T. Douglas was among the 42 passengers who died aboard the steamer *Oberon* when it sank after colliding with the *Arcturus* in the Kattegat on the night of 19 December. The Ministry of Transport had banned motor coaches from certain Central London streets to relieve congestion. It had been announced on 19 December that Lord Willingdon, Governor-General of Canada, was to succeed Lord Irwin as Viceroy of India.

13. Basil Kingsley Martin (1897-1969) took up his post as the first editor of the newly merged *New Statesman and Nation* early in 1931 and retained it until his retire-

Monday 22 December[14]

Horror death of Douglas: Indian Conference. Fog. Intermittent. Weather to be colder.[15]

It occurred to me last night while listening to a Beethoven quartet that I would merge all the interjected passages into Bernard's final speech, & end with the words O solitude: thus making him absorb all those scenes, & having no further break. This is also to show that the theme effort, effort, dominates: not the waves: & personality: & defiance: but I am not sure of the effect artistically; because the proportions may need the intervention of the waves finally so as to make a conclusion.

Tuesday 23 December

I will make this hasty note about being robbed. I put my bag under my coat at Marshall & Snelgrove's. I turned; & felt, before I looked "It is gone". So it was. Then began questions & futile messages. Then the detective came. He stopped a respectable elderly woman apparently shopping. They exchanged remarks about 'the usual one—no she's not here today. Its a young woman in brown fur." Meanwhile I was ravaged, of course, with my own futile wishes—how I had thought, as I put down my bag, this is foolish. I was admitted to the underwor[l]d. I imagined the brown young woman peeping, pouncing. And it was gone my 6 pounds—my two brooches—all because of that moment. They throw the bags away, said the detective. These dreadful women come here—but

ment in December 1960; his first literary editor was R. Ellis Roberts whom he inherited from the *New Statesman*. For an account of the amalgamation of the *N & A* and the *New Statesman* see *The New Statesman. The History of the First Fifty Years* (1963) by Edward Hyams, pp 118-23.

14. On the opposite page VW has copied these lines from Dante, *Inferno*, 26, 94-102:

> Nè dolcezza di figlio, nè la piéta
> del vecchio padre, nè il debito amore
> Lo qual dovea Penelope far lieta
> Vincer poter dentro da me l'ardore
> Ch'i' ebbi a divenir del mondo esperto,
> E degli vizii umani e del valore;
> Ma misi me per l'alto mare aperto
> Sol con un legno e e con quella compagna
> Picciola, dalla qual non fui deserto

15. The Round Table Conference on India was held in London from 12 November 1930-19 January 1931.

not so much as to some of the Oxford St. shops. Fluster, regret, humiliation, curiosity, something frustrated, foolish, something jarred, by this underwor[l]d—a foggy evening—going home, penniless—thinking of my green bag—imagining the woman rifling it—her home—her husband —Now to Rodmell in the fog.[16]

Rodmell.

Saturday 27 December

But whats the use of talking about Bernard's final speech? We came down on Tuesday, & next day my cold was the usual influenza, & I am in bed with the usual temperature, & cant use my wits or, as is visible, form my letters. I daresay 2 days will see me normal; but then the sponge behind my forehead will be dry & pale—& so my precious fortnight of exaltation & concentration is snatched; & I shall go back to the racket & Nelly without a thing done. I cheer myself by thinking that I may evolve some thoughts[?]. Meanwhile it rains; Annie's child is ill; the dogs next door yap & yap; all the colours are rather dim & the pulse of life dulled. I moon torpidly through book after book: Defoe's Tour; Rowan's auto[biograph]y; Benson's Memoirs; Jeans; in the familiar way.[17] The parson—Skinner—who shot himself emerges like a bloody sun in a fog. a book worth perhaps looking at again in a clearer mood. He shot himself in the beech woods above his house; spent a life digging up stones & reducing all places to Camelodunum; quarrelled; bickered; yet loved his sons; yet turned them out of doors—a clear hard picture of one type of human life—the exasperated, unhappy, struggling, intolerably afflicted. Oh & I've read Q.V.'s letters; & wonder what wd. happen had Ellen Terry been born Queen. Complete disaster to the Empire? Q.V. entirely unaesthetic; a kind of Prussian competence, & belief in herself her only prominences; material; brutal[?] to Gladstone; like a mistress with a dishonest footman.

(margin: Diary of a Somerset Rector)

16. LW's diary, 23 December 1930: 'Packed. Drove Marylebone Police Station get V's bag then to Monks.' See also *IV VW Letters* no. 2291 to Vanessa Bell.
17. VW's sickroom reading appears to have been Defoe's *Tour Through the Whole Island of Great Britain* (1724-27); *The Autobiography of Archibald Hamilton Rowan* published in Dublin by the Rev. W. Hamilton Drummond, 1840; *As We Were: A Victorian Peep-Show* by E. F. Benson, 1930; James Jeans' popular *The Mysterious Universe*, or his earlier *The Universe Around Us*; and *The Journal of a Somerset Rector*, edited by Howard Coombs and the Rev. Arthur N. Bax, 1930 (upon which VW based her essay 'The Rev. John Skinner' in *The Common Reader. Second Series*, 1935).

Knew her own mind. But the mind radically commonplace. only its inherited force, & cumulative sense of power, making it remarkable.

Monday 29 December

One of my trial runs to exercise my hands. (Still in bed). Skinner was bred to the Bar, but became, unfortunately, a clergyman. Unfortunately too his wife died, of consumption, leaving him with 3 children. Of these the only satisfactory one was Laura, who inherited her father's love of collecting & tabulating, but also her mother's consumption, so that before she had collected, in a very orderly way, many cabinets of shells, she died; & the other children were unsatisfactory.

Skinner was rector of Camerton in Somerset, & there he remained, year after year, without any aptitude whatsoever for the souls of the living. A clever, upright conscientious man, he did his duty by his flock, by perpetually admonishing them. That they were always bad, seems strange, but was to him true. A colliery was being formed at the village. The morals of colliers are perhaps loose. At any rate, no village in England seems to have contained so many insolent, wicked, ungrateful villagers. And Skinner was forever comparing them with the Romans. His only comfort was to dream himself back into Camelodunum, & to forget 1828. But being a disciplinarian, he was tormented by the need for reproving the living. His conscience refused to let him shut his eyes upon the sufferings of the halfwitted Mrs Goold, or the iniquities practised upon imbecile paupers at the workhouse, & he must perpetually go his rounds among the sick & dying, for accidents among the miners were frequent. He was always on the side of the afflicted; never on the side of the happy. He considered himself one of the worst treated of men, & imagined malignancies & insolences on all sides. Mrs Jarrett, the Squiress, was an arch-hypocrite. All her kindness had deceit behind it. Then he was sometimes asked to a ball—to a dinner party with French dishes. He much preferred solitude to the most brilliant society. Perpetually censorious, he found fault with French dishes, with dressing up, with all enjoyment— save only that of writing & writing, long accounts of places, catalogues of antiquity, & in special, his great work upon Etymology. He met with only ridicule here too. At a parsons dinner, he was asked to explain, on his system, the name of Bumstead, which he did—& then suspected that it was all a joke against him. Suspicion always came after a moments pleasure. Perhaps the only unalloyed pleasure was found in his visits to Stourhead, the seat of [*blank in ms*], where a party of antiquaries stayed for a day or two, giving themselves up to questions of Romans & Britons, of camps & buried cities. There, sitting alone in the luxurious library, he enjoyed the exquisite pleasure of copying extracts from—shall we say?—Ptolemy Theophrastus; & the good Bishop of Bath & Wells made him happy too in spite of a few suspicions—by asking him to spend the week end at Wells. These however were his only alleviations. Home life at Camerton became more & more sordid, humiliating, comfortless & by degrees violent. Jeered at & insulted by the rude peasants & farmers, who told him to his face that he was mad, his treatment was no better in his own vicarage, & from his own flesh & blood. There were terrible scenes with his sons. Once Joseph told him that he was making himself ridiculous by his writings, & was insane. Attempts to keep his son from drinking cider ended—so irritating was his manner—in violent curses. The sons were always being sent to stay with their grandmother at Bath. It was his temper that was at fault, he said; but they were at fault to irritate his temper. The servants left, because he wd. not let them walk out after dinner. The farmers cursed him because he suspected them of stealing his tythes; he nervously, irritatingly & imcompetently tried to exact his due of lambs & haycocks, He knew nothing of farming, nothing of country life. All he knew was that Camerton had been Camelodunum, & his obsession on this point made even the good natured Baronet protest that he carried Camelodunum too far. So at last—all he could do was to write & write & write. The blank pages of his diary alone neither sneered, nor hawked in his face, nor mocked him behind his back, nor plotted his downfall, nor called him mad. Eighty four volumes of antiquarian lumber & daily complaint & journalising were scribbled & put away in certain great iron chests which were bequeathed to the British Museum. At last his confidant was the future—in 50 years after his death, he said, these 84 volumes were to be given to the world—which world would understand his great contribution to etymology, & take his side against the Church-warden, Mrs Jarrett, Owen, the servant girl & all the rest of his ungrateful perpetually afflicting tribe. Fame & comfort would then be his. No doubt this secret confidence kept him going, through the gathering miseries of life. For the unhappy man was not blind to his faults. His chief misery must have come from the struggle of love & irritation. He loved his sons—yet drove them away. They fell ill, & he became all kindness & consideration—& yet how could the unfortunate Owen endure to have his father with him?—his egotistic, exacting, morose, but devoted father? He gave pain even by his affection. And suddenly the diary, written in a crabbed & illegible hand, ceases to be copied out any longer. The brother whose task it was died.

Skinner went on writing, but nobody could read his script. Perhaps the knowledge that even this confidant had failed him finally decided him. At any rate, 7 years later, he went out one December morning in the beechwoods, & fired. They found his dead body & buried it—exacerbated, scarred, covered with infernal irritation—in the grave of his wife & Laura.

Now this little narrative being run off,—& Lord, how difficult to write in bed—I report that the machine is not seriously damaged; & if I can get out, & move about, & yet not get a headache, I daresay in 3 days I shall be beginning to play gently with the waves. I dont have the temptations here of London. Not normal, but being normal is I daresay rather a fetish. All Mrs Dalloway was written with a temp. of 99 I think. How difficult though to get back into the right mental state: what a queer balance is needed. This little Skinner sketch is in the wrong order; but I dont fumble for words. Could let my mind fly, am not as I prove now, used up by an hour's exercise.

It rains. Nessa is driving from Seend today. Vita broadcasting. That bedroom voice, singing Bach, talking of the weather, has come in handy.

Tuesday 30 December

What it wants is presumably unity; but it is I think rather good (I am talking to myself over the fire about The Waves). Suppose I could run all the scenes together more?—by rhythm, chiefly. So as to avoid those cuts; so as to make the blood run like a torrent from end to end—I dont want the waste that the breaks give; I want to avoid chapters; that indeed is my achievement, if any here: a saturated, unchopped, completeness; changes of scene, of mood, of person, done without spilling a drop. Now if it cd. be worked over with heat & currency thats all it wants. And I am getting my blood up. (temp. 99)

But all the same I went to Lewes, & the Keynes's came to tea; & having got astride my saddle the whole world falls into shape; it is this writing that gives me my proportions.

LIST OF
ABBREVIATIONS
AND APPENDIXES
I and II

ABBREVIATIONS

CH, Camb.	Charleston Papers deposited in the Library of King's College, Cambridge
Holleyman	Holleyman & Treacher Ltd: *Catalogue of Books from the Library of Leonard and Virginia Woolf, taken from Monks House, Rodmell, and 24 Victoria Square, London, and now in the possession of Washington State University.* Privately printed, Brighton, 1975
Holroyd	Michael Holroyd: *Lytton Strachey. A Biography*. Revised edition, Penguin Books, 1971
HP Checklist	*A Checklist of the Hogarth Press 1917-1938.* Compiled by J. Howard Woolmer. With a short history of the Press by Mary E. Gaither, Hogarth Press, London, 1976
Kp	B. J. Kirkpatrick: *A Bibliography of Virginia Woolf.* Revised edition, Hart-Davis, London, 1967
LW	Leonard Woolf. Five volumes of his *Autobiography*, Hogarth Press, London.
I LW	*Sowing: . . . 1880-1904.* 1960
II LW	*Growing: . . . 1904-1911.* 1961
III LW	*Beginning Again: . . . 1911-1918.* 1964
IV LW	*Downhill all the Way: . . . 1919-1939.* 1967
V LW	*The Journey not the Arrival Matters: . . . 1939-1969.* 1969
LWP, Sussex	*Leonard Woolf Papers.* University of Sussex Library Catalogue, 1977
M & M	Robin Majumdar and Allen McLaurin: *Virginia Woolf. The Critical Heritage*, Routledge & Kegan Paul, London, 1975
MHP, Sussex	*Monks House Papers.* University of Sussex Library Catalogue, July 1972
N & A	*Nation and Athenaeum*
RF Letters	*Letters of Roger Fry.* Edited by Denys Sutton. Chatto & Windus, London, 1972
I RF Letters	Volume I, 1878-1913
II RF Letters	Volume II, 1913-1934
QB	Quentin Bell: *Virginia Woolf. A Biography*. Hogarth Press, London, 1972
I QB	Volume I: *Virginia Stephen*, 1882-1912
II QB	Volume II: *Mrs Woolf*, 1912-1941
Shone	Richard Shone: *Bloomsbury Portraits*, 1976
TLS	*Times Literary Supplement*

VW   Virginia Woolf

VW Diary   *The Diary of Virginia Woolf.* Edited by Anne Olivier Bell. Hogarth Press, London.

I VW Diary   Volume I: *1915-1919.* 1977

II VW Diary   Volume II: *1920-1924.* 1978

VW Letters   *The Letters of Virginia Woolf.* Edited by Nigel Nicolson. Hogarth Press, London

I VW Letters   Volume I: *The Flight of the Mind* (1888-1912), 1975

II VW Letters   Volume II: *The Question of Things Happening* (1912-1922), 1976

III VW Letters   Volume III: *A Change of Perspective* (1923-1928), 1977

IV VW Letters   Volume IV: *A Reflection of the Other Person* (1929-1931), 1978

NOTE

The Uniform Edition of the Works of Virginia Woolf, published by the Hogarth Press, is used for reference purposes.

APPENDIX I

BIOGRAPHICAL OUTLINES OF PERSONS MOST FREQUENTLY MENTIONED

BELL, Clive (Arthur Clive Heward Bell, 1881-1964), art critic, married Vanessa Stephen in 1907, and thereafter played an important part in VW's life. His marriage had become a matter of convenience and friendship, for since about 1915 Mary Hutchinson held pride of place in his affections. In the period immediately preceding that covered by the present volume Bell published *Poems* (1921), *Since Cézanne* (1922), *The Legend of Monte della Sibilla* (1923) and *On British Freedom* (1923).

BELL, Vanessa ('Nessa'), *née* Stephen (1879-1961), painter, VW's elder sister and, after LW, the most important person in her life. She married Clive Bell in 1907, and though they always remained on amicable terms, from about 1914 and until her death she lived and worked with the painter Duncan Grant. Her children were Julian Heward (1908-1937); Quentin Claudian Stephen (b. 1910); and Angelica Vanessa (b. 1918)—the last-named being the daughter of Duncan Grant.

BIRRELL, Francis ('Frankie') Frederick Locker (1889-1935), critic, elder son of Augustine Birrell, educated at Eton and King's College, Cambridge. He and his friend David Garnett had together served with a Quaker Relief Unit in France during the war. In 1919 he and Garnett entered into partnership to establish a bookshop *Birrell & Garnett* in Taviton Street, near Gordon Square, and subsequently in Gerrard Street. He wrote regularly for the *Nation & Athenaeum* of which LW was the literary editor.

ELIOT, Thomas Stearns (1888-1965), American-born poet, educated at Harvard and Oxford; married in 1915 Vivienne Haigh-Wood. Eliot had known VW since 1918; despite her efforts and those of others to free him, he was until 1925 on the London staff of Lloyds Bank, which he had joined in 1917; he nonetheless edited a literary review, *The Criterion*, founded in 1922. The Hogarth Press had published his *Poems* (1919), *The Waste Land* (1923), and his essays *Homage to John Dryden* (1924).

FORSTER, Edward Morgan (1879-1970), novelist, educated at King's College, Cambridge, 1897-1902, an Apostle. Towards the end of 1921 he had returned from his second visit to India, after which he resumed writing *A Passage to India*, published in 1924. In 1925 he moved with his mother from Weybridge to Abinger in Surrey, and also found a *pied-à-terre* in Brunswick Square,

Bloomsbury. His *Pharos and Pharillon* had been published by the Hogarth Press in 1923.

FRY, Roger Eliot (1866-1934), art critic and painter, descended from generations of Quakers, gained first class honours in Natural Sciences at King's College, Cambridge, where he became an Apostle. He abandoned science for the study and practice of art; he had created a scandal by introducing the British public to Post-Impressionist art, but remained an established and respected figure in the museum and art world in England, France and America. His *Vision and Design* was published in 1920, and *Twelve Original Woodcuts* by the Hogarth Press, in 1921.

GRANT, Duncan James Corrowr (1885-1978), painter, only child of Major Bartle Grant whose sister was Lady Strachey; he spent much of his youth with the Strachey family. From about 1914 until her death in 1961, he lived and worked with Vanessa Bell; their daughter Angelica Bell was born on Christmas Day, 1918.

HUTCHINSON, Mary, *née* Barnes (1889-1977), a first cousin once removed of Lytton Strachey, married in 1910 the barrister and friend to the arts St John ('Jack') Hutchinson (1884-1942). She had for many years been paramount in Clive Bell's affections.

KEYNES, John Maynard (1883-1946), economist, scholar of Eton and King's College, Cambridge, an Apostle, a Fellow and from 1924 First Bursar of the College, and University lecturer in economics; he married in August 1925 the Russian ballerina Lydia Lopokova. In 1923 Keynes had become chairman of the new Board of the *Nation & Athenaeum* and had appointed LW literary editor. His publications up to the present period include *The Economic Consequences of the Peace* (1919), *A Revision of the Treaty* (1922), and his first major work in economics *A Tract on Monetary Reform* (1923).

LOPOKOVA, Lydia (b. 1892), Russian ballerina, studied at the Imperial School of Ballet, St Petersburg: she married Maynard Keynes in August 1925. She had visited London with the Diaghilev Company in 1918, 1919 and again in 1921 when Keynes had fallen in love with her and persuaded her to live in Gordon Square among his friends.

MacCARTHY, (Charles Otto) Desmond (1877-1952), literary journalist and editor, graduate of Trinity College, Cambridge, and an Apostle; married Mary ('Molly') Josefa Warre-Cornish in 1906. In 1920 he became literary editor of the *New Statesman*, for which he wrote a weekly column "Books in General", under the pseudonym "Affable Hawk".

MacCARTHY, Mary ('Molly') Josefa, *née* Warre-Cornish (1882-1953), married Desmond MacCarthy in 1906. Like VW she was a niece by marriage of 'Aunt Anny'—Lady Anne Thackeray Ritchie. In 1924 she published *A Nineteenth-Century Childhood*, a book made from a series of articles contributed to the *Nation & Athenaeum* in 1923-24.

MORRELL, Lady Ottoline, *née* Cavendish-Bentinck (1873-1938), hostess and patroness of the arts, married in 1902 Philip Morrell (1870-1943), barrister and Liberal MP, 1906-18. From 1915-1927 they lived at Garsington Manor in Oxfordshire, where they gave generous hospitality to pacifists, writers, and artists, and thenceforward in Gower Street, Bloomsbury. Their daughter Julian was born in 1906.

MORTIMER, Raymond (b. 1895) critic, a graduate of Balliol College, Oxford. VW first met him in 1923. In the 1920s he was active as a journalist in Paris and in London. He was a close friend of Clive Bell and of the Harold Nicolsons, whom he visited in Persia in 1926.

NICOLSON, Harold (1886-1968), diplomat and author, son of 1st Baron Carnock, married Vita Sackville-West in 1913. In 1925 he was posted to the British Embassy in Teheran, and in 1927 transferred to Berlin. His publications up to the present period include *Paul Verlaine* (1921), *Tennyson* (1923), and *Byron, The Last Journey* (1924).

SACKVILLE-WEST, Victoria ('Vita') Mary (1892-1962), novelist and poet, only child of 3rd Baron Sackville, married Harold Nicolson in 1913. VW first met her at a dinner given by Clive Bell in December 1922. From 1924, the Hogarth Press published thirteen of her books altogether, including her best-selling novel *The Edwardians* in 1930.

STEPHEN, Adrian Leslie (1883-1948), VW's younger brother. Trinity College, Cambridge, 1902-05. A conscientious objector during the war, he married in 1914 Karin Elizabeth Conn Costelloe (1889-1953), a philosophy graduate of Newnham; they had two daughters, Ann (b. 1916) and Judith (1918-72). From 1919-26 they both studied medicine and psychology, and thereafter practised as analysts.

STRACHEY, (Giles) Lytton (1880-1932), critic and biographer, a contemporary and friend of both VW's brother Thoby Stephen and LW at Trinity College, Cambridge, and like the latter an Apostle. Since 1924 he had lived at Ham Spray House in Wiltshire with Carrington and her husband Ralph Partridge. After *Eminent Victorians* (1918), he had published *Queen Victoria* (1921), and *Books and Characters* (1922).

STRACHEY, James Beaumont (1887-1967), psychoanalyst, Lytton's youngest brother; he too went to Trinity College, Cambridge, and became an Apostle. He had married Alix Sargant-Florence in 1920 and with her went in the same year to Vienna to study under Freud; he was to become the English translator and general editor of Freud's works, which the Hogarth Press published.

APPENDIX II

VIRGINIA WOOLF AND 'THAT UNNATURAL FLORENTINE SOCIETY'

VW went with Vanessa and Clive Bell to Florence in April 1909. The notebook recording her impressions of this and other foreign journeys—to Greece in 1906, to Siena and Perugia in 1908, and to Florence in 1909—is lost, but a typed copy (MH/A7) made for Leonard Woolf is among the Monks House Papers in the University of Sussex Library, by whose permission the following passage is printed. It illuminates VW's reflections upon learning of the death of Geoffrey Scott (see Diary, *21 August 1929), and upon reading the life of Alice Meynell (see* Diary, *2 September 1929).*

Today we had another experience of society. We had lunch with the art critic [Bernard Berenson] and his wife; and tea with Mrs Ross. In case space should fail me (the candle gutters intolerably, and the ink oozes) I will describe the tea party. The worst of distinguished old ladies, who have known everyone and lived an independent life, is that they become brusque and imperious without sufficient wits to alleviate the manner. Mrs Ross lives in a great villa, is the daughter of distinguished parents; the friend of writers, and the character of the country side. She sells things off her walls. She is emphatic, forcible, fixes you with her straight grey eye as though it were an honour to occupy, even for a moment, its attention. The head is massive, it is held high; the mouth is coarse and the upper lip haired. Such old women like men, and have a number of unreasonable traditions. Pride of birth, I thought I detected; certainly she has that other pride, the pride which comes to those who have lived among the chosen spirits of the time. A word of family, and her wits were at work at once.

I know not why, but this type . . . does not much attract me. Only one position is possible if you are a young woman: you must let them adopt queenly airs, with a touch of the maternal. She summons you to sit beside her, lays her hand for a moment on yours, dismisses you the next, to make room for some weakly young man. She has them to stay with her for months —likes them best when they are big and strong but will tolerate weakness for the sake of the sex. She has led a bold life, managing for herself, and an English-woman who dictates to peasants is apt to become domineering. However, there can be no question of her spirit—many portraits showed the intent indomitable face, in youth and middle age, it is still the same, beneath white hair. It proved her power that her drawing room filled with guests. She seemed to enjoy sweeping them about, without much ceremony. Parties were bidden to admire the garden; young men were commanded to hand cake. Among the guests was a lean, attenuated woman, who had a face like that of a transfixed hare—the lower part was drawn out in anguish, while the eyes appealed piteously. This was Mrs Meynell, the writer, who somehow made one dislike the notion of women who write. She clasped the arm of a chair, and seemed uncomfortably out of place.

This was no atmosphere for chaste expression—there was nothing to lay hold of. She walked with a curious forward spring which, seeing that the body was spare and bony, encased too in black velvet, had an incongruous air. Once, no doubt, she was a poetess, and trod the fields of Parnassus. It is melancholy to trace even such words as Mrs Meynell's to a lank, slightly absurd and altogether insignificant little body, dressed with some attempt at the fashion. Did Mrs Browning look like that too? And yet, poor woman, had the fire of Sappho burnt in her what else could she have done? These gatherings are brutal things. Or is my theory proved—a writer should be the furnace from which his words come—and tepid people, timid and decorous, never coin true words. The poor thing looked furtive, as though found out—run to earth. She had a plain aesthetic daughter. The wine further watered.

Index

N

Beecham, Sir Thomas: and Ethel Smyth, 306 & n

Beerbohm, Max: his exhibition, 10 & n; a letter from, 173 & n, 174; VW meets, 212, 213; six minutes with, 222; *ref*: ix, 213n

Beethoven: and *The Waves*, 139, 339; *ref*: 246

Bell, Angelica: her accident recalled, 7 & n; perched beside Nessa, 154; acts the Ladies, 158; epitomises womanliness, 167; distracts VW, 211; and school, 220, 254n, 261, 262; admires spangled lady, 284, 285n; whirring & twirling, 312; *ref*: 141, 184 & n, 185, 197, 199, 232, 253, 282, 298, 303, 304, 321

Bell, Clive: for Biographical Note *see* Appendix I; a fling with his Colonel, 10 & n; conspicuously dumb, 15; an ally, 31; but not exalting, 32; pleases and pains, 37; his death imagined, 48; 'The Messiah', 53; on VW's method, 63; his affectionate discrimination, 68; adulterates solitude, 73; back from Paris, 76; to aid Government, 77; on Churchill, 78; laughs at VW's hat, 90, 91; to break with Mary, 126 & n; on VW's haircut, 127; and Mary, 128, 129, 141, 160, 161; remembered abroad, 132 & n; VW angry with, 134 & n; failure & madness, 135, 136; praises *To the Lighthouse*, 136; his smart talk measured, 137, 138; contemplates suicide, 148; 'Don Juan of Bloomsbury', 149; in grand historical picture, 157; and Old Bloomsbury, 162; makes Woolfs feel Bloomsbury-ish, 163; 'incessant', 164; a lady in Leicestershire, 168; off to Germany, 173 & n; is back, and ubiquitous, 175; smacks VW—little upstart, 179; appeals for pity, 182; his book very superficial, 184; denies class distinctions, 190; his inverse snobbery, 198; makes for stridency, 208; 'most honourable' man, 210; intolerably dull, 219; like Lottie *au fond*, 227; sensation-mongerer, 228; inharmonious, 242; VW misses him, 260; compares notes with Lytton, 273; his criticism of VW's books, 275; LW's bugbear, 276; immensely good tempered, 298;

but not intimate, 312; blind of one eye, 328; judges Woolfs 'provincial', 337; *ref*: 7, 17, 35, 36, 49, 57, 58, 67, 69, 79, 80, 82, 85, 93, 101, 108, 133, 140 & n, 146, 147, 151, 165, 169, 174, 176, 201, 236, 274, 310, 332, 338, 352; *Civilization*, 184 & n

Bell, Julian: for Biographical Note *see* Appendix I; shut in pound, 5; utterly cynical, 6; emphatically against buggery, 10; in Clive's eyes, 135; aspiring playwright, 166, 167n; sanity & competence, 187; otherwise like Jem, 190 & n; force & simplicity, 197; benefits lavished on, 200; satisfactory young man, 224; muddles Apostles speech, 235; a mere child, 242; Nessa's escort, 261, 262; to publish poems, 316 & n; no poet, 328; *ref*: 5n, 38, 101, 179, 191, 268, 312, 314, 321; *Winter Movement*, 316n

Bell, Quentin: for Biographical Note *see* Appendix I; kisses Nessa, 5; utterly cynical, 6; his birthday, 38, 311; and 'The Messiah', 53; in Clive's eyes, 135; terrifyingly sophisticated, 158; bound for Germany, 173n, 218; elegant & self-conscious, 197; fetching bottles, 298; natural & gifted, 316; *ref*: 5n, 102, 142, 143, 157, 282, 314, 321

Bell, Vanessa: for Biographical Note *see* Appendix I; kisses Quentin, 5; recalls Angelica's accident, 7; her design mocked, 16 & n; alone with Jack Hills and VW, 33 & n; and Jack's mother, 34 & n; wants Woolfs for Christmas, 47; still most beautiful, her death imagined, 48; what she gives VW, 52; on the Press, 60; on the *N & A*, 69; doesn't consolidate parties, 71; finds fault with VW, 76; her 47th birthday, 87; in quiet black hat, 91; & her children, 107, 108, 110, 158, 167, 168, 189, 241, 254; humming and booming, 111; alarmed by Duncan's illness, 124 & n; her absence felt, 129; remembered abroad, 132 & n; reaction to *To the Lighthouse*, 135, 136n; mutual jealousy over clothes, 137; inscrutable & critical, 140; gossip with, about Clive & Mary, 141; in shabby Renault, 146; sinister

165; lunch party, 166 & n, 222; dinner at a price, 226; loses nest-egg, 265; *ref:* 9 & n, 42, 63, 103, 114, 124, 135, 152, 177, 185, 202, 219, 225, 245, 262, 295, 337

Coleridge, S. T.: 130

Coliseum, The London: 223 & n

Collins, Mrs, and daughter: to replace Nelly?, 146

Columbus, Christopher: Lytton on, 294 & n

Commercio, restaurant: 80

Connaught Rooms: lunch with Desmond at, 21

Conrad, Joseph: George Moore on, 67

Constantinople: 131

Conway, Sir Martin: and strike petition, 83 & n

Cook, Sir John: 166

Cooke, Sidney Russell and Helen *née* Smith: 199 & n

Cookham: 64, 118

Coolidge, Calvin: 69

Cornhill Magazine, The: and Thomas Hardy, 97 & n

Cornwall: 119, 123, 303

Country Life: 16 & n

Couve de Murville, Maurice: 157n

Cowper, William: a good poet, 129; article on, 232 & n; 'The Castaway', 19n

Cox, Miss Catherine: 237 & n

Cox, Ka, *see* Arnold-Forster, Katherine

Cranbourne Chase: 75

Cranium Club: 155 & n, 166

Criterion, The, literary quarterly, later *The New Criterion:* 14n, 41, 46

Croly, Herbert David, editor: 183 & n

Cromer, Evelyn Baring, 1st Earl of: 51 & n

Cromer, Katherine, Countess of: framework of discarded beauty, 51 & n

Cromwell, Oliver: 153, 180 & n, 194 & n, 197

Cruthers, residents of Cassis: 232

Cunard, Lady: stringy old hop-o'-my-thumb, 201-2; *ref:* 202n, 206, 210, 309 & n, 310

Cunard, Nancy: 4 & n, 15, 64; *Parallax,* 4 & n, 5n

Currys, residents of Cassis: 232

Curtis, Mrs, headmistress: 254n, 262

Daglish, Doris, of Wandsworth: 150 & n

Daily Herald: 77

Dalingridge Place, Sussex: 293 & n, 294

Dalloway, Clarissa (fict): disagreeable & limited, 32

Dalton, Hugh: stuffed by LW, 82 & n

D'Annunzio, Gabriele: and Duse, 299 & n

Dante: makes writing unnecessary, 313; *ref:* 103, 179, 283, 320, 326, 339n; *Inferno,* 313, 339n

Darwin (family): 16 & n, 88

Darwin, Bernard: 145 & n

Davidson, Angus: unselfish and charming, 4; like an elder brother, 10; a little languid, 26; wobbles & prevaricates, 29; on Lytton in love, 31; 'He don't do', 116 & n; his cautious alarm, 124 & n; doesn't 'manage', and won't budge, 128; in pink shirt, 154; quarrels about time—and is dismissed, 162; finally to go, 167; his anxieties and gentlemanly reserve, 205 & n; comes for 'character', 211; secretary of London Artists, 269 & n; *ref:* 4 & n, 16, 17, 35 & n, 72, 110, 134

Davidson, Douglas: in perfect trim, 138

Davies, Crompton Llewelyn: 234 & n, 235

Davies, Margaret Llewelyn: in retirement, 23 & n; dishevelled and undistinguished, 296, 297; VW annoyed with, 306, 307; *ref:* 175, 314

Day's Library, Mayfair: 84 & n

Dedman, Mrs, of Rodmell: 321

Defoe, Daniel: 50, 131, 340; *Tour Through the Whole Island of Great Britain,* 340n

De La Mare, Walter: Hardy on, 99 & n; dream talk with Yeats, 329, 330, 332 & n; *ref:* 65 & n, 271; *The Connoisseur and Other Stories,* 99n; *On the Edge,* 332

Dell, Ethel M.: 23 & n

De Quincey, Thomas: VW writing on, 83 & n, 95, 109; 'Suspiria de Profundis', 96 & n

Derby, The: 226

Desborough, Lady: 37 & n

Devonshire, Woolfs tour in: 303

Devonshire, 8th Duke of: Bernard Holland's Life of, 247 & n

Emery, Miss, dog breeder, of Rodmell: 321
Empire Review: 235 & n
Enfield, Dorothy, *née* Hussey: 205 & n
English Association: VW on committee of, 58 & n
Esher, Lady: 337
Esher, Lord (Hon. Oliver Brett): 176n, 335 & n, 337
Esther, unidentified: talking like Macaulay, 231
Etoile Restaurant, Charlotte Street: 36 & n
Eton College: 252 & n, 261, 314
Eve *see* Younger, Eve
Evening Standard: on writing for, 186; VW praised in, 255-6, 256n; *ref:* 309 & n

Faber & Gwyer, publishers: 14n, 41n
Fairbanks, Douglas: 69
Fairlawne, Tonbridge, home of Cazalet family: 252 & n
Faringdon Market: 325
Farquhar, Earl: 283 & n
Farwell, Mr Justice: 273 & n
Fausset, Hugh I'Anson: praises *Common Reader*, 18 & n
Fears, Mr, of Rodmell: 159, 321
Femina-Vie Heureuse, literary prize: awarded to VW, 178 & n, 179, 182, 183 & n; to Rose Macaulay, 185 & n
Fife Settlements: 283 & n
Findlater, Mary: 161 & n
Fisher, Emmeline: 324 & n
Fisher, Herbert Albert Laurens: 42 & n
Fisher, Mary, *née* Jackson: a threat to liberty, 194 & n
Fitzroy Square, No. 29: 267
Fitzroy Street, No. 8 (Vanessa's studio): 220n, 260, 306
Fladgate, Mrs (unidentified): 131
Florence: 243 & n, 244, 352
Fontcreuse, near Cassis: 173n, 179, 231, 232n
Formosa Fishery, near Cookham, home of the Youngs: 35 & n
Forster, E. M. (Morgan): for Biographical Note *see* Appendix I; operation on wrist, 18; his judgment on Mrs D., 22, 24; compliments E. Sitwell, snubs Vita, 28; asks Woolfs out to lunch, 36; his article on VW, 47 & n; his death imagined, 48; his character compared with Lytton's, 48, 49-50; cheers VW, 52 & n; Hardy on, 98, 99; and Tess's picture, 101; on finishing novel, 109; and Abel Chevalley, 114 & n; VW to do, 127 & n; morganatic letter on *Lighthouse*, 137 & n; VW's article on, 149; reacts to criticism, 152 & n; VW reviews, 158 & n; on the Bell children, 158; what he calls 'life', 164; the blue butterfly, 177; on sodomy, and Radclyffe Hall, 193 & n; his articles indistinguishable, 244; and *A Room of One's Own*, 262; in atmosphere of buggery, 299; kept up with, 316; *ref:* 25, 89, 157, 275, 318; *Abinger Harvest*, 47n; *A Passage to India*, 50 & n, 109, 130, 152; *Aspects of the Novel*, 158n
Fortnum & Mason, Piccadilly: 138, 164
Forum, periodical: 58 & n, 127
France: 6, 41, 90, 129, 139, 145, 151, 177, 178, 179, 186, 200, 233, 275, 323, 327
Francis, Mr, at Cassis: 8
Franklin, Sir John: 72 & n
Fred *see* Pape, Frederick
Fry, Joan Mary: 89 & n
Fry, Roger: for Biographical Note *see* Appendix I; an ally, 31; his garden party, 33 & n; his exacerbating egotism, 45; loves Helen Anrep, 52; reports Nessa's criticism of VW, 76; chess with LW, 86; dislikes 'Time Passes', 127 & n; a pure aristocrat, 129; in grand historical picture, 157; and Old Bloomsbury, 162; malicious & vain, 178 & n; a real person, 202; needs Nessa, 224; his life with Helen, 237; hated by critics, 269; ravaged scavenger, 284; *ref:* 34, 38, 53 & n, 125, 164, 166, 173, 203, 217, 218, 227, 236, 259, 262, 275, 282, 283, 293, 323, 332

Gage, 6th Viscount: 102, 198, 199n, 310
Gaige, Crosby: 183 & n
Galsworthy, John: and General Strike, 83 & n; George Moore scorns, 214
Garland, Madge: 12 & n, 184
Garnett, David ('Bunny'): Lytton on, 44; wrong about Julian, 329; *ref:* 208; *A Man in the Zoo*, 44 & n
Garnett, Edward: 204 & n

Garrod, H. W., 92 & n
Garsington Manor, home of Philip and Ottoline Morrell: 13, 90, 91
Garvin, J. L., editor of *The Observer*: 83n
Gathorne-Hardy, Robert: 26 & n, 30
General Election, 1929: draws near, 226 & n; Labour confident, 228; Labour winning, 230 & n; a gamble on, 235
General Strike: exact diary of, 77-85; petition, 81 & n, 82; LW asserts legality of, 83 & n; settlement announced, 84 & n, 85 & n; continuing, 85, 86, 88, 89; *ref:* 77n, 80n
Genji *see* Murasaki, Lady
George V: dispatches Wells, 163 & n; dragging along, 211 & n; at the play, 273, 274
Gerbault, Alain, circumnavigator: misogynist, 299 & n
Gere, Margaret: 290 & n
Gerhardi, William: 71
Germany: and labour relations, 80 & n; *ref:* 173
Germany, Grace: 124n, 333 & n
Gibbons, Stella: 162 & n
Gilbert and Sullivan: 246
Girardin: memoirs, 179
Girton College, Cambridge: its young women, 200 & n, 204; its buildings, 201; *ref:* 199
Gissing, George: 205 & n; 206
Gladstone, William: 340
Gladys, niece? of Nelly Boxall: 153
Goddard, Scott, master at Leighton Park School: 5 & n, 6
Goethe: 186
Goldie *see* Dickinson, Goldsworthy Lowes
Gooch, George Peabody: 82 & n
Goold, Mrs, of Camerton: 341
Gordon Square, No. 37: Nessa's new house, 6, 7n; let, 175n; to let, 220 & n
Gordon Square, No. 46: early days at, 53; *ref:* 26
Gordon-Woodhouse, Violet: 338 & n
Gosse, Sir Edmund: introduces Vita's lecture, 115 & n; mortuary humbug on, 184-5; deprived of Boswell, 238; *ref:* 163, 185n
Gosse, Lady: 115
Gottschalk *see* Riding, Laura
Gould, Barbara Ayrton :70 & n ,71

Gould, Gerald: 70 & n, 71
Grant, Duncan: for Biographical Note *see* Appendix I; on VW, 26; reluctant witness at Keynes's wedding, 38; his death imagined, 48; doesn't consolidate parties, 71; 'commits nuisance', 87; egg in hand, prim and acid, 91; typhoid suspect, 124 & n; and Lytton, 138; on Ethel and Nan, 151 & n; sketchbook under arm, 154; in grand historical picture, 157; about to migrate, 173 & n; and Dante's hell, 179; aloof & supercilious, 191; a real person, 202; exhibits pictures, 217n; visits Germany and Austria, 218; at Cassis, 232; divinely charming, 233; paint and politics, 269 & n; a life of?, 302; sublime ineptitude, 306; easy Bohemian, 316; *ref:* 6, 7n, 15, 47, 53, 127, 133, 147, 203, 231, 242, 282, 304, 305, 323
Granville Barker, Harley: 98 & n
Graphic, The, periodical: 293
Graves, Robert: described, 13-14; *ref:* 13n
Greece: 108, 124, 127, 129, 198, 352
Green, Rev. A. S., vicar of Kingston with Iford, Sussex: 159n
Greenwich: visit to described, 72-3, 269 & n; *ref:* 41, 72n
Gregory, Lady: 284 & n
Grenfell, Florence, *née* Henderson: 210 & n
Greville, Charles: memoirs edited by Lytton Strachey, 294 & n
Grey, Mr, of Rodmell: 155
Grey, old Mrs, of Rodmell: 160 & n
Grey, Viscount: and General Strike, 81 & n
Grizzle, a mongrel dog: 6, 62, 85, 112, 118
Groombridge Place, Kent: 157 & n
Guedalla, Philip: 115 & n
Gumbo *see* Strachey, Marjorie
Gurney, Mr, at Cassis: 8

Hakluyt, Richard: 271
Hall, Radclyffe: petition got up for, 193 & n; the trial, 206 & n, 207; *The Well of Loneliness*, 193n, 201
Hamilton, Mary Agnes ('Molly'): 296 & n
Hammersley, Violet Mary: 214 & n
Hammond, furnishers, of Lewes: 316
Hampstead: recalls Katherine Mansfield,

50 & n; red, sanitary, earnest, 157; *ref*: 49, 80, 204, 286, 306

Hampstead General Hospital: 237 & n

Hampton Court: scene in *The Waves*, 287; *ref*: 224, 324

Ham Spray House, near Hungerford: fire at, 44; *ref*: 89

Handel: 126

Harcourt Brace & Co, publishers, New York: on *Mrs Dalloway*, 9; new edition of *The Voyage Out*, 58; *ref*: 4 & n, 43

Hardy, Florence: conveys husband's pleasure, 25 & n; docile & ready, 96; on serialisation, 97; and London, 98 & n; on T. E. Lawrence and suicide, 100; reads Huxley to Hardy, 101 & n; *ref*: 96n, 99, 102

Hardy, Thomas: takes pleasure in *Common Reader*, 25 & n; George Moore on, 66n, 67; Wells on, 94 & n; VW to visit, 95; portrayed at home, 96-101; 'moments of vision', 105 & n; his funeral, 173-4; VW's article on, 174 & n; a further article, 205 & n; Beerbohm on, 213; *ref*: ix, 96n, 97n, 98n, 99n, 101n, 102, 108, 173n, 206, 210; *The Dynasts*, 98; *Far from the Madding Crowd*, 97 & n, 99; *Jude the Obscure*, 213; *Life's Little Ironies*, 99, 100; *The Mayor of Casterbridge*, 99 & n; *Moments of Vision*, 105n; *Tess of the D'Urbervilles*, 67, 213

Hardy, Thomas, flag captain to Nelson: 72

Harper's Magazine, New York: 127

Harris, Henry ('Bogey'): entertains VW and prime minister, 282, 283 & n; well fed bachelor, 284; *ref*: 166 & n

Harris, Lilian: life with Margaret, 23 & n; mumbling & crumbling, 296, 297

Harrison, Edward, dentist: 78

Harrison, Jane: aged and exalted, 176 & n; her death, 178 & n; and funeral, 181 & n; *ref*: 333; *Reminiscences of a Student's Life*, 176n

Hart-Davis, Rupert: 336 & n

Harvey, Gabriel: 270 & n

Hawkesford, Boen: 159, 160 & n

Hawkesford, Rev. James Boen, rector of Rodmell: described, 159-60; *ref*: 158 & n, 317

Hawkesford, Mrs: 160 & n

Hawthornden Prize: awarded to Vita, 139 & n; and to David Cecil, 304n; *ref*: 71, 303

Hayward, John: praises VW's article, 16 & n

Hazlitt, William: 302, 304 & n, 313, 317

Head, Sir Henry, neurologist: 193 & n

Heal & Son, Tottenham Court Road: 175

Heinemann, publishers: 70, 295 & n

Heliogabalus, Emperor: 308 & n

Hemans, Felicia: 109 & n, 287

Hemingway, Ernest: VW article on, 158 & n; *Men Without Women*, 158n

Henderson, Arthur: at party conference, 258 & n

Henderson, Faith, *née* Bagenal: her reactions imagined, 205; *ref*: 84 & n, 127, 131, 204

Henderson, Hubert: *N & A* arguments, 69 & n; and strike prediction, 80; confident of Labour victory, 228 & n; to give up *N & A*, 260 & n; his perpetual drag, 265 & n; *ref*: 81, 127, 167, 204, 205

Hengist: 274

Herkomer, Sir Hubert von: and Hardy's *Tess*, 101 & n

Heseltine, Philip *see* Warlock, Peter

Herrick, Robert: 40

Highgate Cemetery: 46

Hilda *see* Matheson, Hilda

Hills, John Waller ('Jack'): described, 33-4; *ref*: 33n; *A Summer on the Test*, 34n; *My Sporting Life*, 34n

Hills, Stella, *née* Duckworth: 245 & n, 261

Hogarth Essays: 58 & n

Hogarth House: madness at remembered, 254; *ref*: 132, 267, 327

Hogarth Miscellany: 167 & n

Hogarth News: 293

Hogarth Press: E. Sitwell eager to write for, 24 & n; to be quit of, 40; Eliot and, 42; its compensations, 43; VW to write for, 47; book on fiction for, 50 & n, 107; give it up?, 69; the next question, 70; to strike break?, 77; creaking at hinges, 114; sagging on shoulders, 116; Wells gives boost to, 128 & n; obscure anonymity of, 136; failure with novels, 150; bad year financially, 162; bonuses all round,

221; booming, 260; travelling for, 303; to be stopped, 327; *ref*: 68, 127, 304

Holland, family: history of, 247 & n

Holland, Bernard: 'brilliant young man' portrayed, 244-7; *ref*: 245n, 246n, 247n, 261; *Belief and Freedom*, 247n; *The Lancashire Hollands*, 247n; *The Life of Spencer Compton, 8th Duke of Devonshire*, 247n

Holland, Helen, *née* Duckworth: 245 & n, 246

Holland, the Rev. Canon F. J.: 245 & n

Holland, Mary Sibylla: her letters, 246 & n

Home University Library: 42 & n

Hope, Lottie: wants to return?, 41; discussing marriage, 44; loves cow-man, 45; brings poisonous cold, 88; dismissed amid scenes, 227; to be ruled by?, 230; no more barging in by, 267; dismissed for stealing, 302; *ref*: 3n, 27, 253, 310; 328

Hopkins, Gerard Manley: and Bridges, 93 & n

Horne, Herbert: 282, 283n

Horner, Lady: 90 & n; *Time Remembered*, 90n

Hotel Cendrillon, Cassis: 6, 8, 133

House of Commons: warm debate in, 79; LW's stuffing for, 82 & n; *ref*: 296

Housman, A. E.: 19 & n, 65 & n

Howard, Brian: 268 & n

Howard, Esme: 69 & n

Howards, the, at Cassis: 8

Howe, Beatrice Isabel ('Bea'): 7 & n, 68; *A Fairy Leapt Upon My Knee*, 7n

Hudson, Nan: described, 151 & n; *ref*: 150

Hunt, Mrs, domestic agency: 266, 267, 328

Hunter, Mary, *née* Smyth: 307 & n

Hutchinson, Barbara: her lovely *woman's* eyes, 3; *ref*: 3n, 160, 318

Hutchinson, Jeremy: 3 & n

Hutchinson, Mary: for Biographical Note *see* Appendix I; entertains Woolfs, 3; VW's ally, 31; illumined, 35; her stories 'bad', 52 & n; gives literary party, 66; adulterates solitude, 73; loves VW, 107; VW a success with, 108; Clive to break with, 126 & n; cries for moon, 129; at the opera, 135; and Clive, 136; and Vanessa, 141; no match for motor cars, 146; her book's cost, 150; shadowed by Clive, 160, 161; eats Press profits, 162; loves Lord A, 168; simmers with Jack, 176; and Janet Ross, 243 & n; Clive on, 275; so much unhappiness, 334; *ref*: 3n, 38, 41, 60, 65, 79, 90, 91, 93, 175, 201, 214, 223, 318, 328, 336, 337; *Fugitive Pieces*, 52n, 150n, 162

Hutchinson, St John: for Biographical Note *see* Appendix I; entertains Woolfs, 3; compliment to VW repeated, 35; Eliot's scurvy treatment of, 41 & n; on Tolstoy, 67; simmering with Mary, 176; and George Moore, 214; *ref*: 3n, 90

Huxley, Aldous: gigantic grasshopper, 93 & n; read by the Hardys, 101 & n; approved by Kot, 217-18; *ref*: 90; *Point Counter Point*, 217n; *Two or Three Graces*, 101 & n

Huxley, Maria: 90

Hyde Park: 17, 26, 139

Hyde Park Gate: recollections of, 87; remembered by Hardy, 97; *ref*: 267, 271

Ibbotson, Miss, prospective housekeeper: 318 & n, 319

Ibsen, Henrik: 183n, 210

India, Round Table Conference on: 339 & n

Ingersoll, watch company: 4 & n

Innes, Kathleen E.: *The Story of the League of Nations told for Young People*, 19 & n

International Review: 49 & n

Irvine, Lyn Lloyd: honesty bred of poverty, 249 & n, 250; 'niceness' takes edge off, 269; *ref*: 268, 304, 305, 328

Irving, Mary: killed in Alps, 314 & n

Isaiah, Book of: 294

Italy: 87, 124, 129, 130, 132, 133, 295, 311

Ivy, The, restaurant: 57

Iwerne Minster: 74, 75

James, Charles, Rodmell farmer: 193, 194n, 195

James, Henry: George Moore on, 67; Wells on, 94 & n, 95; his spirit

League of Nations: 19 & n, 60, 123n
Le Bosquet, Audrey: 252 & n, 309
Lee, Vernon: 20 & n, 312
Lehmann, Rosamund: 314 & n; *A Note in Music*, 314n
Leighton, Lord: 142
Leighton Park School: 5 & n, 6
Leverson, Ada: 163
Lewes, Sussex: 42, 169, 179, 230, 241, 303, 313, 324, 343
Lewis, Percy Wyndham: 242, 323; *The Apes of God*, 324n; *Satire & Fiction*, 324n
Leys, Dr Norman: 19 & n; *Kenya*, 19n
Liberal Party: muddle over funds, 283 & n
Life and Letters, periodical: 176n, 178, 185 & n, 195 & n, 335n
Lily, Rodmell housemaid: 44
Lime Kiln Farm, Sussex: 189, 190n
Lion, The, Cambridge hostelry: 204
Littell, Philip: 150 & n
Litvin, Rachel ('Ray'): a Bohemian, 20 & n
Llangollen, Ladies of: 131 & n
Loeb, Sydney J., amateur photographer: 26 & n
Loeffler, Mrs Hennik: 309 & n, 310n
Lomas, Henry, butler: 151 & n
London: street sauntering in, 11; novel writing in, 64; during General Strike, 77, 78, 79, 80; Hardy's view of, 98; article all about, 118; summer in, 132, 140; near end of season, 147; perpetual attraction of, 186; plunged into, 223; out of the window, 230; complete aloofness from, 232; £200 a year in, 249; its imminence, 258; violent shots at, 275; in the stir of, 295; walking alone in, 298; very exciting, 299; *ref:* 3, 6, 14, 22, 24, 25, 40, 44, 53, 61, 90, 101, 113, 144, 152, 155, 157, 161, 179, 217, 224, 239, 255, 256, 281, 301, 303, 318, 319, 327, 343
London Artists Association: 269 & n
Londonderry, Lady: 283 & n, 284
London Library: 82
London School of Economics (LSE): 70
Long Barn, V. Sackville-West's house: no invitation to, 48; 3 days at, 51 & n; clouds of glory from, 52-3; such opulence & freedom at, 144; happy to visit, 187; another visit, 211; Geoffrey

Scott at, 243; in the garden, 252; *ref:* 101, 114, 116, 118, 149, 157, 164, 173, 191, 199, 231, 251, 303, 304, 310, 314
Lopokova, Lydia (wife of Maynard Keynes): for Biographical Note *see* Appendix I; a lark soaring, 18; marriage impending and effected, 38 & n; home from Russia, 43-4; her 'zebra' shoes, 70; would like provostship, 76; performs Stravinsky, 147 & n; sobs at funeral, 164; very sensible, 181; and the Shaws, 276, 277; and true childhood, 312; *ref:* 15, 17, 43n, 102, 110, 157, 168 & n, 198, 210, 211, 223, 253, 259, 281, 315, 343
Lords, cricket ground: 89 & n, 261
Lottie *see* Hope, Lottie
Loune, butler at Long Barn: 164
Lowell, James Russell: 248 & n
Löwenstein-Wertheim, Princess: 'the Flying Princess', 154 & n, 155
Lubbock, Percy: 66 & n, 116
Lubin, David: Wells on, 93, 94 & n
Lucas, Emily Beatrice Coursolles ('Topsy'), *née* Jones: pumps Dadie, 150 & n; leaves husband, 225
Lucas, Frank Laurence ('Peter'): no ascendancy of brain, 64-5; doubts Dadie's fellowship, 66 & n; Dadie doubts his book, 150 & n; leaves wife, 225; an uninteresting mind, 256-7; *ref:* 30 & n, 65n, 255 & n; *The River Flows*, 65n; *Tragedy in Relation to Aristotle's Poetics*, 150n
Lushington, Judge Vernon, and family: 99 & n
Lynd, Robert: 70 & n, 71, 173
Lynd, Sylvia: 70 & n, 71
Lyn *see* Irvine, Lyn
Lynn, Olga, *Lieder* singer: 34 & n
Lyttleton (family): 246 & n
Lyttleton, Dame Edith (Mrs Lyttleton): 308 & n

Mabel, a typist: 336
MacAfee, Helen, of the *Yale Review*: 200 & n
Macaulay, Lord: 231
Macaulay, Rose: described, 60-2; her 'pothouse' dinner-party, 70-1; on women, 76; signs strike petition, 83; on writing, 96; and *Prix Femina*, 185 & n; and the *Evening Standard*, 186

& n; a mere chit, 204; *ref*: 60n, 61n, 70n, 184; *Dangerous Ages*, 185n

MacCarthy, Dermod: 19 & n, 148

MacCarthy, Desmond: for Biographical Note *see* Appendix I; worn & aged, 19-20; gives VW lunch and his 'filth packets', 21; lovable but depressing, 25; a wave that never breaks, 27; and the 'Ireniad', 28 & n, 285; lunching with Woolfs and Wells, 93n, 94; on Wells, 95; talks about Shakespeare, 96; Molly on, and the DM fund, 130 & n; and Henry James, 137; tender and garrulous and confidential, 147-148; his gratitude, 149; and *Life and Letters*, 176 & n, 185 & n; his bubbling lazy mind, 177-8; his homage to Gosse, 185 & n; gold & silver talk, 195-6; his letter annoys VW, 197 & n; his armchair egotism, 203-4; at Bow Street, 207; an adorable man, 234; loses £5 bet, 235; brilliant about Byron and Boswell, 237, 238n; *ref*: 19n, 20n, 71, 78, 79, 82, 195n, 210, 229, 335 & n; *Criticism*, 20n

MacCarthy, Mary ('Molly'): for Biographical Note *see* Appendix I; and Irene Noel-Baker, 28 & n; an ally, 31; warm faithful bear, 72; dusty, diligent, at London Library, 82 & n; her worries and debts, 130 & n; insists on VW memoir, 185; *ref*: 225, 229; *Fighting Fitzgerald and other Papers*, 82n

MacCarthy, Michael: 19 & n

MacCarthy, Rachel: 19 & n, 130, 197, 268, 272

MacColl, D. S.: 178 & n

MacDermott, F. T., printer: 84 & n

MacDonald, Ramsay: at Bogey Harris's dinner party, 283 & n, 284; *ref*: 25, 282

McGlashan, Dr Alan: 322 & n, 332

MacLagan, Mr and Mrs Eric: 148 & n

McLaren, Christabel ('Chrissie'): and the Desmond fund, 130 & n; artificial gambols with, 148; her 'winkle' party, 210; *ref*: 33 & n, 108 & n, 147, 208, 211, 223, 225

Macmillan, Hugh: 263 & n

Malthouse, Henry, Rodmell publican: 154 & n

Manchester Guardian: praises *Common*

Reader, 18 & n; *Orlando* 'a masterpiece', 217 & n

Manning-Sanders, Ruth: 60 & n; *Martha Wish-You-Ill*, 60n

Mansfield, Katherine: recalled, 50 & n; a dream of, 187; Kot's obsession with, 217, 218; on the Meynells, 251

Mansfield, Mrs, Bloomsbury char: 270 & n, 310

Marchand, Jean-Hippolyte: 47 & n

Marsh, Edward ('Eddie'), 63 & n, 294

Marshall, Frances: 76n, 84 & n, 95

Marshall, Thomas Humphrey (Tom): 11 & n, 82

Marshall & Snelgrove: VW robbed at, 339

Marten, Dr, of Freiburg: treats Vivienne Eliot, 15 & n

Martin, (Basil) Kingsley: 338 & n

Marvell, Andrew: 40

Mary, Aunt *see* Fisher, Mary

Mary, Queen: 273, 274

Masefield, John: and Yeats' anniversary, 331 & n; *ref*: 71

Masefield, Judith: 331

Masefield, Mrs: 331

Matheson, Hilda: abroad with Vita, 239 & n; very upset, 241; alters VW's broadcast, secondrate, 267 & n; *ref*: 266, 282, 328

Matisse: exhibited in Russia, 44

Matriarch, The, play, 260 & n

Matthews, Marjorie: 282 & n

Maugham, William Somerset: and Hugh Walpole, 328 & n; *Cakes and Ale*, 328n

Maupassant, Guy de: 108

Maurois, André: 184 & n, 287 & n; *Byron*, 287n

Mauron, Charles: 223 & n, 224, 225, 237, 266

Maxse, Kitty, *née* Lushington: and Clarissa Dalloway, 32 & n

Mayor, Beatrice ('Bobo'), *née* Meinertzhagen: shingles VW, 127 & n

Mayor, F. M.: 27, 28n; *The Rector's Daughter*, 28n

Meen, Reggie, boxer: 338 & n

Meinertzhagen, Elizabeth (Betty Potter): 113 & n

Meleager, see Trevelyan, R. C.

Melinda, unidentified: 148

Melville, Herman: *Moby Dick*, 195, 197

Meredith, George: VW's article on, 174 & n; claimed by Mrs Ross, 243 & n

Meynell, Alice: her life, 250-1; in Florentine Society, 352-3; *ref*: 250n, 251n

Meynell, Viola: memoir of mother, 250 & n, 352; sugar lumps, 251

Meynell, Wilfred: 250 & n

Michelet, Jules, historian: 93

Michelham Priory, Sussex: 154

Millais, Sir John Everett: 154

Milton, John: Yeats on, 330; *ref*: 3 & n, 235; *Lycidas*, 330

Mirrlees, Hope; crossing graveyard, 179; and Jane Harrison's death, 180 & n; sly convert, 268; liberated, 333; *ref*: 89 & n, 208, 269

Monks House, Rodmell: think of selling, 40; resolve shaken, 41; not hub of world, 112; rise in value, 158; unexpectedly nice, 192; gastronomy at, 257 & n; *ref*: ix, 3, 11, 36, 38, 53, 90, 123, 169, 173, 178, 188, 238, 259, 296, 303, 316, 317

Monro, Harold, poet and publisher: 157n

Montaigne: 8 & n

Moore, George: holds forth on writers, 66-7; on Bennett and others, 214 & n; on himself & his books, 226; compliments VW, 227; is liked, 242; Shaw and Zola on, 276; Bennett on, 335; *ref*: ix, 14 & n, 17, 66n, 206, 227n; *Aphrodite in Aulis*, 214n; *Esther Waters*, 67; *The Mummer's Wife*, 335

Morning Post: 21, 156 & n, 200 & n

Morrell, Julian: for Biographical Note *see* Appendix I; part of invasion, 26; cheers up Clive, 37; *ref*: 35, 93

Morrell, Lady Ottoline: for Biographical Note *see* Appendix I; a threat to Chelsea, 20; VW's affection for, 26; gives ghastly party, 30 & n; re-tells old stories, 36 & n; doing a cure, 58; seeking pity, 65-6; dressed like a girl of 18, 66; her dwindling charm, 93; on *To the Lighthouse*, 136 & n; shabby, easy, intimate, 152 & n; acted by Angelica, 158; & Bernard Holland, 246, 247; and conservation, 274 & n; on Henry Brewster, 326; hostess to Yeats, 329; *ref*: 20n, 34, 35, 37, 185, 238, 281, 282, 332

Morrell, Philip: for Biographical Note *see* Appendix I; part of invasion, 26; amorous, 152 & n; *ref*: 35, 37

Morris, William: and his circle, 186 & n; *ref*: 269 & n

Mortimer, Raymond: for Biographical Note *see* Appendix I; wires praise of *Mrs Dalloway*, 22; on Vita, 47; regrets Harold Nicolson's absence, 48; on VW's method, 63; his smart talk, 137-8; on Empire and nationality, 145; on Vita and Harold, 146; to marry?, 168; animated admirable talk with, 181-2; compared to Plomer, 242; his company, 299; shabby and likeable, 323, 324n; *ref*: 15, 24, 27, 35, 59 & n, 64 & n, 102, 129, 148, 179, 185, 208, 298

Mozart: 27, 126, 129, 282n; *Don Giovanni*, 89 & n; *La Finta Giardiniera*, 282n

Muir, Edwin: 109 & n; *The Marionette*, 150 & n; *Transition*, 109n

Murasaki, Lady: *The Tale of Genji*, 30, 31n

Murphy, Bernadette, assistant at Hogarth Press: described, 10; in the glumps, 11; turns crusty, 26; wants to stay, 299 & n; 'going', 35; works like slave, 38; in the basement, 40; *ref*: 10n, 26n

Murray, Mrs Graham, unidentified: 282

Murry, John Middleton: perpetual source of disquiet, vii; on VW's failure, 58 & n; Kot's abuse of, 217; *ref*: 218; *God: an Introduction to the Science of*, *Metabiology*, 263 & n

Napoleon: 329

Natasha (fict), in *War and Peace*: 67

National Gallery: 329

National Maritime Museum, Greenwich: 72 & n

Nation & Athenaeum: to be quit of, 40; LW to resign, 69 & n; richer without it, 70; Thank God to be out of, 71; dallying about, 76; skeleton Strike number, 77 & n, 80; Keynes commands Hogarth Press to print, 82; LW's article for blacked, 83 & n; printers still out, 85; 'The Questionnaire', 108 & n; and Lord Alfred Douglas, 227n; homogeneity of

'well enough', 25; his vanity exposed, 118; pink & spruce, 137 & n; *ref*: 78, 326

Smith, Mrs Reginald John: and Hardy ms, 97 & n

Smyth, Dame Ethel: and LW, viii; VW to put off, 286 & n; a book from, 289; military old woman, 290, 291, 292; cause of quarrel, 298; old Sapphist fires, 306; her home visited, 307 & n, 308; daily letters from, 312; described, 313, 314; valiant old woman, 315; a portrait of, 325, 326; *ref*: ix, 296n, 305, 310, 324, 326n, 328, 332, 335, 338 & n; *The Prison*, 291n, 335; 'Three Moods of the Sea', 326; *The Wreckers*, 291n

Snowden, Lily: 289

Snowden, Margaret (Margery) K.: a character sketch of, 289 & n, 290; *ref*: 290 & n

Southampton Row: 77, 211, 230, 302, 322

Southease, Sussex, property for sale at: 37, 43, 188, 265

Southorn, Bella, *née* Woolf, *quo* Lock: 318 & n, 319

Southorn, Thomas, 318n, 319

Spender, Stephen: 318 & n

Spender-Clay, Phyllis Mary: 93 & n

Spengler, Oswald: 224 & n; *The Decline of the West*, 224n

Sprott, Walter John Herbert ('Sebastian'): 253 & n, 281, 282

Squire, J. C. (Jack): verger with whiskers, 60 & n; won't knuckle under, 83; and insignificant literati, 139 & n; at Hardy's funeral, 173; barks at *Orlando*, 200 & n; *ref*: 91, 206

Stamper, Col. *see* Byng-Stamper, Captain

Star, newspaper: 16 & n

Starr, Mrs, prospective housekeeper: 318 & n, 319

Steer, Philip Wilson: 108 & n

Stein, Gertrude: 89 & n; *Composition as Explanation*, 89n

Stendhal: 33, 37

Stephen, family: mature late, 141; admirable solidity, 235; different from Hollands, 246

Stephen, Adrian: silent & satirical, 71; emerging from analysis, 141 & n; in grand historical picture, 157; moping & glooming, 227; never seen, 316; *ref*: 3n, 28n, 118, 208, 212, 275

Stephen, Ann: 205, 273 & n

Stephen, Dorothea: 245 & n, 246

Stephen, Sir Harry Lushington: 141 & n, 246

Stephen, James Kenneth: 190 & n

Stephen, Judith, 223 & n

Stephen, Julia, *née* Jackson, *quo* Duckworth: and *To the Lighthouse*, 18, 208; Nessa reminiscent of, 33; 'so beautiful', 61; amazing portrait of, 135; Leslie on, 164 & n; most beautiful Madonna, 183; VW obsessed by, 208; George Duckworth on, 293; *ref*: 12n, 245

Stephen, Karin, *née* Costelloe: precipitates VW's headache, 41; face half paralysed, 45-6; stockpiling in strike, 79; gives brisk party, 205, 206; savage & violent, 227; to introduce VW and Geoffrey Scott, 244; dismisses Lottie for stealing, 302; *ref*: 3n, 28 & n, 46n, 118

Stephen, Katherine (Kate): 17 & n

Stephen, Leslie: as 'The Old Man', 3 & n; and *To the Lighthouse*, 18-19, 37, 208; his character, 61; dealings with Hardy, 97 & n; his youth, 160; on Julia, 164 & n; 'my father', 194; would have ended VW's life, 208; deprived of Boswell, 238; *Social Rights and Duties*, 164n

Stephen, Thoby: and Elena Richmond, 40; and VW's suffering, 260; that queer ghost, his letters, 275 & n; his birthday, 317; *ref*: 17 & n, 39n, 286

Stephens, James: 330 & n; *The Crock of Gold*, 330n

Stern, G. B.: *The Matriarch*, 260 & n

Sterne, Laurence: 119, 188 & n; *Tristram Shandy*, 32, 116, 320n

Stevenson, Robert Louis and Mrs: 276

Stiles, Mrs, charwoman: 332

Stolypin, P. A.: 163 & n

Stone, Grace Zaring: *Bitter Tea*, 337, 338n

Storrs, Sir Ronald: 304 & n

Strachan, Miss, Hogarth Press clerk: 323

Strachey, family type: 48

Strachey, (Giles) Lytton: for Biographical Note *see* Appendix I; dismisses Christ, talks of buggers, 10; has drive, 21;

surly in love, 31; on *Mrs Dalloway*, 32; on Bunny's book, 44; his work, Q. Elizabeth, and his character, 47-8; his death imagined, 48; his character —his leathern eyelid, 49-50; his prose, 66 & n; signs Strike petition, 83; his dull harem, 108; his life, 130; love's invalid, 138; in grand historical picture, 157; on Hardy, 174; *Elizabeth and Essex*, a poor book, 208-9; his book discussed—a relief, 233-4; his indistinguishable articles, 244; at Charleston, 255; had VW married him, 273; unexpected visitor, 292; makes Columbus concoction, 294 & n; in atmosphere of buggery, 299; seldom seen, 316; *ref*: 4, 60, 71, 183, 235, 236, 262, 337; *Elizabeth and Essex*, 208 & n, 209, 213, 233, 234, 274n; *Portraits in Miniature*, 337, 338n; *Queen Victoria*, 66 & n

Strachey, James: for Biographical Note *see* Appendix I; 19, 21, 82 & n, 84

Strachey, Lady: 174 & n, 211 & n, 212

Strachey, Julia: 7 & n

Strachey, Marjorie ('Gumbo'): 125 & n, 182, 282

Strachey, Oliver ('Noll'): 7n, 30, 76 & n

Strachey, Pernel: 16 & n, 17, 199, 209

Strachey, Rachel (Ray), *née* Costelloe: 30 & n, 143, 144

Strachey, St Loe: and General Strike, 82 & n, 83

Stravinsky, Igor: 63, 147 & n; *L'Histoire du soldat*, 147n

Studd, Arthur Haythorne: brilliant young man, 260-1; *ref*: 260n

Swift, Dean: 33 & n, 34, 36

Sydney-Turner, Saxon: his great-grand-father's diary, 72 & n, 87; at the opera, 135; going to the Ring, 225; *ref*: 143, 144, 316

Tagore, Rabindranath: 329 & n

Talbot, Rose, of Dollman & Pritchard: 79 & n

Talland House, St Ives: 194

Tauchnitz, Bernhard: 25 & n

Taupin, Mrs, temporary domestic: 304 & n

'Tavistock Cafe' ('Bloomsbury Bar'): 93n

Tavistock Square: dog fight in, 79; won by Grizzle, 85; its most liked inhabi-

tant, 228; *ref*: 4, 18, 21, 46, 59, 64, 70, 81, 88, 132, 327

Tavistock Square, No. 25, possible house: 336

Tavistock Square, No. 52: ix, 5, 46, 57, 123, 133, 173, 195, 244, 259, 273, 281, 322

Taylor, Valerie: 148 & n, 149, 165, 168, 208

Taylor, Sir Henry's, daughters: 248 & n

Tchekhov *see* Chekhov, Anton

Teed, Lt. Col. A. S. H., of Fontcreuse: 173n, 179, 232n

Tennant, Stephen: 265 & n, 299

Tennyson, Lord: 285

Terry, Ellen: 340

Thackeray, Anne *see* Ritchie, Anne, Lady

Thackeray, W. M.: *Pendennis*, 213

Thoby *see* Stephen, Thoby

Thomas, Rev. Walter Webb, of South-ease: 321 & n

Thomas, J. H.: and General Strike, 78 & n; meets Baldwin, 82

Thomas, Margaret Ellen, Girton student: 200 & n, 204

Thompsett, Annie: her life, and VW's, 236; not available, 240; to be servant, 255; her cottage, 258; very sympath-etic, 275; nice, bright, 311; surprises one daily, 317; anxious to stay, 323; *ref*: 236n, 265, 267, 315, 324, 327, 340

Thomsett, George, Nicolsons' butler: 252 & n

Thompson, Francis, poet: 243

Thompson, George Derwent, Apostle: 16 & n

Thompson, Lord, Secretary of State for Air: 322 & n

Thomson, Marjorie, called Joad: 11 & n, 135

Thorndike, Sibyl, in *Othello*: 304

Tilton, Sussex: 102, 106, 110

Time and Tide, periodical: 317 & n

Times, The: fails to mention Nessa's pictures, 217; George Duckworth on pigs in, 293 & n; *ref*: 247

Times Book Club: 80 & n

Times Literary Supplement, The (*TLS*) [Note: VW generally refers to the *TLS* as 'the Times'. Unless the opposite meaning is clearly intended we enter 'Times' under *The Times*

315; with pied hair?, 319; Trim & Uncle Toby, 320

(2) *The Hogarth Press and literary work*: harsh to Murphy, his pamphlet, 11; gives farewell dinner, 16; doing up parcels, 52; *N & A* resignation, 69 & n; and dallying about it, 76; to collect Essays, 90 & n; forging ahead, 114; and Angus Davidson, 116, 128, 162, 167, 211; discusses advertisements, 136; consults about *Orlando*, 212; gives bonuses, 221; works on dust cover, 225; and Lord Alfred's libel, 227n; giving up *N & A?*, 260 & n; freedom draws near, 265 & n; on Press tour, 303; no to *N S & N*, 338

(3) *Political activities*: countless committees, 19, 123n; and lectures, 22 & n, 166, 167n; and R. MacDonald, 25; adored by Irene Noel-Baker, 28; to answer *British Gazette*, 77; labour ... or baptism, 80; tub thumper, 80-1; not a scab, 82; asserts strike's legality, 83; urges Webb over Kenya, 263 & n; Works mentioned: *Fear and Politics*, 11 & n; *Essays on Literature, History, Politics, etc*, 90n

Woolf, Marie (VW's mother-in-law): a child with feelings, 193 & n; non-stop talk, 194 & n, 195; like an old rose, 230-1; grinds one to bits, 253; her charm & dignity, 258; soot, sparks, and tobacco, 271; vainest of women, 320; painfully sensitive, 321; *ref*: 182, 235, 282, 318 & n

Woolf, Marjorie ('Babs') (wife of Philip): 68 & n, 320

Woolf, Philip: 68 & n, 300n, 320

Woolf, Virginia. Entries are divided thus: (1) Early life and relationships. (2) Personality and health. (3) Relationship with LW. (4) Diversions. (5) Domestic matters. (6) Literary activities. (7) Her own published books.

(1) *Early life and relationships*: St Ives and childhood, 18-19; Jack Hills, 33-4; George Young, 35 & n; Katie Cromer, 51 & n; disagreeable memories, 87; history at St Ives, and threats to liberty, 194; scenes of travel, 198; Geoffrey Scott and Florentine society, 243, 352-3; Ber-

nard Holland and Canterbury society, 245-6; Phil Jones in Venice, 248; 'autumn plans', 255; Thoby Stephen, 260, 275, 317; Arthur Studd recalled, 260-1; throwing off chains, 267; early literary loves and endeavours, 271; tremendous desire to write, 315

(2) *Personality and health*: attitude to fame, vii; her own sex, 3; and influenza, 5; past, present, and future, 5, 36; impressions from Cassis, 6, 8, from an accident, 6; on Jacques Raverat's death, 7-8, 34, 47; her version of Montaigne, 8; and her own image, 9, 12, 21, 37, 132; her anti-bugger revolution, 10; Marjorie Thomson and happiness, 11; on clothes, 11, 12, 21, 42, 90-1, 113, 296, 334; party consciousness, 12, 13; fidgety, 15; her reputation, 16, 21, 22; on Kate Stephen's death, 17 & n; jangled, 18, 21; on human fellowship, 22; £50 worth of charm, 27; no lioness, 30; 'I do not love my kind', 33; most beautiful, 35; aristocracy *v.* middle class, 37; faints at Charleston, 38-9; still amphibious, 40-1; to take fences, 42; headache renewed, 44; tumbled into bed, 46; on Madge Vaughan's death, 46, 48; imagines death, 48; K. Mansfield recalled, 50, 187; Sapphist love, 51; wish for maternal protection, 52; measles . . . and Murry, 58; spring and funerals, 59; fanatical like father?, 60; life and discovery, 62-3; headaches and beauty, 64; a horrid gaffe, 68; ten years younger, 69-70; in underworld, 70-1; untrustworthy humanity, 81; transitory reality, 85; 'flu and shivers, 89; integrity and art, 102, 104; miniature nervous breakdown, 103, 110-11; marriage, 105; on parenthood, 107-8; haunting criticism, 109; symbolism and sentimentality, 110; intense depression, 111-12; mystical solitude, 113; emotional battlefield, 114; complete inner composure, 116; vision of death, 117; 'something in me', 123; shingled and bingled, 127; and fearless, 129; headachy, 130; summer disturbances, 132; on opinions, 133, 134, 135-6; in bed, 136;

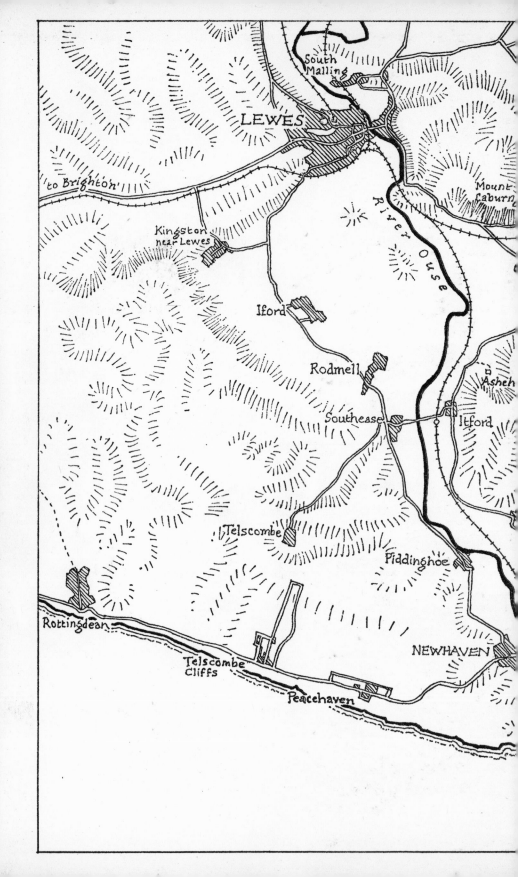